THE MESSIAH TEXTS

THE MESSIAH TEXTS

RAPHAEL PATAI

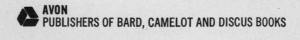

AVON
PUBLISHERS OF BARD, CAMELOT AND DISCUS BOOKS

AVON BOOKS
A division of
The Hearst Corporation
959 Eighth Avenue
New York, New York 10019

First Avon Printing, October, 1979

AVON TRADEMARK REG. U.S. PAT. OFF. AND IN
OTHER COUNTRIES, MARCA REGISTRADA, HECHO EN
U.S.A.

Printed in the U.S.A.

Dedication

It has come to pass in our days that there arose men in the four corners of the earth who exerted themselves to bring us nearer to the Messianic era of peace between Israel and the nations.

In Europe, Nahum Goldmann worked to achieve reconciliation and peace between the remorseful sons of the German Armilus and the surviving children of his victims, the Jews.

In Africa, Anwar el-Sadat stepped forth and went like a lion into the Jerusalem den of Daniels to plead for peace between the embittered sons of Ya'rub and sons of Ya'qub.

In Asia, Menachem Begin fought with his own brethren to convince them that peace with their neighbors means more than retaining land conquered with the blood of the sons of Zion.

In America, Jimmy Carter strove long and hard to bring about a peace agreement between reluctant Egypt and hesitant Israel.

It is to these men that *The Messiah Texts* is inscribed.

DR. RAPHAEL PATAI is a noted anthropologist, Biblical scholar, and author. He taught Hebrew at the Hebrew University of Jerusalem, and has served as Professor of Anthropology at Fairleigh Dickinson University and Dropsie University, and as Visiting Professor at the University of Pennsylvania, Princeton, Columbia, and Ohio State, as well as Director of Research of the Herzl Institute and Editor of the Herzl Press. He was also consultant to the department of Social Affairs of the United Nations Secretariat, and director of the Syria-Lebanon-Jordan research project of the Human Relations Area Files. Dr. Patai is the author of twenty-five books, including *Hebrew Myths* (with Robert Graves), *Man and Temple in Ancient Jewish Myth and Ritual*, *Golden River to Golden Road: Society, Culture and Change in the Middle East*, *Israel Between East and West*, *The Kingdom of Jordan*, *Tents of Jacob: The Diaspora Yesterday and Today*, *Myth and Modern Man*, *The Arab Mind*, *The Myth of the Jewish Race* (with Jennifer Patai-Wing), and *The Jewish Mind*. His book *The Hebrew Goddess* was published by Avon Books in 1978.

Acknowledgments

The author wishes to express his thanks for permission to quote, in the original or in his translation, from the works listed below.

Shalom Asch, *From Many Countries: The Collected Stories of Shalom Asch*. (Copyright 1958 by Ruth Schaffer, Moses Asch, John Asch and the representative of Nathan Asch.)

Rachel Berdach, *The Emperor, the Sages, and Death*, New York-London: Thomas Yoseloff, 1962. Reprinted by permission of A. S. Barnes & Co., Cranbury, N.J.

Martin Buber, *Gog und Magog*, Frankfurt/M and Hamburg: Fischer Bücherei, 1957; and the Jewish Publication Society of America, Philadelphia. (Translated by R. P.)

Efraim Frisch, "Die Legende von Kuty." From Karl Otten (ed.), *Schofar: Lieder und Legenden jüdischer Dichter*, Neuwied am Rhein: Hermann Luchterhand Verlag, 1962; and Mrs. Karl Otten, Minusio, Locarno, Switzerland. (Translated by R. P.)

Hans Jacob Christoffel von Grimmelshausen, *Courage the Adventuress and the False Messiah*, translated and introduction by Hans Speier (Copyright 1964, Princeton University Press), pp. 243–45 and 247–48.

Elie Wiesel, *One Generation After*, New York: Random House, Inc., 1970.

William Zuckerman, *Refuge from Judea*, New York: Philosophical Library, 1961.

Contents

Preface

The purpose of the present book is to put before the reader the texts of Jewish legends dealing with the coming of the Messiah and the events preceding, accompanying, and following his advent. These texts are excerpts from an exceed ingly voluminous literature spanning three millennia, beginning with early Biblical indications and concluding with Messiah legends written, and Messiah dreams dreamt, by modern authors. The material scattered especially in the Talmudic, Midrashic, and Kabbalistic books and presented here is astounding in its riches, even though I cannot be sure that I succeeded in locating all the significant variants on each and every theme. All the non-English texts, except for two or three selections, are given in my own translation from the Hebrew, Aramaic, Arabic, Latin, Ladino, Yiddish, German, and Hungarian originals.

I did not intend to include nonlegendary statements about the Messiah and the Messianic age. The nonlegendary material comprises several categories. There are, in the first place, legal and logical, often casuistic, arguments about whether or not a certain Messianic event, such as the Resurrection—which legend and belief consider an integral part of the Messianic happenings—is referred to in the Bible, whether it will take place, and if yes, when, where, how, and why, and what types of persons, or which individuals, will be involved in it. Then there is the ritual counterpart of the Messianic beliefs and legends. In many ages and many places pious Jews performed Messiah-related rites for the purpose of preparing themselves for the coming of the Redeemer, or facilitating his expected advent, or even forcing him to come. Their observances included fervent recitals of texts, mystical concentrations akin to meditation, mortification of the flesh, other ascetic exercises, and rites of magic and sorcery. Some of these devotions left their traces in legends (such as the one included in chapter 7), but to deal with these rituals as such would have meant to branch out into an area different from the one I staked out for the present book, as would have a presentation of the legal opinions and debates.

A third subject of which again only the legendary reflection is found in this book is that of the calculations of the Messianic advent. However, in this case I could not refrain from at least giving a briefest resumé of the Messianic mathematics of the most prominent among the *m'hashve haqitzim*, or "calculators of the ends," as they were called (see introductory note to chapter 6).

Yet another aspect of Jewish Messianism barely touched upon is the long chain of pseudo-Messiahs whose appearance constitutes some of the psychologically most fascinating pages in Jewish history. But, obviously, the history of Jewish Messianic movements is a very different subject from the legends in which the Coming is always an event of the future, never of the past. Of course, the inner connection between the two must not be overlooked: without the legends which were derived from belief in the Future to Come, and which in turn sustained and nurtured it, no individual Jew would have conceived the idea that he was the expected Redeemer, nor would any such claim have evoked the enthusiastic or even hysterical response that greeted a Reubeni in the sixteenth century or a Shabbatai Zevi in the seventeenth. On the other hand, had these Messianic pretenders not given the people a taste, albeit a fleeting one, of what it would be like for a Jew to live in the Messianic days, the legends and beliefs would perhaps not have proliferated and become the focal concerns they actually were in Jewish consciousness for two millennia.

The present book, then, tells only part of the story of what the concept Messiah has meant in Jewish life. But it tells what, I am convinced, is the essential part. The Messiah legend is the fullest and truest expression of the undying Jewish belief in the Redeemer who has been about to come for two thousand years. The Talmudic term denoting the events which precede the coming of the Redeemer is *'iqvot haMashiah*, literally, "footprints of the Messiah." This is most significant because the Messianic advent is the only event in history which, although it has not yet come to pass, has left its footprints in advance in the soul of a people, and thereby shaped it and sustained it.

A word has to be said about my translations of the texts presented. I attempted to adhere as closely as possible to the original style and manner of writing, even if this meant deviating from modern idiomatic English. The sources excerpted, some of them going back to centuries Before the Common Era (B.C.E.), always have a specific, quite peculiar flavor of their own which, I strongly felt, was part of their charm and character, and which should be retained and reproduced in the English rendering if at all possible.

A further important characteristic of the *Aggadot* ("legends"), most marked in the stories contained in the Talmud and Midrash, is that they are very frequently interspersed with Biblical quotations. Talmudic and Midrashic stories are as likely as not to underpin every statement by adding the phrase "as it is written," followed by a more or less appropriate quote from the Bible. In most cases the purpose of resorting to this method of presentation was to legitimize the idea expressed in the *Aggada*, to harmonize it, however newfangled, original, or even unorthodox, with the undoubted truths contained in Scripture. If, in the course of doing so, the original meaning of the Biblical verse or phrase was twisted beyond recognition, or it was given a diametrically opposed interpretation, this was considered perfectly permissible. In fact, one often feels the pride of the Aggadist in having been able to impart an entirely new meaning to a Biblical verse. However, as far as the story line of the *Aggadot* is concerned, in the great majority of cases the Biblical quotes add nothing to it. Because of this, and also because the frequent Biblical quotes interrupt the flow of the story, I felt it was preferable to omit most of them. They were retained only where a protagonist of the story is made to quote them directly, or where they are necessary for an understanding of what takes place.

The material in this book is organized in the following manner: After a general introduction into the complex world of the Messianic ideology and its significance for Jewish history throughout the ages, the texts themselves are presented. They begin with the Biblical adumbrations of the major themes, namely, the Suffering Servant, the Slain Messiah, Gog of the Land of Magog, the Day of the Lord, the King of Peace, and Resurrection. This is followed by a chapter-by-chapter presentation of the Messianic events, beginning with the preexistence of the Messiah and ending with the universal blessings which were believed to ensue after his advent and victories.

Each chapter opens with a few brief introductory remarks intended to serve as general orientation for the specific topic dealt with, and to provide continuity between it and the subject matter of the preceding chapter. Then follow the texts of the legends in a roughly chronological order.

Chapter 28, "Messiah Dreams," adds a special psychological dimension to the preceding chapters in that it gives a few examples from widely differing periods showing the extent to which the Jewish subconscious was preoccupied with the Messianic idea. The last chapter, entitled "Recapitulation," intends to give two examples of the complete Messiah legend as known to, and believed in, by Aggadists on the one hand and philosophers on the other, representing the two extremes in Jewish intellectual orientation in the Middle Ages. I would have liked to add a third such general statement from the pen of a Kabbalist, but the lack of systematization which characterizes all Kabbalistic writings made it impossible to find a single chronologically ordered description of what the Kabbalists believed would be the sequence of events in the Messianic era.

The first appendix shows how the theme of Redemption figures in the prayers recited to this day by observant Jews three times a day. The second presents what Maimonides, the greatest of Medieval Jewish philosophers, believed would characterize the Messianic era. It is interesting to note that while Sa'adya Gaon largely follows the Aggada in presenting his views of the Messianic times (see Chapter 30), Maimonides dismisses legends and Midrashim and bases himself on Biblical pronouncements only. Appendix III consists of the chapter headings of an extensive collection of Biblical quotations dealing with the Messiah and the Messianic era. They are taken from a hitherto unpublished Hebrew manuscript, dated 1466 and found in the British Library, London. The headings in their totality constitute a Messianic catechism, giving in a summary and systematic form the essential items of belief centering around the Messiah as subscribed to by European Jews in the Middle Ages. Appendix IV presents a letter, purportedly written by a pope to a king of France with the purpose of exonerating the Jews of the sin of deicide. The letter, contained in the same Hebrew manuscript from which Appendix III is taken, is in the form of a typical Midrashic parable about a king, his orchard, and its keeper. Appendix V contains the text of a disputation about the Messiah which took place between a leading rabbi and a leading churchman in the fourteenth century. Appendix VI presents the popular Jewish Messianic beliefs as they filtered through to the seventeenth-century German Gentile author Grimmelshausen.

The scholarly apparatus, relegated to the end of the book, consists, first, of a chronological listing of the sources excerpted. This should enable the interested reader to ascertain the period in which each of the texts was written. It is followed by an annotated bibliography which should prove useful for those wishing to delve further into the subject. In view of the organization and nature of the material, I felt I could dispense with a subject index, and confined myself to an index of proper names.

In conclusion I wish to express my thanks to those who in various ways helped me in the writing of this book. Among them were Dr. Leonard S. Gold, chief of the Jewish Division of the New York Public Library and its knowledgeable staff, who with great patience and competence helped me locate many an obscure source; Consuelo López-Morillas of the Department of Spanish and Portuguese of Indiana University, Bloomington, who helped me with the translation of the two Ladino poems included; Prof. Harry Zohn of Brandeis University, Waltham, Mass., who called my attention to modern writings I might otherwise have missed; Mlle. Madeleine Neige, head of the Service Hebraique, and M. Michel Garel, curator of Hebrew manuscripts, Bibliothèque Nationale, Paris; Dr. David Goldstein, Assistant Keeper, Hebrew Section, Department of Oriental Manuscripts and Printed Books, the British Library, London; Mr. R. A. May, Senior Assistant Librarian, Department of Oriental Books, Bodleian Library, Oxford; and Mr. A. E. B. Owen, Senior Under-Librarian, Cambridge University Library, for their help. Also to the Library of the Jewish Theological Seminary of America, New York; the Bibliothèque Nationale, Paris; the Bibliothèque Municipale, Marseilles; the British Library, London; the Bodleian Library, Oxford; and the Syndics of the Cambridge University Library, for their permission to study the manuscripts in their collections, to copy and translate them, and to publish the translations.

Forest Hills, N.Y.   Raphael Patai
October 15, 1978

Prologue

And when the flames engulfed the Temple, three young priests went up to its roof and threw the keys of the House of God to heaven. A hand reached down and took the keys.

And the priests said: "How long, O Lord, how long?"

And a heavenly voice issued and said: "Not longer than two days, My children."

Then they knew that the exile of the Shekhina and the dispersion of Israel would last two millennia, for it is written, A thousand years in Thy sight are but as yesterday *(Ps. 90:4).*

And they said before Him: "Master of the World! How can Israel endure two thousand years of suffering?"

And He said to them: "Behold, I give them a ray of hope which will pierce the night of their exile. I will give them one whom they will never see but whose presence they will feel all the time; who will never come but will always be a-coming; whom they will seek among the lepers in the gates of Rome and in the golden canopy of the supernal Bird's Nest, but who will be found only in their heart of hearts. I will give them him who will not be but who will sustain them. I will give them the Messiah."

(R. P.)

Introduction

One of the fundamental tenets of Judaism is the belief in the Messiah, the Savior who is to come, redeem the people of Israel from their suffering in exile, lead them back to Jerusalem, and establish the rule of peace over all the nations of the world. The organic growth of the Messiah myth from its earliest Biblical indications resulted, in the course of many centuries, in a burgeoning of ornate elaboration and the addition of many new motifs. But while the particulars of the expected Messianic events and era thus changed from time to time, the basic belief in him who must come remained the same and sustained the Jewish people for two millennia.

I

Remarkably and characteristically, the term *Mashiah*—of which "Messiah" is the Anglicized form—had preceded the Messianic concept by many centuries. Originally, in Biblical usage, it simply meant "anointed," and referred to Aaron and his sons, who were anointed with oil and thereby consecrated to the service of God (Exod. 28:41, etc.). The High

Priest, in particular, was termed "the Anointed [*Mashiah*] of God" (Lev. 4:3, 5, 16; 6:15). With the establishment of the monarchy, the same term was applied to the king: he was "the Anointed of the Lord" because he was installed in his high office by receiving the sacrament of anointment (1Sam. 2:10, 35; 9:16; 24:7, etc.). A third type of the divinely elected, the prophet, would also undergo the ceremony of anointing: Elijah, we read, was commanded by God to anoint Jehu as king over Israel, and Elisha as prophet in his own place (1Kings 19:16).

Still in early monarchic days the person of "the Anointed of the Lord" came to be considered sacrosanct: to harm him, or even to curse him, was a capital offense (2Sam. 19:22). A further development of this concept can be seen in the belief that God provided special protection to His anointed king. The Psalms contain several references to the idea of divine intervention for "the Anointed of the Lord," the idealized Davidic king:

> Now I know that the Lord saveth His Anointed [*Mashiah*],
> He will answer him from His holy heaven
> With the mighty acts of His saving right hand.
>
> (Ps. 20:7)

> The Lord is a strength unto them,
> And He is a stronghold of salvation to His Anointed.
>
> (Ps. 28:8)

While David was king of Israel (tenth century B.C.E.), the belief developed that his House would rule forever, not only over Israel but also over all the nations:

> The God who giveth me vengeance,
> And bringeth down peoples under me....
> Therefore I praise Thee, O Lord, among the nations,
> And will sing unto Thy name,
> Who increaseth the victories of His king
> And dealeth graciously with His Anointed,
> With David and his seed for evermore.
>
> (2Sam. 22:48–52; Ps. 18:42–52)

II

Some two centuries later, the Hebrew prophets began to turn their attention from the troubled present to the promise of the future. Isaiah, who was active from c. 738 to c. 701 B.C.E., envisaged a future era of universal peace which would be ushered in by "a Shoot out of the stock of Jesse" (Isa. 11:1), that is, a king of the Davidic line. At the same time, ideas about the resurrection of the dead also began to take shape. It is Isaiah who mentions it in a tantalizingly brief and enigmatic reference (Isa. 26:19). But there seems to have been no connection at that early date between the belief in resurrection and the expected coming of the "Shoot."

Once Judah became bereft of its king, the veneration of the royal personage who was no more increased. In Lamentations, written shortly after the destruction of Jerusalem (586 B.C.E.), the captive Davidic king is called "the breath of our nostrils" (Lam. 4:20).

The shape of the future occupies a prominent place in the prophecies of Ezekiel, who lived in Babylonia at the same time. Among his prophecies are two which subsequently became the basic building blocks of the Messianic myth. One is that of the great apocalyptic war of Gog and Magog (Ezek. 38 and 39), and the other his famous vision of the dry bones (Ezek. 37; see below, chapters 15 and 21).

About half a century after Ezekiel, there lived in Babylonia the anonymous prophet of consolation and Israel's national restoration, usually referred to as Deutero-Isaiah. This great poet-prophet spoke repeatedly about the "Servant of the Lord," describing the call, mission, sufferings, death, and resurrection of this mysterious individual (Isa. 42:1–4; 49:1–6; 50:4–9; 52:13–53:12). As to the identification of this "Servant," there is no scholarly consensus to this day. However, the Aggada, the Talmudic legend, unhesitatingly identifies him with the Messiah, and understands especially the descriptions of his sufferings as referring to Messiah ben Joseph (cf. below, chapter 17).

III

The latest Biblical books and the earliest apocryphal writings were the products of the second century B.C.E. In them an old Messianic idea, already alluded to by Amos (5:18—20), received new emphasis and was dwelt upon in considerable detail. The eschatological salvation which was to come about in the End of Days now became a cornerstone of the Messianic myth. The great redemption would come, God would directly and miraculously intervene in the affairs of the nations, and would bring about the succor of Jerusalem, the return of the exiles, the conversion of the Gentiles to a belief in the God of Israel, and the resurrection of the dead.

In the prophecies of Daniel (dated from the early Maccabean period, i.e., c. 164 B.C.E.) all these themes are contained, as well as those of the coming of an Anointed Prince, or Prince Messiah (*Mashiah Nagid*), his death, the destruction of the Sanctuary, and wars of desolation (Dan. 9:24—26; 12:1—3). Daniel is the only book of the rich apocalyptic literature which was admitted into the Biblical canon. The other apocalypses (or "revelations"), some contemporaneous with Daniel, were excluded and became part of the apocrypha, or "hidden writings." In all of them "the Day of the Lord" appears as a recurrent leitmotif, but especially so in the so-called pseudepigrapha ("false or spurious writings") which purport to be written by ancient Biblical characters or in long past Biblical days. This apocalyptic Day of Judgment was incorporated into the events of the Messianic era as a concomitant of the resurrection of the dead: once the dead come back to life, they must pass muster to reap rewards for their good deeds or suffer punishment for their evil acts.

IV

This, in turn, led to the next chapter in the great prognostication of Messianic events: the description, in ever greater detail, of the punishment of the wicked in hell, in Gehenna, and of the rewards of the pious in the Garden of Eden. In connection with the latter, the great Messianic banquet was a favorite imaginary event on which the Jewish messianologists lavished attention.

From a lament by El'azar Kallir (c. seventh century) one can form a clear picture of the ideas current in his day concerning the Messianic age. The lament, which is printed in the Mahzor (holiday prayer book) according to the Roman rite, contains twelve stanzas, which describe briefly the Messianic events that were believed to take place in the twelve months of the year of the Messiah's advent. In Nissan, says Kallir, Menahem ben 'Amiel will suddenly appear; in Iyyar, the dead, including Korah and his community, will rise; in Sivan, "the dead of the desert," those Children of Israel who died in the course of the forty years' wandering in the desert after the Exodus from Egypt, will rise; in Tammuz, there will be great wrath and ire everywhere, and a godless king (in whom we recognize the evil Armilus; see chapter 16) will persecute Israel; in Av, "the Pure Father"— i.e. God—"will wrap Himself in the garments of His revenge," the Mount of Olives will be rent from His shout, and Messiah will come in his greatness. In Elul, Ben Shealtiel will announce the coming of the Messiah, and the angels "Michael and Gabriel will descend to wage the war of revenge of God, and will not leave a single one of the enemies of Israel." In Tishri, there will be great confusion and strife among the nations, and they will say, "Let us go and destroy Israel." In Heshvan, Israel will be exiled into the desert; in Kislev, "suddenly a sword will fall from heaven, and blood will flow like rivers of water, and the dead will rise." In Teveth, there will be a famine that will last forty-five days. In Shevat, there will be a great war between Israel and the nations—evidently the War of Gog and Magog—in which each man from Israel will put to flight a thousand of its enemies. In Adar, Jerusalem will be rebuilt and in it Elijah, Menahem and Nehemiah will appear "with the glory of the ministering priest," and all the souls will praise God, Hallelujah![1]

Added to these themes were other related subjects: the splendor of the future Jerusalem, the miraculous universal peace and happiness, the dominion of King Messiah over the nations of the world, all of whom will recognize and worship only the God of Israel, the Holy One, blessed be He, the one and only Master of the Universe. For many centuries, in the midst of persecutions, massacres, expulsions, and humiliations, while living the life of hated and despised pariahs, the Jews in their fantasy saw themselves as kings of the World to Come, enjoying great pleasures of the palate, exquisite luxuries of housing and clothing, wading ankle-deep in floods of diamonds and pearls, studying the new Tora of the Messiah taught to them directly by God, and being entertained by dances performed by God himself to the music of the angels and the heavenly spheres.

In popular imagination, especially during the Middle Ages, the many specific images of rebuilt Jerusalem, of heavenly Jerusalem which would descend to the earth, of the earthly paradise, and of the heavenly paradise all merged into one and became a generalized myth of a kind of cosmic pleasure dome in which the pious would live for ever and ever. Only one feature was missing in this perfervid kaleidoscope of the Messianic bliss. Its absence is the more surprising since in the belief-system of the Muslim environment, in which many of the Jewish Messiah-legends developed, it occupied an important place. In the Muslim descriptions of Paradise, prepared for the pious, a central theme is the pleasure the elect will find in the Houris, those paradisiac maidens with large, fine, black eyes. To quote but one of the several Koranic passages in which this theme is touched upon,

---

1. Kallir's lamentation *BaYamim haHem* ("In Those Days") for Tish'a B'Av, in Mahzor according to the Roman rite, Bologna, 1540, vol. 1, fifth (unpaginated) folio from the end.

They will be reclining, facing each other, on gold-encrusted couches, while permanent attendants will circle among them with goblets and jugs and cups of pure drink that will give them no headache nor make them intoxicated. They will also have fruits of their choice and flesh of fowl that they may desire. All this in the company of fair maidens, pure like hidden pearls, a reward for their deeds (Koran 56:15–24).

The theme is elaborated and amplified in later Arabic literature, which dwells on the carnal joys the Houris will provide the pious, joys which will be a hundred times greater than earthly pleasures.

This has no counterpart in Jewish Messianology. Not only is there no reference whatsoever to sexual pleasures in any of the numerous Messianic legends, but the impression one gets from the invariably sexless mentions of "the pious" is that when the dead are resuscitated, sexuality will not be brought back to life with them. Moreover, the Talmudic and Midrashic view was that in Messianic times the "evil inclination" (*yetzer hara'*), which is identified with the sexual urge, will be uprooted from Israel, or, as one source singularly puts it, will be "slain" (B. Suk. 52a; Pes. Rab. ch. 36).[2]

V

From the first century B.C.E., the Messiah was the central figure in the Jewish myth of the future. The Jewish Messianic mythographers know and expound in minute detail the acts of all the protagonists of the great drama that will unfold in the End of the Days. And more than that: they present verbatim transcripts of the dialogues and discussions that will take place between and among God, the two Messiahs, the prophet Elijah, the people of Israel, the pious and

---

2. Abbreviations such as these are explained in the Annotated Bibliography and Abbreviations, at the end of the book.

the wicked, the nations of the world, Gog and Magog, the satanic Armilus, the archangels Michael and Gabriel, the many ministering angels, Samael the Satan, and even the earth, the mountains, and the waters. Not satisfied even with this, they recount, not unlike the all-informed modern novelist, what the actors in that cosmic drama of the future will feel: their intentions and desires, their hopes and fears, their emotional ups and downs, all are presented in elaborate, and often astounding, detail.

The complexity of interaction between Israel and its enemies on earth, and on high between the supernatural forces of good and evil represented by angels and devils, by seraphim and demons, is such that God himself must needs play a part far from the one usually taken in Jewish religion by the absolute ruler of the world, the supreme will in the universe, the omnipotent, omniscient, and omnipresent Creator and Master of all. In the Messianic myth cycle God is often depicted as being frustrated in His intentions and desires, as being successfully opposed by other divine beings and even by human heroes and protagonists, as a deity who wants to, but cannot, help His beloved people Israel, and who in His great compassion suffers with His children, sheds bitter tears over the cruel pain His elect, the Messiah, must endure, and seems powerless to change the march of events that inexorably lead to their death many of the Children of Israel, among them Messiah ben Joseph.

Because man invariably projects his own image onto his gods, these legends contain an indirect admission of the Jews' own inability to take the crucial step leading from a mere knowledge of the future (which they claimed to possess) to shaping the destiny that awaited them in the End of the Days. They knew what would happen but had no way of preventing its horrors, its bloodshed, its holocaust. In a sense, the Messianic movements (about which more will have to be said later) were desperate attempts to break out of this fated futurity and to take an active role in bringing about and transmuting the End of Days. They were doomed to

failure because a future known to consist of a certain sequence of events can, of course, not be changed.

Once the belief in the Messiah as the future Redeemer
became firmly entrenched in Jewish consciousness, another,
more immediate, problem arose: how to find justification for
his failure to come, year after year, decade after decade,
century after century. Had not the cup of Israel's sufferings
long run over? Was not God's promise to send His True
Messiah irrevocable and the basis of the enduring passionate
relationship between Him and the Community of Israel, or,
as the Kabbalists put it, between the King and His exiled
spouse, the Matronit? Psychologically, the expected and
hoped-for Coming was simply indispensable for the continued existence of Israel. Hence the delay in his advent had
to be explained in a manner that was at once acceptable
logically and sustaining emotionally. Despite all the ingenuity that went into finding an explanation, the answers
proffered were few and poor. The Messiah was prevented
from coming because the generation was unworthy; because
there were too many sinners in Israel; because of the machi-
nations of Satan; because the pious were unable to complete
the prayers that would have brought his advent; because he
could come only after all the unborn souls were born and the
celestial Hall of the Souls, the mystical *Guf*, was emptied;
etc. Again, what lies behind all these lame explanations is the
notion, or rather the vague sense—which was never allowed
to rise above the threshold of consciousness—that God was
not a free agent but was unable to do what He undoubtedly
would have liked to do: to redeem His beloved Israel right
away. If we substitute here too, as we have just done above,
the people of Israel for God, the notion becomes psychologically inevitable and theologically inoffensive.

VI

Rarely is a myth as perfectly prefigured in a tradition many centuries older as is the Jewish Messiah myth in the life of Moses. For it is a remarkable fact that the major features comprised in the myth of the Messiah, which developed fully between the second and the twelfth centuries C.E., are outlined in the Biblical story of Moses, whose main materials were set forth certainly not later than the sixth century B.C.E. A quick rundown of the main ingredients of the Messiah myth and their analogues in the Moses story will show to what extent this indeed is the case.

The Messiah is of the most noble royal blood known in Israel, that of the House of David; Moses is of the noblest line that existed in those early days among the Children of Israel, the priestly family of Levi. The great task both the Messiah and Moses are destined to fulfill is the redemption of their people from bondage—the bondage of the exile and dispersion in the case of the Messiah, and the bondage of the Egyptian slavery in the case of Moses. Both lead their people back to the Promised Land, the Holy Land, the land of the fathers. At the time of the advent of both, the people have suffered for a long time, for many generations, but, in the absence of divine help, they have been unable to better their lot. Both Moses and the Messiah spend an inordinately long time waiting for the divinely ordained moment when they can embark on their mission of salvation.

As the Midrash succinctly indicates, both Moses and the Messiah spent their years of waiting in the very place upon which they were to bring divine retribution. This is stated in several versions:

> The daughter of Pharaoh brought up him [Moses] who was to bring retribution upon her father. Thus also King Messiah, who will bring retribution upon Edom [i.e. Rome], dwells with them in their country.... (Ex. Rab. 1:26)

> The daughter of Pharaoh brought up him who was destined to take revenge on her father and his land. Likewise the Messiah, who is destined to take revenge on the idolaters, will grow up among them in that country [i.e. in Rome].... (Tanhuma Sh'mot 8)

> Moses grew up in the house of Pharaoh and thought
> that he was a son of his house.... And likewise the Mes-
> siah who will in the future take revenge on Gog and Magog
> and their armies, will grow up together with them in that
> country [i.e. in Rome].... (Tanhuma Tazri'a 8)

Moses is eighty years old when God speaks to him from
the Burning Bush and instructs him to go to Pharaoh; for
forty years he lived in the court of Pharaoh as a prince, for
another forty he was a shepherd in the Wilderness of Midian,
and we can assume—must assume—that all that time,
whether he knew it or not, he was waiting for the Call. The
Messiah, of course, has to wait much longer, for centuries at
least, but wait he does, in the gates of Rome among the sick
and the leprous, in the mysterious Bird's Nest in the supernal Garden of Eden, and in the anguished hearts of many a
Tzaddiq and of the simple, pious folk.

Nor does the Redemption follow immediately upon the
appearance of the Redeemer. After he is revealed, he is
hidden, and only upon his second appearance does the great
global process of Redemption begin. Thus R. Berekhya is
reported to have said:

> As the first Redeemer [i.e. Moses], so the last Redeemer
> [i.e. the Messiah]. Just as the first Redeemer was revealed
> [to the Children of Israel] and then again hidden from
> them...for three months...so the last Redeemer will be
> revealed and then again hidden from them. And how long
> will he be hidden from them? R. Tanhuma in the name of
> the rabbis said, "For forty-five days..." R. Yitzhaq ben
> Qatzarta in the name of R. Yona said, "Those are the
> forty-five days during which Israel will pluck salt-worth
> and eat it." (Job 30:4; Ruth Rab. 5:6; cf. Num. Rab. 11:2)

In conclusion of this theme it must be mentioned that
several Talmudic sages felt that there was a cosmic relationship, or rather equivalency, between Moses and the Messiah. According to Sh'muel the world itself was created only
for the sake of Moses, while according to R. Yohanan it was
created only for the sake of the Messiah (B. Sanh. 98b).
When, at long last, the Call comes, the Redeemer,

whether Moses or the Messiah, has to face a mighty oppo-
nent in relation to whom his own strength is nil. Moses is
opposed by the forces of a stone-hearted Pharaoh, his armed
hosts, and his magicians' millennial knowledge; the Messiah,
by the monstrous and satanic Armilus, the son of the stone
woman, with his numberless legions gathered from the four
corners of the earth. The unequal battle is joined. The
sufferings of the Redeemer are intensified, the outcome is
hopeless, or, rather, would be were it not for divine intervention in the last moment: the ten plagues and the miraculous
parting of the sea assure Moses the victory over the Egyp-
tians, and the even more awesome manifestations of divine
partisanship in the form of great atmospheric fireworks,
earthquakes, thunder and lightning, horrifying giant stars,
and warrior angels and Seraphim make the legions of Armilus buckle under the Messiah.

However, the Redeemer himself cannot escape tragedy
either. After leading and teaching, nursing and coaxing, and,
when need be, forcing and coercing his people for forty years
and bringing it to the very gates of Canaan, Moses must die.
He is denied what he wants most: entry into the Promised
Land. The greatest master, the greatest of men ever known
to Jewish history, who fearlessly and zealously championed,
not only the cause of God to an often rebellious people, but
also the cause of the people to an impatient and irate deity,
who spoke face to face to God and was so enveloped by
divine effulgence that he had to cover his face with a veil, to
hide it behind a mask, lest it frighten to death the people who
beheld it, this man of God himself had to die. The Biblical
account of the death of Moses is enigmatically silent about
the feelings that must have assaulted the man Moses when he
was informed by an inexorable deity of his impending de-
mise, so near the goal of his forty years of ministry in the
service of God and people, and yet so unattainably far. But
the Midrash enlarges upon the missing theme, and the
legends describing how Moses fought off the Angel of Death
and implored God to let him enter the Land of Promise, at

least in the shape of a deer or a bird, are among the most moving in the entire Midrashic literature.

The Messiah, too, is haunted, pursued, and overtaken by the problem of the Redeemer who is not allowed to see, let alone taste, the fruits of his labors. But the medieval messianologists who faced the issue solved it in a manner different from the one presented by the death of Moses. The Messiah, too, must die before his mission is completed, but he also must live in order to sit on the throne of David in Jerusalem. Therefore, two Messiahs must appear, one after the other. The first, Messiah son of Joseph, dies in the global wars of Gog and Magog in which he leads the modest forces of Israel against the juggernaut of Armilus. He fights valiantly, and so do his men, but the satanic powers prevail and slay many or most of them while putting the rest to flight and forcing them to hide in caves and crevices, in deserts and marshes. Messiah ben Joseph himself is killed by Armilus, and his body remains unburied in the streets of Jerusalem for forty days.

But then he comes to life. The legend tells us that Messiah ben David appears, and as one of the first of his Messianic acts, he resuscitates him. Since nothing more is said about him after his revival, one suspects that what one must understand is that the request which was denied to Moses will be granted to the Messiah: he, as the Son of Joseph, will die on the threshold of the End of Days, but then will come back to life as the Son of David and complete the mission he began in his earlier incarnation.

With the death of Moses, the earthly career of Israel's first Redeemer comes to an end. In the Other World, of course, he continues to keep a watchful eye on his people, continues to intercede in their behalf. Messiah ben David, too, nears the end of his ministry with his victory over the armies of Gog and Magog and over their satanic master Armilus, whom he kills with the breath of his mouth. This latter detail, incidentally, is an eloquent indication of the kind of victory Jewish legend envisaged would be achieved by the Messiah. There was to be, first of all, a holocaustal sequence of wars, myriads would be killed in actual combat, or by earthquakes and other great cataclysms, but the greatest of victories, that over Armilus himself, the evil incarnate, would be a spiritual one: his annihilation would be brought about by a breath from the pure mouth of the Son of David, the elect of God, the Messiah.

This greatest feat of the Messiah is, at one and the same time, also his last one. Just as Moses had brought the Children of Israel to the threshold of the Promised Land and then died, so the Messiah leads them to victory over Gog and Magog, culminating in the elimination of Armilus, and then fades away, disappears from the scene. Nothing more is heard about him except some very vague and generalized statements to the effect that he would continue to rule over his people for an indeterminate period. In all the great events which follow the victory over Armilus, the Messiah plays no role whatsoever. We know, or at least we are led to believe, that he is present at the Resurrection of the dead, at the Last Judgment, at the Messianic banquet, at the House of Study of the future in which the new, Messianic, Tora will be taught, but if he is, no mention is made of his presence and he plays no role at all. In all those great occurrences and processes it is God, the Holy One, blessed be He, who Himself takes the central place on the stage. It is God who resuscitates the dead, who judges the pious and the wicked, who sits with the saintly at the great feast, who pours wine into their cups, who entertains them by dancing before them, who teaches them the new Tora, and who receives the homage of the entire rejuvenated, reformed, and sanctified world. Where is the Messiah in all this? We are told nothing of him, and were it not that in the earlier phases of the Messianic myth we were assured that he would, after the ultimate victory, reign in Jerusalem as the Prince of Peace, we would not even suspect that he is present.

Thus, and in this primarily, the Messiah proves to be essentially a Moses figure, and Moses to be the accurate prefiguration of the Messiah. Both are Redeemers, but neither of them has a part in the great era to whose threshold they lead their people at the price of their lifeblood.

VII

Corresponding to his truncated career, the waiting for the Messiah, the millennial yearning for him, has also concentrated, not on his rule and sway over the world, but on his *coming*. The Messiah myth has much to say about the condition of the world and of the Jews in it which must obtain before the Messiah can come. Sufferings, evils, horrors are the main themes whose somber colors must fill the global canvas before the Messianic ray of light can illuminate it. Much speculation is devoted even to his forerunner, the prophet Elijah. When will he come, how will he appear, what will he do, how will he announce the coming of King Messiah?—these are momentous questions to which much attention is given by the messianologists. The history of the Messiah prior to his coming is also dealt with in great detail. We are told about his being created prior to, or during, the six days of Creation; about his waiting patiently, and then again impatiently, for the time when he can come; about his willingness to take upon himself unspeakable suffering so as to ease thereby the anguish of his people; about his attempts, and the attempts of the spiritual leaders of the people, to "hasten the end," as the oft-recurring phrase has it, that is, to bring about his coming, soon, quickly, today, by performing acts of utter piety, or else magic acts, or in some other way creating conditions which must result in his coming. And we hear a lot about the lack of success in which all these attempts inevitably end.

When, in God's own good time, the End of Days finally arrives and the Messiah appears, the lore of centuries knows and recounts in remarkable detail what will happen—until the moment, that is, that he ascends the throne of his father

David in Jerusalem. The wars, the victories, the resurrection, the ingathering, the judgment, the rebuilding of the Temple—all this is detailed in many sources, in many versions, with baroque embellishments and frills. But then—like a novel which regales the reader with the most hair-raising adventures of its hero, but only to the point where he emerges victorious, and leaves him there with one of the many variants of the traditional "and then he lived happily ever after"—the story stops, and we must take it on faith that after all the miraculous global events the Messiah would sit on his throne, serenely, peacefully, and happily ever after.

There is, of course, no reason to expect otherwise. Sufferings, adventures, misadventures, wars, defeats, victories, are the stuff stories are made of. To them can be added, in the case of myths and legends, miraculous happenings such as those enumerated above. But once Gog and Magog are defeated, Armilus killed, the dead resurrected, the wicked punished and the pious rewarded, the exiles ingathered, the throne of David restored, and the Temple rebuilt, what else remains? Whatever does, can be stated in a sentence ending with "ever after." Therefore the Messiah myth must end where it does, for it would be ludicrous to start chronicling the day-to-day details of King Messiah's administration governing from Jerusalem a submissive, happy, and God-fearing family of nations. The Messiah myth is, in essence, a myth of the great struggle between good and evil, with all its miraculous concomitants, the story of an upheaval greater than mankind has ever known in the past or will experience in the future, of the most stupendous holocaust one can imagine, which was deemed inevitable so that the old world array, or disarray, of evil could be eliminated and replaced by a new global order of goodness.

That in this great cataclysm the Jewish people, led by their long-suffering divine king, the Messiah, and protected by their Father in heaven, should be assigned the central role was likewise inevitable considering the social, political, and religious conditions of the Diaspora Jews who authored and elaborated the Messiah myth—and, more specifically, considering the mental image the Jews had of the triangular relationship between God and the nations, God and the Jews, and the Jews and the nations. Living as they did in a state of dispersion among the nations and of oppression by the Gentiles, the Jews nevertheless remained firmly convinced of the centrality of the Jewish people in the divine scheme with all that this meant in imaginary privileges and onerous obligations.[3] Thus the Redemption in the End of Days, too, could not but be centered on the Jewish people, whose role, however, was conceived as that of the divine instrument in imposing God's rule over the entire world.

Since the process was the thing, no wonder that by the time the story reached the end of the struggle and of the miraculous events, its mythopoeic élan was exhausted. We are, of course, given to understand that the Messiah was to settle down in Jerusalem to enjoy the fruits of his victory, and let the people enjoy them with him. But the millennial Jewish waiting and yearning for the *coming* of the Messiah and for the global upheaval and havoc he was expected to wreak among the Gentiles was satisfied by the account of the process, of the great Messianic cataclysm, of the traumatic replacement of global evil by global good. Once this was accomplished, the Messiah's mission was completed, his role ended. What he thereafter would go on doing as the king of peace could no longer hold the popular interest which for so long was focused on his superhuman heroics.

VIII

The enduring fascination of the Messianic idea for Judaism can best be gauged by two phenomena: one scholarly, the other popular. The scholarly phenomenon was the irresist-

---

3. On the Jewish view of history and the place of the Jewish people in it, cf. Raphael Patai, *The Jewish Mind*, pp. 28–37.

ible attraction the "Calculation of the End" had for the minds of many of the most learned rabbis and religious scholars in every generation from the first to the eighteenth century. While opponents of these mathematical pyrotechnics were never absent, the calculators of the time of the Messianic advent were always much more numerous, and included some of the greatest Talmudic sages, authors of Midrashim, philosophers, poets, commentators, Kabbalists, and statesmen. The list of those who, in the first few centuries of the Common Era, engaged in such calculations and found that the Messiah was about to come in just a few years include leaders in the days of the destruction of the Temple by the Romans (70 C.E.), the Tannaïtes Yohanan ben Zakkai, Eliezer ben Azariah, Yose the Galilean, and many other Talmudic sages.[4] The ingenuity with which scholars especially in the Middle Ages and down to the eighteenth century calculated the time of the Messianic advent is as astounding as is the fact that they mostly arrived at a date which lay only a few years or a few decades beyond their own time.[5] Evidently, the common motivation of all these mystico-mathematical efforts was the irrepressible desire of the calculators to find scriptural basis for the belief that the Messiah would indeed come soon, not in a distant indefinite future, but in their own lifetime.

The great Maimonides (1135–1204) himself, although he repeatedly and emphatically went on record decrying any attempt to fix the time of the coming of the Messiah, nevertheless succumbed to the temptation of interpreting certain Biblical passages as containing an indication of the date of the Redemption. Thus, on the one hand, in his commentary on the Mishna, he says:

---

4. Cf. Josephus Flavius, *Wars of the Jews* 6:5:4; B. Ber. 28b (where it is stated that Yohanan ben Zakkai expected the Messiah in the person of King Hezekiah of Judah); B. Sanh. 99a; Mid. T'hillim 90:17, ed. Buber, p. 393; Pes. Rab. 1; etc.

5. A detailed discussion of these calculations is found in Abba Hillel Silver, *A History of Messianic Speculations in Israel*.

The twelfth [of the thirteen principles of the Tora] pertains to the days of the Messiah: it is to believe and to hold true that he will come, and not to say that he is delayed, for even though he tarry, wait for him. But one must not fix a time for him, nor interpret Biblical passages so as to derive from them the time of his coming. And the sages said, "May the spirit of the calculators of the Ends be blown away."[6]

On the other hand, in his letter to the Yemenite Jews, after reiterating his criticism of those who calculate the date of the coming of the Messiah, Maimonides goes on to quote, and to subscribe to, an old family tradition concerning that very issue:

As for the precise determination of the time [of the advent of the Messiah]—it is not known. But I have a wondrous tradition which I received from my father [who got it] from my grandfather, from his father, from his grandfather of blessed memory, in this manner until the beginning of our exile from Jerusalem. . . . And it is, that in the wording of the prophecy of Balaam there is an allusion to the return of [the gift of] prophecy to Israel after its cessation. . . . Balaam said that after a lapse of time one will tell Jacob and Israel *What hath God wrought* (Num. 23:23). There is a secret in this: from that time on one must count as long a period as had passed from the six days of Creation until that time, and then prophecy will return to Israel and the prophet will tell them *What hath God wrought*. And that saying was [uttered by Balaam] in the thirty-eighth year after Israel's Exodus from Egypt; that is, from the beginning until that day 2485 years had elapsed. For they were redeemed [from Egypt] in the year 2448. And according to this conclusion and this explanation, prophecy will return to Israel in the year 4970 of the Creation [i.e., 1210 C.E.]. And there is no doubt that the return of prophecy is one of the preludes of the Messiah, as it is said, *And it shall come to pass afterward that I will pour out My spirit upon all flesh, and your sons and your daughters shall prophesy* . . . (Joel

6. Maimónides, *Commentary on the Mishna*, Seder N'ziqin, Tractate Sanhedrin, chapter 10, p. 216. My translation from the Arabic. The quoted saying of the sages is found in B. Sanh, 97b; its author is Sh'muel bar Nahmani in the name of Rabbi Jonathan.

3:1). And this is the clearest end which was told us, and we say that this is the authentic one. . . .[7]

That is to say, Maimonides actually expected the coming of the Messiah within a few years, and certainly hoped that he would see him with his own eyes. It so happened, however, that he died in 1204 (at the age of sixty-nine), just six years before the date of the advent as he calculated it.

IX

So much for members of the Jewish intellectual elite and their Messianic calculations. Their popular counterpart was the readiness of the masses to give credence to any imposter or self-deluded dreamer who claimed to be the Messiah. The list of these pseudo-Messiahs is as long as that of the calculators of the End, and the Messianic movements they triggered punctuate Jewish history from earliest times down to the eighteenth century.

The Biblical Zerubbabel, grandson of King Jehoiachin of Judah and thus a scion of the House of David, was the leader of one of the groups that returned from Babylonia to Jerusalem. He was for some time governor, but then mysteriously disappeared (c. 519/18 B.C.E.). Some historians consider him as having stood at the center of the first Messianic movement. In any case, the prophet Zechariah has God call Zerubbabel *"My servant the Shoot [Tzemah]"* who *"shall bear the glory and sit and rule upon his throne"* (Zech. 3:8; 6:12–13), all concepts with definitely Messianic connotations in the style of Isaiah (Isa. 11).

The Maccabean uprising (166 B.C.E.) definitely had Messianic overtones. Jesus of Nazareth (born between 9 and 6 B.C.E., died in 29 or 30 C.E.) was one of many Jews who claimed to be divinely inspired redeemers, although his

---

7. Maimonides, *Epistle to Yomen*, ed. Abraham S. Halkin, pp. 80–84. My translation from the Arabic.

ministry did not arouse a mass movement until a century or
so after his execution by the Romans as a seditionist. More
popular in his day was a certain Theudas, who (as Josephus
puts it) "persuaded a great part of the people" to follow him
to the river Jordan which, he promised, would part at his
command, and who was captured and beheaded by the
Romans together with many of his followers, in about 45
C.E.[8]

Somewhat later lived Menahem ben Judah ben
Hezekiah, a leader of the Jewish uprising against the Romans
who also had royal and Messianic pretensions but was killed
by the Jewish insurgents in Jerusalem (c. 68 C.E.). The name
Menahem, as we have seen, continued to have Messianic
connotations for many centuries. Other military leaders of
the period, too, considered themselves, or were considered
by the people, Messianic figures—the most famous among
them being Shim'on bar Kokhba (originally ben Kozba),
who first beat the legions of Rome and then held out against
them for three years before he was overwhelmed and slain in
battle (135 C.E.). When such a warlord fell, this very fact was
construed as proving that he was indeed Messiah ben Joseph,
who was destined to fight and be killed prior to the coming of
Messiah ben David.

The belief in these self-proclaimed Messiahs and in their
power to perform miracles could be so strong that it could
override all normal instincts of self-preservation. Thus in
about 448 a Jew appeared on Crete announcing that he was
Moses and that he would repeat on a much larger scale the
miracle performed by Moses at the Red Sea: he would part
the waters of the Mediterranean and lead the Jews of the
island dryshod to Judaea! When the hour he fixed for the
miracle arrived, he ordered his followers to jump into the
sea, which they did, with the result that many of them
drowned in the waves.[9]

---

8. Josephus Flavius, *Antiquities* 20:5:1; cf. also Acts 5:35–39.

9. Socrates Scholasticus, *Historia Ecclesiae* 12:33, as quoted in *Encyclopaedia
Judaica*, s.v. Messianic Movements.

This type of fanatical belief could be self-induced and self-centered as well, as shown by the example of a certain Yemenite pseudo-Messiah who appeared toward the end of the twelfth century. As Maimonides recounts the events, many Jews and Arabs rallied around this man, until finally he was apprehended by the Arab authorities. When asked for a proof of the divine source of his message, he answered: "Cut off my head and I shall come back to life immediately." Thus he died, but many people in Yemen continued to believe that he would rise and lead them yet.[10]

Throughout the Middle Ages and well into modern times, Messianic movements periodically energized the sluggish wheels of Jewish history. More than that: during that long period these movements were the only manifestations of the will of the Jewish people to assume an active role in their historical destiny. It has repeatedly been pointed out by historians that throughout the long centuries of the Diaspora the Jews in all the lands of their dispersion never acted but were always acted upon by the state, the principality, the city, or whatever other Gentile power held sway over them. Their own role was a passive one: one of accommodation, adjustment, petitioning, propitiation, supplication, submission, acceptance, and, if need be, laying down their lives. The Messianic movements were the one exception to this rule of one-sided power relationship. When seized by the Messianic fervor, the Jews became recklessly active: they sold or abandoned their property, moved to points of embarkation, bought or chartered ships, dared to resist or challenge the authorities, and made themselves ready to set sail under a moment's notice to the distant land of their fathers to join the forces of the Messiah and help him establish God's rule over Israel and the rest of the world.

The disappointment which inevitably followed these frantic preparations was heartrending. It hurled them from the pinnacles of ecstasy to the bottomless pit of despair. And

---

10. A. Marx, in *Hebrew Union College Annual* 3 (1926):356.

yet, such is the remarkable psychology of disconfirmation[11] that the failure of the particular Messianic pretender of the moment never resulted in a disbelief in the Messiah who was to come, and in his divine Father who would bring him. The thousands of Jews who remained stranded in many port cities and way stations, who were rendered destitute and homeless, who were ridiculed by the Gentiles as well as by their own unbelieving brethren, nevertheless held on to their age-old belief in the Messiah who would come, who must come. The firmness of their belief was succinctly expressed in the credo formulated by Maimonides: "And even though he tarry, nevertheless I shall wait for him every day that he should come." Within a few years the bitter experience was forgotten, and the next Messianic pretender was given as much credence as his predecessors, was greeted with as much enthusiasm, and was able to plunge his contemporaries into the same kind of frenzied belief, manic activism, and abandoned recklessness. From 1087 to 1172, a short span of eighty-five years, Jewish history records no less than nine Messianic movements which shook the communities in such widely scattered places as Morocco, Spain, France, Byzantium, Khazaria, Palestine, Babylonia, and Yemen.

The number of men who, in the course of the long Diaspora history, claimed to be the Messiah is unknown and cannot even be estimated, for those who left their traces in historical records can only be a fraction of the many more who arose, created a stir, gathered a following, and then met a violent end or disappeared.

X

However, it was not until great national catastrophes had

11. On the effect of disconfirmation on the belief in an expected miraculous superhuman intervention, cf. Leon Festinger, Henry W. Riecken, and Stanley Schachter, *When Prophecy Fails*, pp. 25ff. 43ff., 103, 140, 169, 180ff., 208, 212tf.; R. Patai, *Myth and Modern Man*, pp. 318–19.

overtaken Diaspora Jewry that the Messianic movements they engendered assumed really large dimensions. This was entirely in keeping with the generally prevalent old Jewish belief that the greater the sufferings of Israel, and, incidentally, the more complete its dispersion in all the countries of the world, the closer the date of the Messiah's coming. In 1492 the Jews were expelled from Spain—the greatest national disaster since the destruction of Jerusalem in 70 C.E. and the defeat of Bar Kokhba in 135—and at the same time Messianic hopes rose to a high pitch, centering upon the legendary Ten Lost Tribes of Israel. These tribes, stout warriors all, were believed to dwell somewhere to the east of Palestine, beyond the great desert, at a distance of some fifty days' journey, on the other side of the river Sambatyon, which threw up stones and sand throughout the six days of the week, making passage impossible, and rested on the Sabbath (hence its name Sambatyon). On the Sabbath, of course, it was forbidden to Jews to travel, let alone cross a river.

The legend of the Ten Tribes prepared the ground for the appearance of David Reubeni in 1523 in Venice. He was at the time a man of about forty years of age, small of stature and swarthy of complexion. He claimed that he was sent by his brother Joseph, the king of a country in the Desert of Khabur—the name perhaps echoes that of the great Arabian oasis of Khaibar—whose people comprised 300,000 men of the tribes of Gad, Reuben, and half of Manasseh—the two and a half tribes of Israel that, according to the Biblical account, *have received their inheritance beyond the Jordan at Jericho eastward, toward the sunrise* (Num. 34:15). Reubeni asserted that he was entrusted by his brother with the mission of proposing to the Pope that the Christian countries join forces with his brother to liberate the Holy Land from Turkish rule. For eleven years Reubeni kept the Jews of Italy, France, and Germany in turmoil, and was initially given a friendly reception by the Pope and kings. In Portugal, Marranos began openly to return to Judaism. Among them was Diego Pires, who circumcised himself, assumed the name Sh'lomo Molcho (1500–1532), and ultimately came to consider himself the Messiah. In 1532 Molcho and Reubeni went together to Regensburg, where they were received by the emperor Charles V, but instead of convincing him of their Messiano-political scheme, they aroused his suspicions, and he had both of them imprisoned. Molcho was burned at the stake, and Reubeni was taken in chains to Spain where he perished a few years later in an auto-da-fé. The origins of Reubeni are still debated by historians: some think he was a Falasha Jew from Ethiopia; others, that he was a Central European Ashkenazi Jew.

The next century witnessed the greatest Messianic movement in all Jewish history. Shabbatai Zevi, a Sephardi Jew, was born in Smyrna in 1626, on the ninth of Ab, the traditional date of the birth of the Messiah ever since early Talmudic times (see chapter 13). Suffering from manic-depressive states, he immersed himself in the study of the Kabbala, and after the horrors of the Chmielnicki massacres (1648–49) he became convinced that he was the Messiah. In 1662, after having twice married and immediately divorced his brides, he married in Cairo a young woman named Sarah who had survived the Polish massacres as a child, grown up to live a dissolute life, and let it be known that she was destined to become the wife of the Messiah. The shades of David Reubeni briefly flitted across the scene in the form of rumors that a Jewish army was ready to march out of the Arabian desert to conquer Palestine.

Shabbatai Zevi's antinomian acts, but even more so his personal beauty and extraordinary charm, made people accept his Messianic pretensions unquestioningly, and the popular enthusiasm he evoked was unprecedented. His fame rapidly spread beyond the borders of the Ottoman realm. By 1665 the whole Diaspora was under his spell. From Poland emissaries were sent to pay him homage, and in Holland entire Jewish communities liquidated their positions and waited for his word in the harbors to set sail for the Holy

Land.

As the Messianic year of 1666 drew nigh, Shabbatai Zevi announced that he would go to Constantinople, depose the Sultan, and assume the rule over the Ottoman Empire, among whose many far-flung dependencies was Palestine, the Holy Land. He sailed from Smyrna to Constantinople, but on February 6, 1666, his ship was intercepted. He was arrested and confined to the fortress of Gallipoli, where he managed to hold court in the grandest style for several months. Finally his behavior incurred the wrath of the Sublime Porte, and on September 16 of the same year he was brought before the Divan and given the choice between immediate death and conversion to Islam.

He chose the latter alternative, but put forward a mystical explanation of his apostasy: his conversion to Islam, which he equated with degradation and suffering—although in reality he received a respectable stipend from the Sultan—was a form of atonement for Israel. This was in accordance with the old Jewish legend which held that prior to his coming the Messiah must voluntarily undertake sufferings in order to ease the sufferings of Israel (see chapter 12). The new twist Shabbatai Zevi gave to this old Messiah legend proved acceptable to some of his followers. In further explanation of his apostasy, both Shabbatai and his followers adduced certain Kabbalistic tenets to the effect that he had to descend into the impure realm of the "husks" in order to redeem the scattered sparks of the divine light entrapped by them. The success of this ingenious mythical-theological reinterpretation of the disconfirmation of Shabbatai Zevi's mission can be gauged by the fact that after his death in 1676 a sect of Muslim Shabbatians, the so-called Doenmeh, survived until the nineteenth century.

For the rest of the Jewish world the shock of Shabbatai Zevi's apostasy was profound. Little is known about what the common people felt, but the rabbis in their wisdom decided on a course which, they thought, was most likely to heal the wounds in the nation's psyche: the course of minimizing what had happened, and of covering it with the veils of silence and disregard. The strategy succeeded: within a hundred years Judaism produced a new great religious movement, that of Hasidism, in which Messianic expectations were tamed, kept in their place, and never again allowed to get out of hand.

XI

In the nineteenth century, Messianism influenced two modern Jewish movements: Reform Judaism and Zionism. One of the basic tents of Reform is that it is the mission of Judaism to spread pure, rational, and ethical monotheism in the world. This, of course, is but a modern version of the old Messianic notion which holds that in the End of Days, after the victory of Israel over the nations, the whole world will come to believe in the one and only God. The old myth envisaged a catastrophic defeat for the nations at the hand of Israel, or, rather, their God—an idea that struck a familiar chord in the minds of Jews in the Middle Ages whether they lived in the Muslim orbit carved out from the world by the Arabs in accordance with their famous tenet, *din Muhammad bis-sayf*, "the religion of Muhammad by the sword," or in the shadows of the Christian *ecclesia militans*. The Reform Jewish doctrine, developed in the pseudoliberal atmosphere of nineteenth-century Central Europe, substituted example, suasion, and precept for the sword and militancy as the method of spreading the true faith in the world, but it retained the same Messianic vision: the filling of the earth with the knowledge of the Lord as the waters cover the sea.

The Messianic antecedents of Zionism are even clearer. The aim of Zionism was, of course, much more modest than the old Messianic dream. The defeat of the nations of the world and Messiah ben David's rule over them played no role in it. But the one purpose of Zionism, the establishment of an independent Jewish state in Palestine, was identical with the central feature in the Messianic myth, the final achievement it envisaged. The Jewish background of Theodor Herzl, the founder of modern political Zionism, was wanting, but it so happens that the concept of the Messiah was familiar to him, as we know from a childhood dream he later remembered and recounted (see chapter 28). But even though Messianic ideas may have been present in his subconscious, Herzl reached his solution of the Jewish problem, the establishment of a *Judenstaat*, through a political and sociological approach. His secularist attitude, to be sure, did not keep the enthusiastic East European Jewish masses from hailing him as "King Messiah." Others, too, felt that Herzlian political Zionism was a secularized Messianism, divested of its miraculous, superhuman elements, and centering instead on diplomatic negotiation with the modern-day heirs of Armilus—the Tsarist government of Russia, the Sublime Porte of Turkey, the Pope of Rome, the Kaiser of Germany.

In Herzl's days, as well as after his time, the Zionist movement had Messianic overtones whose strength depended on the depth of the roots in Jewish tradition. In the west, where these roots were shallow or withered, Zionism acquired the coloration of a social movement or a philanthropic undertaking; in Eastern Europe, where Jewish life was nourished by a vital and throbbing tradition of Judaism, the movement had a pronounced Messianic character. When, fifty years after the First Zionist Congress (1897), the State of Israel became a reality, as Herzl had foretold it in a prophetic exclamation,[12] Yemenite and other Oriental Jews greeted the event as the undoubted Messianic fulfillment of

---

12. On September 3, 1897, Herzl wrote in his Diaries: "Were I to sum up the Basel [Zionist] Congress in a word—which I shall guard against pronouncing publicly—it would be this: At Basel I founded the Jewish State. If I said this out loud today, I would be answered by universal laughter. Perhaps in five years, and certainly in fifty, everyone will know it." Cf. *The Complete Diaries of Theodor Herzl*, ed. by R. Patai, p. 581. It might be mentioned here in passing that the Chief Rabbi of Sofia considered Herzl the Messiah, and that in January 1904 Herzl told the King of Italy that when he was in Palestine, "I had avoided mounting a white donkey or a white horse, so no one would embarrass me by thinking I was the Messiah." *Ibid.*, pp. 310, 1599.

the ancient Biblical promise about the Return and the Ingathering.

XII

A few points need elucidation before we can conclude these
introductory remarks. One pertains to my use of the term
"myth," which may appear improper when used as a referent
to the sacred fantasies woven by millennial Jewish belief
around the figure of the Messiah. I therefore wish to em-
phasize that throughout this introduction I never use the
term in its popular or journalistic sense, familiar to many
readers from such headlines as "The Loch Ness Monster—
Truth or Myth?" All serious students of myth always use the
term in the sense of a story possessed of a deep inner truth for
those who believe in it. There are many definitions of myth,
but the belief in its truth is always part of them. I myself am
still satisfied with the one I arrived at several years ago:
"myth is a traditional religious charter, which operates by
validating laws, customs, rites, institutions, and beliefs, or
explaining socio-cultural situations and natural phenomena,
and taking the form of stories, believed to be true, about
divine beings and heroes."[13] This definition, arrived at after
lengthy study of the myths of many nations, fits the Messiah
myth perfectly.

First of all, the "traditional religious charter" character of
the Messiah myth is clearly indicated by the fact that this
myth has for more than two thousand years served as a basic
document outlining and defining the position of the Jewish
people in relation to God, to the world of the nations, to its
own Holy Land, to the forces of good and evil, and to the
issues of pleasures and sufferings, merits and sins. The
Messiah myth operates by explaining the one overriding
socio-cultural situation in which the Jews have found them-

---

13. R. Patai, "What Is Hebrew Mythology?" *Transactions of the New York Academy
of Sciences*, November, 1964, Ser. II, vol. 27, no. 1, p. 73.

selves ever since the destruction of Jerusalem: that of the Diaspora, the exile and the disperson, of being a prey to the Gentiles, whose will made them suffer and at whose whim they lived or died. While the origin of this condition is set forth in another myth, that of the great national sin which brought about the retribution of the exile, its continued duration through the centuries is explained and made bearable by the Messiah myth which demonstrates its provisional nature and its impending end through the Messiah whose coming is expected to take place any day. In other words, the Messiah myth validates the Jewish belief in a great and glorious Jewish national future. At the same time, the Messiah myth differs from the run-of-the-mill myths inasmuch as they speak of fateful events that took place in the past, and whose effect was to determine the course of happenings in succeeding generations and down to the present time; the Messiah myth, on the other hand, describes events equally fateful but future that will take place in the End of Days and which, through their expected occurrence, influence the course of events in the present. What the Messiah myth says, in essence, is that because the Messianic Redemption will come and has not yet arrived, therefore events and conditions in the present, and in the past that has led up to the present, are what they are and as they are.

That the stories comprised in the Messiah myth speak about divine beings and heroes does not even have to be pointed out. In fact, in comparison with other myths, this feature is most intensively and emphatically present in the Messiah myth. Other myths speak not only of divine beings and superhuman heroes, but also of simple men and women, flesh-and-blood humans, whose interaction with the wonderful and much more powerful divinities and heroes lends the myth much of its tension, power, and enduring, fateful influence. In the Messiah myth, human individuals appear only as passive onlookers who are granted, here and there, a glimpse of what is going on in the realm inhabited by divine beings and superhuman heroes. If humanity participates at all in the events, it is represented only by anonymous masses: armies, crowds, swarms of refugees, and other large human aggregates. This is how we hear in these myths about Israel, the nations of the world, the pious, the wicked, and the like. All the active protagonists who are referred to as individuals are divine beings and heroes whose acts determine the fate of the masses they protect, attack, or direct. We hear about God, angels, the heavenly princes (or patrons) of the nations, Satan, Armilus, the prophet Elijah come back to earth, and, of course, the Messiah himself, whose superhuman portraiture begins with the mythologem of his being called into existence by God in the six days of Creation.

Because the drama of the Messianic end takes place in the interaction among these divine beings and heroes, to which the holocaustal carnage of the armies and the civilians serves merely as a foil, we remain curiously unmoved by the latter. That myriads are slain by Gog and Magog touches us far less than the death of the one hero, Messiah ben Joseph. But perhaps this structural feature of the Messiah myth—the emphasis on the individual superhuman hero and the submerging of all individual men into one undifferentiated human mass—contributed to its effectiveness as a charter for life in exile: it placed individual suffering, of which there was plenty, into perspective, it made people realize and understand that their own personal tragedy was but one of many, and made them find some comfort in this thought, as well as in the concentration it demanded on the great agony and tragedy of the superhuman protagonist of the Redemption myth, the person of the Messiah himself.

All myths must be believed to be true in order to be effective. The truth of the Messiah myth was taken so seriously that, as we have seen, belief in the coming of the Messiah was made a cardinal tenet of Judaism. True, no sage, rabbi, or teacher ever demanded belief in the truth of all the details comprised in the medieval proliferation of the Messiah myth. But it was precisely the folkloristic frills, the colorful embroideries, the grossly exaggerated fantastic features which assured its effective hold on the popular mind. Just as the belief in the Other World made suffering less painful for the individual, so the belief in the collective Future to Come rendered the national tragedy of the exile less excruciating. Whether or not this belief exploded into a Messianic movement, as it did from time to time, its very presence helped divert attention from the dismal present to the glorious future. While the myth of the Messiah was alive—that is, while the belief in his impending coming was an actuality—it was a powerful sustaining force in the life of the Jewish people. When it declined and became moribund, as it did in the nineteenth century, Jewry had to produce new concepts and precepts to assure its own continued existence.

XIII

A word must also be said about my use of the term "legend." Legend, which originally meant something that was read at a religious service or at meals, usually a story of a saint's or martyr's life, has come to mean a story supposedly based on fact, and therefore told as true. The truth content, that is, is common to myth and legend. Where the two differ is in their protagonists. The protagonists of the myth, as stated above, are divine beings and heroes; those of the legend were people who actually lived at some point in the past. Nor does the legend have the *general* explanatory function of the myth: it is often tied to a place, explaining some local feature of geography, or a name, a custom, or a tradition, by recounting what a person did there in the past. The myth, on the other hand, typically deals with great all-human issues, such as the origin of the world, of man, of death, of suffering, and other basic features of the human condition. Legend can thus be viewed as a myth in a minor key, treating of matters of lesser importance. Despite these typological differences, the line between myth and legend is often vague, and the same story can be considered myth by some and legend by others.

Because of this fluidity of the boundary line between myth and legend, I have used the two terms rather loosely. In my unconcern with consistency in this respect I was also influenced by the fact that the traditional Talmudic term "Aggada" means, even at its narrowest, both legend and myth. Still, a closer look at the Messiah texts reveals that some of them have the definite characteristics of myth, others bear the stamp of legend. The wars of Gog and Magog, the encounter between the Messiah and Armilus, the resurrection of the dead, the Last Judgment, the great banquet, and many more, are unquestionably myths. The story about the man who plows his field and then goes to Bethlehem to seek out the mother of the Messiah has the earmarks of legend. The Hasidic stories about the Ba'al Shem entering a half-ruined house and meeting there a leper who, as the Ba'al Shem later asserted, was the Messiah, or of various rabbis' encounters with a poor beggar who was the Messiah in disguise—these again are legends. In general it can be said that in the type of material we are dealing with in the Messiah stories, the taxonomical distinction between myth and legend is immaterial. However different in character, all the Messiah stories express the one basic belief that the Messiah does exist at present, is in a state of waiting and suffering, and is ready to come when the End of Days arrives. Whether this belief is poured into the form of myth or into that of legends, or whether the stories fall into the first or the second category, is insignificant in relation to the great central concern informing them all: the undaunted will to believe in his coming.

1

The Biblical Preamble

The writings of the Hebrew prophets are replete with descriptions of, and references to, the Messianic era. Obviously, only a small selection from them can be presented here. However, the excerpts which follow contain the main features of the Biblical Messianic idea that were subsequently elaborated and augmented in the Apocrypha, the Talmudic and Midrashic literature, and later Jewish writings.

It also must be pointed out that several of these Biblical Messianic prophecies are Messianic only in the light of these later interpretations. At the time of their composition, these passages may have had other meanings. The important prophecies of Deutero-Isaiah about the Suffering Servant, for instance, are considered by Jewish as well as Christian scholars as referring to the people of Israel as a whole. In Isaiah 49:3 the Suffering Servant is explicitly identified with Israel (see the full passage below). On this basis, as well as on the basis of certain other features, all the so-called "Servant Songs" (Isa. 42:1—4; 49:1—6; 50:4—9; and 52:13—53:12) have long been taken to speak of the sufferings of exiled Israel as personified in "the Servant of the Lord." Yet these same passages became in Talmudic times identified with the Messianic theme, and so they have remained in Jewish folk

consciousness throughout the ages. In fact, it is quite proba-
ble that the concept of the suffering Messiah, fully developed
in the Talmud, the Midrash, and the Zohar, has its origin in
the Biblical prophecies about the Suffering Servant, as
shown by the direct references to Isaiah 53:5 in describing
the sufferings of the Messiah in the Talmud, the Midrash
Konen (eleventh or twelfth century), and the Zohar (thirteenth century; see below, chapter 12).

The Suffering Servant

Behold, My Servant whom I uphold, My Elect whom My
soul wanteth: I have put My spirit upon him; he shall send out
justice to the nations. He shall not shout, neither lift up his voice
nor let it be heard abroad. He shall not break [even] a bruised reed,
not a dim wick shall he quench, [but] he shall in truth send out
justice. He shall not grow dim, nor shall he be crushed, until he
puts justice in the earth, and the isles shall hope for his teachings.

(Isa. 42:1–4)

Listen, O isles, to me, and hearken, O nations from afar! The
Lord hath called me from the womb, from my mother's bowels He
mentioned my name. And He made my mouth like a sharp sword,
in the shadow of His hand He hid me, and He made me into a
bright arrow, in His quiver He concealed me. And He said to me:
Thou are My Servant, Israel, in whom I will be glorified. And I
said: In vain have I labored, for naught and in vain have I spent my
strength, yet surely my right is with the Lord, and my recompense
with my God! And now, saith the Lord, my Creator from the
womb to be His Servant, to bring Jacob back to Him, so that Israel
be gathered to Him, and I be honored in the eyes of the Lord, and
my God become my strength—and He said: It is a light thing for
thee to be My Servant, to raise up the tribes of Jacob, and to bring
back the offspring of Israel; I will also give thee for a light of the
nations, to be My salvation until the end of the earth.

(Isa. 49:1–6)

The Lord God hath given me a trained tongue, to know how to sustain the weary; He awakens at morn, at morn He awakens my ear to hear what is taught. The Lord God opened my ear and I have not rebelled, neither did I turn backward. My back I gave to the smiters and my cheeks to those who pluck, my face I have not hid from shame and spitting. And the Lord God helped me, therefore I was not ashamed, therefore I set my face like a rock and I knew that I would not be abashed. Near is He who justifieth me; who, then, can contend with me? Let us stand up together, who is mine adversary? Let him come near me! Behold, the Lord God will help me; who, then, shall condemn me? Behold, they all shall wax old as a garment, the moth shall eat them up.

(Isa. 50:4—9)

Behold, My Servant shall prosper, he shall be exalted and lifted up, and be very high. Even as many were appalled at thee— as his visage was marred more than any man's, and his form more than the sons of Adam,—so shall he startle many nations, kings shall shut their mouths before him, for that which had not been told them shall they see, and that which they had not heard shall they perceive.

Who would have believed our report, and to whom hath the Lord's arm been revealed? For he shot up as a sapling before him, and as a root out of parched earth, he hath neither form nor comeliness that we could see in him, and no appearance that we would desire. He is despised and forsaken of men, a man of pains and acquainted with disease, and as one from whom faces are hidden, despised was he and we esteemed him not. Verily he hath borne our diseases, and our pains—he carried them, and we thought him stricken, smitten of God, and afflicted. But he was wounded because of our transgressions, bruised because of our iniquities, the chastisement of our welfare was upon him, and with his stripes we are healed. All of us, like sheep we went astray, each man turned to his own way, and the Lord inflicted upon him the sin of us all. He was oppressed and tortured, and yet he opened not his mouth, as a lamb led to slaughter, and as a sheep dumb before her shearers, and he opened not his mouth. From prison and judgment was he taken, and who can reason with his generation? For he was cut off out of the land of the living because of the transgression of my people, plague upon them! And they made his grave with the wicked, and with the rich his tomb, although he hath done no violence, and no deceit was in his mouth. Yet it pleased the Lord to crush him by disease. Oh, make not his soul a guilt-offering, let him see his seed, prolong his days, and let the purpose of the Lord prosper in his hand! He shall see his soul free of travail, he shall be satisfied with knowledge, and shall turn the righteous to righteousness, My Servant of the many, and he shall bear their iniquities. Therefore I will give him a portion among the great ones, and with the mighty shall he divide the spoil, because he hath bared his soul unto death and was counted among the transgressors, and he bore the sin of many, and interceded for the transgressors.

(Isa. 52:13—53:12)

The Slain Messiah

Seventy weeks are decreed upon thy people and upon thy holy city to imprison the transgression and to put a seal on sin, and to atone iniquity, and to bring everlasting righteousness, and to seal vision and prophet, and to anoint the Holy of Holies. Know therefore and discern: from the issuance of the word about the return and rebuilding of Jerusalem until the [coming of] the Messiah the prince, seven weeks [shall pass]; and for sixty-two weeks it shall be built again, [with] broad place and moat, but in troublous times. And after the sixty-two weeks the Messiah will be cut off and be no more; and the city and the Sanctuary shall be destroyed by a people, a prince who shall come. But his end will be in a flood. And until the end of the war, desolations are determined....

(Dan. 9:24—26)

Gog of the Land of Magog

And the word of the Lord came unto me saying: Son of Man, set thy face toward Gog, of the land of Magog, the chief prince of Meshekh and Tubal, and prophesy about him, and say: Thus saith the Lord God: Behold, I am against thee, Gog, the chief prince of Meshekh and Tubal. And I will turn thee about, and put hooks into thy jaws, and will bring thee forth and all thy army, horses, and riders, all of them clothed most gorgeously, a great company with buckler and shield, all of them handling swords. Persia, Cush, and Put with them, all with shield and helmet. Gomer with all its bands, the house of Togarmah in the uttermost north with all its bands, and many peoples with thee. . . . In the end of the years thou wilt come against the land saved from the sword, gathered from among many peoples upon the mountains of Israel which have been a continual ruin; it was brought out from peoples, and all of them dwelt safely. And thou shalt ascend like a storm, come like a cloud to cover the land, thou and all thy bands, and many peoples with thee.

Thus saith the Lord God: And it shall come to pass in that day that things shall come up into thy heart, and thou shalt think an evil thought. And thou shalt say: I will go up against the open land, I will come upon the quiet who dwell safely, all of them dwell without walls, and they have no bars and gates. To take spoil and to take the prey, to turn thy hand against the ruins, now inhabited, and against the people gathered from among nations, that make cattle and goods, dwell upon the navel of the earth. Sheba and Dedan and the merchants of Tarshish and all her villages will say to you: Comest thou to take the spoil? Hast thou assembled thy company to take the prey? To carry off silver and gold, to take cattle and goods, to take great spoil?

Therefore prophesy, Son of Man, and say to Gog: In that day, when My people Israel dwelleth safely, shalt thou not know it? That thou comest forth from your place, from the uttermost north, thou and many peoples with thee, riders of horses all of them, a great company and a mighty army? And thou comest up against My people Israel like a cloud to cover the earth. In the end of the days it shall be, and I will bring thee to My country that the nations may know Me, when I will be sanctified through thee before their eyes, O Gog!

Thus saith the Lord God: Art thou he of whom I spake in ancient days through My servants the prophets of Israel who prophesied in those days for years, to bring thee against them? And it shall come to pass in that day, in the day in which Gog shall come upon the land of Israel, saith the Lord God, My wrath shall rise in My nostrils. And in My jealousy in the fire of My fury did I speak: Surely in that day there shall be a great trembling upon the land of

Israel. And the fish of the sea and the fowl of heaven, and the beast of the field, and all the creeping things that creep upon the ground, and all the men that are upon the face of the earth shall tremble at My presence, and the mountains shall collapse, and the terraces shall tumble, and every wall shall fall to earth. And I will call for a sword against him, saith the Lord God, and each man's sword shall be against his brother. And I will punish him with pestilence and with blood, and I will rain torrential rains, and hailstones, and fire and brimstone upon him and upon his bands and upon the many peoples that shall be with him. And thus I will magnify Myself and sanctify Myself, and I will make Myself known before the eyes of many nations, and they shall know that I am the Lord.

(Ezek. 38)

And thou, Son of Man, prophesy about Gog and say: Thus saith the Lord God: Behold, I am against thee, Gog, chief prince of Meshekh and Tubal. And I will turn thee about and lead thee on, and will bring thee up from the edges of the north, and will bring thee upon the mountains of Israel. And I will knock thy bow out of thy left hand, and make thy arrows drop from thy right. Upon the mountains of Israel wilt thou fall, thou and all thy bands, and the peoples that are with thee; and I will give thee unto the birds of prey of all sorts and to the beasts of the field, to be devoured. Upon the face of the field shalt thou fall, for I have spoken, saith the Lord God.

And I will send a fire on Magog and on them that dwell safely in the isles, and they shall know that I am the Lord. And I will make known My holy name in the midst of My people Israel; and will not desecrate My holy name any more, and the nations shall know that I am the Lord, holy in Israel.

Behold, it cometh and it shall be, saith the Lord God. This is the day whereof I have spoken. And the inhabitants of the cities of Israel shall go forth, and shall burn the weapons and use them as fuel, the shield and the buckler, the bow and the arrows, the hand-stave and the spear, and they shall burn fire of them seven years. And they shall not carry wood from the field, and shall not hew of the forests, for they shall burn fire of the weapons, and they shall spoil their spoilers and rob their robbers, saith the Lord God.

And it shall come to pass in that day that I will give unto Gog a place of burial in Israel . . . and they shall bury there Gog and all his multitude, and shall call it the Valley of Gog's Multitude. And the house of Israel shall bury them that they may cleanse the land, seven months....

And thou, Son of Man, thus saith the Lord God: Say to the bird of every sort and to every beast of the field: Assemble and come, gather around My sacrifice which I sacrifice for you, a great sacrifice upon the mountains of Israel, that ye may eat flesh and drink blood. The flesh of the mighty shall ye eat, and the blood of the princes of the earth shall ye drink.... And ye shall be filled at My table with horse and rider, the mighty and the man of war, saith the Lord God.

And I will set My glory among the nations, and nations shall see My judgment that I have executed, and My hand that I have laid upon them. And the house of Israel shall know that I am the Lord their God, from that day and forward. And the nations shall know that the House of Israel was exiled for their iniquity, because they broke faith with Me....

Therefore thus saith the Lord God: Now I bring back the captivity of Jacob, and have compassion upon all the House of Israel, and I will be jealous for My holy name.... When I bring them back from the peoples and gather them from the lands of their enemies I will be sanctified in them in the sight of many nations. And they shall know that I am the Lord their God....

(Ezek. 39)

The Day of the Lord

Behold, a day of the Lord cometh, and thy spoil shall be divided in thy midst. For I will gather all the nations against Jerusalem to battle, and the city shall be taken and the houses rifled, and the women ravished, and half of the city will go into captivity, but the residue of the people shall not be cut off from the city. Then shall the Lord go forth and fight against those nations as when He fighteth in the day of battle....

(Zech. 14:1−3)

Behold, I will send to you Elijah the prophet before the coming of the Day of the Lord, the great and terrible one. And he shall return the heart of the fathers to the sons and the heart of the sons to their fathers, lest I come and smite the land to destruction.

(Mal. 3:23–24)

The Victory

I see him, but not now,
I behold him, but not from nigh:
A star shall step forth from Jacob,
And a scepter shall arise from Israel,
And shall crush the corners of Moab,
And break all the Children of Seth,
And Edom shall be his possession,
And Seir a possession of its enemies,
And Israel shall do valiantly!

(Num. 24:17–18)

The Ingathering

I will bear you on the wings of eagles and bring you unto Myself. . . . [1]

(Exod. 19:4)

And when all these things are come upon thee, the blessing and the curse, and thou shalt turn to thy heart among all the nations whither the Lord thy God hath driven thee, and thou shalt return unto the Lord thy God and hearken to His voice. . . . then the Lord thy God shall bring back thy captivity and have compassion upon thee, and He will gather thee from all the peoples whither the Lord thy God hath scattered thee. If thy dispersed be in the ends of heaven, from thence the Lord thy God shall gather thee, and from thence will He fetch thee. And the Lord thy God shall bring thee into the land which thy fathers possessed, and thou shalt possess it, and He shall do thee good and shall multiply thee above thy fathers.

(Deut. 30:1–5)

---

1. This is not the literal, but the popular, interpretation of the verse.

And the children of Judah and the children of Israel shall be gathered together, and they shall appoint themselves one head....

(Hos. 2:2)

And it shall come to pass in that day
That the Lord will set His hand a second time
To recover the remnant of His people
That shall remain from Assyria and Egypt,
From Pathros and Cush, from Elam and Shinar,
From Hamath and the islands of the sea.
And He will raise an ensign for the nations,
And assemble the dispersed of Israel,
And gather the scattered of Judah
From the four winds of the earth.

(Isa. 11:11−12)

And I will let you find Me, saith the Lord, and I will return your captivity, and I will gather you from all the peoples and from all the places whither I have driven you, and will bring you back to the place whence I have caused you to be exiled.

(Jer. 29:14)

For thus saith the Lord:
Sing to Jacob with joy
And shout at the head of nations,
Announce ye, praise ye, and say:
Save, O Lord, Thy people,
The remnant of Israel.
Behold, I bring them from the north country
And gather them from the ends of the earth....
In a great company shall they return hither....
For I am become a father to Israel,
And Ephraim is My firstborn.

(Jer.31:7–9)

Thus saith the Lord God: I will gather you from the peoples and assemble you out of the countries in which ye have been scattered, and will give you the soil of Israel....

(Ezek. 11:17)

And I will bring you out from the peoples, and gather you from the countries wherein ye are scattered, with a mighty hand and with an outstretched arm, and with fury poured out.

(Ezek. 20:34)

With sweet savour will I accept you when I bring you out from the peoples, and gather you out of the countries wherein ye have been scattered, and I will be sanctified in you in the sight of the nations. And ye shall know that I am the Lord when I bring you to the soil of Israel, to the land which I lifted up My hand to give to your fathers.

(Ezek. 20:41—42)

For thus saith the Lord God: Behold, here am I, and I will search for My sheep and seek them out. As a shepherd seeketh out his flock in the day that he is among his sheep that are separated, so will I seek out My sheep and I will deliver them out of all places whither they have been scattered in the day of cloud and thick darkness. And I will bring them out from the peoples, and gather them from the countries, and will bring them into their own land, and I will let them graze on the mountains of Israel, by the streams and all the habitations of the country. . . .

(Ezek. 34:11—13)

For a small moment have I forsaken thee,
But with great compassion will I gather thee;
In a flush of wrath I hid My face from thee
But with mercy eternal will I pity thee,
Saith thy Redeemer the Lord.

(Isa. 54:7—8)

Thank the Lord, for He is good,
Forever is His mercy—
Thus will say the redeemed of the Lord
Whom he redeemed from the hand of the foe
And gathered out of the lands,
From east and from west,
From the north and from the sea.

(Ps. 107:1—3)

The King of Peace

A child will be born to us,
A son will be given to us,
And the dominion will be upon his shoulder,
And his name will be called
"Wonderful Counselor, Mighty God,
Eternal Father, Prince of Peace."
The dominion will be increased
And of peace there will be no end
Upon the throne of David
And upon his kingdom,
To establish it and uphold it
In justice and righteousness
From henceforth and forever....

(Isa. 9:5–6)

A Shoot will come forth out of the stock of Jesse,
And a twig shall grow forth from his roots.
And the spirit of the Lord shall rest upon him,
A spirit of wisdom and understanding,
A spirit of counsel and might,
A spirit of knowledge and the fear of the Lord.
And his delight shall be in the fear of the Lord,
And he shall not judge after the sight of his eyes,
And not after the hearing of his ears shall he decide.
But he shall judge the poor in righteousness
And decide with equity for the meek of the land,
And shall smite the land with the rod of his mouth
And with the spirit of his lips shall he slay the
    wicked.
And righteousness shall be the girdle of his loins,
And the faithfulness the girdle of his reins.
And the wolf shall dwell with the lamb,
And the leopard lie down with the kid,
And the calf and the lion and the fatling together,
And a little boy shall lead them.
And the cow and the bear shall feed,
Together their young ones shall rest,

And the lion like the ox shall eat straw.
And the suckling child shall play on the asp's hole,
And over the basilisk's den the weaned shall pass his
    hand.
They shall neither hurt nor destroy in all My holy
    mountain,
For the earth shall be full of the knowledge of the
    Lord
As the waters cover the sea.
And it shall come to pass on that day
That the root of Jesse which standeth as the peoples'
    ensign
Unto it shall nations seek
And its resting place shall be glory.
And it shall come to pass on that day
That the Lord shall set His hand a second time
To recover the remnant of His people
That shall remain from Assyria and Egypt,
From Pathros and Cush, from Elam and Shinar,
From Hamath and the islands of the sea.
And He will raise an ensign for the nations,
And assemble the dispersed of Israel,
And gather the scattered of Judah
From the four winds of the earth.

                        (Isa. 11:1–12)

And it shall come to pass in the end of days
That the mountain of the Lord's House
Shall be established at the head of the mountains
And exalted above the hills,
And peoples shall stream unto it.
And many nations shall go and say:
Come, let us go up to the Lord's mountain
And to the House of Jacob's God
And He shall teach us of His ways
And we will walk in His paths,
For out of Zion shall come forth the Law
And the word of the Lord from Jerusalem.
And He shall judge among many peoples

And decide for nations mighty and far off,
And they shall beat their swords into ploughshares
And their spears into pruning hooks,
Nation shall not raise sword against nation
And they shall not learn war any more.
But each man shall sit under his vine
And under his fig tree, and none shall frighten,
For the mouth of the Lord hath spoken.

(Mic. 4:1–4; cf. Isa. 2:2–4)

Behold, days come, saith the Lord,
When I will raise unto David a righteous shoot
And he shall reign as king and prosper,
And do right and justice in the land.
In his days Judah shall be saved
And Israel shall dwell in safety.
And this is the name he shall be called:
The Lord is our justice.

(Jer. 23:5–6)

Rejoice greatly, O daughter of Zion,
Shout, O daughter of Jerusalem,
Behold, thy king cometh unto thee,
Righteous and victorious is he,
Lowly, and riding upon an ass,
Upon a colt, an ass's foal.
And I will cut off chariots from Ephraim
And horses from Jerusalem,
And off shall be cut the battle bow,
And peace shall be his word to the nations
And his dominion shall be from sea to sea,
And from the River to the ends of the earth.

(Zech. 9:9–10)

I saw in a night vision, and, behold, with the clouds of heaven came one like unto a son of man, and he went to the Ancient One [God], and he was brought near before Him. And to him was given dominion and glory and kingship, and all the peoples, nations, and languages will serve him. His dominion shall be an everlasting dominion which shall not pass away, and his kingdom shall not be destroyed.

(Dan. 7:13—14)

Resurrection

Thy dead shall live,
My corpses shall arise,
Awake and sing
Ye dwellers of the dust,
For a dew of light is thy dew
And the earth shall bring forth the shades.

(Isa. 26:19)

And at that time Michael the great prince shall stand up, he who standeth over the children of thy people. And it shall be a time of trouble such as never was ever since there was a nation and until that time. And at that time thy people shall be delivered, all those who shall be found written in the book. And many of them that sleep in the dust of the earth shall awaken, some to eternal life and some to reproaches and everlasting abhorrence. And the wise shall be resplendent as the splendor of the firmament, and they that turn many to righteousness as the stars for ever and ever.

(Dan. 12:1—3)

The Vision of the Dry Bones

The hand of the Lord was upon me, and He carried me out in the spirit of the Lord and set me down in the midst of the valley, and it was full of bones. And He caused me to pass all around them, and, behold, they were very many upon the face of the valley, and, behold, they were very dry. And He said to me: Son of Man! Can these bones live? And I said: Lord God, Thou knowest. And He said to me: Prophesy, Son of Man, about these bones and say to them: O ye dry bones, hear the word of the Lord! Thus saith the

Lord God to these bones: Behold, I bring spirit into you and ye shall live! And I will put upon you sinews, and will bring flesh upon you, and will stretch skin over you, and will put spirit into you, and ye shall know that I am the Lord. And I prophesied as I was commanded, and there was a sound as I prophesied, and, behold, a commotion, and the bones came together, bone to its bone. And I saw, and behold, there were upon them sinews, and flesh came up, and skin stretched upon them on the top, but spirit was not in them. And He said to me: Prophesy to the spirit, prophesy Son of Man, and say to the spirit: Thus saith the Lord God: From the four winds come, O spirit, and breathe into these slain ones so that they may live! And I prophesied as He commanded me, and the spirit came into them and they lived, and they stood upon their feet, an army, very, very great. And He said to me: Son of Man! These bones are all the House of Israel. Behold, they say: Our bones are dried up, and lost is our hope, we are cut off! Therefore prophesy and say to them: Thus saith the Lord God: Behold, I open your tombs and I will bring you up from your graves, O My people, and will take you to the Land of Israel. And ye shall know that I am the Lord, I spoke and I did it, saith the Lord.

(Ezek. 37:1—14)

2

Preexistence and
Names of the Messiah

Jewish authors and sages had a very specific way of emphasizing the great importance they attached to certain central values in Jewish life and thought: they made statements to the effect that the features in question were preexistent in the sense that they were either actually created in the six days of Genesis or their idea came up before God at that seminal time. Among them they mentioned the Tora, Repentance, the Garden of Eden and Gehenna, God's Throne of Glory, the Fathers, Israel, the Temple—and the Messiah. Of these various entities to which preexistence was ascribed, the Messiah is mentioned in a much earlier literary source than the others. He first appears as preexistent in the apocryphal First Book of Enoch, which was originally written in Hebrew or Aramaic about 150 B.C.E. From that period on, the concept of the Messiah who was created in the six days of Creation, or even prior to them, or who was born at variously stated subsequent dates (see chapter 3) and was then hidden to await his time, became a standard feature of Jewish Messianic eschatology. In one version it is the name of the Messiah which was created in the Beginning; in another, his spirit or his soul; in a third, he himself was actually born and even his celestial throne was fashioned.

The concept of the preexistence of the Messiah accords

with the general Talmudic view which holds that "The Holy One, blessed be He, prepares the remedy before the wound" (B. Meg. 13b). By this token, of course, the preexistence of the Messiah means that the exile of Israel (the wound) was predetermined by God in the very six days of Creation. Only if this was so did the creation of the Messiah, the ultimate healer of the great national disaster of Israel, at that early date make sense, and more than that, become a mythical necessity.

The names by which the Messiah is called are revealing. In the First Book of Enoch he is called, first of all, "Head of Days," an epithet alluding to his preexistence, or to the emergence of his name before God prior to the creation of the world. In the same source he is also called "Son of Man," an old Biblical appellation heavy with theosophical symbolism. Ever since Ezekiel, "Son of Man" has been a designation signifying special nearness to God of the person so called. Some of the Messiah's names contain historical allusions (e.g. David), others are symbolic ("Shoot," Menahem [i.e. "Comforter"], Light, Peace). Some rabbis insisted that the Messiah's name was identical with, or similar to, the name of the sage whose students they were (R. Shelah—Shiloh; R. Hanina—Hanina; R. Yannai—Yinnon). Some engaged in rather forced interpretations (Hadrakh—Had and Rakh). Others applied to him the name of God, a daring procedure in the Jewish context. Most remarkable is the opinion according to which the Messiah's name is "The Leprous of the House of Study," on the basis of Isa. 53:4, *Verily he hath borne our diseases*, etc. (see below; cf. also the Hasidic legend on the Leper Messiah included in chapter 3).

In any case this multiplicity of names indicates one thing very clearly: The image of the Messiah was very much in the forefront of rabbinical—and undoubtedly also of popular—thought from the second century B.C.E. on.

Preexistence

And there I saw him who is the Head of Days,
And his head was white like wool,
And with him was another one whose countenance
    had the appearance of a man
And his face was full of graciousness, like one of the
    holy angels.
And I asked the angel who went with me and
    showed me all the hidden things about that Son
    of Man: Who is he and whence is he, and why
    did he go with the Head of Days? And he
    answered and said to me:
This is the Son of Man who has righteousness,
With whom dwells righteousness,
And who reveals all the treasures of the crowns,
For the Lord of Spirits chose him. . . .

                       (1 Enoch 46:1−3)

He shall be a staff for the righteous,
Whereon to lean, to stand and not to fall,
And he shall be a light unto the nations,
And hope for the troubled of heart.
And all the earth-dwellers before him shall fall
    down,
And worship and praise and bless
And sing to the Lord of Spirits.
It is for this that he has been chosen
And hidden before Him, even before
The creation of the world and for evermore.

                       (1 Enoch 48:4−6)

From the beginning the Son of Man was hidden,
And the Most High has preserved him
In the presence of His might,
And revealed him to the elect.
And the congregation of the elect and the holy shall
    be sown,
And all the elect shall stand before him on that day.
And all the kings and the mighty and the exalted and

the rulers of the earth
Shall fall down before him on their faces,
And worship and set their hope upon the Son of
    Man,
And petition him and ask for mercy at his hands.
                            (1 Enoch 62:7−9)

It was taught: Seven things were created before the world was created, and these are they: the Tora, Repentance, the Garden of Eden, Gehenna, the Throne of Glory, the Temple, and the name of the Messiah.... The name of the Messiah, as it is said: *May his name endure forever, may his name blossom before the sun* (Ps. 72:17).
                            (B. Pes. 54a; B. Ned. 39a)

Six things preceded the creation of the world. Some of them were [actually] created, and some of them [merely] arose in the thought [of God] to be created. The Tora and the Throne of Glory were created.... The Fathers, Israel, the Temple and the name of the Messiah arose in the thought to be created....
                            (Gen. Rab. 1:4)

R. Shim'on ben Laqish explained: "*and the spirit of God hovered over the face of the water* (Gen. 1:2)—this is the spirit of King Messiah, as it is written, *And the spirit of the Lord will rest upon him* (Isa. 11:2). By what merit will it [the spirit of the Messiah] come?... By the merit of repentance."
                            (Gen. Rab. 2:4)

You find that at the beginning of the creation of the world King Messiah was born [and] that he emerged in the thought [of God] even before the world was created....
                            (Pes. Rab. ed. Friedmann, p. 152b)

In that hour [in the days of Creation] the Holy One, blessed be He, appointed four animals for him [the Messiah] to carry the Throne of Honor of the Messiah. In that hour his enemies and the [celestial] princes of the kingdoms said: "Come, let us bring charges against the generation of the Messiah, so that they may never be created." But the Holy One, blessed be He, said to them: "How dare you accuse that generation which is beloved and dear,

and in which I rejoice, and which I desire? I shall support it and
want it. . . . And how dare you accuse it? Behold, I shall destroy all
of you. . . ."

(Pes. Rab. ch. 35)

The Names of the Messiah

> In that hour in which the Son of Man was named
> In the presence of the Lord of Spirits—
> And his name is Head of Days—
> Ere the sun and the signs were created,
> Ere the stars of heaven were made,
> His name was named before the Lord of Spirits.

(1 Enoch 48:2—3)

Some say: "Menahem son of Hezekiah is his name. . . ." And
the rabbis say: "The Leprous of the House of Study is his name, as
it is said, *Verily, he hath borne our diseases, and our pains—he carried them,
and we thought him stricken, smitten of God, and afflicted* (Isa.
53:4)." . . . Rav said: "If he is of those who live [today], then he is
like our Holy Master [Rabbi Y'huda the Prince], and if he is of those
who have died, then he is like Daniel the beloved man."

(B. Sanh. 98b)

The rabbis said: "King Messiah, if he is of those who are alive
[today], David is his name, and if he is of those who have died,
David is his name. . . ." R. Y'hoshu'a ben Levi said: "*Tzemah*
[Shoot] is his name." R. Yudan the son of R. Aybo said: "*Menahem*
[Comforter] is his name."

(Y. Ber. 5a)

Rav Y'huda said: "Rav said that the Holy One, blessed be He,
will in the future raise for them [for Israel] another David, for it is
said, *They shall serve the Lord their God and David their king whom I will
raise up unto them* (Jer. 30:9). It does not say 'raised up,' but 'will
raise up.'"

Rav Papa said to Abbaye: "But it is written, *And David My
servant shall be their prince forever* (Ezek. 37:25)?" [He answered:

"They will be] like Caesar and vice-Caesar."[1]

(B. Sanh. 98b)

R. Sh'muel bar Nahmani said in the name of R. Yohanan: "Three are called by the name of the Holy One, blessed be He, and they are: the righteous, the Messiah, and Jerusalem...."

(B. Bab. Bath. 75b)

R. Yose the Galilean said: "The name of the Messiah is Peace, for it is said, *Everlasting Father, Prince Peace* (Isa. 9:5)...." R. Yose the Galilean said: "Great is peace, for in the hour in which King Messiah is revealed to Israel, he begins with peace, for it is said, *How beautiful upon the mountains are the feet of the messenger of good tidings who announceth peace* (Isa. 52:7)."

(Pereq Shalom, p. 101)

R. Y'huda expounded: "*The burden of the word of the Lord: In the land of Hadrakh and in Damascus shall be His resting place...* (Zech. 9:1). This [the word Hadrakh] is [a reference to] the Messiah who will be sharp [had] towards the nations of the world, and soft [rakh] toward Israel."

(Sifre Deut. ed. Friedmann 65a)

What is the name of King Messiah? R. Abba bar Kahana said: "LORD [*Adonai*] is his name, for it is written, *I will raise unto David a righteous Shoot.... In his days Judah shall be saved.... And this is the name whereby he shall be called: The Lord is our righteousness* (Jer. 23:5–6)." For R. Levi said: "Happy is the country whose name is like the name of its king and the name of whose king is like the name of its God...." R. Y'hoshu'a said: "SHOOT [Tzemah] is his name, for it is written, *Behold a man whose name is Shoot and who shall shoot up out of his place and build the Temple of the Lord* (Zech. 6:12)." R. Yudan in the name of R. Aybo said: "MENAHEM ['Comforter'] is his name, for it is written, *Because the Comforter is far from me* (Lam. 1:16)." In the house of R. Shela they said: "SHILOH is the name of the Messiah, for it is written, *Until Shiloh will come* (Gen. 49:10), and the word is spelled Shela." In the house of R. Hanina they said: "HANINA is his name, for it is written, *For I will show you no favor*

---

1. I.e. the second David will be like a king, and the first David will be like a viceroy under him.

[*hanina*] (Jer. 16:13)." In the house of R. Yannai they said: "YIN-NON is his name, for it is written *May his name be continued* [*yinnon*] *as long as the sun* (Ps. 72:17)." R. Biva of Srungaya said: "NEHIRA ['Light'] is his name, for it is written, *And the light* [*nehora*] *dwelleth with Him* (Dan. 2:22), and it is spelled *nehira*." R. Y'huda ben R. Shim'on said in the name of R. Sh'muel ben R. Yitzhaq: "This King Messiah, if he is of those who are alive, his name is DAVID, and if he is of those who have died, his name is DAVID." R. Tanhuma said: "I shall tell you the reason: [it is written] *He giveth great salvation to His king, and showeth mercy to His anointed* (Ps. 18:51). [Thereafter] it is not written 'and to David,' but *to His anointed to David and his seed....*"

(Lam. Rab. 1:51, p. 36, ad Lam. 1:16)

Rav Huna said: "The Messiah is called by seven names and they are: Yinnon, Tzidqenu ['Our Justice'], Tzemah ['Shoot'], Menahem ['Comforter'], David, Shiloh, and Elijah."

(Mid. Mishle, ed. Buber, p. 87)

The Messiah is called by eight names: Yinnon, Tzemah, Pele ["Miracle"], Yo'etz ["Counselor"], Mashiah ["Messiah"], El ["God"], Gibbor ["Hero"], and Avi 'Ad Shalom ["Eternal Father of Peace"].

(S. Buber's note, ibid. p. 87)

There is yet another fragrance, and that is King Messiah who is called Fragrance. For it is written, *And He shall make him fragrant with the fear of the Lord*[2] (Isa. 11:3). And therefore he is called Fragrance.

(Zohar Hadash, Mid. haNe'elam to Songs, p. 64c)

---

2. This is the Kabbalist's literal reading of the passage, which usually is understood to mean, *And his delight shall be the fear of the Lord.*

3

Early Messiahs

Jewish legend knows of several men of great merit who almost became the Messiah, or who, for all too brief a time, fulfilled the role of the Redeemer. In a sense these legendary heroes continued the line of those royal figures who in Biblical times were styled "The Anointed [*Mashiah*] of God." Saul and David were "Messiahs of God" in this older, more realistic sense, as were other kings of Judah who followed them, and so was Cyrus the Great, who enabled the Jews to return to Jerusalem from their Babylonian captivity. An interesting variant on this theme is the legend which calls Esther "Redeemer"—the only woman in Jewish literature to be given this epithet. The Midrash draws a parallel between her and Abraham: both were seventy-five years old when their historic mission began; and compares her to Israel: both were orphans.

The earliest Biblical figure who in later literature was endowed with a superhuman Messianic character is Enoch, about whom it is said in Genesis (5:24) that *he walked with God, and he was no more, for God took him.* This brief enigmatic statement sufficed to turn Enoch into a superhuman figure: after his translation he became Metatron, the chief of all angels, and, according to the Book of Enoch (which was preserved in Ethiopic), he became the Messiah (see below).

The list of legendary Redeemers, or quasi-Messianic charismatic figures, includes Moses, Elijah (see chapter 14), King Hezekiah, Menahem ben 'Amiel (who was born when the First Temple was destroyed), Menahem ben Hezekiah (who was born on the very day the Second Temple was destroyed; see chapter 13), and Bar Kokhba (c. 135 C.E.). In later times, Kabbalistic masters, such as Yitzhaq Luria, the great sixteenth-century mystic, and his leading disciple Hayyim Vital, claimed Messianic status. Still later, Hasidic lore found the Messiah in unknown and hidden saints; among them is the Leper Messiah, to whom reference is made in the Talmud (see chapter 2) and whom the Ba'al Shem Tov is reported to have encountered 1500 years later. Finally, the fervor of their believers clothed several Hasidic rabbis in Messianic colors.

To this context belong the legends which grew up around pseudo-Messiahs. Of the rich literature describing the miracles they were believed to have performed, and explaining the circumstances and hidden significance of their failure, we can present here only a few examples. Of all the false Messiahs, Shabbatai Zevi was the one who created the greatest stir among both Jews and Gentiles. His manic-depressive states were interpreted as mystical manifestations, and his ultimate conversion to Islam (in 1666) was justified and legitimized by explaining it in terms of the Lurianic concept of the divine sparks caught among the "husks" of impurity.

Enoch

And he [the "Head of Days"][1] came to me [Enoch] and greeted me with his voice, and said unto me:

---

1. Above, in chapter 2, we met the "Head of Days" as a term referring to the Messiah. Here the Head of Days is an intermediary between the Lord of Spirits (God) and the Son of Man (the Messiah-Enoch), that is, has the role which the Shekhina (the personified presence of God) fulfills in the Midrash.

"You are the Son of Man [i.e. the Messiah] who is born unto righteousness, and righteousness abides over you, and the righteousness of the Head of Days forsakes you not!"

And he [the angel who leads Enoch] said unto me: "He [the Head of Days] proclaims unto you peace in the name of the World to Come...."

And so there shall be length of days with that Son of Man, and the righteous shall have peace and a straight way in the name of the Lord of Spirits forever and ever.

(1 Enoch 71:14–17)

Moses

My beloved is like a gazelle (Song of Songs 2:9). R. Yitzhaq said: "Just as this gazelle can be seen and then again hides itself, so the first Messiah [i.e. Moses] revealed himself to the Children of Israel and then again hid himself from them." For how long did he hide himself? Y'huda ben Rabbi said: "For three months...."

(Pes. diR. Kah., ed. Mandelbaum, pp. 91–92)

Hezekiah

R. Tanhum said: Bar Kappara expounded in Sepphoris: The Holy One, blessed be He, wanted to make Hezekiah [king of Judah] the Messiah and Sanherib [king of Assyria] Gog and Magog. But the [divine] attribute of Justice said before the Holy One, blessed be He: Master of the World! Even though David sang many songs and praises before You, You did not make him the Messiah, and now you want to make Hezekiah the Messiah although You worked for him all these miracles, and he never sang a single song before You? Therefore [the matter remained] undecided. Instantly the Earth opened [her mouth] and said before Him: Master of the World! I shall sing a song in place of this saintly man [Hezekiah]: make him the Messiah. And she opened her mouth and sang a song before Him.... Then the [celestial] Prince of the World said before Him: Master of the World! Fulfill the wish of this saintly man! A heavenly voice issued and said: *I waste away, I waste away*

(Isa. 24:16). What the prophet meant was this: Woe is me, woe is me! How long [until the Redemption]?

(B. Sahn. 94a)

R. Gidel said: "Israel will in the future enjoy the years of the Messiah." R. Yosef said: "This is self-evident. Who else should enjoy them? Perhaps Hileq and Bileq [two imaginary persons] should enjoy them? [However, the point in R. Gidel's statement was to] exclude what R. Hillel said, namely that Israel has no Messiah because they already consumed him in the days of Hezekiah.

(B. Sanh. 98b, 99a)

Menahem Ben 'Amiel

The name of the Messiah of the Lord is Menahem ben 'Amiel, and he was born in the days of David king of Israel.

(Sefer Zerubbabel, BhM 2:55)

(Zerubbabel questions Metatron:) And I said to him [to the angel]: "I have a question to ask." And he said to me: "Ask and I shall tell you." And I said to him: "Are you Metatron?" And he answered with a pleasant voice and said to me: "I am Metatron Michael, the prince of the host of the Lord. And he placed me over His people and over those who love Him. I am he who led Abraham across the whole land of Canaan, and I blessed him in the name of the Lord. I am he who redeemed Isaac when the angels wept over him and the Ariels cried. And I am he who struggled with Jacob beyond the river. And I am he who led Israel in the desert for forty years in the name of the Lord the God of Israel. And I am he who appeared to Joshua in Gilgal. And I am he who caused brimstone and fire to rain upon Sodom and Gomorrah from heaven, from the Lord who sent me and who made my name like unto His name. And now, Zerubbabel, ask and I shall give you the answer." And I said to him: "This man said to me, 'I am the Messiah of the Lord,' and I was amazed at him." And Metatron said to me: "Yes, this is the Messiah of the Lord, who was born to the house of David. And the Lord expected him to be the prince of the covenant of the holy people. This is Menahem ben 'Amiel who was born when Nebuchadnezzar came to Jerusalem. And He lifted him up with the spirit of the Lord and put him in this place until the time of the end...."

(Manuscript from Yemen, no. 890, Add. 3381
Cambridge University Library)

Cyrus

Thus saith the Lord...that hath said of Cyrus: "He is My shepherd, and shall perform all My pleasure, even saying of Jerusalem, 'She shall be built,' and to the Temple, 'Thy foundations shall be laid.'"

Thus saith the Lord to His Anointed [Messiah] to Cyrus whose right hand I have holden to subdue nations before him...: "I will go before thee and make the crooked places straight...."

(Isa. 44:28–45:2)

Thus saith the Lord to His Anointed [Messiah] to Cyrus (Isa. 45:1). Was then Cyrus the Messiah? No, but the Holy One, blessed be He, said to the Messiah: "I complain to you about Cyrus. I said he should rebuild My House [the Temple] and gather My exiles, but [all he did was to] say: *Whosoever there is among you of all His people...let him go up to Jerusalem* (Ezra 1:3).

(B. Meg. 12a)

Elijah, Manasseh, Ephraim,
and the Son of David

There is much discussion about the Anointed Ones [Messiahs]. Some say they are seven, as is written, *Then shall We raise against him seven shepherds* (Mic. 5:4); and some say, eight—*And eight princes among men* (ibid.)...

David came and explained: *Gilead is Mine* (Ps. 60:9), this refers to Elijah who was of the inhabitants of Gilead: *and Manasseh is Mine* (ibid.), this refers to the Messiah who arises from among the Children of Manasseh....*Ephraim also is the defence of My head* (ibid.), this refers to the Anointed of War who comes from Eph-raim....*Judah is My scepter* (ibid.), this refers to the Great Re-deemer who is from among the Children of David.

(Num. Rab. 14:1)

Esther

R. Berekhya said: "The Holy One, blessed be He, said to Abraham: 'You left your father's house when you were seventy-five years old; by your life, also the Redeemer [Esther] whom I shall cause to rise for your children in Media, she too will be seventy-five years old.'" R. Berekhya [further] said in the name of R. Levi: "The Holy One, blessed be He, said to Israel: 'You wept, *We are become orphans and fatherless* (Lam. 5:3); also the Redeemer whom I shall make rise for you in Media, she too will have neither father nor mother.'"

(Mid. Abba Gorion, BhM 1:5)

Bar Kokhba

R. Shim'on ben Yohai taught: "My master Akiba used to explain: *A star [kokhav] shall step forth out of Jacob* (Num. 24:17)—this means Kozba [i.e. Bar Kokhba] shall step forth out of Jacob." When R. Akiba saw Bar Kozba, he said: "This is King Messiah!" R. Yohanan ben Torta said to him: "Akiba, grass will come out of your cheeks and still the Son of David will not have come!"

(Y. Ta'an. 68d)

About the Messiah it is written, *And the spirit of the Lord shall rest upon him, the spirit of wisdom and understanding, the spirit of counsel and might, the spirit of knowledge and the fear of the Lord* (Isa. 11:2). And further it is written, *And He will let him have delight in* [lit.: "will let him scent"] *the fear of the Lord* (ibid. v. 3). R. Alexandri said: "This teaches us that they burdened him with commandments and sufferings like millstones."[2] Rava said: "[This teaches us] that he will scent [the truth] and will adjudicate, as it is written, *And he shall not judge after the sight of his eyes . . . but with righteousness shall he judge the poor, and decide with equity for the meek of the land* (ibid. vv. 3—4). Bar Kozba who ruled for two and a half years said to the sages: "I am the Messiah." They said to him: "Of the Messiah it is said that he will scent and judge. Let us see whether he scents and judges." When they saw that he neither scented nor judged, they killed him.

(B. Shabbat 93b)

Yitzhaq Luria

And behold, before my Teacher of blessed memory passed away, one day we went with him to the tomb of Sh'ma'ya and Avtalyon [in Gush Halav] and we prayed there. And they [Sh'ma'ya and Avtalyon] said to my Master that he should tell us that when we recite [the blessing of] "The Throne of David" in the Eighteen Benedictions, we should concentrate [on the request] that Messiah ben Ephraim should not die through the wicked Armilus. For Messiah ben Ephraim is the Throne of David which is mentioned in the Zohar, and this is the mystery of *He asked life of Thee* (Ps. 21:5). And my Teacher cautioned us very emphatically that we should concentrate on this. And we did not understand the words of my Teacher when he cautioned us about this. And his end proved [the meaning of] his warning, for my Teacher died because of our many and great sins. . . . And the companions did not know that it was about the Master himself that those Tannaites [Sh'ma'ya and Avtalyon] said what they said. And in his modesty the Master did not explain the matter to the companions. And when the Master passed into the House of His World, they understood belatedly that he was Messiah ben Ephraim.

(Benayahu, *Sefer Toldot haAri*, pp. 199, 258)

---

2. R. Alexandri explains the Hebrew *hariho* (lit.: "he will let him scent") as being derived from *rehayim*, millstones.

Hayyim Vital

In the year 5334 [1574 C.E.] came Mas'ud haKohen from Der'a to Safed, and told me that before his departure he had gone to take leave from a great man who knew the future and his name was Abraham Shalom. And he said to him: "Go in health and peace," and he told him the meaning of [secret] words, [and instructed him] to come to me, R. Hayyim, and give me peace in his name, and he gave him all the signs by which I can be recognized. And he said to him: "Tell him in my name that he is Messiah ben Joseph, and that he should go to Jerusalem and dwell there for two years without fail. And in the third year the choice will be in his hand: if he wishes, let him stay there. And after the first year the spirit of the Lord will begin to agitate him, and from then on there will be a conflict about him between the people of Jerusalem and of the Galilee, and the people of Egypt will side with Jerusalem. But with all this, the Galileans will win and will make him return to dwell there in the Galilee. And there thousands and myriads of Israel will gather around him, and he will rule over them and will teach them Tora. And thereafter I myself shall go there, and I shall be Messiah ben David, and he will be Messiah ben Joseph, if the generation will merit it. And when he goes to Jerusalem let him beware that he should not gather people around him, because this would result in great harm to him, and also because of this reason he would be put in the jailhouse. And what the sages of blessed memory said about Messiah ben Joseph—that he will be slain—I shall try with all my strength to save him from that fate, for about him it is said, *He asked life of Thee, Thou gavest it to him* (Ps. 21:5), which means that Messiah ben David will ask of the Name, blessed be He, that He should give life to Messiah ben Joseph who is called Hayyim [i.e. Life], and the Name, blessed be He, will give him life."

In the year 5337 [1577 C.E.] I went to Egypt, and a scholar came from Der'a and told me everything just as R. Mas'ud had told me, in the name of the aforementioned R. Abraham Shalom.

(*Shivhe R. Hayyim Vital*, pp. 2b–3a)

The Leper Messiah

[One Friday afternoon a young Talmudic scholar was riding with the Ba'al Shem in a cart across the open field, when] all of a sudden he espied a village in the distance, and he was filled with joy, for he thought that they would surely spend the Sabbath there, and not out in the open. And in that very moment they entered the village, and, behold, the horse went on of its own through the village and did not stop at any house. The youth became saddened by this, for [it seemed that] they would, after all, not spend the Sabbath in the village. But when the horse reached the end of the village, it stopped in front of a ruin. The youth thought that they would spend the Sabbath in that ruin and became filled with joy, for it was better than being in the field. And the Ba'al Shem entered the ruin, and the youth went after him. And, behold, in the ruined house lived an old man, a leper; from head to foot there was no hale spot in his body, he was so full of wounds and boils. And his wife and children walked about in torn and tattered garments. And when the Ba'al Shem opened the door, the old man became filled with joy, and ran up to the Ba'al Shem, and said to him, "Peace be unto you, my Master and Teacher!" And he who saw not their joy has never seen joy in his life. And they went into a separate room, and talked there about half an hour. And then they took permission from each other, and parted from each other in fierce love, like the love of David and Jonathan. And then the Ba'al Shem took his seat in the cart, and the horse trotted along on its own....

[On the way back home the youth asked the Ba'al Shem: "What was the meaning of] the joy which the encounter with the old leper caused to both of you?..." And the Ba'al Shem said to him: "... As for what happened between me and the old man in the village, as it is known, there is a Messiah in every generation in This World, in reality, clothed in a body. And if the generation is worthy, he is ready to reveal himself; and if, God forbid, they are not worthy, he departs. And behold, that old man was ready to be our True Messiah, and it was his desire to enjoy my company on the Sabbath. But I foresaw that he would depart at the Third Meal [which is taken at the outgoing of the Sabbath], and I did not want to endure any pain on the Sabbath [and therefore I took my leave from him before the arrival of the Sabbath]."

(Kadaner, *Sefer Sippurim Noraim*, pp. 9a−b,10b)

The Beggar Messiah

Rabbi Zvi Elimelekh dwelt in the city of Dinov, and he had a son, [who was] the rabbi of Strizev, [but] who always sat with his father in Dinov. Once a poor beggar came to the city of Dinov for the holy Sabbath, and that poor man was the Messiah. He went to a ruinous house, for they did not let him enter a respectable lodging. He left his things with a poor baker whose boys plagued him very much. On the Sabbath the boys chased after him at the time of prayer, so that one could not pray. At the outgoing of the Sabbath the rabbi of Strizev invited his Hasidim to the meal ushering out the Queen Sabbath, and the aforementioned poor man also came with them to the meal. And there, too, the boys made fun of him, and also plagued him. And when the rabbi of Strizev saw this, he arose and said to the poor man: "Go, please, to Rabbi David Ries; he, too, is having a rich meal ushering out the Queen, and there you can eat and drink to your heart's desire." But he answered: "My intention is not to eat and drink, but to hear words of Tora." The rabbi of Strizev thereupon rose and drove him from his house, lest he cause them a disruption in celebrating the ushering out of the Queen. While they sat at the ushering out of the Queen, the rabbi of Dinov was already asleep, and [his son] the rabbi of Strizev locked the door from the outside. After they ate, the rabbi of Strizev said: "Let us recite the grace after meals, for I must go to open the door." And when he went to open the door, [he found that] the door was locked from the inside as well. And as he [tried to] open it, he heard that inside the house people were discussing mysteries of the Tora. And it came to pass in the morning that he asked his father: "Who was there [with you]?" He told him that it was the aforementioned poor beggar, who was Messiah ben David. When his son heard this, he fell to the ground and fainted. And [when he came to] he instantly ran to the baker to find out whether he [the poor man] was there, but he found him not, for a pillar of fire had come and taken him from there. May the merit of the pious protect us!

(Sofer, *Sippure Ya'aqov*, pp. 35−36)

The Stoliner Rebbe

Among the Stoliner Hasidim there was a tradition that the Stoliner Rebbe was the Messiah, but that God did not give him permission to reveal himself.

(Mintz, *Legends*, p. 201)

Shabbatai Zevi

In the year 5426 [1665 C.E.], on the twenty-second of Kislev, rumors came from the corners of the East, from Egypt and her neighbors, that in Gaza, which is near Jerusalem, a prophet arose, announcing good tidings and salvation. They said about a scholar whose name is Shabbatai Zevi, of the inhabitants of Izmir [Smyrna], who sojourned there in Jerusalem, that he was the Messiah of the God of Jacob, and that within a year and a few months he would take the kingship from the hand of the Togar [the Sultan], not with an army and not by force, but the king, the Togar, himself would place the royal crown on his head. And thereafter he [Shabbatai Zevi] would go to the River Sambatyon to take for himself from there a wife, a thirteen-year-old daughter of our Master Moses, peace be upon him. And he will come with the Ten Tribes, riding a lion, and the halter which will be pulled across its mouth will be a tortuous serpent with seven heads. And thereafter he will make great wars with the nations for five years. And at that time it will be a time of trouble for Jacob, and those are the pangs of the Messiah.

And these words entered the heart of the masses, and made an impression also upon some of the sages, and all Israel was aroused to great repentance, both the nearby and the faraway in the whole world, and they accepted the words of the prophet Nathan [of Gaza] as words of truth....

(Sasportas, *Tzitzat Novel Tz'vi*, p. 1)

All these things were revealed only to proclaim the greatness of our lord [Shabbatai Zevi], may his majesty be exalted, [and to show] how he will annul the power of the Serpent which is rooted in strong supernal roots which incessantly enticed him. And after he would labor hard to extract great holiness from the husks [i.e. the evil physical world], they would be able to seize him when his illumination was stopped up. And they would show him that they had dominion. And [as for] his faith in the [Sefira of] Beauty, they showed him that their power was equal to his power, and that they had a *Merkava* [Chariot] like he, as Pharaoh had said, *Who is the Lord* (Exod. 5:2). But at the time of his illumination Shabbatai Zevi again subdued the Serpent.... And I have already stated that the Scripture says that the name of the Messiah is Job, for he has sunk deep in the midst of the husks. And this would happen in the days of the darkness which are days of anguish. But when he had an illumination, which are days of rest and joy...then he emerges from the midst of the husks....

(Nathan of Gaza, *Treatise on the Dragons*)

In the year 5434 [1674 C.E.] of the Creation of the world, in the night of Rosh haShana, a Maggid ["heavenly herald"] came to a young man, not in a dream and not while he was awake. He was from the city of Meqnes in the Land of Barbary, and his name was R. Yosef ben Tzur. And he was an ignoramus but a fearer of heaven. And [the Maggid] announced to him the coming of the Redeemer, and raised him up on his feet and poured over him the water which was in a jar, and the water increased to such an extent that he was forced to change his clothes. And he showed him our lord our king Shabbatai Zevi in heaven. And they [the heavenly company] said to him: "This is the true Redeemer, Messiah ben David, and R. Nathan Benjamin [of Gaza] is his true prophet, and you are Messiah ben Joseph." And the angel Raphael handed him an alphabet which read: ANY MLK H'WZ STH DRG MQTz ShBT TzMKh NF.[3] And he said that this was its original order when it was given from Sinai, and that when the Children of Israel made the Golden Calf the letters became mixed up, and this is why our alphabet has a different order. And Yosef ben Tzur learned from him the entire Tora, with supernal mysteries, so that none like him could be found among all the sages of the West [i.e. Morocco]. And they also told him that the End is hinted at in the Tora and in Daniel....

---

3. The first three words into which this Messianic alphabet is grouped read *ani melekh ha'oz*, i.e., "I am the king of power." The meaning of the remaining letter groups is not clear.

Men of wisdom and learned Kabbalists from the city of Fez—a great city of wise men and scribes—went there to see him [Yosef ben Tzur] and to talk to him; and also from Tetuan, Salé, and other places. And they recognized and knew that his knowledge was divine Knowledge. And he showed them from the Book of Zohar and from Daniel and from the story of Creation that the true Redeemer of Israel was our lord Shabbatai Zevi, may his majesty be exalted, and that the time of the Redemption would be on the eve of Passover in the year 5435 [i.e. 1675], after the cleaning out of the *hametz* [the leavened bread]. The sages said to him: "Ask the Maggid for a sign or a portent concerning this." He said to them: "What could be a greater sign and portent than that which you already know, namely, that formerly I could not study even Rashi,[4] and now I am telling you supernal mysteries which you have never known and never heard? If you wish, I shall go out into the streets of the city and shall proclaim and say that Shabbatai Zevi is the Messiah of Israel, and you will see that no harm will come either to me or to anyone of Israel."

Because of this many sages who had spoken sedition against our lord, may his majesty be exalted, felt great regret and turned away from the thought of their heart, and now they believed in him. And in all the Land of Barbary they were aroused to a greater repentance than they had been when our lord, may his majesty be exalted, first revealed himself.[5]

And our Father Abraham said to him that the Redemption had been intended to come to pass ten years earlier, but the exile had been extended because our lord, may his majesty be exalted, had prayed for it before the Holy One, blessed be He, lest the pangs of the Messiah come upon Israel and lest those who had not believed in him die, for already death had been decreed for them from heaven. And the Maggid also explained the reason for the turban which our lord, may his majesty be exalted, put on his head,[6] and said that this [was done] so that they should mock him, and thus he would carry all the Messianic pangs of Israel. And he also said than an additional advantage would be derived from this

---

4. The commentary of Rashi to the Bible is taught to small children.

5. Shabbatai Zevi first revealed himself in 1648. He converted to Islam in 1666 in order to escape execution, and died in 1676.

6. I.e. has converted to Islam.

[postponement of the Redemption], and that is that the sparks of holiness which are caught among the nations in the husks would be drawn out, for since the Messiah is among the husks, the sparks of purity would enter into him, into our Messiah, for they would find [in him] their own kindred and would be aroused and thus would cling to him.

And should you say, why did he turn into a Turk and not into one of Edom [i.e. a Christian], be it known to you that all the sparks of holiness which are in Edom were gathered by the Turk [i.e. the Sultan] into him, for this is the mystery of *And He will set up an ensign for the nations and will assemble the dispersed of Israel* (Isa. 11:12). And its explanation is that all the sparks are impressed into the Turks, since you find that the Turkish Sultan receives by lot many young boys from the Christians and turns them into Turks.[7] And it is from God that the lot falls only on those who have a spark of holiness. The result is that all the sparks of holiness are sunk into the Turkish Sultan. This is why he [Shabbatai Zevi] turned into a Turk, and this is a great miracle....

('*Iny'ne Shabbatai Zevi*, pp. 73–74)

---

7. The reference is to the periodical levy of young Christian boys for training to fill the ranks of the Janizaries (the Sultan's guard) and to occupy posts in the palace service and in administration. Our story is mistaken in stating that casting of lots was involved. In fact, the best children were carefully selected by Janizary recruiting officers.

4

The Ancestry of the Messiah

In the preceding two chapters we got acquainted with two mythical ideas: one which attributes preexistence to the Messiah, and the other which assigns Messianic status to several historical figures. Jewish legendary proclivity was not satisfied with these details about what can be termed the prehistory of the Messiah, and proceeded to invent stories about the time and circumstances of his creation.

According to one of these legends, God intervened in human affairs as early as in the days of Jacob and brought together his son Judah with Tamar for the express purpose of bringing about the birth of Perez, who was the ancestor of David and thus of the Messiah. A brief Midrashic statement has it that the Messiah himself was born even before Pharaoh, the first enslaver of the Children of Israel. A long folk-tale-like story tells how God caused King Solomon to be removed from his throne, and to wander about in the world, until He caused him to arrive in the court of the king of Ammon. There Solomon worked as a waiter and cook, and was seen by the daughter of the king, the pious Naamah, who promptly fell in love with him. All this was engineered by God in order to have Solomon and Naamah become the ancestors of the Messiah. Zerubbabel, a late scion of the House of David, is also specified in a brief Aggadic passage as a forebear of the Messiah. In order to make Zerubbabel worthy of becoming an ancestor of the Messiah, God gave exceptional greatness to him, referred to by his contemporary, the prophet Zechariah.

These legends about the ancestry of the Messiah achieve several purposes. They make it clear that God planned for the birth and coming of the Messiah throughout the history of Israel, from the days of Jacob onward. They assign the descent of the Messiah to the noblest royal line that ever existed in Israel, that of King David. And they instill the hope, nay, the certainty, in the hearts of all that the Messiah, whose birth was prepared by God with such long planning and such loving care, will certainly, unfailingly, come, even though the waiting for him may seem endless.

R. Sh'muel bar Nahman began: *"For I know the thoughts that I think toward you, saith the Lord, thoughts of peace, and not of evil, to give you a future and a hope* (Jer. 29:11). The tribes [i.e. the sons of Jacob] were busy with the selling of Joseph; Jacob was busy with his sackcloth and his fasting [mourning over Joseph]; Judah was busy with taking a wife; and the Holy One, blessed be He, was creating the light of the Messiah."

(Gen. Rab. 85:1)

Before she travailed she brought forth (Isa. 66:7). Before the last enslaver [Titus] was born, the first Redeemer was born.

[Another version:] Before the first enslaver [Pharaoh] was born, the last Redeemer [the Messiah] was born.[1]

(Gen. Rab. 85:1; variant given by Theodor, p. 1030)

When [because of his sins] Solomon had to go into exile for three years, Ashmodai took his ring [upon which was engraved the Ineffable Name of God] and threw it into the sea. And a fish came and swallowed it. Then he [Ashmodai] flung him [Solomon] four

---

1. The reference is to the birth of Perez, son of Judah, whose descendant was David, and through him the Messiah.

hundred parasangs into the land of the nations, and drove him away from his kingdom. And all his glory was lost, for he threw him far away, and he went begging at the doors and said: "I, Solomon, was king in Jerusalem."[2] And they laughed at his words and said: "Would such a king come begging at the doors?"

And he had to endure this suffering for three years, because he had transgressed three precepts of the Tora: [namely, that a king] should not take him many wives, and should not acquire many horses, and should not accumulate too much silver and gold.[3] And he stumbled over all three.[4] And at the end of this time, at the end of three years, the Holy One, blessed be He, wanted to have mercy on him for the sake of his servant David, and for the sake of the pious woman, Naamah, the daughter of the king of Ammon, from whom the Messiah was destined to issue.[5] And so that he should join himself to her and bring her with him to the Land of Israel, the Holy One, blessed be He, led him to the Land of Ammon, and he came to the royal city whose name is Mashkemam.[6] And he stood in the streets of the city of Mashkemam, and the king's butler, the chief of the cooks who prepared and cooked the food for the king, came to buy what was necessary for his work, and found Solomon standing there, and he took him and pressed him into service [among those] who carried what he had bought. And he brought him into the kitchen. And he [Solomon] saw what he did and said that he would stay with him and serve him, and that he wanted nothing but food to eat. And he [the butler] agreed. And he [Solomon] stayed with him and served him and helped him.

After a few days he [Solomon] said to him that he would like to cook for the king dishes according to his custom, since he was a great artist in these dishes. And the butler agreed, and he prepared and cooked royal delicacies. And when the king ate those tasty dishes which the butler brought him, and tasted those dishes, the king asked the butler: "Who cooked these dishes, for until now you

---

2. A paraphrase of Eccles. 1:12, which reads, *I Koheleth was king over Israel in Jerusalem.*

3. Cf. Deut. 17:16—17.

4. Cf. 1 Kings 10:14, 26; 11:3.

5. According to 1 Kings 14:21, Naamah the Ammonitess was the mother of Rehoboam, the son and heir of Solomon, and thus an ancestress of Messiah ben David.

6. A fantastic name. The well-known Biblical name of the capital city of Ammon was Rabbat Ammon (full form: Rabbat B'ne Ammon, i.e. Rabba of the Children of Ammon), today Amman, capital of Jordan.

have never brought before me anything like these?"

And he [the butler] told him all that had happened, that that man cooked them, and he [the king] commanded his servants that they should call him. And he came before the king and he [the king] said to him: "Do you wish to be my butler?" And he said: "Yes." And he dismissed the butler from before him and put him [Solomon] in his place to cook for him all his food.

And it came to pass after these things that the daughter of the king of Ammon, whose name was Naamah, saw him and said to her mother that it was her wish to take this man, the butler, to be her husband. And her mother rebuked her and said to her: "There are in the kingdom of your father many princes and notables, among whom you can take him whom you like." And she importuned her very much, but it did not help, for she said: "In any case, I want no other man but this one." Finally her mother was forced to divulge the matter to her husband the king, that his daughter wanted to take the butler as her husband. And when he heard this thing, it enraged him very much, and he wanted to kill both of them.

But this was not the will of the Holy One, blessed be He, and it happened to them that the compassion of the king was kindled over them, and he did not want to spill innocent blood, and he called one of his servants and commanded him that he should take them to the desert where they would die of themselves. And the eunuch did as the king had commanded, and left them in the desert, and went his way [back] to the king to serve him as before.

And they went from there to find food to keep their souls alive, and they came to a city which was on the seashore. And he went to search for food for their souls, and found fishermen selling fish, and he bought one from them, and brought this fish to his wife that she should cook it. And when she opened the fish, she found in it the ring on which was engraved the Ineffable Name, and she gave the ring to her husband. And he instantly recognized the ring, and put it on his finger, and instantly his spirit returned to him and his mind became reassured. And he went up to Jersualem and expelled Ashmodai, and sat on his royal throne, and put the royal crown on his head. And then he sent for her father who was the king of the Children of Ammon, and said to him: "Why did you kill two souls without permission?" And he was afraid and said: "God forbid, I did not kill them but expelled them into the desert. I do not know what has happened to them." King Solomon said to him: "And should you see them, would you recognize them? Be it known to you that I am the butler, and your daughter is my wife." And he sent for her, and she came and kissed his hands, and he rejoiced greatly and returned to his country.

(Ma'aseh biSh'lomo haMelekh, BhM 2:86–87)

It is written, *Who art thou, O great mountain? before Zerubbabel thou shalt become a plain* (Zech. 4:7). What does it mean, *Who art thou, O great mountain?* This is King Messiah. And why does he call him *great mountain?* Because he is greater than the Fathers... loftier than Abraham... more elevated than Moses... and higher than the ministering angels.... And from whom will he issue? From Zerubbabel....

(Mid. Tanhuma, ed. Buber 1:139)

5

The Waiting

One of the most moving of all Messiah legends is the one that tells how, in a splendid heavenly palace, Elijah takes the head of the crying Messiah in his lap and says to him: "Be silent. Suffer the chastisement of your Master, for He punishes you for the sins of Israel. Be silent, for the end is near." But the Messiah cannot silently bear the anguish of waiting, and the fathers of Israel, the greatest historical leaders of the people, Moses and Aaron, David and Solomon, come to him, and while admonishing him, like Elijah, to bear his pain silently and patiently, raise their own voices and weep with him, lamenting his sufferings and those of their children (see chapter 12). This myth of the waiting, suffering, and crying Messiah can be regarded as the classical Aggadic example of the projection onto the concrete, personal image of the Messiah of the Jewish people's anguish in the long exile, of its impatience, its tottering on the brink of despair, and its eternal return to the hope of Redemption without which it can have no life. No other legend in the great Messiah cycle shows as clearly as this one that the Messiah is none other than Israel personified. When the legend describes how he sits and waits, how he suffers among the sick and the poor in the gates of Rome (see chapter 12), it in fact speaks of the waiting and suffering of Israel. When the legend tells that the

Messiah voluntarily undertook the sufferings in order to ease the fate of Israel, we understand that it actually speaks of Israel and of the sufferings it voluntarily has taken upon itself in every generation by remaining true to its God and its Tora. The Messiah who waits to be released from his chains is Israel waiting for Redemption. The Messiah comforted by the soothing words of Elijah, telling him that the end is near and that he should lean on God, is again Israel finding spiritual sustenance in the only hope that has remained with it ever since the destruction of the Temple: that the inscrutable will of God will, any time now, see fit to bring about the miraculous end, and that the day of salvation is about to dawn.

Of the numerous reasons put forward by Jewish inventiveness as to why the Messiah has not yet come, none are more ingenious than the following. For one, the Messiah can come only after all the souls sojourning in a secret heavenly hall called *Guf* ("Body"), and waiting for incarnation, are come down to earth and clothed in bodies, and the *Guf* remains empty. For another, the Messiah can come only after all the sinners have repented; should he come earlier, the unredeemed sinners would become liable to eternal punishment. This latter reasoning was used, in a twisted form, by the followers of Shabbatai Zevi in trying to justify his failure to bring about Redemption ten years after he had first revealed himself: he wanted to give time to those who did not believe in him, and whom God consequently condemned to death, to repent and to become true believers in him (see chapter 3).

In Hasidic circles the waiting for the Messiah became a matter of primary concern and concentration. It was considered such a great *mitzva* (meritorious religious act) that even a complete ignoramus, who because of his ignorance could not observe most commandments, if his heart was truly filled with longing for the Messiah, was considered to have achieved a higher spiritual level than many a scrupulously observant Tzaddiq (see below the story about R. Levi Yitzhaq of Berdichev).

Some Tzaddiqim took the Maimonidean principle of waiting for the Messiah every day quite literally, and numerous stories tell about this or that Tzaddiq whose whole life was devoted to this incessant waiting, expecting, hoping. A prototype of such a Tzaddiq was R. Moshe Teitelbaum (1759–1841), who was rabbi of Sátoraljaujhely (in Hasidic literature Ujhely or Uhel), Hungary, from 1808 to his death, and was the founder of the dynasty of Tzaddiqim whose last scion is the present rabbi of Satmar, residing in Williamsburg, Brooklyn. In his 1912 book, B. Ehrman included a brief factual statement about the ritual developed by R. Moshe to express his fervent expectation of the coming of the Messiah on the eve of Passover. This theme served as the basis of my father's moving story about "The Messiah-Dreamer of Ujhely" (see chapter 29).

R. Yirm'ya commanded: "[When I die] clothe me in a white shroud, dress me in my socks, put shoes on my feet and the staff in my hand, and lay me on the side [of the road], so that when the Messiah comes, I shall be ready."

(Y. Kil. 32b; Gen. Rab. 100:2)

Once R. Hiyya Rabba and R. Shim'on ben Halafta were walking in the Valley of Arbel [in the Galilee] at daybreak, and they saw the Hind of the Dawn whose light burst forth. R. Hiyya Rabba said to R. Shim'on ben Halafta: "O Rabbi, thus will be the Redemption of Israel: at first, just a little; then, as it will progress, it will grow greater and greater."

(Y. Ber. 2c mid.)

Rabban Gamliel, R. El'azar ben 'Azarya, R. Y'hoshu'a, and R. Akiba were walking on the road, and they heard the noise of the city of (Babylon) [Rome] from its streets at a distance of 120 mil. They began to cry, but R. Akiba smiled. They said to him: "Why are you smiling?" He said to them: "And you, why are you crying?" They said to him: "These pagans, who worship idols and burn incense to statues, dwell in safety; and we—the house of the footstool of our God is burnt in fire, how could we not cry?" He said to them: "This is why I smile: If this is [the lot] of those who disobey His will, those who fulfill His will how much more so!"

Again, once they were going up to Jerusalem, and when they reached Mount Scopus they rent their garments. When they reached the Temple Mount they saw a fox as it was running out of the House of Holy of Holies. They began to cry, but Akiba smiled. They said to him: "Why are you smiling?" And he said to them: "Why are you crying?" They said to him: "The place about which it is written, *The common man that draweth nigh shall be put to death* (Num. 1:51), now foxes walk in it, and shall we not cry?" He said to them: "This is why I smile. For it is written, *I will take unto Me faithful witnesses to record, Uriah the priest and Zechariah son of Berechiahu* (Isa. 8:2). What is the connection between Uriah and Zechariah, since Uriah [lived] in [the days of] the First Temple, and Zechariah in [those of] the Second? However, Scripture made the prophecy of Zechariah dependent on the prophecy of Uriah. It is written that Uriah said, *Because of you Zion shall be plowed as a field* (Mic. 3:13; Jer. 26:18, 20). And it is written that Zechariah said, *There shall yet old men and old women sit in the streets of Jerusalem* (Zech. 8:4). Before the prophecy of Uriah was fulfilled I was afraid lest the prophecy of Zechariah would not be fulfilled. Now that the prophecy of Uriah has been fulfilled, I know that the prophecy of Zechariah will be fulfilled in this language [i.e. literally]." They said to him: "Akiba, you have comforted us; Akiba, you have comforted us."

(B. Makkot 24a–b)

In the hour in which Israel was exiled, the Fathers of the World with the Mothers gathered and came to the Holy One, blessed be He, and began a great mourning there. In that hour the Holy One, blessed be He, joined them from the heaven most high and said to them: "Why are my lovers making a mourning for the dead?" They said to Him: "Master of the World! What sins did our children commit that You did this to them?" He said to them: "They did wickedness; and all that holiness which was in their flesh, they removed it from themselves. Because of this they were punished by exile." The Fathers said to Him: "Perhaps You will become oblivious of them among the nations of the World!" He said to them: "I swear by My great name that I shall not forget them among the nations of the world, but shall bring them back to their place...." Instantly the Holy One, blessed be He, comforted the fathers, and they returned and lay down in their tombs. Therefore, when the Bringer of Tidings comes, he will first go to the Cave of Machpela....

(Pes. diR. Kah., ed. Mandelbaum, p. 464)

R. Hiyya bar Abba said in the name of R. Yohanan: *"Hope deferred maketh the heart sick, but desire fulfilled is a tree of life* (Prov. 13:12). When a man expects something but his expectation is not given him, his heart becomes sorrowful; but when his expectation is fulfilled he is like one to whom life is given. Thus the Community of Israel says: 'Master of the World! All the hopes in the world have a time limit, and does the hope for the Messiah have no time limit?' The Holy One, blessed be He, says to her:'Come, and I shall comfort you, as it is written, *For the Lord hath comforted Zion, He hath comforted all her waste places* (Isa. 51:3).' And what does He say to her? *'Arise, shine, for thy light is come, and the glory of the Lord is risen upon thee'* (Isa. 60:1).... And with what will the Holy One, blessed be He, comfort her in the future? With the ingathering of her children in her in joy...."

(Ped. diR. Kah., ed. Mandelbaum, p. 465)

R. Y'hoshu'a ben Levi said: "When I came to the Messiah, he asked me and said: 'What are Israel doing in the world from which you came?' I said to him: 'They are waiting for you every day.' Instantly he lifted up his voice and cried."

(Ma'ase diR. Y'hoshu'a ben Levi, BhM 2:50)

A parable. There was a king who married a Matronit (lady), and went to a country overseas. He tarried there many days, and her women friends said to her: "The king has left you and will not return to you. How long will you wait?" But she went into the house and took out her marriage contract and read it and found consolation in it. After a time the king, her husband, returned and said: "My daughter, I am amazed that you have waited for me all these years." And she said to him: "My lord the king, were it not for my marriage contract, which provides a great settlement, my women friends would have caused me to be lost to you."

Thus Israel in This World. The nations of the world say to them: "How long will you wait for the Salvation? Look, how despised you are among us, and how much pain and suffering has come upon you. Come, be like one of us, and we shall make you dukes and princes and chiefs!" But Israel enters the synagogues and houses of study, and takes out the Tora scroll and reads in it, *And I will turn to you and make you fruitful* (Lev. 26:9), and in this they find consolation. And in the hour when the end comes, the Holy One, blessed be He, will say to Israel: "I am amazed, how were you able to wait for such a long time?" And Israel will say: "Master of the World! Were it not for the Tora which You gave me, the nations of the world would have caused me to be lost...."

(Pes. Hadta, BhM 6:43—44; also Mid. Ekha)

I believe with complete faith in the coming of the Messiah, and even though he should tarry, nevertheless I shall wait for his coming every day.

(Maimonides, *Thirteen Principles of the Faith*, 12th principle)

A Judaean [traveler] said to R. Y'huda: "This is what my father told me when he was about to depart from the world: 'Do not expect the feet of the Messiah until this rainbow appears in the world adorned in splendid brilliant colors and radiates into the world. Then you should expect the Messiah.'" From where [do we learn this]? It is written, *And I will look upon it* [the rainbow] *that I may remember the everlasting covenant* (Gen. 9:16). At present, when the rainbow appears in dull colors, it appears [merely] as a reminder that no deluge would come; but in That Time it will appear in brilliant colors and will be adorned like a bride who adorns herself for her bridegroom, in order to *remember the everlasting covenant*, and the Holy One, blessed be He, will remember that covenant which is in exile, and will raise it from the dust....

(Zohar 1:72b)

The Fifth Hall [of the Seven Heavenly Halls of Holiness]. The function of this Hall is to light up those Halls which are below it. And this is the Hall whose function is to shed light with the mystery of faith.

There is one gate to this Hall, and over it is appointed one named *Sanegoria* ["Defense"]. He stands over that gate in order to plead the defense of Israel before their Master, and so that the Other [i.e. Evil] Side should not rule over them. In this Hall there is one spirit who comprises four, for this spirit comprises four colors, white and black, green and red. And this is the spirit who exists completely in everything, and his name is *Suriya*. He is lord over all the armies of below, and all of them stand under him and are under his hand. This is the spirit who locks and opens all supernal locks. All of them are in his hands three times a day. All the armies of below are comprised and exist under him, and are nourished from him. He knows all the secrets of his Master: all the supernal hidden things are delivered into his hands. This spirit is [also] called *Ahava* ["Love"], and because of that, this Hall is called the Hall of Love; because here are hidden all the mysteries of mysteries for those who need to cling to him. . . .

This spirit guards all the treasures, and is [also] called the Guardian of Israel, the Guardian of the Covenant. For here he keeps guard over all the supernal treasures, and all the treasures of his Master are hidden in him. From here issue paths and roads to those who are below in order to arouse in them the spirit of love. Those four colors which are in him are comprised one in the other. And when they want to surround [him] they tread on one another, and from all of them issues a holy animal called *Zohar* ["Splendor"]. . . . From this Hall come forth all holy spirits which owe their existence to the supernal kisses. For from those kisses issues the air of the spirit for the existence of the soul, for all those supernal souls which were given to the children of man. . . . For in this Hall exist all the souls and all the spirits that are destined to descend into the children of man from the day that the world was created. And because of that, this Hall takes all the souls issuing from that river which flows and streams [from above], and therefore this Hall is never empty. And from the day on which the Temple was destroyed no more souls entered this Hall. And when the Hall will run out of souls that are in it, it will remain empty, and then it will be remembered from Above, and then King Messiah will come, and will arouse that Hall. . . .

(Zohar 2:253)

IMMANUEL HAROMI

Sonnet on the Messiah

Hurry, Messiah of God, why do you tarry?
Behold, they wait for you with flowing tears,
Their tears of blood are like mighty streams,
For you, O prince, yearns every heart and tongue!

Take up a rope of flax and measure Zion,
The crown of beauty: her sons will be found
Better in all the graces. The evil foe
Will be cast out. But you remain here standing!

Awake, our Messiah, rise and shine, mount
A galloping horse, hitch up a royal carriage,
Woe, all my bones are broken and are scattered.

But should you ride an ass, my lord, here's my advice:
Go back to sleep, our prince, and calm your heart,
Let the end wait and the vision be sealed.

(From Haberman, *Mahb'rot 'Imanuel*, 1946, p. 269)

Just as the man gives to his wife male waters which flow from his brain, so also from the woman, from her brain, female waters descend into her womb, and from these female waters and male waters which flow down from the brain of the female and the male, from them, actually, is the child fashioned, for they are the souls. . . .

[In the days of Adam] there was as yet no devastation in the world, but it was then as it will again be in the days of the Messiah, [may he come] quickly in our days. For about those days it is written, *He will swallow up death forever* (Isa. 25:8), [and "death" refers to] the husks whose existence is in the nature of female waters, and those husks were not sifted out but are still inside the female waters. And when they will be sifted out entirely, all the vitality will be removed from them and they will die totally. And this is the meaning of [the saying that] the Son of David will come only when the *Guf* will be emptied of all the souls. For when all the holy souls will be finished coming forth from there, and will ascend in the nature of female waters from which the souls are fashioned, as it has been said in the beginning of this section, the husks will no longer have vitality and they will die and be annulled. And this is the meaning of *He will swallow up death forever*, for the husks are called death and they will be swallowed up altogether.

(Vital, *Sefer 'Etz Hayyim* 2:129–30)

When the Seer of Lublin[1] passed away, his son, the Tzaddiq R. Joseph of Torchyn, received as his share of his inheritance the silken Sabbath garments, the belt, and the clock which was always hanging on the wall of the room in which the Seer used to sit. On his way back from Lublin to his home, rain began to fall, and it was impossible to go on. R. Joseph was forced to stay in a village in the house of a Jew who lived there. The rain fell for several days, and when it stopped, he wanted to continue his voyage, but the villager asked payment for the lodging. R. Joseph said: "I have no money, but I have with me a few holy things." He took out of his sack everything he had received in inheritance, and told the villager that he should choose whatever he wanted instead of the money he demanded. The villager called his wife to consult her as to what to choose, and she said: "The clothes and the belt are of no value for us, but the clock is something we can use in order to know every day in the morning that the time has come to milk the cow." And so they did: they accepted the clock for the debt.

Some time later, the Holy Old Man, the rabbi R. Ber of Radoshitz,[2] passed through that same village, and since it was late in the evening he stayed there. He entered the house of that Jew to spend the night there. The villager gave him the room in which that clock was hanging. All night the Rabbi of Radoshitz did not sleep, but paced back and forth in the room, joyously, with dancing steps. In the morning the villager asked him why he did not sleep all night and why was he so joyful. The rabbi said to him: "Tell me, please, where did you get this clock?" And he told him that he had received the clock in payment for the lodging from a man who had no money to pay. The Holy Old Man said:

"When I heard the chimes of the clock I instantly recognized that this was the clock of our Holy Master of Lublin. For from

---

1. Jacob Isaac haHoze miLublin (the Seer of Lublin; 1745–1815), was one of the founders of the Hasidic movement in Poland and Galicia.

2. Issachar Baer of Radoszyce (1765–1843), a disciple of the Seer of Lublin, was famous as a miracle healer.

every clock one hears a note which tells its owner that he is one hour nearer his death. And although he needs this knowledge, still the note is one of sadness and sorrow. But the clock of the Rabbi of Lublin issued notes of joy and jubilation that an hour has passed until the coming of our true Messiah. This is why I could not sleep, and for sheer joy I danced."

(Zevin, *Sippure Hasidim*, 2:292−93)

Once the holy rabbi, R. Levi Yitzhaq of Berdichev,[3] cele-brated the Seder on the first night of Passover, and it seemed to him that he had achieved complete concentration, and he became boast-ful about it in his heart. And they revealed to him from heaven: "Why should you be boastful about your Seder, when there is here in this town R. Hayyim Treger, who celebrates the Seder in a more accomplished way than you?" In the meantime many Hasidim came to listen to the benedictions of the Seder from the mouth of the rabbi. The rabbi of blessed memory said to them: "Do you know R. Hayyim Treger?" One of them said: "I know him, but I don't know where he lives." The rabbi said to them: "If it were possible to invite him here, how good that would be." The Hasidim spread out in the streets of Berdichev to find R. Hayyim Treger, until they found out where R. Hayyim Treger lived. They went there and knocked on his door. His wife opened the door and said: "What do you want? My husband is drunk and he is asleep." But the Hasidim roused him from his sleep and carried him off, literally on their shoulders, until they came with him to the rabbi of blessed memory. And the rabbi commanded them that they should give him his own chair to sit on, and said to him: "Dearest R. Hayyim, have you recited this past Sabbath 'We were slaves to Pharaoh in Egypt'?[4] R. Hayyim answered, "Yes." "Have you searched for *Hametz?*" He answered, "Yes." "Did you burn the *Hametz?*" R. Hayyim began to think and then answered: "No, for I forgot, and the *Hametz* is still there on a beam of wood."[5] The rabbi

---

3. Levi Yitzhaq ben Meir of Berdichev (c. 1740−1810) was a leading Tzaddiq.

4. Deut. 6:21. This Biblical quotation introduces the recitation of the story of the miraculous deliverance from Egypt before the Seder meal.

5. On the eve of the fourteenth of Nisan, that is, about twenty-four hours prior to the beginning of Passover, the house is searched for any *Hametz* (leaven). The *Hametz* found is put in a safe place overnight (hence the reference to the beam in our story), and is burnt next morning.

said to him: "Did you celebrate the Seder?" He answered him:
"Rabbi, I shall tell you the truth, I have heard that it is forbidden to
drink brandy eight days [of Passover], so I drank brandy in the
morning that it should be enough for me for eight days, and I
became very sleepy and fell asleep. And my wife aroused me from
my sleep and said to me, 'Why don't you celebrate the Seder like
every other Jew?' And I said to her, 'What do you want of me, you
know that I am an ignoramus ['am ha'aretz], and also my father was
an ignoramus, and I know nothing except that the Jews were in
exile among the *Tziganers* ["gypsies," i.e. Egyptians], and we have
our God who brought us out from there to freedom, and even now
we are again in exile, and God will bring us out now again from this
exile.' And I saw on the table *matzot* and wine and eggs, and I ate
the *mazot* with the eggs and drank the wine, and because of
drowsiness I had to go back to sleep." And the rabbi of blessed
memory commanded that they should go back with him to his
house. And these words [of R. Hayyim Treger] were well [re-
ceived] in heaven, for he said them in truth, without any intention,
for he really knew nothing more.

(Ma'asiyyot w'Sihot Tzaddiqim, p. 68)

The greatness of the belief of R. Moshe Teitelbaum[6] of
Ujhely in the coming of the Messiah is well known to everybody.
He commanded his attendant, R. Mikhel Glazer of blessed memory, that should he hear at night any noise in the town, he should
wake him from his sleep, for perhaps it is the voice of the Messiah.
And on every Passover eve he would take a bundle of *matzot* (he
would take six *matzot*) and a bottle of wine and a cup, and put them
in a basket, and tie it to his staff, and put it over his shoulder, and he
would stand and look out the window and listen whether he could
hear the sound of the shofar, the shofar of the messiah.

(Ehrman, *Sefer P'er w'Khavod* 2b—3a)

The rod of Judah is in distress and pain,
When will the lion roar in the forest?
For your salvation yearn fathers and sons,

---

6. R. Moshe Teitelbaum (1759—1841) was rabbi of Sátoraljaujhely (in Hasidic
literature Ujhely or Uhel), in Hungary, from 1808 to his death. He was the founder
of the dynasty of Tzaddiqim, the last scion of which is the present Rabbi of Satmar,
who has his headquarters in Brooklyn.

The poor ones and the desolate.
Let our supplication rise up on high,
O God, King, sitting on the throne of mercy.
(Sephardi penitential song, from Idelsohn,
Gesänge der orientalischen Sefardim, p. 156)

_____

6

Counting the Days

It was inevitable that the long wait for the Messiah should engender impatience, and that this impatience, in turn, should lead to attempts at calculating the precise time of his coming. All these calculations were, of course, predicated on the assumption that the date of the coming of the Messiah had long been predetermined by God, and that while He did not divulge the date to His people, He allowed His prophets to perceive veiled hints at it in their visions. Thus the Messianic calculators managed to find Biblical bases for their arithmetic, and—a psychologically most significant fact—in most places and ages they figured that the Messiah would come within a few decades, or even a few years.

Rabban Yohanan ben Zakkai, the founder of the Talmudic Academy at Jabne (70 C.E.) stated shortly before his death that he expected the coming of the Messiah—whom he identified with King Hezekiah—within a very short time (cf. B. Ber. 28b). The rabbis of the first and second centuries of the common era in general took it for granted that the Messiah would come soon, and devoted their attention to the question of how long his rule would last. R. Eliezer believed that it would last forty years, R. El'azar ben 'Azarya said seventy years, and R. Y'huda haNasi (c. 135–220) said three generations, or, according to another tradition, 365 years (B.

Sanh. 99a). R. Dosa said four hundred years, and R. Abimi, the son of R. Abbahu, said seven thousand years. Rav Y'huda in the name of Sh'muel said: "The days of the Messiah will last as long as the time that has passed from the creation of the world until now." Rav Nahman bar Yitzhaq said: "As long as the time that has passed from the days of Noah until now" (ibid.). The last two statements ("until now") only make sense if the rabbis who made them assumed that "now," or very soon, the Messianic days would begin.

Historical upheavals could not fail to leave their impress on these Messianic calculations. The destruction of Jerusalem by Titus (70 C.E.), Bar Kokhba's uprising (132–135 C.E.), the Sassanian attacks on the Romans (third century), the disintegration of the Roman Empire (fifth century), the conquest of Palestine by the Persians (614–628), were all interpreted as harbingers of the coming of the Messiah. The appearance of the Arabs on the horizon and their rapid conquest of the lands of the east (in the mid-seventh century) were seen as Messianic wars (see chapters 15–18) which would be followed by the appearance of the Messiah. Thus the *Pirqe R. Eliezer*, a Midrash of Palestinian origin edited in the eighth century but containing much earlier material, gives several Messianic dates in the seventh century.[1]

Of the many Messianic calculators of the Middle Ages we can mention only the most outstanding ones. Rashi (1040–1105) figured that the Messiah would come in 1352 or in 1478.[2] Maimonides (1135–1204), as we have seen in the Introduction (section VIII), expected him in 1210. In the same period (from 1087 to 1172) there were at least nine Messianic movements in various parts of the Jewish world (see Introduction, section IX).

Nahmanides (1194–1268) calculated that the Messiah would come in 1403.[3] R. Moses de Leon (1240–1305), the

---

1. Cf. Abba Hillel Silver, *A History of Messianic Speculation*, pp. 37–42.

2. Ibid., pp. 66–67.

3. Ibid., p. 84.

author of the Zohar, gives various dates: 1300, 1306, 1324, 1334, 1340, 1608, and 1648.[4] The last mentioned date, which coincided with the Cossack massacres, was the one that supplied the mystical validation for the greatest of all Messianic movements that convulsed Israel, that of Shabbatai Zevi (1626–76).

In the seventeenth century, Kabbalists and non-Kabbalists alike engaged in Messianic speculations and variously fixed the date of Redemption for 1648 (Isaiah Horowitz, Yom-Tov Lippmann Heller, Shabbatai Cohen, Joseph Sambari), 1713 (Isaac Cohen), 1725 (Nathan Nata Spira), etc.[5] In the eighteenth century, pseudoprophets and pseudo-Messiahs continued to appear in Germany and Poland, the most infamous among them being Jacob Frank (1726–91).

In Eastern Europe, the inclination to Messianic calculations remained alive long after it had disappeared in other parts of the Diaspora. As late as 1868, the chief rabbi of Rumania, Meir Loeb ben Y'hiel Mikhael Malbim (1809–79) calculated that the beginning of the Redemption would take place in 1913. He wrote:

> The time of the end will come in the year 5673 [i.e. 1913].... The growing of the horn of the House of David and the building of the Temple, and all the promises of the prophets will come true at once, and their light will shine from the year 5673 [1913] until 5788 [1928], for then the Temple will already stand and the city [of Jerusalem] will be built on her hill, and the palace will sit over its judgment, and all the promises of the prophets will come true, and the kingship shall be the Lord's, *and the Lord shall be King over all the earth* (Zech. 14:9).[6]

The foregoing brief survey allows no more than a fleeting glimpse of the permanence, ubiquity, and power of the Messianic idea in Jewish history as manifested in unceasing

---

4. Ibid., pp. 90–92.

5. Ibid., pp. 184ff.

6. Cf. the Malbim's commentary on Dan. 7:25 and at the very end of his comments on Daniel.

calculations of the date of the Messiah's coming, and in the long string of Messianic movements centered on the person of one pseudo-Messiah after the other. As against the many rabbis and scholars who calculated the days of the advent and also the duration of the Messianic era, those who opposed such attempts were few and far in between. Let me mention here only one of them. R. Y'huda heHasid ("The Pious"; c. 1150–1217), principal author of the important ethical work *Sefer Hasidim* (Book of the Pious), went so far as to equate Messianic calculations with witchcraft. He wrote:

> When you see a person prophesying about the Messiah, you should know that he is either engaged in witchcraft, or has dealings with demons, or has adjured them with the Ineffable Name. Because such a sorcerer importunes the angels or the spirits, they say to him: "Speak not in this manner, [rather] reveal [the coming of the Messiah] to the whole world." But at the end he will be put to shame before the whole world, because he importuned the angels or the demons. And in its place misfortunes come because of him who adjured. And demons come and teach him calculations and secrets, to his shame and the shame of those who believe his words...for no man knows about the coming of the Messiah.[7]

The texts that follow are taken from the Talmud, the Midrash, and the Zohar. To them is appended a Hasidic story (as rewritten by Martin Buber) which illustrates how some Hasidic rabbis found a way to reinterpret and dilute the idea of the Messiah until it dissolved into a vague and amorphous feeling of "Light of Redemption" which was supposed to hover about Israel bowed by the burden of exile.

Israel has been assured that Elijah would come neither on the eve of a Sabbath nor on the eve of a holy day, because of the trouble [they would interrupt the preparations for the Sabbath or holy day and would go to receive him].... However, the Messiah can come [on those days], because when the Messiah comes, all [the nations]

---

7. *Sefer Hasidim*, pp. 76–77.

will be servants to Israel [and they will do the Sabbath preparations].

(B. 'Er. 43b, and Rashi)

The Master said: "In the sixth year [of the Messianic septenary], sounds will be heard; in the seventh, there will be wars, and at the end of the seventh, the Son of David will come. Wars are the beginning of Redemption."

(B. Meg. 17b)

And this is for you the sign [of the coming of the Messiah]: that you see a septenary which begins with rain; in the second year, arrows of famine are sent out; in the third, there is great famine; and in the fourth—neither hunger nor plenty; in the sixth—great plenty, and a star will grow from the east with a staff on its head, and that is the star of Israel... and if it lights up, it is for the benefit of Israel, and then will sprout up Messiah ben David. And this is the sign for you: When you see that the eastern Nero [i.e., emperor] in Damascus has fallen, and the kingdom of the Children of the East has fallen, then will salvation sprout up for Israel, and Messiah ben David will come, and they will ascend to Jerusalem and enjoy it.... May God in His mercy send us the Redeemer rapidly in our days, Amen.

(Nistarot R. Shim'on ben Yohai, BhM 3:82)

Once Y'huda and Hizqiya, the sons of R. Hiyya, sat at a banquet before Rabbi [Y'huda the Prince] without saying anything. Whereupon Rabbi said: "Give the boys much wine, so that they say a word." When they felt the wine, they started to speak and said: "The Son of David will not come until two houses disappear from Israel, and they are [those of] the Exilarch in Babylon and the Prince in the Land of Israel, for it is said, *And He shall be for a sanctuary and for a stone of stumbling and for a rock of offense to both the houses of Israel* (Isa. 8:14)." He said to them: "My sons, you are sticking thorns into my eyes." R. Hiyya said to him: "Rabbi, let this not be bad in your eyes... when wine goes in, secret comes out."

(B. Sanh. 38a)

His disciples asked R. Yose ben Qisma: "When will the Son of David come?" He said: "I am afraid that you will ask me for a sign." They said to him: "We shall not ask you for a sign." He said to them: "When this [city] gate will fall and will be rebuilt, and fall again, they will have no time to rebuild it again until the Son of David comes." They said to him: "Our Master! give us a sign!" He said to them: "Did you not tell me that you would not ask me for a sign?" They said to him: "Nevertheless." He said to them: "If so, let the waters of the Cave of Pamias [the source of the Jordan River] turn into blood!" And they turned into blood. In the hour of his death he said to them: "Dig a deep grave for my coffin, for [in the wars of Gog and Magog] there will be no palm tree in Babylon to which the Persians will not tie their horses, and no coffin in the Land of Israel from which a Persian horse will not eat straw."

(B. Sanh. 98a–b, with Rashi's comments)

The rabbis taught: "The proselytes and those who play with children hold back the Messiah." This is understandable as far as the proselytes are concerned, for R. Helbo said: "The proselytes are as bad for Israel as a sore on the skin"; but why those who play with children?... This refers to those who marry little girls who are not yet able to bear children, for R. Yose said: "The Son of David will not come until all the souls are emptied from the *Guf* [lit.: "body"; the celestial place where the souls of the unborn are kept], for it is said: *For the spirit that enwrappeth itself is from Me, and the souls which I have made* (Isa. 57:16)—that is: The spirits that I destined to be born are thus kept back...."

(B. Nid. 13b and Rashi ibid.)

R. Tanhum son of R. Hiyya, and some say the rabbis, said: "King Messiah will never come until all the souls which came up in the thought [of God] will be created. These are the souls that are enumerated in the Book of Adam."

(Gen. Rab. 24:4)

R. Levi said: "[God made Israel swear that they] should not reveal the [Messianic] end, and should not reveal the secrets [of the Tora] to the idolaters."

(B. Ket. 111a)

Rav Qetina said: "For six thousand years the world will exist, and for one thousand years it will lie waste...." Abbaye said: "It will lie waste for two thousand years..." It was taught in accordance with Rav Qetina: "Just as in the Sabbatical year [the fields] lie fallow for one year every seven years, so the world will lie waste for one thousand years in seven thousand years...." In the school of Elijah it was taught: "For six thousand years the world will exist: [there will be] two thousand years of *Tohu* ['void'], two thousand years of Tora, and two thousand years of the Messiah. But because of our sins, which are many, several of these [Messianic years] have already passed."

Elijah said to Rav Y'huda the brother of Rav Sala the Pious: "The world will exist for no less than eighty-five jubilees [that is, 4,250 years], and in the last jubilee the Son of David will come." He asked him: "In its beginning or at its end?" He answered: "I do not know." [Rav Y'huda then asked:] "Will it be complete or not?" He said to him: "I do not know." Rav Ashi said: "This is what Elijah told him: 'Until the last jubilee expect him not; from then on expect him.'"

(B. Sanh. 97a–b)

Rav Hanan bar Tahlifa sent [a message] to Rav Yosef: "I encountered a man who has in his possession a scroll written in Assyrian [Hebrew] characters in the Holy Language. I said to him: 'How did you get this?' He said to me: 'I hired myself out to the Roman armies and found it among the hidden treasures of Rome.' And in it was written: 'After 4,291 years from the creation of the world, the world will be orphaned. In some of them [the ensuing years] will be wars of sea monsters, in others the wars of Gog and Magog, and the rest will be the days of the Messiah. And the Holy One, blessed be He, will renew His world only after seven thousand years.' Rav Aha son of Rava said: "After five thousand years."

(B. Sanh. 97b)

R. Sh'muel bar Nahmani said in the name of R. Yohanan: "May the bones of those who calculate the [Messianic] end be blown away! As soon as the time [calculated by them] arrives and the Messiah does not come, they say: 'He will no longer come at all.' Rather, wait for him, for it is said, *Though he tarry, wait for him* (Hab. 2:3)."

(B. Sanh. 97b)

Rav said: "All the [calculated] ends have already expired, and the matter [of the coming of the Messiah] now depends only on repentance and good deeds." And Sh'muel said: "It is sufficient for the mourner that he abide in his mourning." This is like [the dispute of] Tannaites: R. Eliezer says: "If Israel repents, it will be redeemed; if not, it will not be redeemed..." R. Y'hoshu'a said to him: "[Can it be that] if they do not repent they will not be redeemed? [No,] but the Holy One, blessed be He, will cause a king to arise against them whose decrees will be cruel like [those of] Haman, [whereupon] Israel will repent and turn to be good."

(B. Sanh. 97b)

A Sadducee once asked R. Abbahu: "When will the Messiah come?" He answered: "When darkness will envelope you people." He said to him: "Are you threatening me?" He said: "It is an explicit verse: *For, behold, darkness shall cover the earth, and gross darkness the peoples, but upon thee the Lord will arise, and His glory shall be upon thee* (Isa. 60:2)."

(B. Sanh. 99a)

We learned: R. Eliezer said: "The days of the Messiah will be forty years...." R. El'azar ben 'Azarya said: "Seventy years...." Rabbi said: "Three generations...." R. Dosa said: "Four hundred years...." Rabbi said: "Three hundred and sixty-five years like the number of the days of the sun...." Abimi the son of R. Abbahu taught: "The days of the Messiah will be for Israel seven thousand years...." Rav Y'huda in the name of Sh'muel said: "The days of the Messiah will be as from the day in which the world was created until now...." Sh'muel said: "There is no difference whatsoever between this world and the days of the Messiah except the enslavement by the governments."

(B. Sanh. 99a)

Elijah used to frequent the academy of Rabbi [Y'huda the Prince]. One day— it was the new moon—it got dark but he did not come. [Next day, when Elijah did come, Rabbi said to him:

"Why did the Master not come?" He said to him: "I had to awaken Abraham, and wash his hands, and he prayed, and then I made him lie down; and likewise with Isaac, and so with Jacob." "But could they not be awakened together?" "I knew that their [joint] supplication would be so overwhelming that they would bring the Messiah before his time." He said to him: "And is there anybody like them in This World [whose prayer would be heeded]?" He said to him: "There is R. Hiyya and his sons." Rabbi [thereupon] proclaimed a fast, and R. Hiyya and his sons were called upon to lead in the prayers. When R. Hiyya said, "He causeth the wind to blow," a blast of wind came; when he said, "He causeth the rain to fall," a shower came; when he was about to say, "He quickeneth the dead," the world shook, and they said in heaven, "Who revealed the secret in the world?" They said: "Elijah." They brought him and gave him sixty lashes of fire, and he went and appeared like a bear of fire, and went in among them [in the synagogue] and scattered them.

(B. Bab. Metz. 85b)

R. Sh'muel taught in the name of R. Y'huda: "If somebody tells you when the end, the Redemption, will come, believe him not, for it is written: *For the day of vengeance was in My heart* (Isa. 63:4). The heart did not reveal it to the mouth; how could the mouth reveal it?"

(Mid. Teh. Buber, pp. 80–81)

R. Yose entered a cave and found in it a book which was stuck into a cleft in the rock at the far end of the cave. He brought it out, and when he opened it, he saw the shapes of the seventy-two letters which were given to Adam the first man, and through which Adam knew all the wisdom of the supernal Holy Beings and of all those who [sit] behind the millstones that turn behind the Veil of the Supernal Lights, and [knew] all the things that were to come to pass in the world until the day when a cloud that is on the west side would arise and cast darkness upon the world. R. Yose called R. Y'huda, and they began to study the book. But as soon as they had studied two or three pages of those letters, they found themselves looking at that Supernal Wisdom. When they came to delve into the mysteries of the book, and began to discuss them among themselves, a fiery flame and a gust of wind came and struck their hands, and the book disappeared. R. Yose wept and said: "Perhaps, God forbid, we are guilty of a sin, or is it that we are not worthy to know these things?" When they came to R. Shim'on and told him what had happened, he said to them; "Perhaps you were trying to learn about the Messianic end from those letters?" They said to him: "That we do not know, for we have forgotten all of it." R. Shim'on said to them: "It is not the will of the Holy One, blessed be He, that too much be revealed to the world. But when the days of the Messiah approach, even the children of the world will be able to discover secrets of wisdom, and to know through them the Ends and the Calculations, and in that time it will be revealed to all. . . ."

(Zohar 1:117b–118a)

R. Shim'on began and said: "*I will remember My covenant with Jacob* (Lev. 26:42). [The name Jacob is here written] fully, with a *vav*. Why? . . . This verse speaks about the exile of Israel. For when they are in exile, at the time in which they will be remembered [and redeemed], they will be remembered in the mystery of the [letter] *vav*, that is, in the sixth millennium [for the *vav* has the numerical value of six]. And the period of the remembrance of the *vav* will be six moments and one half of a moment. When sixty years will have passed beyond the bolt of the threshold of the sixth millennium, God of heaven will turn with remembrance to the daughter of Jacob [the people of Israel]. And from that time [there will pass] another six years. . . . In the sixty-sixth, King Messiah will reveal himself in the Land of Galilee, and a star on the east side will swallow seven stars from the north side. And a flame of dark fire will be suspended in heaven for sixty days, and wars will be stirred up in the world toward the north side, and two kings will fall in those wars. And all the peoples will join together against the daughter of Jacob in order to drive her from the world. . . . And then the *Guf* [the heavenly chamber that contains the unborn souls] will be emptied of all the souls that seek to be renewed. . . . In the seventy-third, all the kings of the world will gather in the great city of Rome, and the Holy One, blessed be He, will shower them with fire and hailstones and rocks, and they will perish from the world, except for those kings who will not [yet] have arrived there, and they will return to wage other wars. And from that time on King Messiah will be revealed in the whole world, and around him will assemble many nations and many armies from all the ends of the world, and all the Children of Israel will gather in all their places, until the count of those years will reach a hundred.... And the Children of Ishmael [the Arabs] will at that time arise with all the nations of the world to go forth against Jerusalem.... Happy will be all those who will remain in the world at the end of the sixth millennium to enter into [the millennium of] the Sabbath....

(Zohar 1:119a)

R. Y'hoshu'a said: "...We have learned that there will be three categories [of people]: one of the totally saintly, one of the wicked, and one of the intermediate. The totally saintly will arise at the rising of the dead of the Land of Israel... in the fortieth year of the ingathering of the exiles. And the last ones [will arise] in the four hundred and eighth year of the sixth millennium...." R. Y'huda said: "The saintly ones will arise two hundred and ten years earlier than all other people." R. Yitzhaq said: "Two hundred and fourteen years earlier...."

(Zohar 1:140a, Mid. haNe'elam)

A friend once asked the Rabbi of Sadagora: "How can this be? A number of holy men who lived before our time alluded to a date on which redemption was to come. The era they indicated has come and gone, but redemption has not come to pass."

The Tzaddiq replied: "My father, may his memory be a blessing to us, said this: 'In the Talmud we read that all the calculated dates of redemption have passed. But just as the Divine Presence left the Sanctuary and went into exile in the course of ten journeys, so she cannot return all at once, and the light of redemption loiters between heaven and earth. At every date it descended one rung. The light of redemption is now dwelling in the lowest heaven, which is called Curtain.' That is what my father said. But I say: The light of redemption is spread about us at the level of our heads. We do not notice it because our heads are bowed beneath the burden of exile. Oh, that God might lift up our heads!"

(Buber, *Tales* II:72)

7

Hastening the End

Occasionally, outstanding Kabbalists and Hasidic adepts in the secret lore could not restrain their desperate impatience with the delay in the coming of the Messiah, and felt impelled to take matters into their own hands. These men were convinced that the esoteric doctrines they had mastered, and the powers of saintliness they had acquired by years of ruthless mortification of their flesh, would enable them to "hasten the End," as the traditional phrase goes. Their attempts, inevitably doomed to failure of course, form the subject of a type of legends which tell about the measures taken by these saints to force the Redemption. The basis of these stories is the belief that it is possible for men of exceptional saintliness to force the hand of God, and that they would have succeeded in making the Messiah come had it not been for interference by Satan, the ancient enemy of God and Israel.

The most popular of these stories, extant in several versions, is that of R. Joseph della Reina (i.e., "of the Queen"), also known as R. Joseph Dolphina (i.e., "[of the] Dauphine"), who is said to have lived in the thirteenth and fourteenth centuries, when the Zohar "was discovered in the world," and who, after his unsuccessful attempt to destroy Satan, went astray and became guilty of one of the three greatest sins, that of fornication. The woman whom the demons brought to his bed every night was the queen of France (or, in another version, of Greece)—hence his surname.

A rather different variant of the same theme of "hastening the End" is the legend that tells, of various Hasidic rabbis, that they tried to force the coming of the Messiah by deciding during their lifetime to refuse to enter heaven after their death unless the Messiah would come. Since, in the Hasidic world view, merits must without fail get their reward, such a refusal on the part of a great saint causes an intolerable disruption in the heavenly order of things, which must instantly be remedied by letting the Messiah commence his mission. But this pious blackmail, too, is doomed to failure. "Those in Heaven" manage to play a trick on the soul of the saint and entice it to enter heaven against its will. (See below, "Four Stories of Impatient Tzaddiqim," stories 2 and 3.)

Yet another variant on the same theme is based on the belief that if two or three saintly men join forces they can bring the Messiah. In the preceding chapter we saw the Talmudic origin of this belief: had Abraham, Isaac, and Jacob prayed together, they could have brought the Messiah before his time, and prayers in unison by R. Hiyya and his sons would have had the same effect. In the Hasidic versions of this legend the story hinges on the circumstances— brought about by the forces of evil—that prevent the saintly men from meeting and storming the gates of heaven with their joint supplication. (See below, R. Nahman of Bratzlav's story, "How Satan Prevented the Coming of the Messiah," and "Four Stories of Impatient Tzaddiqim," story 4.)

Often it is the death of one or more of these impatient saints, which, according to the story, prevents them from attaining their great goal, the Hastening of the End. Commenting on these remarkable occurrences (for the stories frequently had a basis in fact), Martin Buber wrote:

Some of the Tzaddiqim actually attempted, by means of theurgic acts (the so-called practical Kabbala), to make Napoleon into Ezekiel's "Gog of the land of Magog," whose wars, as set forth in some eschatological texts, will be followed by the coming of the Messiah. Other Tzaddiqim opposed these attempts and warned that the beginning of the Redemption must be prepared, not by external gestures, but solely by a turning around of man as a whole. And the decisively remarkable thing was that all of them, the darers and the warners, actually died within one year. One can hardly entertain any doubt that the sphere which they entered, even though from different sides, burned up their earthly lives. It was not the imagination of legend but the simple fact that there was a struggle in which both parties were annihilated. One issue, above all, was at stake in that struggle: whether it was permitted to importune the Powers on High that they bring about that for which we yearn. Next to it there was the other one: whether the way for the fulfillment should be paved by magical procedures or by an inner transformation. And the questions were not a subject of discussion, but a matter of life and death.[1]

In a different type of stories the Hasidic rabbi is reported, not to have engaged in any special act with a view to hastening the end, but to have reproached his followers for not having followed certain, to him elementary, patterns of pious behavior which would have brought the Messiah. In one of these stories the Ba'al Shem Tov is left to pray alone; had his disciples remained with him and joined him in his supplication, he could have captured the wonderful bird of his parable which, of course, is none other than the Messiah. In three others, the erring people are reproached for asking only simple material benefits in their prayers (because they are caught up in the world of the "husks," the physical, material aspects of existence), whereas they could and should have asked for the ultimate benefit, Redemption. (See below, "Four Stories of Men of Small Faith.")

---

1. Buber, *Gog und Magog*, p. 232.

The Story of R. Joseph Dolphina

A pious man lived in the Holy Land, in Hebron, may it be rebuilt quickly. He was a great scholar, versed in the Tora and in piety. This pious man delved deep in reading and studying the science of truth, the science of the Kabbala. And in his days was found the holy book Zohar, which was discovered at that time in the world, and he rejoiced greatly over the Zohar. And R. Joseph sought for himself companions excelling in the Tora and in piety, ten great scholars, and they studied the Kabbala day and night, and mortified themselves so severely that it cannot be told. But R. Joseph exceeded all of them, for he spent all his days fasting, and sought great solitude. And when his companions would leave him, he would lock himself in a separate room and recite great prayers with utmost devotion. This he would do day after day.

And at night he would lie on the bare earth, and strew ashes upon his head, and cry and mourn with great cries over the destruction of the Temple. This he did for a long time, until the Prophet Elijah appeared to him and taught him many mysteries and gave him many combinations of Holy Names. Thus Elijah of blessed memory would come to him every day. And R. Joseph would pray very great prayers, and weep and cry every day imploring God that He reveal him the end and send us the True Redeemer soon to gather the exiled of Israel. And from that time on, the Prophet Elijah withdrew from him and no longer showed himself to him.

Now when this R. Joseph saw that Elijah no longer came to him, he was greatly distressed, and he cried in prayers and supplications, and undertook great self-mortifications and fasts and submersions, and he subjected himself to great torture for forty days, and incessantly cried: "Elijah, Elijah! Where are you? Why are you staying away? Why do you not show yourself to me?" When the forty days of fasting were over, Elijah came to him and said to him: "You putrid drop! You dust and ashes! Why did you storm the supernals and the infernals with your prayer? Do you not know that this thing you ask has never been revealed to any man, not even to the holy prophets? And how many sages and pious men and holy men have prayed for it but achieved nothing? Therefore, give it up. These are mysteries and secrets which cannot be revealed to anybody. You will achieve nothing with all your weeping and crying."

When the pious man heard these words, he began to lament and said: "I shall not let you go until you answer the question I want to put to you." And he began to adjure him by the great and terrible Name of God that he leave him not until he gave an answer to his question. And this is the thing which he wanted Elijah to tell him: What kind of acts should he perform in order to bring about Redemption, and to eject the uncleanness and the evil spirits and the accusers from the world.

And Elijah answered him and said: "Your weeping and crying and your prayers of great devotion were heard in heaven. So I shall tell you all that I have permission to tell. If you really want to perform the act, you must go, with your companions the pious men, to the Mountains of Darkness by means of the Holy Names which I shall reveal to you now. And there you will find a completely black dog, a dog blacker than black. But you must be very, very careful lest he deceive you in any manner. And here, I am giving you a chain upon which is engraved the Ineffable Name of the Lord God of Hosts. And here, I am giving you pure frankincense, which you should sniff; this is from the eleven spices which were used for the incense in the Temple, so that it will give you strength to stand the horrible stench of the black dog. For he is none other than Samael. And while doing this you must all concentrate most intensively on the devotions which I herewith give you. And this chain with the Ineffable Name engraved upon it, hurl it at the black dog; thus he will be caught and chained. And then you must instantly slaughter him, without the slightest delay. And I shall be with you to lead you the way to the Mountains of Darkness which you must follow, after you have done all this. And as for the manner in which you must thereafter conduct yourselves, that I shall teach you later. But one thing I am telling you again: Beware, and beware, very, very much, of the black dog, that he should not deceive you in any way. And be very, very careful to chain him instantly with this chain and to slaughter him immediately, without any compassion whatsoever, and do not give in to him in any matter, lest he deceive you. This is what I have received permission to tell you, and nothing more."

And then Elijah gave this R. Joseph the Names and the utterings and the combinations of Names on which they would have to concentrate in order to do all this. And then the prophet Elijah disappeared from him.

Now this pious man, R. Joseph, was in a very happy and joyous mood, and he went to his companions, the righteous, and related to them that which Elijah had told him, and he showed his friends the chain and the pure frankincense which he had given him. And when they saw them they believed him and rejoiced greatly that they would merit to destroy Samael and to bring about Redemption.

And all of them instantly began to prepare themselves in holiness and in purity, in fear and in tremor, to combine the Holy Names and the utterances. And as soon as they combined and uttered those Holy Names as Elijah had taught them, they found themselves in the Mountains of Darkness and instantly they found there the black dog. And as the prophet Elijah had told them, they threw at him the chain with the Ineffable Name and chained him with great cruelty. And the black dog began to weep and to cry, and to implore them that they have pity on him and let him go. But they did not listen to his crying and begging, and handled him with great cruelty. But he did not cease crying and begging. And they took him with force, with cruelty, to slaughter him, and with great devotion they uttered the Holy Names which Elijah had taught them. When now the black dog saw that all his weeping and moaning did not help, and that they would have no pity on him, he sought another ruse and said to R. Joseph: "I am in your power. You can do with me as you wish. I shall keep quiet." And the pious men were busy with their devotions and combinations of the Holy Names in order to slaughter him. A moment later the black dog said: "Let me smell a little of this pure frankincense before I die." And because of their preoccupation and confusion, they let him have a whiff of the pure frankincense. Instantly the black dog stood up on his feet and said: "Master of the World! You wrote in Your Tora 'Thou shalt not bow down to other gods nor serve them,' and these people here have served me, they offered their pure frankincense to me." And instantly he was able to snap the chain with great strength, and broke it into many pieces, and he hurled those righteous men far away, some of them on mountains and hills, others into the desert, each one to a different place, so that no two of them remained together. But each one of them was able to save himself through the Holy Names and utterances, which they all knew well. So each of them reached inhabited places, but several of them died within the year, and some of them lost their minds, and some of them returned to the Land of Israel, and returned to their studies. But never did they reveal anything of all this, and they refrained from again following such paths, and never again engaged in such things.

And R. Joseph was thrown very far away on top of a mountain, near the kingdom of France, and he too lost his mind. One day he reached France, and he went to a place near the place where the king of France lived. Jews lived there, but nobody knew him. But they recognized that he was a great man, outstanding in the Tora and a great Kabbalist, only there was a madness in him. So the Jews there made an arrangement to let him have a livelihood, and put him in a house before the city, and gave him several books which he needed. So he stayed in that house several months and studied.

Thereafter he began to perform miraculous acts with Holy Names, and he mentioned many names, and performed wondrous things which cannot at all be told here. And he also adjured angels so that they had to bring to him the Queen Dolphina [Dauphine], who was a great beauty. And the king of France was her husband. And they brought her every night to his house, to his bed, and he lay with her. And the queen lay in great fear, for she was not at all aware that she was brought there by force, for she saw no men nor any creature in the world who brought her or led her to the bed of this R. Joseph. She saw only him lying there each time with her. Therefore she was very much afraid, for she did not know how she got there, and because of her fear she could not utter a word. And in the morning, at dawn, she was again taken back to her house. R. Joseph did this for two months. Every night he had the Queen Dolphina brought to him through the Names. This is why he is called R. Joseph Dolphina, after the name of the queen.

Finally, however, the queen went to the king and told him everything that had happened to her. The king was greatly frightened by what he heard, and said to the queen: "Would you recognize the man to whom you were carried every night?" The queen said: "Yes, my lord King, if the man should come before us, I would recognize him. And thus and thus is his appearance." And she told him all the marks, as he was. And the king had done all the investigations and searches which were at all possible to be undertaken in the kingdom. Finally it became known that the man was R. Joseph who lived before the city, for enough had been heard about the wondrous acts he performed, and his appearance was exactly as the queen described him.

Instantly the king of France sent messengers to this R. Joseph to bring him right away to the king. When these messengers came to the house of R. Joseph, they looked for him but could not find him. And he shouted at them and said: "Whom do you want? Here I am. What do you want of me? Go to the king and tell him I do not want to go to him. If he has something to say to me, let him send word through you." And the messengers said: "Where are you? Show yourself to us!" For they only heard his voice but saw nobody. He said: "Go to the king and say to him what I commanded you to say, and fulfill your mission, for you cannot achieve anything with me."

And the messengers grew frightened, and were very astonished at this thing, and they went to the king and told him everything that had happened and the message he had sent to the king, and they said to the king that this man was a Jew. When the king heard this, he instantly sent word to the Jews and ordered them to bring this R. Joseph to him. And this was a time of troubles for the Jews, because they knew that R. Joseph could perform many acts with Names. And they were sore afraid: how could they bring him before the king? And who knew what he would do when there? God forbid, a cruel decree could result from this.

And right away the Jews sent to this R. Joseph, telling him that he should know that he must not bring such a calamity upon the community of Israel, that he should go to the king and should not disobey the king, and that they would try to save him with all the means at their disposal. But should he refuse to do so, they would pronounce the ban upon him in all the synagogues and houses of study with the blowing of shofars and with the Holy Names, and then all his acts would help him nothing. And when R. Joseph heard this he understood that this time he could not save himself, in particular since this time he had the Jews against him. For he was not afraid of the king, but against the Jews he could do nothing. So he went up a high mountain and threw himself down and died. The Jews instantly informed the king that he was dead, and that he had been insane, and that he had killed himself in his insanity. The king instantly commanded that they bury him with great honors, for he had heard that once R. Joseph had been a great man, and that everything he did, he did in his insanity. So the king was satisfied, and the land rested.

(Z. Rubashov, pp. 97–118.)

How Satan Prevented the Coming of the Messiah

It happened to a rabbi who had no children that after a long while an only son was born to him. He brought him up and took a wife for him. The son sat on the upper floor and studied, as is the wont of the sons of rich men. He always studied and prayed. Nevertheless he felt it in himself that he was deficient in something, but he did not know what it was he lacked. He felt that his study and his prayer had no meaning for him. He told about this to two youths, who advised him to go to a certain Tzaddiq. Once the son performed a *mitzva* [an important religious deed] through which he achieved the rank of a Small Luminary.[2]

The son went and told his father that he found no meaning in his study and in his service [of God], and that he lacked something but did not know what, and therefore he wanted to go to that Tzaddiq. His father replied to him: "Why should you want to go to him, when you are a greater scholar than he and are of nobler descent? It is not seemly that you go to him. Give up this plan!" Thus he prevented him from going.

The son returned to his studies, and again felt a deficiency in his soul. He again took counsel with the same men, and they again advised him to go to the Tzaddiq. He went again to his father, and his father prevented him from going to the Tzaddiq this time too.

The son continuously suffered from his deficiency and desired greatly to remedy it, but he did not know what it was and how to remedy it. Finally he went to his father and entreated him very much that he should let him go to the Tzaddiq. His father could not refuse him, and was forced to travel with him, for he did not want to let his only son travel alone. And his father said to him: "Behold, I shall go with you and show you that there is no substance in him!"

They hitched up the cart and departed. His father said to him:

---

2. An individual who achieved a very high degree of spiritual power, second only to that of a Great Luminary. See below.

"Let this be a sign for us: if our journey goes smoothly, the thing is from heaven. But if not, it is not from heaven, and we shall turn back."

They traveled. They came to a small bridge. One of the horses fell and the cart turned over, and they almost drowned. His father said to him: "You see, our journey is wrong. It is not from heaven." They returned home.

The son returned to his studies, and again felt the deficiency, and did not know what it was. He again importuned his father about the journey. His father was forced to go with him a second time. And again made a condition as he did the first time: "If the journey goes smoothly, fine; but if not, it is not from heaven." The axle of the cart broke. His father said to him: "Again our journey has proved to be wrong. The matter is not from heaven." So they turned back again.

The son returned to his studies but they did not progress satisfactorily. His deficiency gave him no rest. He importuned his father that he should go with him this time without any condition and without any sign. The signs mean nothing—it is quite an ordinary thing that a horse should fall occasionally, or that the axle of a cart should break.

They traveled and came to an inn to stay overnight. They met there a merchant, and began to talk to him as is the wont of merchants. They did not tell him that they were on their way to that Tzaddiq, for the rabbi was ashamed to divulge such a thing. They talked about the affairs of the world. In the course of their talk the matter of Tzaddiqim came up, and where Tzaddiqim were found. The merchant told them that here lived a Tzaddiq, and there, and there. They began to talk about the Tzaddiq to whom they were going. The merchant said: "That one! He is of little worth. I am just coming from him. I was there and saw that he was guilty of a transgression." The father said to his son: "Do you see? This merchant is talking casually, and he has just come from there!" And they returned home.

The son fell ill, and departed from the world. Then he came in a dream to his father. His father saw him standing in great wrath. He asked him: "Why are you angry?" He answered him: "Go to that Tzaddiq, and he will tell you why I am angry." The father woke up and thought: "It happened by chance." Then he dreamt a second time. He said: "This, too, happened by chance." And so it happened three times. Finally he took the matter to heart and went to that Tzaddiq. On the way he entered an inn to rest. It so happened that it was the same inn where he stayed with his son the previous time. He also met there that merchant whom he and his son had met the first time. He recognized him and asked him: "Are you he whom I saw then?" The merchant replied: "Certainly you saw me then."

And then the merchant opened his mouth and said: "Do you remember, when you traveled with your son, at first the horse fell on the bridge, and you turned back. Then the axle broke, and you turned back. The third time you met me and I told you that he [the Tzaddiq] was of no value, and you turned back. Now that I have dispatched your son, now you are permitted to complete your journey. For be it known to you: Your son had the rank of a Small Luminary, and that Tzaddiq has the rank of a Great Luminary. Had they met and joined forces, the Messiah would have come. But since I dispatched him, you are permitted to go on." Thus he spoke and disappeared. The rabbi stood amazed. There was nobody with whom he could have spoken.

He continued his journey to the Tzaddiq. He came to him and cried: "Woe, woe! Woe for those who are lost and cannot be found!"

May the Name, blessed be He, return our exiles soon, Amen!
(Nahman of Bratzlav, *Sippure Ma'asiyyot*,
story no. 4, pp. 22–24.)

Four Stories of Impatient Tzaddiqim

1

Before his death he [the author of *Yitav Lev*[3]] said: "My sons! I should have had many more years to live, but I have become very obstinate about the coming of the Messiah. I did not have to suffer all this anguish [of constantly expecting him], but I accepted it with strong love." And he passed to his world on the eve of the holy

3. R. Jekuthiel Judah Teitelbaum (1808–1883), grandson of Moshe Teitelbaum, became rabbi of Ujhely in 1841. His book, *Yitav Lev*, containing sermons on the Five Books of Moses, was published in Mármaros-Sziget in 1875.

Sabbath of the weekly portion of *Shoftim*, on the sixth of Elul, 5643 [i.e. 1883].

(Ehrman, *Sefer P'er w'Khavod*, 11b)

2

Before he passed away, Reb Mendele of Rymanov[4] said that after his death he would make great efforts that the time of Redemption should come, and that he would not enter the Garden of Eden until they promised him this. And so it was. And they showed him many different things, but they were unable to get him to enter the Garden of Eden. But it was not yet the time for the Messiah to come. So they showed him the harp as the musician, David our king, peace be upon him, was playing on it. And he went after the sweetness of the sound of the harp, and he forgot everything that was before him, and entered the Garden of Eden. This happened to the rabbi R. Mendele.

The rabbi of Ujhely[5] said that they would not be able to entice him to enter; the fiddle of David would not help. [But when he died] they honored him with delivering a sermon, and said to him that when he finished the discourse, the Messiah would come.[6] But he is still preaching his sermon. And the rabbi of Sanz[7] said: "Perhaps there is an exaggeration in what you say?" No, it is true, he is still talking, presenting the sermon. For in the Supernal Realm there is a great abundance of wisdom and knowledge without limit, and they always inspire him with wonderful new interpretations. And he in his mind thinks that he has only started to speak, for there he is above time, and the past and the future are one. So they captivated him as well.

(Ibid., 16a—b)

Before his death the Rabbi of Apt[8] said: "The Rabbi of

---

4. Menaham Mendel of Rymanov (d. 1815) saw the Napoleonic wars as the wars of Gog and Magog.

5. See chapter 5, note 6.

6. This is a reference to the tradition which requires that all sermons conclude with the quotation from Isa. 59:20: *And a Redeemer will come to Zion, and unto them that turn from transgression in Jacob, saith the Lord.*

7. Hayyim Halberstam (1793-1876) was rabbi of Sanz (Zanz, Nowy Sacz), Galicia, from 1830, and became founder of a famous Hasidic dynasty.

8. R. Abraham Joshua Heschel (d. 1825), was rabbi of Apt (Opatow).

Berdychev[9] said that before he would enter into That World he would, when he came into heaven, urge and demand Redemption until they would send the Messiah. But when he reached the Heights, the angels knew how to lead him into a hall of highest pleasure so that he forgot his promise. But I promise you that if I get up there I shall not let myself be enticed by pleasures and shall force the coming of the Messiah."

(Chajim Bloch, *Die Gemeinde*, p. 230)

4

Three Hasidic Rebbes, the Lubliner, Rimanover, and Medzhibozher, made a pact that they would force the Messiah to come. They set a date for Simhat Tora in the year 5575 (1815 C.E.).

However, just before Rosh haShana, the Medzhibozher Rebbe took sick and passed away. This was twenty-two days before Simhat Tora. The Rebbe of Lublin did not know about it, and on Simhat Tora he danced with the Tora-scroll, doing his part. Then he went up to a room on the upper floor and closed the door. He remained there alone for several hours, and the Hasidim did not know what happened. Suddenly they heard a great cry in the courtyard. They rushed out, and found their Rebbe lying there, hurt.

"I was praying my part," he said to them, "when someone grabbed my arm and pushed me out the window. I would have been killed, but the Medzhibozher Rebbe came and spread out his Tallis [prayer shawl] like a net and caught me. So the fall was not so hard. Then I knew that he was dead. Had I known it earlier, I would not have started [the prayer to bring the Messiah].

Some time thereafter the Lubliner Rebbe, too, took sick, and he died on the Ninth of Av, the day when the Temple was destroyed.

(After Mintz, *Legends*, pp. 179-80)

Four Stories of Men of Small Faith

1

Once the Ba'al Shem Tov was praying in the company of his

---

9. See chapter 5, note 3.

followers with exceedingly great love, and he prolonged the Eighteen Benedictions very much, and his followers could not wait for
him to finish, and each of them went his way. And after each of
them took care of his affairs they returned and gathered around
him. And the Besht said to them that they caused a great separation
by leaving him and going their way. And he explained it to them
with a parable:

As is well known [he said] it is in the nature of birds that each
winter they fly to warm countries, to dwell there all the days of the
winter. Once the people of the country saw that a bird, most
glorious in its many colors, came and perched on a very big and tall
tree, so that no man could reach it. And when the king heard about
it, he commanded that several thousands of men should gather at
that tree, and should stand one on top of the other, higher and
higher, until the topmost could stretch forth his hand and take the
bird from the tree and bring it to the king. And so they did. And as
they were standing one on top of the other, those who stood below
moved here and there and did not join themselves strongly to those
who stood above them, and because of this all of them fell down.
And the bird which was in the tree flew away, and the whole
matter came to naught, and the wish of the king was not fulfilled.

Thus, had you been attached and tied to me in prayer, the
matter would have been totally good. But since you left me, and
each of you went to take care of his affairs, the whole matter
collapsed, and what I wanted to achieve flew away from me.

(Abraham, *Mid. RIBaSh Tov*, p. 42)

2

Once on Rosh haShana our master, my grandfather, R.
Sh'muel Shmelke haLevi Horowitz of Nikolsburg,[10] came to the
synagogue before the blowing of the shofar, weeping desperately,
and spoke in this language: "Master of the World! All the people
sigh and weep and beseech You and cry before You. But what have
we with this kind of supplication? They request bread, [other]
corporeal things, and not [the end of] the exile of the Shekhina...."
This happened on the first day.

And on the second day he again came before the blowing of
the shofar and again cried and wept as he recited the verse, *Where-*

---

10. Hasidic rabbi, d. 1778.

fore cometh not the son of Jesse to the meal, neither yesterday nor today?
(1 Sam. 20:27). And he said: *"Wherefore cometh not the son of Jesse—*
this refers to King Messiah who is of the stock of Jesse—neither
yesterday, on the first day of Rosh haShana, nor today, on the
second day of Rosh haShana? [Because] they pray for bread, only
for corporeal things, and not for [the end of] the exile of the
Shekhina."

(Michelsohn, *Sefer Shemen haTov*, p. 44)

3

The holy rabbi, R. Bunem of Przysucha,[11] said in the name of
his father the Tzaddiq, the Preacher of Wadislav[12]:

A parable...about a prince who sinned. And his father expelled him from his house. And he went erring about, aimlessly, in
the company of cardplayers and drunkards. And all the time he
sank lower and lower. Finally he joined a group of peasant villag-
ers. Of their bread he ate and at their work he worked. One day the
king sent one of his lords to search for his son, for perhaps he had
improved his ways and was worthy of being returned to his father's
house. The lord found him plowing in the field. And he asked him:
"Do you recognize me?" "Yes," answered the prince. And the lord
said: "And what is your request of your father the king? I shall tell
him." The prince answered: "How good would it be if my father
took pity on me and sent me a garment like those the peasants wear,
and also heavy shoes which are suitable for a villager." "O, you
fool, you fool," cried the lord, "it would have been better for you to
ask of your father that he should take you back to his house and his
palace. Is, perchance, anything lacking in the house of the king?"[13]

Thus they [the Jews] cry, "Give us this and give us that...." It
would be better to request and to pray that He should lead us back
to our country and build our Temple, and there we shall have
everything we need.

(Ibid., p. 142)

---

11. R. Simha Bunem of Przysucha (1765–1827).

12. R. Simha Bunem's father, R. Zevi, was an itinerant preacher in Poland and
Western Europe.

13. I.e., once you are there, you would have everything you want.

4

When Yom Kippur ended, R. Levi Yitzhaq [of Berdychev] beckoned to a tailor and asked him to relate to the congregation the argument he had that day with the Master of the World. The tailor began in a trembling voice:

"I told the Master of the World, Today is the Day of Judgment. One must repent. But I did not sin much. I took a little left-over cloth from the rich.... And once I drank a small glass of brandy in the house of the *Poretz* [lord] and took a bite of bread without washing my hands. These are all my transgressions.

"But You, Master of the World, how many are Your transgressions! Why have You taken away small children who had not sinned? And from others You have taken the mothers of such children! But, Master of the World, I shall forgive You Your transgressions, and may You forgive me mine, and let us drink *L'Hayyim* [to life]!"

And as he related all this, the tailor drank *L'Hayyim* to the Master of the World.

The rabbi said after Yom Kippur:

"The tailor with his arguments saved the Jews. But a tailor remains a tailor. In exchange for a little left-over cloth he forgave the Master of the World such great sins! I, in that hour, would have asked another thing—that He send us His Messiah to redeem the Jews...."

(Yitzhaq Ashkenazi, *Otz'rot*, p. 20)

8

Son of the Clouds

As we have seen in chapter 1, the idea that the Messiah ("Son of Man") would come "with the clouds of heaven" is Biblical: it appears in the second part of the Book of Daniel, which was written in 165 B.C.E. This concept was elaborated in the Fourth Book of Ezra (also known as the Second Book of Esdras), an apocryphal text written about the time of the destruction of Jerusalem by the Romans (70 C.E.). In the Babylonian Talmud (compiled c. 500 C.E.), R. Nahman ascribes to the Messiah the name *Bar Nifle*, which, in all probability, means "Son of the Clouds," although he does not refer in this context to Daniel. In a passage in the Targum, the Messiah is called *'Anani*, that is, "He of the Clouds," and in a Midrash fragment he is described as "riding on the cloud," which, of course, recalls the Biblical descriptions of God as *riding upon the heaven* (Deut. 33:26), *riding upon a swift cloud* (Isa. 19:1), *riding upon the skies*, and *riding upon the heavens of heavens* (Ps. 68:5, 34). To this context belongs also the song in which the psalmist thanks God who *Rode upon a cherub and did fly, yea, He did swoop down upon the wings of the wind* (Ps. 18:11; with some variations also in 2 Sam. 22:11).

It was perhaps this well-known image of God riding on the cloud which made the Aggadists, beginning with 4 Ezra, exercise great restraint in attributing the same divine feat to the Messiah as well. In any case, where we would expect rich Aggadic embellishment, we find no more than fleeting allusions to the Messiah who rides on a cloud and who is called "Son of the Cloud."

And it came to pass after seven days that I dreamed a dream by night: and I beheld, and lo! there arose a violent wind from the sea, and stirred all its waves. And the wind caused the likeness of a form of a man to come out of the heart of the seas. And this Man flew with the clouds of heaven. And wherever he turned his countenance to look, everything seen by him trembled; and whithersoever the voice went out of his mouth, all that heard his voice melted away, as the wax melts when it feels the fire. And after this I beheld that there was gathered from the four winds of heaven an innumerable multitude of men to make war against that Man who came up out of the sea.... And I saw that he cut out for himself a great mountain and flew up upon it.... And when he saw the assault of the multitude as they came, he neither lifted his hand, nor held spear nor any warlike weapon; but I saw only how he sent out of his mouth as it were a fiery stream, and out of his lips a flaming breath, and out of his tongue he shot forth a storm of sparks.... And these fell upon the assault of the multitude...and burned them all up....

These are the interpretations of the vision: Whereas you did see a Man coming up from the heart of the sea: this is he whom the Most High is keeping many ages and through whom He will deliver His creation, and the same shall order the survivors....

But he shall stand upon the summit of Mount Zion. And Zion shall come and shall be made manifest to all men, prepared and built, even as you did see the mountain cut out without hands. But he, My Son, shall reprove the nations that are come for their ungodliness....

(4 Ezra 13:1–9, 25–26, 35–36)

R. Nahman said to R. Yitzhaq: "Have you perhaps heard when Bar Nifle ['Son of the Clouds'] will come?" He answered: "Who is Bar Nifle?" R. Nahman said: "The Messiah." R. Yitzhaq said: "You call the Messiah Bar Nifle?" He said: "Yes, for it is written, *On that day I shall raise up the Tabernacle of David that is fallen* [*nofelet*] (Amos 9:11)."

(B. Sanh. 96b–97a)

R. Alexandri said: "R. Y'hoshu'a ben Levi explained:.... 'If they will be righteous, [the Messiah will come] *on the clouds of heaven* (Daniel 7:13); if they will not be righteous, [he will come] as *a poor man riding upon an ass* (Zech. 9:9).'"

King Shabur [Sapur] said to Sh'muel: "You say that the Messiah will come upon an ass; I shall send him a well-groomed horse." He answered: "Do you, perchance, have a horse of a hundred colors?"

(B. Sanh. 98a)

'Anani ["He of the Clouds"] is King Messiah, who will in the future reveal himself.

(Targum to I Chron. 3:24)

And now let us speak in praise of King Messiah who will come in the future with the clouds of heaven and two Seraphim [fiery angels] to his right and to his left, as it is written, *Behold, with the clouds of heaven came one like unto a son of man* (Dan. 7:13).

(Pirqe Mashiah, BhM 3:70)

The tenth sign [of the signs of the Messiah]: God will liberate Menahem ben 'Amiel, Messiah ben David, from the jailhouse .... and make him ride on the cloud.... The marks of King Messiah are: He is tall of stature, his neck is thick, his face is like the wheel of the sun, his eyes are radiant, the soles of his feet are thick.... He will rule over all the lands, and to him will be given kingdom and honor and greatness....

(Midrash fragment, ed. Marmorstein, *REJ* 52 (1906), p. 184.)

9

The Bird's Nest

"If a bird's nest chance to be before thee in the way, in any tree or on the ground, [with] young ones or eggs, and the mother [bird] sitteth upon the young or upon the eggs, thou shalt not take the mother with the sons. Thou must send away the mother, and the sons thou [mayest] take unto thyself, that it may be well with thee and that thou mayest prolong thy days" (Deut. 22:6–7).

This Biblical commandment—one of the first animal-protection laws in the world—was reinterpreted by the Kabbalists, who sensed a mystical meaning in it. The "Bird's Nest" became the hidden abode of the Messiah, while the mother bird was understood to represent the community of Israel, or the Shekhina, the Presence of God. In addition to several passing references to this mystical "Bird's Nest" in the Zohar, there is one passage that deals with it in detail. This long passage, which is presented here in full, describes a series of highly dramatic events in heaven, a powerful interplay between divine, human, and cosmic forces, in the sense of the Biblical book of Job and Goethe's *Faust*. The main protagonists are God and the Messiah, with Rachel, the *mater dolorosa* of Israel, mourning in the background, and a fearsome star flashing overhead. Samael, the heavenly prince and patron of Evil, unnamed but clearly alluded to, is also present, but, in contrast to Job and *Faust*, plays but a subordinate role. The Fathers and Moses appear, various divine voices are heard, alternately there is desperate lamentation and joyful dancing, the firmaments shake, God kisses the Messiah time and again, and finally the whole Bird's Nest comes down to earth in a magnificent epiphany, to position itself at Rachel's tomb on the road to Bethlehem.

Since ultimately all this grand commotion leads to no tangible result—the exile continues and the Messiah "returns to his place"—one gets the impression that the message of this entire elaborate sequence is the movement itself. It teaches us—to use Midrashic language—that the powers on high, the Supernal Family, do not merely rest and wait in resigned passivity, but, quite to the contrary, are engaged in energetic, even feverish, activity, which, although for the moment frustrated, must ultimately lead to the yearned-for result, the Messianic advent.

R. Shim'on said to his son, R. El'azar: El'azar, at the time when the Messiah will be stirred up, many signs and other miracles will occur in the world. Come and see: In the Garden of Eden of Below there is a secret place, hidden and unknown, which is embroidered with many colors, and in which are hidden a thousand halls of yearnings. And there is none who enters it except the Messiah who dwells always in the Garden of Eden. And the whole Garden is surrounded by many groups of the pious. And the Messiah is appointed over them and over many hosts, and over many camps of the souls of the pious. And on New Moons and holy days and Sabbaths the Messiah enters that place to enjoy himself in all those halls. And within all those halls there is another place, hidden and secret, which is not known at all, and it is called Eden, and there is none who can find it. And the Messiah is hidden outside the limits of that place, until a place is revealed to him which is called Bird's Nest. That is the place which is proclaimed by that bird which is stirred up in the Garden of Eden every day. And in that place they embroider effigies of all the nations that banded together against Israel to harm her. The Messiah enters that place, lifts up his eyes, and sees the Fathers coming to the ruins of the House of God, and then he sees Rachel with tears on her face, and the Holy One, blessed be He, comforting her, but she does not want to accept consolation.... Then the Messiah lifts up his voice and weeps, and the whole Garden of Eden trembles, and all the pious who are there cry and weep with him. When he cries and weeps the second time, the firmament which is above the Garden shakes, and the fifteen hundred myriads of supernal hosts [tremble], until [the voice] reaches the Supernal Throne. Then the Holy One, blessed be He, beckons that bird, and it enters its nest, and comes to the Messiah, and it calls what it calls, and stirs up what it stirs up, until that Bird's Nest and the Messiah are called three times from inside the Holy Throne, and all ascend. And the Holy One, blessed be He, swears to them that He will destroy the wicked kingdom [Rome] from the world by the hand of the Messiah, and will avenge the vengence of Israel, and will give to His people all those benefits which He destined for them. And the Bird's Nest and the Messiah return to their place. And the Messiah returns and becomes hidden in that place as before.

And at the time when the Holy One, blessed be He, bestirs Himself to perfect the world, the letters of His name [YHWH] will radiate in perfection, the Y with the H, and the W with the [second] H, in order to become united in perfection. Then a fearsome star will rise in the middle of the firmament: by day it will radiate and glow like purple before the eyes of the whole world. And the flame of the fire [that is, Samael] will arise from the north side of the firmament, and they shall face each other for forty days, and all the children of the world will be affrighted. At the end of forty days the star and the flame will give battle to each other before the eyes of all. And that flame will spread a great conflagration from the north side in the firmament, and will seem to swallow that star. And many rulers and kings and nations and peoples will be sore afraid. Then that star will move to the south side and will overcome that flame and that flame will be swallowed up little by little in the firmament before that star, until it will no longer be seen at all. Then that star will make paths in the firmament, in twelve areas, and they will remain luminous in the firmament for twelve more days. After the twelve days all the children of the world will tremble, and the sun will become dark at noontime as it grew dark on the day in which the Temple was destroyed, until the heaven and the earth will not be seen. And a voice will be stirred up with thunder and lightning, and the earth will shake from that voice, and many armies and camps will die from it. And on that day a flame of fire will be stirred up by that voice in the city of Great Rome. And it will be stirred up in the whole world, and it will consume many towers and many palaces, and many towers will collapse, and many princes and potentates will fall on that day. And all will gather to harm her [Israel]. And none of the children of the world will be able to escape.

From that day on for twelve months all the kings will take counsel and will issue many evil decrees and will persecute Israel and they will prevail over her.... Happy is he who will be there, and happy is he who will not be there! And the whole world will be in great confusion.

At the end of twelve months a scepter will arise out of Israel—this is King Messiah, who will be stirred up in the Garden of Eden. And all the pious will surround him, and gird him with weapons inscribed with the letters of the Holy Name. And a voice will burst forth among the branches of the trees in the Garden, and will call powerfully and say: "Awaken, Supernal Saints, rise before the Messiah! This is the time for the Wife [Israel] to join her Husband [God], and her Husband seeks vengeance for her in the world, and lets her shake off the dust." Then all will rise and gird him [the Messiah] with weapons as before. Abraham on his right, Isaac on his left, Jacob before him, and Moses, the faithful shepherd of all these saints, will go and dance in the Garden of Eden.

As soon as the Messiah is installed by the saints in the Garden of Eden, he enters that place which is called Bird's Nest, as before, and there he sees the image of the destruction of the Temple and of all the saints who were slain in it. Then he takes from there ten garments, which are the ten garments of zeal, and he hides himself there for forty days, [during which] he does not reveal himself at all. And at the end of forty days a voice is stirred up from the Supernal Throne and calls that Bird's Nest in which King Messiah has hid himself. And then they carry him aloft, and when the Holy One, blessed be He, sees King Messiah clothed in garments of vengeance and girded with weapons, He takes him and kisses him on his forehead. Then three hundred and ninety firmaments shake, and the Holy One, blessed be He, beckons to one firmament from among them which is hidden ever since the six days of creation, and from a sanctuary which is in that firmament He takes a crown engraved with holy names. It is the crown with which the Holy One, blessed be He, crowned Himself when Israel passed through the sea to take vengeance on all the chariots of Pharaoh and his horsemen, and with it He crowns King Messiah. As soon as he is crowned and supplied with all these embellishments, the Holy One, blessed be He, takes him and kisses him as before. Who can see the holy chariots and supernal hosts which surround him and give him presents and many gifts! And he is adorned by all of them, and enters a sanctuary and sees all those supernal angels who are called the Mourners of Zion, because they constantly cry over the destruction of the Temple. And they give him a red-purple cloak so that he can carry out his vengeance. Then the Holy One, blessed be He, [again] hides him in that Bird's Nest, and he remains hidden there thirty days.

After thirty days in that Bird's Nest, he comes down adorned with all those embellishments from Above and from Below. Many holy hosts surround him, and the whole world will see a light suspended from the firmament to the earth and it will stay seven days. And all the children of the world will see it and will marvel and will be frightened. And none will understand it, except those wise men who know these mysteries. Happy is their portion! And all those seven days the Messiah will be crowned on earth in that Bird's Nest. In what place? "*On the way,*" that is, at Rachel's tomb, which stands at the crossroads. And he will bring her glad tidings and will comfort her, and she will accept consolation, and will arise and kiss him. Then that light will arise from that place, and rest over Jericho, the city of trees....

And the Messiah will be hidden in that light of the Bird's Nest for twelve months. After the twelve months that light will shoot up between heaven and earth and rest in the Land of Galilee. For there was the beginning of Israel's exile. And there he [the Messiah] will reveal himself in that light of the Bird's Nest, and then he will return to his place. And on that day the whole earth will tremble as before from one end of heaven to the other. And then the whole world will see that King Messiah revealed himself in the Land of Galilee. And all those who study the Tora—and they will be very few in the world—will gather around him. And because of the merits of the little children of the schoolhouse, his army will gain strength, and this is the mystery of the *"young birds."* And if such should not be found, then [the Messiah will be'strengthened through] the sucklings who sit in the strength of their mother and suck. To them refers the verse when it says, *"or eggs,"* because it is for their sake that the Shekhina rests on Israel in exile, for indeed very few sages will be found at that time.... And those children and sucklings will give strength to King Messiah, and the Supernal Mother who is *"sitting upon the young or upon the eggs"* will be stirred up toward her Husband [God]. He will tarry for another twelve months, and then Her Husband will come and raise her from the dust.... On that day King Messiah will begin to gather the exiles from one end of the world to the other.... From that day on all the signs and miracles and portents which the Holy One, blessed be He, performed in Egypt He will [again] perform for Israel....

(Zohar 2:8a−9a)

Once when Rabbi Menahem Nahum of Chernobyl[1] was in our town...he said that the Messiah had said to the Ba'al Shem Tov: "I know not whether you will open [the gate], but if you do, redemption will certainly come to Israel." He said further that this was the gate of the palace of the Bird's Nest, which no one has ever entered save the Messiah, as it is said in the holy Zohar. And he said that he heard God's voice saying to him: "What can I do with you, since I must fulfill your will?"[2]

(Shivhe haBeShT, pp. 64−65)

---

1. R. Menahem Mendel Twersky (1730−1787), *maggid* (preacher) at Chernobyl, was the founder of a Hasidic dynasty in the Ukraine.

2. The idea that God must fulfill the will of a saintly man is Talmudic. Cf. R. Patai, *Man and Temple*, pp. 187−88.

10

Contest in Heaven

The preceding chapter has introduced us to the idea that much of the Messianic drama filling the eons of waiting takes place in heaven rather than on earth. Even when the Messiah finally comes, the major contest between his forces and the opposing forces of evil is played out in heaven above. Or, to put it differently, the Messianic wars between Israel and the nations (see chapters 15 to 18) will have their prototype, or heavenly reflection, in contests between God and Samael, in struggles between celestial manifestations of radiant light and the fires of evil, or, more concretely, between the gigantic star of the Messiah and other, lesser and evil, stars which repeatedly attack it. The celestial victory of the forces of good over those of evil will signal the triumph of the Messiah over his opponents.

Part of the contest—and this is typical of the Aggadic mind—is not a combat between opposing powers as indicated above, but a legal conflict between Michael, the celestial prince of Israel, and Samael, the celestial prince of Edom-Rome, epitomizing the nations of the world. Samael accuses Israel of the same sins for which Michael demands the punishment of Edom. Finally it is only God Himself who can present the clinching argument in defense of His children. This is in keeping with the old Jewish idea that the fate of Israel and the relations between Israel and the nations depend on the degree of piety of Israel. The exile is a punishment for Israel's sins; the conditions under which Israel must live in the exile are determined by whether or not Israel repents, and the coming of the Messiah is contingent on a total change of Israel's heart to the good. Thus the claim Israel has on the Messianic victory over the nations can be substantiated only by furnishing proof before the divine seat of judgment that it deserves the Redemption. The cataclysmic manifestations in heaven, the stars, the fires, the quakes, are all but reflections of what takes place in the august halls of that supernal court of justice.

Once the Prophet Elijah of blessed memory came to the study house of Rabbi Yose. When Rabbi Yose arrived, he found that Elijah was sad. Rabbi Yose asked him: "Why are you sad?" He answered: "I have come from before the Holy One, blessed be He, and He and the Messiah were occupied with the consolations of the Prophet Isaiah, and Samael, the [celestial] prince of Rome, came and brought accusations against Israel. I said to Samael: 'The Holy One, blessed be He, and His Messiah are occupied with the consolations of Isaiah, and you dare to accuse Israel? [Rather] wipe me out, and slay me, and banish me!' But he answered me nothing...."

After the Holy One, blessed be He, delivers Samael into the hands of Michael, Samael will say before Him: "Why did You deliver me into the hands of Michael? Let him come and argue with me before You!" Instantly the Holy One, blessed be He, says to Michael: "Go and argue with him!" Samael begins by saying: "If the nations of the world are guilty of sins, so is Israel guilty of sins; if these commit incest, these too commit incest; if these shed blood, these too shed blood." Instantly Michael falls silent. But the Holy One, blessed be He, says to Michael: "You fell silent, but I shall speak in defense of My children, and all the acts of Samael will be of no avail...."

(Pirqe Mashiah, BhM 3:68)

R. Shim'on lifted up his hands and wept and said: "Woe to him who will live at that time, and happy is the lot of him who will live and be present at that time! Woe to him who will live at that time because when the Holy One, blessed be He, will come to remember the Hind [i.e., the Shekhina], He will seek out those who stand by her among all those who are found with her. [And He will search] all the deeds of each one, and they will not be found worthy.... And how many troubles will befall Israel! And happy is he who will live and be present at that time, for he who will stand in that time in faithfulness will deserve the radiant joy of the King [God]...."

And thereafter sufferings will overtake Israel, and all the nations and their kings will consult together against her, and many evil decrees will arise and will bring trouble upon trouble, and each subsequent one will cause the earlier to be forgotten. And then a pillar of fire will appear, positioned from Above to Below for forty days, and all the nations of the world will see it. At that time King Messiah will be stirred up to come forth from the Garden of Eden, from that place which is called Bird's Nest. And he will arise in the Land of Galilee. And on the day on which he comes there the whole world will tremble, and all the children of the world will hide in caves and crevices, and will think that they cannot be saved.... The Messiah will arise and reveal himself in the Land of Galilee because that was the first place to be destroyed in the Holy Land; therefore he will first reveal himself there of all places, and from thence he will stir up battles in the whole world. And after the forty days in which the pillar [of fire] will stand from the earth to heaven in the sight of the whole world, and the Messiah will reveal himself, there will arise from the east side a star flaming with all colors. And seven other stars will surround that star and attack it in battle from all sides, three times every day, for seventy days, and the children of the world will see it. And that star will wage war against them with arrows of flaming fire which will erupt on all sides, and it will crush them until it swallows them every evening. And in the morning it will disgorge them, and they will again wage war [against it] in the sight of the whole world, and thus every day for seventy days. And after seventy days that star will be hidden, and the Messiah will be hidden for twelve months. And that pillar of fire will return as before, and in it the Messiah will be hidden, and that pillar will not be visible. After twelve months they will raise the Messiah in that pillar to the firmament, and there he will receive power and the crown of kingship. And when he [again] descends, that pillar of fire will again be visible as before to the eyes of the whole world. And thereafter the Messiah will be revealed, and many nations will gather against him, and he will stir up wars in the whole world. And at that time the Holy One, blessed be He, will manifest His power against all the nations of the world, and King Messiah will become known in all the world, and all the kings of the world will rise up to wage war against him. And many of the wicked among the Jews will join them and come with them to wage war against King Messiah. And then the whole world will darken for fifteen days, and many of the People of Israel will die in that darkness....

(Zohar 2:7b)

Above all these firmaments there is a firmament which is hidden and concealed...and in it are...windows.... The sixth window is the window which is called *Nagha* ["Radiance"], and a star called *Gazron* ["Decreer"] enters through it, for when it rules the world it issues many severe decrees and many chastisements. Day after day decrees are being renewed against the world, and even before these are carried out, new ones are enacted. And this [star] has [at present] no great power over the world, but close to the days of the Messiah this window with this star will rule the world. And because of this, beasts and evil diseases will rule the world, and evil events will be renewed one after the other, and Israel will be in distress. And when they will be in great straits in the darkness of exile, the Holy One, blessed be He, will cause the light of day to shine upon them...and then the seventh window will be opened upon the whole world, and its star is the star of Jacob...and this star will shine for forty days and forty nights. And then King Messiah will be revealed and all the nations of the world will gather around King Messiah, and then the verse will be fulfilled: *The root of Jesse which standeth as the peoples' ensign, unto it shall the nations seek, and his resting place shall be glory* (Isa. 11:10).

(Zohar 2:172b)

I see him but not now (Num. 24:17). Of these words, some were fulfilled in that very hour [when Balaam uttered them], some later, and some [will be fulfilled] at the time of King Messiah. We have learned: The Holy One, blessed be He, is ready to rebuild Jerusalem and to reveal to her a star which is fixed and sparkles with seventy rays and seventy flames streaming from it in the middle of the firmament... and it will shine and flame for seventy days. It will appear on the sixth day [of the week], on the twenty-fifth day of the sixth month; and on the seventh day, at the end of seventy days, it will disappear. On the first day[1] it will appear in the city of Rome. And on that day three lofty walls of that city of Rome will collapse, and a mighty palace will fall, and the ruler of that city will die. Then that star will spread out so as to be seen in the [whole] world. And at that time mighty wars will be stirred up in the world, on all four sides, and no faith will be found among the nations. And in the middle of the world that star will shine in the center of the firmament. A great king will arise and rule the world, and his spirit will be proud over all kings, and he will stir up wars on two sides, and he will vanquish them. And on the day on which the star appears, the Holy Land will tremble to [a distance of] forty-five miles around the place in which stood the Temple. And a cave will be revealed under the earth, and from that cave a mighty fire will come forth to consume the world. And from that cave a great supernal branch [or bird] will spread which will rule the whole world. And to it will be given the kingship, and the supernal saints will gather around it. Then will be revealed King Messiah in the whole world, and to him will kingship be given. And in the hour in which he will be revealed the children of the world will be in the midst of one calamity after another, and the enemies of Israel will wax strong. And then the spirit of the Messiah will be stirred up against them, and he will destroy sinful Edom and burn the whole Land of Seir with fire.... And at that time the Holy One, blessed be He, will raise up the dead of His people and death will be forgotten by them....

(Zohar 3:212b)

---

1. That is, on the twenty-fifth of Elul, which is the sixth month. Adolf Jellinek, in his BhM 3:xxxvii–xxxviii, calculated that this passage refers to the death of Pope Nicholas III on August 22, 1280, which date corresponds to Elul 25 in the Jewish calendar, and which fell on a Thursday. However, since in the Jewish calendar the evening of a day counts as the beginning of the next day, the evening and night of August 22 counted as the beginning of Friday ("the sixth day") mentioned in the text. The Zohar, from which the above excerpt is taken, was written between 1270 and 1300 (see bibliography).

11

The Pangs of Times

It is impossible for Israel as a whole to be wholly righteous. Any generation may have individual saintly men living in it, but the people as a whole cannot be saintly, pious, or righteous. This pessimistic insight into the human condition is reflected in that part of the Messiah legend which tells about the pangs of the Messianic times which must come upon Israel because of its wickedness. Once the idea became entrenched that the coming of the Messiah will be preceded by greatly increased suffering, and that even the beginnings of the Messianic era itself will be an age of great trials and tribulations, apocalyptic fantasy went to work with a vengeance on elaborating in gruesome detail what would happen at the onset of the days of the Messiah.

Again, as in the depiction of the contest in heaven (see preceding chapter), the pangs of the Messianic times are imagined as having heavenly as well as earthly sources and expressions. From Above, awesome cosmic cataclysms will be visited upon the earth: conflagrations, pestilence, famine, earthquakes, hail and snow, thunder and lightning. These will be paralleled by evils brought by men upon themselves: insolence, robbery, heresy, harlotry, corruption, oppression, cruel edicts, lack of truth, and no fear of sin. All this will lead to internal decay, demoralization, and even apostasy. Things will come to such a head that people will despair of Redemption. This will last seven years. And then, unexpectedly, the Messiah will come.

Because of this gloomy picture of the beginnings of the Messianic era, which by Talmudic times was firmly believed in, some sages expressed the wish not to see the Messiah (cf. excerpt below, from B. Sanh. 98b). However, the teaching which gained general acceptance was that by occupying oneself with Tora study and deeds of charity, one can escape the Messianic sufferings. In any case, both the people and its religious leaders continued to hope for the coming of the Messiah, much like a woman who hopes and waits for the birth of her child, even though she knows that she will have to go through severe pangs of childbirth before she can enjoy the pleasures of motherhood.

And He [God] said to me [Abraham]: "What is desired in thine heart I will tell thee, because thou hast sought to see the ten plagues which I have prepared for the heathen, and have prepared beforehand at the passing over of the twelfth hour of the earth [i.e. the last hour of the present age]. Hear what I divulge to thee, so shall it come to pass: the first [is] great distress; the second, conflagration of many cities; the third, destruction and pestilence of animals; the fourth, hunger of the whole world and of its people; the fifth, destruction among its rulers, [and] destruction by earthquake and the sword; the sixth, multiplication of hail and snow; the seventh, the wild beasts will be their grave; the eighth, hunger and pestilence will alternate with their destruction; the ninth, punishment by the sword and flight in distress; the tenth, thunder and voices and destructive earthquake.

"Then I will sound the trumpet out of the air, and will send mine Elect One [i.e. the Messiah], having in him all my power, one measure [of each of my attributes]; and this one shall summon my despised people from the nations, and I will burn with fire those who have insulted them and who have ruled over them in this Age.

"And I will give those who have covered them with mockery to the scorn of the coming Age; and I have prepared them to be food for the fire of Gehenna and for ceaseless flight to and fro through the air in the underworld beneath the earth."

(Apocalypse of Abraham, pp. 82 ff.)

In the footsteps of the Messiah [i.e. when the Messiah is about to come], insolence will multiply and honor will disappear, the vine will give its fruit but wine will be expensive, the government will be transformed into heresy, and there will be no admonishing, the Council House will become [a house of] harlotry. The Galilee will be destroyed, the Gavlan will be devastated. The people of the frontier will make the round of the city [begging] and will find no mercy. The wisdom of the scribes will become corrupt. The fearers of sin will be despised. The truth will disappear. Youths will shame the faces of the old, old men will stand up before children. *The son dishonoreth the father, the daughter riseth up against her mother, the daughter-in-law against her mother-in-law, a man's enemies are the people of his own house* (Mic. 7:6). The son will not be ashamed from his Father. And on whom can we lean? On our Father who is in heaven.

(M. Sota 9:15)

R. Yitzhaq said: "Thus spoke R. Yohanan: The generation in which the Son of David comes, the scholars will diminish in it, and as for the rest, their eyes will be consumed because of sorrow and sighs. And many woes and cruel decrees will be renewed; even before one is over the next will hasten to come."

The rabbis taught: The septenary in which the Son of David comes, in its first year the verse will be fulfilled, *I shall cause it to rain upon one city and shall cause it not to rain upon another city* (Amos 4:7). In the second year arrows of famine will be sent out; in the third, there will be great famine, and men, women, and children, the pious and the men of [good] deeds, will die, and the Tora will be forgotten by its students. In the fourth, there will be plenty and yet no plenty. In the fifth, there will be great plenty, they will eat and drink and rejoice, and the Tora will return to her students. In the sixth, there will be sounds [of trumpets]. In the seventh there will be wars, and at the end of the seventh the Son of David will come. Rav Yosef said: "Many septenaries like this have come and gone, and he did not come." Abbaye said: "Were there in the sixth year sounds, and in the seventh wars? Moreover, did these events ever occur in this order?"...

The rabbis taught: The Son of David will not come until the informers multiply. Another opinion: Until the students diminish. Yet another opinion: Until the penny disappears from the pockets. And still another opinion: Until they despair of the Redemption.... When, as it were, Israel will have neither supporter nor helper. For this is how R. Zera used to say when he found the rabbis occupying themselves with it [the coming of the Messiah]: "I beg you, I ask of you, do not delay it, for we have learned: Three [things] come unexpectedly: the Messiah, a find, and a scorpion."

(B. Sanh. 97a)

R. Hanina said: "The Son of David will not come until they will seek a fish for the sick and will find none...." R. Hama son of R. Hanina said: "The Son of David will not come until even the slightest royal authority will disappear from Israel...." R. Simlai in the name of R. El'azar son of R. Shim'on said: "The Son of David will not come until all the judges and officers will disappear from Israel...." 'Ula said: "Jerusalem will be redeemed only through charity...." Rav Papa said: 'When there will be no more haughty people, there will be no [Persian] magi; when there will be no more judges, there will be no [Persian] officers...." R. Yohanan said: "If you see a generation whose numbers become more and more reduced, expect him [the Messiah]...." R. Yohanan said: "If you see a generation beset by many sufferings like a river, expect him...." And R. Yohanan said: "The Son of David will not come except in a generation which is either totally righteous or totally guilty...."

(B. Sanh. 98a)

Rav said: "The Son of David will not come until the [wicked] rule will spread over [all] Israel for nine months...."

'Ula said: "May he come, but I do not wish to see him."

Likewise Rava said: "May he come, but I do wish to see him."

Rav Yosef said: "May he come and may I sit in the shadow of his ass's droppings."

Abbaye said to Rava: "Why [do you not wish to see him]? If because of the Messianic sufferings, have we not learned that R. El'azar was asked by his disciples: What should a man do in order to escape the Messianic sufferings, [and he answered them:] Let him occupy himself with the Tora and with deeds of charity? And you, O Master, you have both Tora and deeds of charity." Rava said: "But, perhaps the sin will cause it [that I shall not escape the sufferings]...."

[In the days of the Messianic sufferings] *All faces will be turned into paleness* (Jer. 30:6). R. Yohanan said: "This refers to the Upper Family [the angels] and the Lower Family [Israel], in the hour when the Holy One, blessed be He, will say: 'These [the nations of the world] are My children, and these [Israel] are My children. How can I destroy these because of these?' [and, hearing this, the angels and Israel will become pale with fear]."

(B. Sanh. 98b)

Abbaye said: "We have been taught that Babylonia will not experience the Pangs of the Messiah."

(B. Ket. 111a)

R. Zera said in the name of R. Yirm'ya bar Abba: "In the generation in which the Son of David comes, there will be accusations against the sages. When I said this before Sh'muel, he said: 'Cruel edicts shall follow one another.'" R. Yosef taught: "There will be robbers, and robbers of robbers...."

(B. Ket. 112b)

R. Berekhia in the name of R. Levi: "The Last Redeemer [the Messiah] will be like the First Redeemer [Moses]. Just as the First Redeemer was revealed and then again was hidden from the Children of Israel...for thirty days...so the Last Redeemer will be revealed to them and then will be hidden from them...for forty-five days...." R. Yitzhaq ben Qatzarta in the name of R. Yona: "Those are the forty-five days in which Israel will pluck salt-wort and eat it, as it is written, *They pluck salt-wort with wormwood and the roots of the broom are their food* (Job 30:4)." Where will he lead them? From the Land [of Israel] into the desert of Judah, to the desert of Sihon and of Og.... And he who does not believe in him will go to the nations of the world and they will kill him. R. Yitzhaq ben Marion said: "In the end the Holy One, blessed be He, will reveal Himself to them and will cause manna to descend for them, [for] *There is nothing new under the sun* (Eccles. 1:9)."

(Ruth Rabba 5:6)

R. Yishmaʿel said: "Fifteen things will the Children of Ishmael do in the land at the End of Days, and they are: They will measure the land with ropes; and will turn the cemetery into a pasture for the flocks; and they will pour their refuse over the top of the mountains[1]; and the lies will multiply; and truth will be suppressed; and law will be removed from Israel; and sins will multiply in Israel; and worm-scarlet will be as wool; and the paper and the pen will wither; and the rock of kingship will be hewn down; and they will rebuild the desolate cities; and they will sweep the roads; and they will plant gardens and orchards; and they will repair the breaches in the walls of the Temple; and they will erect a building in the Temple place.

"And two brothers will rise as princes over them at the end, and in their days will arise the Shoot son of David...."

And R. Yishmaʿel further said: "The Children of Ishmael will wage three wars of discomfiture in the land at the End of Days. ... One in the forest in Arabia... and one in the sea... and one in the great city which is in Rome [i.e. Byzantium], and this last one will be heavier than the other two.... And from there the Son of David will sprout up, and will witness the destruction of the idolaters, and from there he will come to the Land of Israel...."

(Pirqe R. Eliezer, ch. 30, end)

In that hour the right hand of the Holy One, blessed be He, cried, and five rivers of tears issued from its five fingers and fell into the Great Sea and shook the world.... And when the Holy One, blessed be He, sees that there is no righteous in the generation and no pious in the land, and no charity in the hands of man, and that there is no man like Moses and no one to entreat as Samuel who asked mercy before the Place [i.e. God]... instantly the Holy One, blessed be He, remembers His own charity, compassion, and mercy, and helps Himself with His Great Arm....

In that hour the Holy One, blessed be He, uncovers to the world His Great Arm whose length is like the length of the world from one end to the other, and whose width is like the width of the world, and whose radiance is like the splendor of the sun in its strength in the season of Tammuz [midsummer]. Instantly Israel

---

1. The Hebrew text of this sentence is corrupt in the original. The above is a mere approximation of its meaning.

are redeemed among themselves, and the Messiah becomes visible
to them, and he will take them up to Jerusalem from the four winds
of the world, and the nations of the world will not eat with them.

(Sefer Hekhalot, BhM 5:189−90)

The wise men of Egypt foretold signs which would come to
pass in the future when all the planets will be in conjunction, and
the tail of Draco with them in the sign of Libra, in the month of
Elul. On the twenty-ninth day of that month, according to the
Hebrews in the year 4946 from the beginning of the world [1186
C.E.], on Sunday night, about midnight, will begin the signs to
come, and they will last until the subsequent Wednesday noon.

At that time from the sea will rise a very strong wind, which
will strike terror in the hearts of men, and it will raise sand and dust
from the surface of the earth, until it will cover the trees and the
towers. And all this because the conjunction of the planets will be
in Libra, that is to say, in the sign of air and winds. And according
to the view of the same sages, this conjunction signifies *A great and
strong wind which will rend the mountains and rocks* (1 Kings 19:11).
And there will be heard in the air quakes and thunders and voices
which will strike terror in the hearts of men, and all the countries
will be covered with sand and dust, that is to say, those which are
in the fifth clime. For that wind will rise from the west corner and
will reach until the east corner, encompassing all the countries of
Egypt and Ethiopia, that is to say, Mecca, Basra, and Aleppo, and
Shinar, and the lands of the Arabs, and the whole land of Elam,
and Rama, Carmen, and Segesta [Sidon?], and Calla [Acre?], and
Nazareth, and Kabul, and Tiberias, and Beerot, for all those
countries and regions are comprised under the sign of Libra, and
also the lands of Rome.

And after those events of the winds, five miracles will come to
pass one after the other.

First, a most wise man will arise from the east, versed in secret
wisdom, that is, in wisdom which is beyond man. And he will walk
in justice and will teach the law of truth, and he will cause many to
return to straight mores from the darknesses of ignorance, and
from unbelief to the way of truth, and he will instruct the sinners in
the way of righteousness (cf. Ps. 25:8; Prov. 16:31), and he will not
pride himself with being counted among the prophets.

Secondly, a man will come forth from Elam and will assemble

a multitude of great forces (Dan. 11:1), and will wage a great war against the nations (Zech. 14), and he will not live long.

Thirdly, up will rise another man who will say that he is a prophet. He will hold a book in his hand and will say that he was sent by God and by His prophets. And with his preachings he will cause many nations to go astray, and will seduce even more. But that which he will prophesy to the nations will come upon his own head. And he, too, will not live long.

Fourthly, a comet will be seen in heaven—a star, that is, with a tail or an appendage—and this apparition will signify destructions and tumults and hard strifes, and the withholding of rains, and dryness of the earth, and mighty battles, and the flowing of blood upon the earth of the east, and from beyond the River Habor it will reach to the very end of the west. And the just and the truly religious will be oppressed or will suffer persecutions, and the house of prayer will be destroyed.

Fifthly, there will be an eclipse of the sun, like the color of fire, until the whole body of the sun will be obscured, and at the time of the eclipse there will be such darkness over the earth as there is at midnight on those nights on which there is no moonlight, in the days of the rains. . . .

(Rigord of St. Denis, pp. 114—15)

I heard from an old Hasid that once there was a summer of drought. And they entered before him [the Tzaddiq of Przysucha[2]] that he should pray for rain. He spoke in this language: "There will be a time before the coming of the Redeemer, when there will be students without Tora, Hasidim without Hasidut ['charitableness'], princes without money, summer without heat, winter without cold. And there will be growth without rain."

I heard from an old man that once, at the time of the *havdala*,[3] after he [the Tzaddiq of Przysucha] had taken the Havdala cup into his hand, he put it down again and spoke in this language: "I can now see the time before the coming of the Redeemer. Jews will

---

2. The reference is to R. Simha Bunem (1765—1827), who, before he became the Tzaddiq of Przysucha, was a clerk in a timber firm and a pharmacist. The words quoted as having been said by him are in Yiddish, the rest of the story in Hebrew.

3. *Havdala* ("Separation") is the ceremony performed at the outgoing of the Sabbath to separate the holy day from the weekdays. A cup of wine, a container of spices ("*b'somim biks'l*"), and a braided, multicolored candle are used.

have no livelihood from their stores, each one will have to search for a side income. My hair and nails stand on edge...."

(Rakatz, Siah Sarfe Qodesh, p. 129)

The whole world and that which fills it were created only for the sake of Israel.... For Israel are called Beginning. And everything belongs to them and is subordinated to them. As it was to some extent in the days of David and Solomon, when the main kingship was that of Israel, and as it will be in the future when our True Messiah will come. For then the kingship will return to Israel, and all will be subordinated to Israel.... But now, in the exile, because of our many sins, things have turned upside down, for the idolaters are kings and rulers, and Israel are, heaven forfend, like slaves.

(R. Nathan Sternhartz, in R. Nahman of
Bratzlav, Sippure Ma'asiyyot, 1973 ed., p. 171)

12

The Suffering Messiah

The sufferings Israel must face in the days of the Messiah are temporary and transitory. They will last, according to the Talmudic view quoted in the preceding chapter, seven years; a later Aggada, of which we shall hear more anon, reduces this period to a mere forty-five days. The Messiah himself, on the other hand, must spend his entire life, from the moment of his creation until the time of his advent many centuries or even millennia later, in a state of constant and acute suffering. Despised and afflicted with unhealing wounds, he sits in the gates of Great Rome and winds and unwinds the bandages of his festering sores; as a Midrash expresses it, "pains have adopted him." According to one of the most moving, and at the same time psychologically most meaningful, of all Messiah legends, God, when He created the Messiah, gave him the choice whether or not to accept the sufferings for the sins of Israel. And the Messiah answered: "I accept it with joy, so that not a single soul of Israel should perish" (see excerpt from Pes. Rab. below). In the later, Zoharic formulation of this legend, the Messiah himself summons all the diseases, pains, and sufferings of Israel to come upon him, in order thus to ease the anguish of Israel, which otherwise would be unbearable.

In all this the Messiah becomes heir to the Suffering

Servant of God, who figures prominently in the prophecies of Deutero-Isaiah (see chapter 1), and who suffers undeservedly for the sins of others. While some scholars maintain that the Suffering Servant is the Messiah, at least one passage in the Biblical text itself identifies the Suffering Servant with Israel (see Isa. 49:3). There can be little doubt that psychologically the Suffering Messiah is but a projection and personification of Suffering Israel. This is especially clear in the legend which describes the Suffering Messiah in the "house of frivolity in the marketplace" of Great Rome, that is, the world of the exile. It is, of course, Israel itself that is kept "captive in prison" in exile among the nations of the world, and that, when the redemption comes, will be transformed from the despised and wounded figure seen by Zerubbabel in Rome into a "youth in the perfection of his beauty" (see below, excerpt from Sefer Zerubbabel). Similarly, the Leper Messiah and the Beggar Messiah, with whom we have become acquainted above in chapter 3, are but variants on the theme of Suffering Israel personified in the Suffering Messiah figure. And it is undoubtedly true in the psychological sense that, as the Zohar states, the acceptance of Israel's sufferings by the Messiah (read: their projection onto the Messiah) eases that suffering which otherwise could not be endured.

The stories of R. Nahman of Bratzlav (1772–1811), one of which was presented above in chapter 7, have a special place in Hasidic literature. The founder of a new school of Hasidism, R. Nahman began to tell stories only in the last few years of his short life (he died of tuberculosis at the age of thirty-nine). He told the stories in Yiddish, and after his death his disciple and successor, R. Nathan Sternhartz (1780–1845) wrote them down, translated them into Hebrew, and published them in a bilingual edition with his introduction and explanatory notes. The first of R. Nahman's thirteen stories, presented below in my meticulously literal translation from the Yiddish, was considered so important that practically the entire introduction of R.

Nathan is devoted to a discussion of its mystical and symbolic meaning. As R. Nathan repeatedly states, its meaning is Messianic:

> The King's daughter is an epithet for the Shekhina and the Community of Israel. . . . It is clear to the eyes that the exile of the Shekhina and of the Community of Israel is like the loss of the king's daughter and her removal from her lover. . . . And, behold, the first story about the king's daughter who was lost is the mystery of the Shekhina in exile. . . .
>
> The exile of the Shekhina actually began before the creation of the world, and Adam should have remedied it by causing all the worlds to ascend to their proper places and by revealing the kingship of God instantly in the hour of the creation of the world, just as His kingship will be revealed soon at the time of the coming of our Messiah, [may he come] quickly in our days. But he became negligent by eating from the Tree of Knowledge, which is, as told in the aforementioned story, like unto the Viceroy who failed the test and ate of the aftergrowth, and thereby caused damage in all the worlds. And the Shekhina again descended and went down below among the Other [Evil] Side. . . .
>
> And this story is about every man in every time, for almost this entire story occurs to every man individually, for everyone of Israel must occupy himself with this perfection [*tiqqun*], namely to raise up the Shekhina from the exile, to raise her up from the dust, and to liberate the Holy Kingdom from among the idolators and the Other Side among whom she is caught. . . . Thus one finds that everyone in Israel is occupied with the search for the King's Daughter, to take her back to her Father. . . . For Israel as a whole has the character of the Viceroy. . . . [1]

A few comments may be added to these traditional explanations. R. Nahman took considerable liberties with his characters and the events he described. Thus while the king

---

1. R. Nathan's introduction to R. Nahman of Bratzlav's *Sippure Ma'asiyyot*, 1973 ed., pp. 7–8.

is undoubtedly God, he attributes to him rather limited powers: the king tries to, but cannot, find his daughter. The daughter, as R. Nathan explains, is the Shekhina and also the Community of Israel—the identity of these two is an old Midrashic idea—but, for a captive princess, she is surprisingly free to come and go in her carriage, and she occupies the position of queen in the castle of the king who has captured her. The environment which holds the princess (i.e., Israel) captive is described as a friendly, pleasant place: the princess enjoys royal honors, orchestras entertain her, great luxuries are at her disposal, she drives out in a carriage accompanied by many retainers, etc. This is a surprisingly rosy picture of Israel's exile. But at the bottom of it all is the typical Hasidic attitude to the mundane aspect of the world of the nations: Israel is captive in it, and thus is dominated by the "husks," the Other Side, the evil, physical-material aspect of existence.

The most enigmatic character is the Viceroy. He is, according to R. Nathan's explanation, everyman in Israel; but he also bears unmistakable similarity to the Messiah: at first, he waits patiently, then misses two opportunities to liberate the princess, then sleeps for seventy years, then wanders in fantastic deserts, and encounters there three skeptical but friendly giants with superhuman powers. Throughout, he is maintained by an unshakable faith in the existence of the mysterious castle of pearls on a golden mountain in which he would find the princess. Is the Viceroy's belief in the existence of the castle a mystical reversal of the enduring faith of Israel in the coming of the Messiah? While the Viceroy resembles to some extent the Biblical Suffering Servant, he has other features, especially his stubborn perseverance in his search for the princess, reminiscent of Israel's unceasing expectation of the Redemption. The greatest paradox, of course, is that of the contrast between the life of ease and luxury enjoyed by the princess and her all-eclipsing despair at the failure of the Viceroy to liberate her.

While these and many other details in the story that have
no readily apparent meaning can be given various interpretations, it is not at all certain that each of them was invented by
R. Nahman with a specific symbolic meaning in mind. One
rather gets the impression that, in the manner of many a
masterly storyteller, he let himself be carried away by the
flow of his own narrative, and added detail upon detail, not
unlike a jeweler who fashions a kingly crown and embellishes
it with many a decorative lobule pleasing to the eye but of no
import in relation to the symbolic significance of the crown
itself.

In the explanations by R. Nahman of Tcherin (whose
father was a disciple of R. Nahman of Bratzlav), appended to
the volume, the Messianic connotations of another story are
spelled out:

I heard from my father of blessed memory that after
our Master [R. Nahman of Bratzlav] told the story about
the merchant, there was then a great and mighty rejoicing
among his men. And they sang the verse, *For the Lord hath
comforted Zion* (Isa. 51:3), for they understood then from
his holy discourses which he uttered thereafter, and which
are explained at the end of the story, that the story of the
youth and the princess alludes to the soul of the Messiah
and the Community of Israel, who are now separated from
each other. And the whole community of Israel and the
kingship of holiness which flows from her fell and sank
down under the hands of the husks of the wrath of the
murderer, as told in the story. He inspires such fear and
dread in man that he dares not cry to the Name, blessed be
He, and he says to him, "If you cry, I shall strangle you
instantly!" And indeed they [the souls of the Messiah and
the Community of Israel] fell and sank down under the
hands of the husks of insolence.... And also the soul of the
Messiah is subjugated in the exile among the husks, in a
place of desert and desolation where no man walks. And
the storm wind spread and became strong and caused such
confusion that he [the Messiah] lost all the signs which
were given to him from the roots of the souls of Israel.
Until it was totally impossible for them to recognize him.
For as a result of the many tribulations that have come

over him from being oppressed under their hands, and, as a result of their powerful sucking from him, some of the mysteries of the signs and portents and marvels were given over to them as well. Until there were found also among them some who imitated [the Messiah] like an ape before a man, calling themselves by the name Messiah. For this is the whole issue of the false Messiahs who were in the world. And thereafter, once their lies and wantonness were known, it had become very difficult to believe in the light of the truth of his [the Messiah's] own selfness when it was revealed to them. For also about the first one, too, they imagined that it was as clear as the sun that he was he [the Messiah]. And so about the second, and so also about the third, as it is told in the story. And now, from where should their succor come to recognize him, himself, since each of the liars, who wanted to attach themselves to her [the Community of Israel], also had such signs and portents? (And this matter caused damage also in the disputes and quarrels which came about concerning the great real Tzaddiqim, such as the Ba'al Shem Tov and our Master [R. Nahman of Bratzlav], for not the whole world merited to recognize the height of their greatness; and had all Israel drawn near them, there would have surely been complete Redemption.) And from that time until now the sinking down of the Community of Israel has become intensified and she is caught among murderers and the licentious who deprived her of all the glory of her precious garments, until her face has changed so that she cannot be recognized at all, as told there [in the story]. And therefore let the Cause of all Causes be exalted and glorified, for He will turn even such descents into ascents... and she herself [the Community of Israel] will find the signs and recognize with her own eyes that they are the true ones, until they will be exalted and brought back to their place, and the kingship will be given to them forever and ever, *for the Lord hath comforted Zion.*[2]

The above excerpt is a typical example of the attention paid in subsequent generations to R. Nahman's stories, of the convoluted style of the explanations appended to them, and of the reading of complex, mystical, Kabbalistic mean-

2. R. Nahman of Tcherin in R. Nahman of Bratzlav, *Sippure Ma'asiyyot*, 1973 ed., pp. 276–77.

ings into them (such as the descent of the Shekhina into the world of the "Other Side," the evil "husks," the "sucking" out by the "husks" of the spiritual substance of Israel, etc.). Noteworthy is the mystical explanation given to the temporary successes of the false Messiahs, and the warning of the danger they represent to Israel by making it difficult for them to recognize the True Messiah when he finally comes.

R. Y'hoshu'a ben Levi once found Elijah standing at the entrance of the cave of R. Shim'on ben Yohai.... He asked him: "When will the Messiah come?" He said to him: "Go, ask him himself." "And where does he sit?" "At the entrance of the city [of Rome]." "And what are his marks?" "His marks are that he sits among the poor who suffer of diseases, and while all of them unwind and rewind [the bandages of all their wounds] at once, he unwinds and rewinds them one by one, for, he says, 'Should I be summoned, there must be no delay.'" R. Y'hoshu'a went to him and said to him: "Peace be unto you, my Master and Teacher!" He said to him: "Peace be unto you, Son of Levi!" He said to him: "When will the Master come?" He said to him: "Today." R. Y'hoshu'a went to Elijah, who asked him: "What did he tell you?" R. Y'hoshu'a said: "[He said to me:] Peace be unto you, Son of Levi!" Elijah said to him: "[By saying this] he assured the World to Come for you and your father." R. Y'hoshu'a then said to Elijah: "The Messiah lied to me, for he said 'Today I shall come,' and he did not come." Elijah said: "This is what he told you: *'Today, if you but hearken to His voice'* (Ps. 95:7)."

(B. Sanh. 98a)

[Zerubbabel ben Shealtiel said:] On the eleventh of Adar, God spoke to me and said to me: "Come to Me, ask of Me!" And I said: "What shall I ask? The days of my end are short, let me live to the fill of my days." And He said to me: "I shall let you live." And the spirit carried me between heaven and earth and took me to Nineveh, the great city, which is the city of blood. And I suffered greatly, and rose up from suffering to pray and to beseech the face of the God of Israel, and confessed my sins and transgressions, and said: "O, Lord, I sinned and transgressed, and pains have adopted me. You are the God of Israel who made everything with the spirit of Your mouth, and by Your word the dead shall live." And the

Lord said to me: "Go to the house of frivolity in the marketplace."
And I went as He had commanded me. And He said to me: "Turn
and go on." And I turned and He touched me, and I saw a man,
despised and wounded. And the wounded and despised man said
to me: "Zerubbabel, what have you here?" And I answered and
said: "The spirit of God brought me to this city which I know not,
and led me to this place." And he said to me: "Fear not, for you
were brought here in order to be shown." And when I heard his
words I was comforted and I asked him: "What is the name of this
place?" And he said to me: "This is Great Rome, in which I am
kept captive in prison until my end comes." And when I heard this
I hid my face for a moment from him, and then again looked at him,
and again hid my face, for I was afraid. And he said to me: "Fear
not and dread not, why are you silent?" And I said: "I have heard
your tidings, that you are the Messiah of my God." And forthwith
he appeared to me like a youth in the perfection of his beauty and
pleasing, a young man the like of whom there is none. And I said to
him: "When will the lamp of Israel light up?" And as I said these
words, and lo, a man with wings [Metatron] came to me and said to
me that he was the celestial prince of the army of Israel who fought
against Sanherib and the kings of Canaan, and will in the future
fight the war of the Lord with the Messiah of the Lord against the
insolent king, Armilus, son of the stone, who will issue from the
stone.... And he said to me: "This is the Messiah of the Lord who
is hidden here until the time of the End...."

(Sefer Zerubbabel, BhM 2:54-55)

R. Hosha'ya said: "In the future Jerusalem will be a lantern for
the nations of the world, and they will walk in her light...."

In Thy light do we see light (Ps. 36:10). This is the light of the
Messiah, as it is written, *And God saw the light that it was good* (Gen.
1:4). This teaches us that the Holy One, blessed be He, saw the
generation of the Messiah and its deeds prior to the creation of the
world. And He hid the light for the Messiah and his generation
under His Throne of Glory.

Satan said before the Holy One, blessed be He: "Master of the
World! The light which is hidden under Your Throne of Glory,
for whom is it [destined]?" He said to him: "For him who will turn
you back and disgrace you, and shame your face." He said to him:
"Master of the World! Show him to me!" He said to him: "Come

and see him!" When Satan saw the Messiah, he trembled and fell upon his face and said: "Surely this is the Messiah who in the future will cast me and all the princes of the nations of the world into Gehenna...."

In that hour the nations became awestruck and said before him: "Master of the World! Who is he into whose hand we shall fall, what is his name and what his nature?" The Holy One, blessed be He, said to them: "His name is Ephraim, My True Messiah. He will raise his stature and the stature of his generation, and will light up the eyes of Israel, and will save his people, and no nation and language shall be able to stand up against him.... All his enemies and adversaries will be affrighted and will flee from him... and even the rivers will cease to flow into the sea...."

[When He created the Messiah,] the Holy One, blessed be He, began to tell him the conditions [of his future mission], and said to him: "Those who are hidden with you [your generation], their sins will in the future force you into an iron yoke, and they will render you like unto this calf whose eyes have grown dim, and they will choke your spirit with the yoke, and because of their sins your tongue will cleave to the roof of your mouth. Do you accept this?"

The Messiah said before the Holy One, blessed be He: "Master of the World! Will that suffering last many years?" The Holy One, blessed be He, said to him: "By your life and the life of my head, it is a septenary of it that I decreed upon you. But if your soul is troubled, I shall banish them as from this moment."

He said before Him: "Master of the Worlds! With gladness in my soul and with joy in my heart I accept it, so that not a single one of Israel should perish; and not only those who will be alive should be saved in my days, but even the dead who have died from the days of Adam the first man until now. And not only they, but even the stillborn should be saved in my days; and not only the stillborn, but even those to whose creation You gave thought but who were not created. This is what I want, this is what I accept!"

(Pes. Rab. pp. 161a–b)

They said: In the septenary in which the Son of David comes they will bring iron beams and put them upon his neck until his body bends and he cries and weeps, and his voice rises up into the Heights, and he says before Him: "Master of the World! How much can my strength suffer? How much my spirit? How much my soul? And how much my limbs? Am I not but flesh and blood?..."

In that hour the Holy One, blessed be He, says to him: "Ephraim, My True Messiah, you have already accepted [this suffering] from the six days of Creation. Now your suffering shall be like My suffering. For ever since the day on which wicked Nebuchadnezzar came up and destroyed My Temple and burnt My sanctuary, and I exiled My children among the nations of the world, by your life and the life of your head, I have not sat on My Throne. And if you do not believe, see the dew that is upon My head...."

In that hour he says before Him: "Master of the World! Now my mind is at rest, for it is sufficient for the servant to be like his Master!"

(Pes. Rab. 162a)

The Fathers of the World [Abraham, Issac, and Jacob] will in the future rise up in the month of Nissan and will speak to him: "Ephraim, our True Messiah! Even though we are your fathers, you are greater than we, for you suffered because of the sins of our children, and cruel punishments have come upon you the like of which have not come upon the early and the later generations, and you were put to ridicule and held in contempt by the nations of the world because of Israel, and you sat in darkness and blackness and your eyes saw no light, and your skin cleft to your bones, and your body dried out and was like wood, and your eyes grew dim from fasting, and your strength became like a potsherd. All this because of the sins of our children. Do you want that our children should enjoy the happiness that the Holy One, blessed be He, allotted to Israel, or perhaps, because of the great sufferings that have come upon you on their account, and because they imprisoned you in the jailhouse, your mind is not reconciled with them?"

And the Messiah answers them: "Fathers of the World! Everything I did, I did only for you and for your children, and for your honor and for the honor of your children, so that they should enjoy this happiness the Holy One, blessed be He, has allotted to Israel."

Then the Fathers of the World say to him: "Ephraim, our True Messiah, let your mind be at ease, for you put at ease our minds and the mind of your Creator!"

R. Shim'on ben Pazi said: "In that hour the Holy One, blessed be He, raises up the Messiah unto the heaven of heavens and spreads over him the splendor of His Glory [to protect him] from the nations of the world, from the wicked Persians. And He says to him: 'Ephraim, Our True Messiah, be you the judge over these peoples, and do to them whatever your soul wishes'. For had it not been for My compassion for you which became strong, they would have caused you to perish from the world in one moment...." [God] has mercy on him while he is imprisoned in the jailhouse, for every day the nations of the world gnash their teeth and blink their eyes and shake their heads and shoot out their lips...and roar against him like lions and want to swallow him.... [And God says:] "I shall have mercy on him when he comes out of the house of prisoners, for not only one kingdom, or two kingdoms, or three kingdoms will come against him, but one hundred and forty kingdoms will surround him." And the Holy One, blessed be He, says to him: "Ephraim, My True Messiah, fear them not, because all of them will die from the breath of your lips."

Instantly the Holy One, blessed be He, makes seven canopies of precious stones and pearls for the Messiah, and from each canopy four rivers issue forth, of wine and milk and honey and pure balsam. And the Holy One, blessed be He, embraces him in front of the pious, and leads him under the canopy, and all the pious and the saintly and the heroes of the Tora in every generation see him. And the Holy One, blessed be He, says to the pious: "Pious of the world! So far Ephraim, My True Messiah, has not taken [compensation for as much as] one half of his sufferings. I still have one measure that I shall give him, which no eye has ever seen...." In that hour the Holy One, blessed be He, calls the North Wind and the South Wind, and says to them: "Come, honor Ephraim, My True Messiah, and spread before him all kinds of spices from the Garden of Eden...."

(Pes. Rab. ch. 36)

The fifth house [in the heavenly Paradise] is built of onyx and jasper stones, and inlaid stones, and silver and gold, and good pure gold. And around it are rivers of balsam, and before its door flows the River Gihon. And [it has] a canopy of all trees of incense and good scent. And [in it are] beds of gold and silver, and embroidered garments. And there sit Messiah ben David and Elijah and Messiah ben Ephraim. And there is a canopy of incense trees as in the Sanctuary which Moses made in the desert. And all its vessels and pillars are of silver, its covering is gold, its seat is purple. And in it is Messiah ben David who loves Jerusalem. Elijah of blessed memory takes hold of his head, places it in his lap and holds it, and says to him: "Endure the sufferings and the sentence of your Master who makes you suffer because of the sin of Israel." And thus it is written: *He was wounded because of our transgressions, he was crushed because of our iniquities* (Isa. 53:5)—until the time when the end comes.

And every Monday and Thursday, and every Sabbath and holiday, the Fathers of the World [i.e. Abraham, Isaac, and Jacob] and Moses and Aaron, David and Solomon, and the prophets, and the pious come and visit him, and weep with him. And he weeps with them. And they give him thanks and say to him: "Endure the sentence of your Master, for the end is near to come, and the chains which are on your neck will be broken, and you will go out into freedom."

And even Korah and all his company entreat him every Wednesday and say to him: "How long until the miraculous end? When *will you bring us back to life and bring us up again from the depths of the earth* (Ps. 71:20)?"

And he says to them: "Go and ask the Fathers of the World." And they are ashamed and return to their place.

(Mid. Konen, BhM 2:29–30)

The souls which are in the Garden of Eden of Below roam about on every New Moon and Sabbath, and go to that place which is called Walls of Jerusalem, where there are many officers and detachments which watch over those walls.... And they go to that place, but do not enter it until they are purified. And there they prostrate themselves, and enjoy that radiance, and then return to the Garden. [And again] they go forth from there and roam about in the world, and they see the bodies of the sinful suffering their punishment.... And then they [continue to] roam and view those afflicted with sufferings and disease, and those who suffer for the Oneness of their Master, and then they return and tell [all this] to the Messiah. In the hour in which they tell the Messiah about the sufferings of Israel in exile, and [about] the sinful among them who seek not the knowledge of their Master, the Messiah lifts up his voice and weeps over those sinful among them. This is what is written: *He was wounded because of our transgressions, he was crushed because of our iniquities* (Isa. 53:5). Those souls then return to their places. In the Garden of Eden there is a hall which is called the Hall of the Sons of Illness. The Messiah enters that hall and summons all the diseases and all the pains and all the sufferings of Israel that they should come upon him, and all of them come upon him. And would he not thus bring ease to Israel and take their sufferings upon himself, no man could endure the sufferings Israel has to undergo because they neglected the Tora.... As long as Israel dwelt in the Holy Land, the rituals and the sacrifices they performed [in the Temple] removed all those diseases from the world; now the Messiah removes them from the children of the world....

(Zohar 2:212a)

Once he [R. Mordecai of Lechivitsh[3]] asked: "Do you know what are the pangs of the Messiah?" And he answered: "All the sufferings of the pangs of the Messiah which our sages of blessed memory have enumerated, have already been endured by the Children of Israel in the course of the long *Galuth* [Exile]. But these are the pangs of the Messiah: Time will come when *Grace is deceit and beauty is vanity* (Prov. 31:30)—that is, deceit be considered a grace, and vanity will be considered beauty....And then a man will be found whose heart will burn like fire in the fear of God, and he will be restrained with ropes—that will be the suffering of the Messiah."

(Kleinman, *Sefer Or Y'sharim*, p. 19)

The King's Lost Daughter

There was once a king. The king had six sons and one daughter. The daughter was very dear in his eyes and he loved her very much, and he used to play with her a lot. Once he was together with her one day and he became angry with her. A word

---

3. Mordecai ben Noah of Lachowicze (1742–1810), Hasidic rabbi, founder of a dynasty of Tzaddiqim.

escaped from his mouth, "The Not Good [i.e., the Devil] take you!" At night she went to her room, and in the morning they did not know where she was. Her father was very upset and went to look for her here and there. Up stood the Viceroy, because he saw that the king was in great sorrow, and asked that they give him a servant with a horse and money for expenses. And he went to search for her. And he searched much, a very long time, until he found her. (Now he tells how he searched for her until he found her.) And he went a long time, in deserts and fields and forests, and searched for her a very long time. And as he was walking in the desert he saw a path from one side. He considered: "Since I have been going such a long time in the desert and cannot find her, let me follow this path, perhaps I shall come to a place of settlement." And he went a long time, after which he saw a castle and many troops standing around it. And the castle was very beautiful, and the troops stood around it in order, very neatly. And he was afraid of the troops: perhaps they will not let him enter. And he considered, "I shall try." And he left the horse and went to the castle. They let him. Nobody prevented him at all. He went from room to room without hindrance. He came to a hall and saw that a king was sitting there with a crown, and many troops were standing around him, and many musicians with instruments before him, and it was very pleasant and beautiful there. And neither the king nor anybody else asked him anything. And he saw there good food, and he went and ate. And he went and lay down in a corner to see what will happen there. And he saw that the king commanded that they bring the queen. They went to bring her, and there was a great commotion and great rejoicing, and the orchestras were playing and singing as they brought the queen. And they placed for her a chair and seated her next to him. And she was the daughter of the king. And he saw her and recognized her. Then the queen looked and saw somebody lying in the corner. She recognized him, and stood up from her chair and went there and touched him and asked him, "Do you recognize me?" And he answered her, "Yes, I recognize you. You are the king's daughter who was lost." He asked her, "How did you get here?" She answered, "Because that word escaped from the mouth of my father. And this is the place of the Not Good." He told her that her father was very sad, and that he had been looking for her for many years, and he asked her, "How can I get you away?" She answered him, "You cannot get me out, except if you choose yourself a place and dwell there for a year. And throughout the year you must yearn for me, to bring me out, and when you will have time you must only yearn and wish and hope to bring me out. And you must fast, and on the last day of the year you must fast, and not sleep for a full day." And he went and did so. And at the end of the year, on the last day, he fasted and slept not. And he rose and went there. And he saw a tree on which very beautiful apples grew. And he became very desirous and he went and ate of them. And as soon as he ate the apple, he fell down and sleep snatched him away. And he slept for a very long time. And the servant tried to wake him, but could not wake him. Then he raised himself from his sleep and asked the servant, "Where in the world am I?" And he told him the whole story: "You have been sleeping a very long time. It has been several years that you have slept, and I sustained myself from the fruits." And he was in despair. And he went there and found her. And she complained to him very much and was full of sadness. "Because of one day you have lost. For had you come on that day, you could have taken me away from here. But since not to eat is a very difficult thing, especially on the last day, for then the Evil Inclination becomes very powerful, therefore again choose yourself a place, and dwell there again for a year, but on the last day you will be allowed to eat. But do not sleep and do not drink wine, lest you fall asleep, for the sleep is the main thing." And he went and did so. On the last day he went there and saw a spring flow, and the appearance of the spring was red, and the smell that of wine. He asked the servant, "Do you see this source? There should be water in it, but its appearance is red and its smell is that of wine." And he went and tried some of the spring. And he fell down instantly, and slept many years, seventy years. Many troops went by with their *obazin* [baggage train] which went after them. And the servant hid because of the troops. Then a carriage came by, and in it sat the daughter of the king. She stopped there near him, and got off, and sat down next to him, and recognized him. And she shook him very strongly but he awoke not. She began to complain of him: "You have made so many and so many efforts and had troubles for so many years, and suffered so much toil so long in order to get me out, and because of that day on which you could have taken me away, you lost." And she wept greatly and said: "It is a great pity for you and for me! I have been here for such a long time and cannot get out," etc. Then she took the kerchief from her head and wrote on it with her tears and put it down next to him, and stood up, and returned to her carriage and drove away.

Thereafter he woke up, and asked the servant, "Where in the world am I?" And he told him the whole story, and that many troops had passed by, and that there was here a carriage, and that she wept over him, and cried, "It is a great pity, for you and for me," etc., as mentioned. Meanwhile he looked and saw the kerchief lying next to him, and asked, "From where is this?" He answered him, "She wrote on it with her tears." He took the kerchief and lifted it up against the sun, and he saw the letters, and he read what was written there, her complaints and cries, as mentioned, and that now she was no longer in that castle, but that he should search for a golden mountain with a castle of pearls, "There you will find me."

And he left behind the servant, and went alone to search for her. And he went and searched for her several years. He thought for himself that certainly a golden mountain and a castle of pearls can not be found in an inhabited place. Since he was versed in maps, therefore, "I shall go to deserts to search there." And he went to search for her in the deserts many, many years. Then he saw a very big man whose size was not at all human and he was carrying a big tree the like of which in size cannot be found in an inhabited place. And that man asked him, "Who are you?" He said, "I am a man." The big man was amazed and said, "I have been in the desert for a long time and have never seen a man here." And he told him the whole story, as mentioned, and that he was looking for a golden mountain with a castle of pearls. He answered him, "Certainly it does not exist!" And he put him off and said to him, "They deluded you with a foolish thing for it surely does not exist." And he began to cry very much, "It surely exists, yes it must exist somewhere." But he put him off (that is the wild man put him off) and said, "They deluded you with a foolish thing." And he said, "It surely exists somewhere." He said to him, "To my mind it is nonsense. But since you insist, behold, I am in charge of all the animals, I shall do you a favor and shall call all the animals. They run about in the whole world. Perhaps one of them will know about the mountain with the aforementioned castle." He called all the animals, from the smallest to the biggest, and asked them. All of them answered that they had not seen. He said to him, "You see, they deluded you with nonsense. If you will listen to me, turn back, for surely you will not find it, for it does not exist in the world." And the Viceroy insisted very very much and said, "It surely must exist!" He said to him (the wild man to the Viceroy), "I have a brother in the desert, and he is in charge of all the birds. Perhaps they know, since they fly high in the air. Perhaps they saw the mountain with the castle. Go to him and tell him that I sent you to him." And he went many, many years searching for him. He found again a very big man, as mentioned, and he too carried a big tree, and he also asked him as did the first one. He answered him, telling him the whole story, and that his brother had sent him to him. And he too put him off, for surely it does not exist. And the Viceroy pressed also him very much, "It surely does exist." He told him, "I am in charge of all the birds, I shall call them, perhaps they know." He called all the birds and asked them, from the smallest to the biggest. They answered him that they did not know of the mountain with the castle. He said to him, "You see, it surely does not exist in the world. If you will listen to me, turn back, for it surely does not exist." And he insisted very much and said, "Surely it exists in the world." He said to him: "Farther in the desert lives my brother who is in charge of all the winds, and they run across the whole world. Perhaps they know." He went for many, many years, searching. He found a big man, as mentioned, and he too carried a big tree. And he asked also him as mentioned, and told him the whole story as mentioned. And the man, too, put him off. And the Viceroy begged him very much. He said to him that he will do him a favor and will call all the winds for his sake, and will ask them. He called them, and all the winds came and he asked all of them. But none of them knew about a mountain with the castle. He said to him: "You see that they told you nonsense." The Viceroy began to cry very much and said: "I know that it surely exists." Meanwhile he saw that one more wind came, and the man in charge was angry with him, "Why did you come so late? Did I not command that all the winds should come, why did you not come with them?" He answered him, "I came late because I had to carry a king's daughter to a golden mountain with a castle of pearls." And he rejoiced greatly. And the man in charge of the winds asked the wind: "What is expensive there?" He said, "All things are very expensive there." The man in charge of the winds said to the Viceroy: "Since you have been searching for such a long time, and you have had so many troubles, perhaps now you will be hindered by lack of money, therefore I give you a jar so that if you dip your hand into it you will take money out of it." And he commanded the wind that it should carry him there. The storm wind came and carried him there, and brought him to the gate. And there stood troops who would not let him enter the city. And he put his hand into the jar and took out money and bribed them, and entered the city. It was a beautiful city, and he went to a lord and made arrangements for meals, for [he knew] he would have to tarry there. For one needed much thought and wisdom to bring her out. (And how he brought her out he [R. Nahman] did not relate.) At the end he did bring her out. Amen. Selah.

(R. Nahman of Bratzlav (1973 ed.), pp. 11–15)

13

The Mother of the Messiah

In contrast to Christianity, in parts of which the Mother of the Messiah became a central divine personality whose popular worship frequently tended to overshadow that of her son, in Judaism the Mother of the Messiah remained a shadowy and enigmatic human figure to whom little attention was paid. In fact, there is only one Talmudic legend in which she appears: her name is not stated, but her husband's name is said to be Hezekiah—evidently so named after the king of Judah whom some sages considered to have been an early Messiah (see chapter 3). Her son's name is Menahem ("Comforter"). This Messiah was born on the very day the Second Temple of Jerusalem was destroyed by the Romans (70 C.E.), but some time later a storm wind snatched him from his mother's arms and he disappeared. As for the Midrash literature, in it too only a very few legends speak about the Mother of the Messiah. In one, similar to the Talmudic story, the Mother of the Messiah remains anonymous. In another, she is called Hefzibah, and is the wife of the prophet Nathan. Her son Menahem, the Messiah, is, however, not the son of Nathan but of a certain 'Amiel.[1] He was born in the days of

---

1. In a Midrash fragment published by Wertheimer, *Bate Midrashot*, 2:504, the genealogy of Hefzibah and Menahem is even more confusing. There it says: "And thereafter will come the wife of the prophet Nathan son of David, Hefzibah, mother of Menahem son of 'Amiel son of David'..."

King David, and ever since has been waiting, hidden in the city of Rome. Before the time comes for Menahem to reveal himself, his mother Hefzibah will slay two kings, gather all Israel, and cause confusion in the enemy camp. In another Midrash she is the Widow of Zarephath, and in yet another Naamah the Ammonite, wife of King Solomon, is identified as the Messiah's early ancestress. Finally, in the Zohar, there is a myth-fragment according to which the mother of both Messiahs, the Son of Joseph and the Son of David, is none other than the Shekhina, the personified female aspect of God, who is also identified with the Community of Israel.

The Anonymous Mother

R. Yudan son of R. Aybo said: It happened to a Judean [a Jew] who was standing and leading his ox. His ox lowed before him. An Arab passed by and heard its voice. He said to him: "Son of Judah, Son of Judah! Untie your ox, untie your plow, for the Temple has been destroyed!" The ox lowed a second time, and the Arab said: "Son of Judah, Judaean! Tie your ox and tie your plow, for the King Messiah has been born!" He asked him: "What is his name?" "Menahem." He asked him: "And what is the name of his father?" "Hezekiah." He asked him: "From where is he?" He answered: "From the royal fort of Bethlehem in Judah." He went and sold his ox and sold his plow, and became a seller of infant's clothes, and went from town to town until he came to that town. And all the women bought [clothes from him], but the mother of Menahem did not buy. He heard the talk of the women saying: "Mother of Menahem! Come, buy clothes for your son!" She said: "I wish that the enemies of Israel [euphemism for 'my son'] should suffocate, for on the day in which he was born the Temple was destroyed." He said to her: "We are sure that if it was destroyed because of him, it will be rebuilt because of him." Then she said to him: "I have not a penny." He said to her: "I do not mind, come and buy for him. If you have no money today, another day I shall return and get it." Days later he returned to that town and said to her: "How is your baby?" She said to him: "Since you have seen me last, winds and storms have come and snatched him from my hands."

(Y. Ber. 5a)

Until the day that Jerusalem was taken (Jer. 38:28). Even that day was not anguish but rejoicing, for on that day was born Menahem [the Messiah], and on that day Israel received full payment for all their sins. For R. Sh'muel bar Nahmani said: "On the day on which the Temple was destroyed, Israel received great retribution for their sins, for it is written, *The punishment of thy iniquity is accomplished, O daughter of Zion* (Lam. 4:22). And from whence [do we know] that on that day was the Messiah born? For it is written, *Before she travailed she brought forth* (Isa. 66:7).

On the day on which the Temple was destroyed Elijah of blessed memory was walking along the road. He heard a heavenly voice cry out and say: "The holy Temple has become a ruin, the children of the King went into captivity, the wife of the King remained a widow...." As soon as Elijah heard this, he said to himself: "It is His will to destroy the world!" He went and found people plowing and sowing, and said to them: "The Holy One, blessed be He, is wroth with His world and wants to destroy His house and to exile His children among the nations of the world, and you occupy yourselves with transitory matters?" A heavenly voice was heard and said: "Let them be, for already their Savior has been born." Elijah then said to the heavenly voice: "Where is he?" She said: "In Bethlehem of Judah." He went and found a woman who was seated at the door of her house, and her son, soiled with blood, was lying in front of her. He said to her: "My daughter, did you give birth to a son?" She said: "Yes." He said to her: "Why is he soiled with blood?" She said: "A great evil! For on the day on which he was born the Temple was destroyed." He said to her: "My daughter! Rise and take him up, for a great salvation will come to you through him." Instantly she arose and lifted him up. And he gave her clothes to dress him and ornaments to decorate him, but she did not want to accept them. He said to her: "Take these from me, and after a time I shall come and get their price."

He left her and went away. Five years later he said: "Let me go and see the Savior of Israel, whether he is growing up to look like kings or to look like ministering angels." He went and found the woman standing at the door of her house. He said to her: "My daughter, how is that boy?" She said to him: "Rabbi, did I not tell you that his luck was bad? On the day on which he was born the Temple was destroyed. And although he had feet, he did not walk; he had ears, but did not hear; he had eyes, but did not see; he had a mouth, but did not speak; but was lying there like a stone. Then a wind bore down upon him from the four corners of the world and blew him into the great sea."

Elijah rent his clothes and tore his hair and cried and said: "Woe, lost is the salvation of Israel!" A heavenly voice was heard and said: "Elijah, it is not as you think, but for four hundred years he will dwell in the great sea, and eighty years in the smoke ascent of the Sons of Korah, and eighty years in the gates of Rome, and the rest of the years he will wander in all the great countries until the end."

(B'reshit Rabbati, pp. 130–31)

Hefzibah

[Metatron addresses Zerubbabel in Rome:] "I am he who led Abraham all over the Land of Canaan, and I am he who redeemed Isaac, and who struggled with Jacob at the Ford of Jabbok, and I am he who led Israel in the desert for forty years in the name of the Lord, and I am he who appeared to Joshua in Gilgal, and I am he whose name is like the name of my Master, and His name is in me. And you, Zerubbabel, ask me and I shall tell you what will happen to your people at the end of the days." And he said to me: "This is the Messiah of the Lord who is hidden here until the time of the End, and his name is Menahem son of 'Amiel, and he was born in the days of David king of Israel, and the spirit carried him and hid him here until the time of the End." And I asked Metatron and he said to me: "The Holy One, blessed be He, will give the staff of salvation to Hefzibah, the mother of Menahem, and a star shall shine before her, and Hefzibah will go out and slay two kings, one is Nof from Yemen, and the other's name is Asarno of Antioch. And these signs will come to pass on the feast of Shavu'ot, and the thing is true. And when the city [of Jerusalem] will be rebuilt [after] four hundred and twenty years, it will be destroyed a second time. And when Rome will be built, seventy kings will rule in it, and the tenth of them will destroy the Temple, and daily sacrifices will cease. And from that day count nine hundred and ninety years—then will be the salvation of the Lord, and He will remember His holy people to redeem them and to take them and to carry them and to gather them."

And the staff which the Lord will give to Hefzibah the mother of Menahem is of an almond tree, and it is hidden in Raqat, a city of Naphtali. And it is the staff of Aaron and Moses and David king of Israel. And it is the staff which flowered in the Tent of Meeting, and brought forth blossoms and produced almonds. And Elijah son of El'azar hid it in Raqat, which is Tiberias, and there was hidden the Messiah son of Ephraim. And Zerubbabel son of Shealtiel said to Michael: "If it please my Lord, when will come the light of Israel? And what will be after all this?" And he said to me: "Messiah son of Joseph will come five years after Hefzibah, and will gather all Israel as one man, and then the king of Persia will come up against Israel and there will be great distress in Israel. And Hefzibah the wife of the prophet Nathan will go out with the staff which the Lord will give her, and the Lord will make a spirit of confusion enter them, and they will slay one another, and there the wicked will die."

And when I heard his words I fell upon my face and said to him: "Tell me the truth about the holy people!" And he adhered to me and showed me a stone in the shape of a woman and said to me: "This stone, Satan will lie with it and from it will come forth Armilus, and he will rule over the entire world, and there will be nobody to stand up against him. And all those who do not believe in him will die by his cruel sword. And he will come to the land of Israel with ten kings, to Jerusalem, and there they will slay the Messiah son of Joseph, and with him sixteen pious men. And they will exile Israel into the desert. And Hefzibah the mother of Menahem will stand there, and that wicked one will not see [her]. And this war will be in the month of Av. And then there will be trouble in Israel the like of which never was in the world. And they will flee into crevices and caves in the deserts. And all the nations of the world will go astray after that wicked one, the Satan Armilus, except for Israel. And Israel will mourn over Nehemiah son of Hushiel, who will be killed, and his corpse will be cast before the gates of Jerusalem, but the wild animals and birds will not touch it."

And when I heard his words it grieved me very much, and I

rose to pray before the Lord. And the Lord heard and sent his angel to me, and I knew that it was the angel who spoke to me and I prostrated myself before him. And he said to me: "What is the matter with you, Zerubbabel?" And I said to him: "A spirit frightened me." And Metatron arose and said: "Zerubbabel, ask me before I go from you." And I asked and said: "When will come the light of Israel?" And he answered me and said: "As the Lord lives who sent me that I tell you the acts of the Name, blessed be He, the Holy Voice sent me to tell you all that you will ask." And Michael said to me: "Approach me and incline your heart to that which I shall tell you, for it is true in the name of the Living God." And he said to me: "Menahem ben'Amiel will come suddenly in the month of Nissan, and will stand in the plain of Arbel. And all the sages of Israel will go out to him, and he will say to them: 'I am the Son of 'Amiel, the Messiah, whom the Lord has sent to give you tidings and to save you from the hand of your oppressors.' And the sages will look and will despise him as you despised him, and will not believe him. And his wrath will be kindled in him, and he will put on garments of vengeance, and will come to the gates of Jerusalem, and with him Elijah. And they will awaken and resuscitate Nehemiah the son of Shealtiel who was slain, and [then] they will believe him."

And thus Metatron swore to me that after nine hundred and ninety years will be fulfilled for the ruins of Jerusalem will come the salvation of the Lord. Menahem and Elijah will stand on the Great Sea and will call His prophets. And all the corpses of Israel who threw themselves into the sea because of their captors will come out. And then the community of Korah will ascend and will come to Moses, and the dead of the desert will come to life, and he will gather the banner of the Korahites. And the Name, blessed be He, will descend upon the Mount of Olives, and the mountain will split asunder from His shout, and He will fight those nations like a man of wars, and He will awaken zeal. And Messiah ben David will come, and will blow upon the face of Armilus and slay him. And all Israel will see the Lord when Zion returns, eye to eye, like a man of wars, and a helmet of deliverance will be on His head, and He will be clothed in armor, and He will fight Armilus and his soldiers, and all of them will fall dead in the plain of Arbel, and [only] remnants will escape. And on the Rock of the Lord will gather 1,500 [warriors], and 100,000 men wearing armor, and 500 from Israel with Nehemiah at their head, and they will slay them.

And after this will come Menahem ben 'Amiel and Nehemiahu and Elijah, and they will go up to Jerusalem. And in the month of Av the ruins of Jerusalem will be settled, and there will be great rejoicing for Israel. And they will offer up their sacrifices, and the offering of Judah and Israel will be sweet for the Lord as in the beginning, and He will smell the sweet savor of our sacrifices. And He will rejoice very much in the pomp of the Temple built above, and He will enlarge it in its length and its width, and it will extend from the east and from the Great Desert until the Last Sea and until the Great River, the River Euphrates. And also the Sanctuary will be built on the tops of five mountains.

And I asked him: "What are their [the mountains'] names?" And he said to me: "Lebanon, Mount Moriah, Tabor, Carmel, and Hermon."

And these are the names of the ten kings who will arise over the nations in those seven years: one is Seleucos of Aspamia. The second, Armanus (or Artimus) of the Land of the Sea. The third, Qilus (or Telis) of Gita. The fourth, Peloos (or Paulas) of Gallia. The fifth, Rometrus of Moratia. The sixth, Makellanus of Zalatia (or Murculus of Italia). The seventh, Archetonis of Adames (or Achtunus of Rodama). The eighth, Mesaplisnes (or Apelastus) of Mesopotamia. The ninth, Paros of Parsi (or Shiron of Persia). The tenth, Armilus son of Shafon.... And immediately after him, *the kingdom shall be the Lord's* (Obad. 21). And may our eyes see the anointed city which has been dragged into exile because of our sins, and until now the hope continues.

(Sefer Zerubbabel, BhM 2:54–57)

The Widow of Zarephath

Once our Masters were sitting and discussing from whom did Elijah descend? Some of them said from the seed of Rachel; others said from the seed of Leah. While they were thus sitting and discussing, Elijah came and stood before them. He said to them: "My Masters, I am descended from the seed of Rachel, for thus it is written in the genealogy of Benjamin (that among his descendants were) *Jaareshiah and Elijah and Zichri, the sons of Jeroham* (1 Chron.

8:27).'' Thereupon they said to him: "If so, you are not a Kohen [priest]. How, then, could you say to the widow [of Zarephath], *Make me a little cake first and bring it forth to me* [which is the prerogative of a Kohen] *and afterwards make for thee and thy son* (1 Ki. 17:13)?'' He said to them: "That child [the son of the widow] was none other than Messiah ben Joseph, and I wanted to give a signal to the world that first I shall go down to Babylonia, and thereafter will come the Messiah.''

(Seder Eliyahu Rabba 18, ed. Friedmann, pp. 97–98)

The son of the widow of Zarephath was [the prophet] Jonah, and he was Messiah ben Joseph.

(Yalqut Hadash, Mashiah, par. 22)

Naamah

After the three years [of Solomon's exile] ended, the Holy One, blessed be He, wanted to have mercy on him for the sake of His servant David and for the sake of the righteous Naamah, daughter of the king of Ammon (cf. 1 Kings 14:21, 31), that the Messiah son of David should come forth from him, and that he should join her and bring her with him to the Land of Israel. Therefore the Holy One, blessed be He, made him go the Land of Ammon....

(Naphtali Hirsh ben Elhanan, *'Emeq haMelekh*, 14d–15a)

The Shekhina

The Faithful Shepherd said: "At that time [there will come] pangs and pains upon the woman in childbirth, that is, the Shekhina.... And through these pains, which will make her cry out, seventy supernal Sanhedrins will be aroused, until her voice reaches the Lord.... And from those voices which she gives forth ...her womb opens—and her womb consists of two houses—to give birth to two Messiahs...and she bends her head betwixt her knees: her head is the Middle Column and her two thighs are

Eternity and Majesty . . . and from there are born two Messiahs. In that time the forests will be denuded, and the Serpent will pass from the world.

(Zohar, Ra'aya Mehemna, 3:67b–68a)

14

Elijah the Great Forerunner

In the Bible, Elijah is depicted as a zealous prophet of God who waged a ruthless war against Canaanite idolatry in Israel, defeated the prophets of Ba'al on Mount Carmel in a great rainmaking contest in which he proved the power of God,[1] retraced the footsteps of Moses to Mount Horeb (traditionally identified with Mount Sinai), and ascended to heaven in a chariot of fire (1 Kings 18, 19; 2 Kings 2). By the end of the Biblical period, Elijah had become an immensely popular mythical figure whose return was expected *before the coming of the great and terrible day of the Lord* (Mal. 3:23–24), that is, the day of the Last Judgment. By the first century B.C.E. it was a solidly established tenet that Elijah would be the forerunner of the Messiah.[2]

In this chapter we confine ourselves to the Aggadic role of Elijah in connection with the Messiah. The excerpts presented tell about Elijah comforting the Messiah in his long and painful wait for the call, chronicling the deeds of every generation, and predicting the coming of the Messiah. When the time for Redemption arrives, it is Elijah who introduces the Messiah to the people—evidently because he is well

---

1. Cf. R. Patai, "The Control of Rain in Ancient Palestine," *Hebrew Union College Annual*, vol. 14, 1939, pp. 251–86.

2. On Elijah's Messianic role, cf. L. Ginzberg, *Unbekannte Sekte*, pp. 351 ff.

known to them while the Messiah is unknown. Elijah forces Israel to repent, which is a prerequisite of Redemption. Like Moses and the Messiah, Elijah too appears, then hides, then appears again in the Future to Come. In the critical period of forty-five days between the death of Messiah ben Joseph and the appearance of Messiah ben David, Elijah will take the legendary Book of Yashar, "of which the whole Tora is but a line"; we are not told what he does with the book, but the mere appearance of it seems to be sufficient to make the earth swallow the enemies of Israel. Then, three days prior to the coming of the Messiah, Elijah announces the advent of the Redeemer from the mountains of Israel, slaughters the celestial prince of Edom (Rome), becomes the spokesman of Moses, settles all the disputes, and pleads Israel's case before God. He also provides Israel with miraculous sources of sustenance, and, finally, achieves himself the rank of a Redeemer.

Elijah differs from all other Biblical figures in that he alone has remained—in popular belief—a live, charismatic personality who follows with deep paternal concern the fate of Israel in general and of every individual Jew in particular. He is said to have appeared and conversed with many a Talmudic sage, arranged for meetings between them and the Messiah, explained his words to them, and taught them much of the secret lore of the Tora. More important from the point of view of popular psychology is the widely prevalent belief that Elijah is always ready to extend his helping hand to people in distress, has the power to chase away the Angel of Death, and appears to the poor and the troubled in the most unexpected guises—as a beggar, a Persian, an Arab, a horseman, a Roman court official, a harlot, and (in a story by Peretz) a magician. At the Passover Seder meal, he is welcomed in every Jewish home with a large goblet of wine placed in the middle of the festive table especially for him. At circumcision ceremonies the chair on which the *Sandaq* (god-father) holding the child sits is called the Chair of Elijah, because the prophet is believed to appear and hold the child.

Elijah is celebrated in prayer, legend, and song. An old *piyyut*, sung at the Havdala ceremony at the outgoing of the Sabbath, which describes his past deeds and the acts he is expected to perform in the Messianic age, has kept his image constantly in the mind of everybody. Its stanzas with Messianic connotations are as follows:

Elijah the prophet, Elijah the Tishbite, Elijah the
     Gileadite,
Quickly let him come to us with Messiah ben David,
The man who was zealous for the name of God
The man to whom the tidings of peace were given by
     Yekutiel,[3]
The man who approached and atoned for all the Children
     of Israel.[4]

Elijah, etc.

The man who will be sent from the heights of heaven,
The man who is appointed over all good tidings,
The man who is a faithful messenger to turn the heart of
     the sons to the fathers,

Elijah, etc.

Happy is he who saw his face in a dream,
Happy is he who greeted him and to whom he returned
     the greeting,
May God bless His people with peace.
                (Seder 'Avodat Yisrael, pp. 310–11)

Early Traditions

Behold, I send to you Elijah the prophet before the coming of the day of the Lord, the great and terrible one. And he will return

---

3. One of the names of Moses, according to the Aggada.

4. Reference to Pinhas son of Eleazar son of Aaron, who *was jealous for his God and made atonement for the Children of Israel* (Num. 25:13), and whom the Aggada identifies with Elijah. Cf. below, under "Elijah the Peacemaker."

the heart of the fathers to the sons, and the heart of the sons to their
fathers, lest I come and smite the land to destruction.

(Mal. 3:23–24)

How terrible are you, O Elijah....
Who were taken in a whirlwind up high,
And in hosts of fire to the heights....
To sooth the wrath before the fierce anger [of God],
To return the heart of fathers to the sons,
And to prepare the tribes of Israel.
Blessed is he who sees you and dies....

(Ben Sira 48:9–11)

Elijah Hides Himself

The voice of my beloved, behold, it cometh (Songs 2:8). These are
the voices which will come in the future before the Messiah.... For
the door [of Redemption] will not be opened completely at once,
but Elijah will come to one city and remain hidden to another, and
will speak to one man and remain hidden to his neighbor....

(Mid. Zuta, Shir haShirim 2:8)

In the second year of [King] Ahazia, Elijah was hidden, and
he will not be seen again until King Messiah comes. And then he
will be seen but will be hidden a second time, and seen again only
when Gog and Magog will come.

(Seder 'Olam Rabba, ch. 17)

Elijah the Recorder

[While waiting for the coming of the Messiah, Elijah] writes
the deeds of all the generations.

(Seder 'Olam Rabba, ch. 17)

At the outgoing of the Sabbath, Elijah sits under the Tree of
Life and writes the merits of all the Sabbath keepers.

(Maharil, *Hilkhot Shabbat*, end)

Elijah Comforts the Messiah

The fifth house [in Paradise] is built of silver and gold and pure gold and fine gold and glass and crystal, and the River Gihon flows through it, and its beams are gold and silver, and it emits all the fragrances of Lebanon. There are in it couches of silver and gold and scents, purple-blue and purple-red, woven by Eve, and worm-scarlet and goat [hair] woven by the angels. And in it dwell Messiah ben David and Elijah of blessed memory. And there is a *canopy of the wood of Lebanon, he made its pillars of silver, its top of gold, its seat of purple* (Songs 3:9–10). And in the canopy dwells the Messiah who is the love of the daughters of Jerusalem. *Its inside is inlaid with love* (ibid.). And Elijah of blessed memory takes the head of the Messiah and places it in his lap and says to him: "Be silent, for the end is near!" And the Fathers of the World, and all the Tribes [i.e. the twelve sons of Jacob], and Moses and Aaron, David and Solomon, and all the kings of Israel and of the House of David come to him every Monday and Thursday and every Sabbath and holiday, and weep with him, and hold him and say to him: "Be silent, and lean on your Creator, for the end is near...."

(Ma'ase diR. Y'hosu'a ben Levi, BhM 2:49–50)

Elijah Predicts the Coming of the Messiah

Elijah said to Rav Y'huda the brother of Rav Sala the Pious: "The world will exist for no less than eighty-five jubilees [that is, 4,250 years], and in the last jubilee the Son of David will come." He asked him: "In its beginning or at its end?" He answered: "I do not know." [Rav Y'huda then asked:] "Will it [the last jubilee] be complete or not?" He said to him: "I do not know." Rav Ashi said: "This is what Elijah told him: 'Until the last jubilee expect him not; from then on expect him.'"

(B. Sanh. 97b)

Elijah Makes Israel Repent

R. Y'huda said: "If Israel does not repent, they will not be redeemed. And Israel will not repent except because of the sufferings, and because of the oppression, and because of the harassment, and because they will have no livelihood. And there will be no great repentance in Israel until Elijah of blessed memory comes, as it is said, *Behold I will send you Elijah the prophet before the coming of the great and terrible day of the Lord, and he shall turn the heart of the fathers to the children and the heart of the children to their fathers* (Mal. 3:23).

(Pirqe R. Eliezer, ch. 43)

Elijah Reads the Book of Yashar

God opens a door for Elijah, and he goes out to Midian and leaves the sages who are in Jerusalem. And what does Elijah do? The whole desert which he traverses from Jerusalem to Midian is full of crags and wild beasts. But God makes miracles for him, and he comes and stands before the Messiah in Midian, and the Messiah goes away from there but Elijah stays. In that hour he takes out the Book of Yashar,[5] of which the whole Tora is but one line. The earth opens up beneath them [the enemies of Israel] and burns them, and becomes a great tomb for them.... And the Messiah comes to Midian and takes all its spoils. And thus to Damascus, and takes its spoils.... Until the kingdom of Edom falls. And from there the door opens to Rome....

The kings of the east gather in Tadmor [Palmyra], and Israel comes from Rome and offers up sacrifices in Jerusalem for seven days. And the Holy One, blessed be He, makes the wind blow and says to Israel: "Return to Tadmor against the kings of the east." And the kings of the nations say: "Shall we permit Israel to rebuild the Temple?" And they come to burn it, but the Holy One, blessed be He, goes and fights them.... And the Messiah comes to Tyre and Sidon and to Tadmor and Biri.... And all the nations will hear it and will gather and come against [Beth] Page and Acco, and they

---

5. The *Sefer haYashar* ("Book of the Straight") is quoted twice in the Bible (Josh. 10:12f. and 2 Sam. 1:19–27). It seems to have been an ancient book of heroic songs describing great events in the nation's history. In Biblical times the *Sefer haYashar* was well known, but then it was lost, and in the retrospect of legendary imagination it grew to gigantic proportions.

cry in the environs of Acco.... And the Holy One, blessed be He, rends the firmaments and shows Israel the Throne of Glory... and they pray and He receives them [their prayers]....

(Mid. Zuta, Shir haShirim 5:2)

Elijah Announces the Coming of the Messiah

In the hour when the Holy One, blessed be He, redeems Israel, three days prior to the coming of the Messiah, Elijah will come and will stand on the mountains of Israel and lament over them and say: "Mountains of the Land of Israel! How long will you stand dry and parched and desolate?" And his voice will be heard from one end of the world to the other. And he says to them: "Peace has come to the world," as it is said, *Behold upon the mountains the feet of the messenger who announceth peace* (Nah. 2:1). When the wicked hear this, they all rejoice and say to one another: "Peace has come to us."

On the second day Elijah comes and stands on the mountains of Israel and says: "Goodness has come to the world," as it is said, *The harbinger of goodness* (Isa. 52:7). On the third day he comes and says: "Salvation has come to the world," as it is said, *Announceth salvation* (ibid.). And when he sees the wicked, that they say thus, he says, "*Unto Zion thy God reigneth* (ibid.)," to teach you that salvation comes to Zion and her children but not to the wicked.

In that hour the Holy One, blessed be He, shows His glory and His kingship to all those who walk in the world, and He redeems Israel, and reveals Himself at their head.

(Pes. Rab., p. 161a)

In that hour Elijah will fly all over the world and will give tidings to Israel....

(Pirqe Mashiah, BhM 3:72)

Elijah the prophet and Messiah ben David
Will come to us and give us tidings
Of the building of the Temple
And the restoration of Jerusalem,
And let us say, Amen.
Elijah the prophet, the man who was zealous

For the name of God
The man who was given tidings of peace by Yekutiel,[6]
The man who will come and atone for the Children of Israel,
Elijah the prophet.
                    (Yemenite Sabbath-song. From Idelsohn,
                         N'ginot Y'hude Teman, p. 20.)

Elijah Introduces the Messiah

At that time Michael the great [celestial] prince will rise and
blow the shofar three times...and Messiah ben David and Elijah
will be revealed. And the two of them will go to Israel who will be
[at that time] in the desert of the peoples, and Elijah will say to
them: "This is the Messiah." And he will return their heart [which
will be faint] and will strengthen their hand....
                    (T'fillat R. Shim'on ben Yohai, BhM 2:125)

[After Israel has spent forty-five days in the desert] Elijah of
blessed memory will sprout out for them, and King Messiah with
him. And from there he will announce and say to them: "What
have you here, O Israel?" They say: "We are lost, we are annihilated, we are destroyed!" He says to them: "Arise, for I am Elijah,
and [this is] King Messiah." And they will not believe him. And he
says to them a third time: "Do you wish that I perform signs for
you as Moses did?" And Israel says: "Yes." Elijah of blessed
memory will perform for them seven miracles in that hour. The
first miracle: he brings Moses and his generation from the desert.... The second miracle: he brings up Korah and his whole
community.... The third miracle: he resurrects Nehemiah ben
Hushiel, who was killed in the gates of Jerusalem. The fourth
miracle: he reveals to them the hiding place of the [Holy] Ark and
of the vial of manna, and the pure Menorah with its seven lamps on
it, and the vial with the anointing oil. The fifth miracle: the Holy
One, blessed be He, will give him a rod of strength into his
hand.... The sixth miracle: he will grind all the mountains of Israel
like flour.... The seventh miracle: he will reveal to them the secret,

---

6. Another of the legendary names of Moses.

as it is written, *This is the covenant that I will make with the house of Israel after those days, saith the Lord, I will put My law in their inward parts, and in their heart I will write it, and I will be their God and they shall be My people* (Jer. 31:33).

(Pereq R. Yoshiyahu, BhM 6:115)

Elijah the Avenger

R. Aha expounded: "In the future, all the nations of the world will betray the Fourth Kingdom [Rome] and expel him from their midst, and they will leave him neither a city nor a country, and will chase him from nation to nation until he will reach Bet Guvrin and find there King Messiah. And he will surrender the kingship to him, and then he will flee to Bozrah. And the Holy One, blessed be He, will reveal Himself to him to slay him. And he says [to God]: "Did You not command that *fleeing to one of these cities* [of refuge] *he* [the manslayer] *might live* (Deut. 4:42)?" And the Holy One, blessed be He, answers him: "You did not read what is written next to it: *The avenger of blood shall put the murderer to death* (Num. 35:21). And it is written, *Israel is My son, My firstborn* (Exod. 4:22), and it is written, *My brethren and companions* (Ps. 122:8), and it is written, *The Children of Israel, a people near* [or related] *unto Him* (Ps. 148:14), and it is written, *My beloved* [dodi] *is white and ruddy* (Songs 5:10), and it is written, *His uncle* [dodo] *or his uncle's son should redeem him* (Lev. 25:49)."[7] Instantly the Holy One, blessed be He, seizes his [Rome's celestial] prince by the lock of his head and Elijah slaughters him, and his blood is dashed at his garments as he returns from there, as it is said, *Who is this who cometh from Edom, with crimsoned garments from Bozrah?* (Isa. 63:1).

(Yalqut Sim'oni par. 143, to
WaYishlah 33)

The Holy One, blessed be He, said to Israel: "In This World I sent an angel to put to flight the nations of the world before you.

---

7. The legend makes God quote all these Biblical verses in order to prove to Rome that He indeed is a close relative of Israel, and that therefore it is His right to act as the avenger of blood and mete out death punishment to Edom for his murder of the Children of Israel.

But in the Future to Come I Myself shall lead you and shall send Elijah before you...."

(Mid. Tanh. Mishpatim 18, end)

Moses and Elijah

The Holy One, blessed be He, said to Moses: "Moses, by your life, just as you have given your soul for Israel in This World, so in the Future to Come, when I bring them the prophet Elijah, the two of you will come as one... In that hour he will come and comfort Israel...."

(Deut. Rab. 3:17)

At times a master has an expert disciple.... They all arose and said [to Moses]: "Certainly you are the master, O Faithful Shepherd, about whom it is said, 'Moses received the Tora on Mount Sinai,' and from then on all are your disciples, from Joshua to the end of all generations. This is what is said, 'and he handed it on to Joshua, and Joshua to the elders, and the elders to the prophets,'[8] until the end of them all. Who is your expert disciple? We have seen that it is said, 'everything should be put aside until Elijah comes.'"[9] He said to them: "Certainly so it is, for he is a knowledgeable disciple.... As it is said of Aaron, *He shall be thy spokesman* (Exod. 4:16)... for I was *slow of speech and slow of tongue* (Exod. 4:10), for the Holy One, blessed be He, made me slow of speech in the Oral Law, and slow of tongue in the Written Law... [so in the Future to Come,] Elijah will be my spokesman. He will come and settle all the doubts and explain them to us at That Time...."

(Zohar 3:27B–28a)

Elijah the Messiah's Interpreter

And the Messiah will sit in the future in the Yeshiva, and

---

8. The quotation is from M. Avot 1:1.
9. I.e., Elijah is your expert disciple who can and will solve all the problems with which your other disciples could not cope.

those who walk on earth will come and sit before him to hear his new Tora and new commandments, and the deep wisdom which he will teach Israel.... And Elijah of blessed memory will stand before him as the interpreter. And when he expounds, his voice goes from one end of the world to the other.... In that hour [all the generations] rise from their graves in the Holy Spirit and come and sit in the Yeshiva before the Messiah to hear Midrashim and Halakhot [rulings] from his mouth.... And the Holy One, blessed be He, will reveal to them, through the mouth of Elijah of blessed memory, Halakhot of life, Halakhot of peace, Halakhot of piety, Halakhot of charity.... And he who hears a Midrash from the mouth of the Messiah never forgets it, because the Holy One, blessed be He, reveals Himself in the House of Study of the Messiah and pours out His Holy Spirit upon all those who walk in the world....

(Yemenite Midrash, pp. 349-50)

Elijah the Peacemaker

R. Shim'on ben Laqish said: "Pinhas is Elijah. The Holy One, blessed be He, said to him: 'You established peace between Israel and Me in This World,[10] even so in the Future to Come you will be the one who will establish peace between Me and My children....'" R. Eliezer said: "The Holy One, blessed be He, changed the' name of Pinhas to Elijah of blessed memory from among the inhabitants of Gilead. [This] teaches [us] that he made Israel repent on the Mount of Gilead...."

(Yalqut Shim'oni, par. 771)

Elijah the Arbitrator

R. Y'hoshu'a said: "I am in receipt [of a tradition] from Rabban Yohanan ben Zakkai, who heard it from his master, and his master from his master, [as] a Halakha of Moses from Mount Sinai, that Elijah does not come to declare things impure and pure, nor to remove and to bring near [i.e., settle problems of purity of

---

10. The reference is to the story told in Num. 25; cf. note 4 above.

descent]...." R. Shim'on said: "[He comes] to settle disputes."
And the sages said: "Neither to remove nor to bring near, but to
make peace in the world...."

(M. 'Eduyot 8:7)

[Concerning problems of ritually permitted food,] R. Yohanan said: "Elijah will in the future render a decision about this...."

(B. Menahot 45a)

Elijah the Pleader

R. Y'huda said: "The small children who were hidden during
their lifetime [i.e. died early] because of the sins of their fathers in
This World will rise in the World to Come in the midst of the group
of righteous. And their fathers [will rise] in the midst of the group
of wicked. And they [the children] will say before Him: 'Master of
the World! We died only because of the sins of our fathers. [Now]
let our fathers come [to join the righteous] for the sake of our
merits!' And He says to them: 'Your fathers sinned after you [had
died], and their sins serve as their accusers.'" R. Y'huda bar Ilai in
the name of R. Y'hoshu'a ben Levi [said]: "In that hour Elijah of
blessed memory sits and pleads their defense and says to them:
'Say before Him: Master of the World! Which is the greater
[divine] attribute? The attribute of goodness or the attribute of
chastisement? Certainly the attribute of goodness is ample and the
attribute of chastisement is scant. We died because of the sins of
our fathers. If the attribute of goodness is ample, should our fathers
not be allowed to join us?' God says to them: 'Well did you plead
your fathers' defense. Let them come to you....'" And thus they
will be saved for the sake of their children's merits. Therefore
every man is in duty bound to teach his son Tora, so that the son
may save him from Gehenna.

(Eccl. Rab. 4:1)

Elijah the Provider

These are the three signs that Elijah will in the future reveal to

Israel: The flask of the manna, the flask of water, and the flask of the anointing oil.[11]

(Mekh. diR. Yishm'el, p. 80)

Elijah Awakens the Dead

The resurrection of the dead will come through Elijah of blessed memory, Amen.

(M. Sota 9:15)

The resurrection of the dead will bring about [the coming of] Elijah of blessed memory.

(Y. Sheqalim 47c bot.)

Elijah of blessed memory will come and give good tidings to Israel, to those who will be alive and to the dead. He will rebuild the Temple of the Lord, and Egypt will be made desolate, and the Temple will stand firmly established.

Messiah ben David, Elijah, and Zerubbabel, peace be upon him, will ascend the Mount of Olives. And Messiah will command Elijah to blow the shofar. The light of the six days of Creation will return and will be seen, the light of the moon will be like the light of the sun, and God will send full healing to all the sick of Israel. The second blast which Elijah will blow will make the dead rise. They will rise from the dust and each man will recognize his fellow man, [and so will] husband and wife, father and son, brother and brother. All will come to the Messiah from the four corners of the earth, from east and from west, from north and from south. The Children of Israel will fly on the wings of eagles and come to the Messiah. A pillar of fire will come forth from the Temple and will be a portent to all those who see it, [proving] that just now the Temple has been completed, so that they will know and be convinced. At the third blast which he will blow, the Shekhina will appear. At the fourth blast, the mountains will become a plain and fall silent before the whole earth: Tabor and Carmel, Hermon and the Mount of Olives. And the distance between the mountains will

11. According to the Aggada, these three miraculously inexhaustible flasks were in the possession of Israel, but were hidden by King Joshiah when the imminent destruction of the Temple was announced to him.

be eighty parasangs. And the Temple will appear as Ezekiel prophesied it. And two angels will bring up the Golden Gate [of the Temple] which was hidden in the earth, as God commanded them, and will set it up as it was in the first days....

(Ma'ase Daniel, pp. 225–26)

Elijah the Redeemer

And the Lord showed me four craftsmen. Then I said: "What come these to do?" And He spoke saying: "... These are come to frighten them, to cast down the horns of the nations which lifted up their horns against the land of Judah to scatter it..." (Zech. 2:3). Who are these four craftsmen? R. Hana ben Bizna said in the name of R. Shim'on the Pious: "Messiah ben David, Messiah ben Joseph, Elijah, and the Priest of Justice...."[12]

(B. Sukka 52b)

Two prophets arose for Israel from the tribe of Levi: Moses was the first and Elijah the last. And both redeem Israel on a mission [of God]. Moses redeemed them from Egypt... and Elijah will redeem them in the Future to Come.... Moses redeemed them from Egypt in the beginning, and they still have not returned and not been subjugated in Egypt. And Elijah, when he redeems them from the Fourth [Kingdom], from Edom [Rome], they will never again be subjugated, but it will be an everlasting salvation. Thus you find that Moses and Elijah are equal to one another in everything.

(Pes. Rab., p. 13a)

Everywhere in the Bible the name of Jacob is spelled without the letter *vav* [i.e. Y'qv], except for five places; and everywhere the name of Elijah is spelled with a *vav* [i.e. Eliyah*u*], except for five places. Why? To teach you that Elijah will come and redeem the seed of Jacob. Jacob took the *vav* from the name of Elijah as a pledge that Elijah would come and announce the redemption of the world to his children.

(Mid. Haser w'Yater, pp. 16, 42, and Rashi ad Lev. 26:42)

---

12. On the four craftsmen see L. Ginzberg, *Unbekannte Sekte.*

15

Gog and Magog

Ezekiel's great prophecy about Gog of the Land of Magog (see chapter 1) became the basis in Talmudic and Medieval times of the myth of the global Armageddon between the armies of Gog and Magog and the forces of the Messiah. Especially in the Middle Ages, the theme was elaborated and built up into detailed accounts chronicling the horrors of holocaustal battles which would be fought at the End of Days. The forces of the Messiah are almost crushed by the overwhelming power of Gog and Magog, aided by all the nations of the world, but in the end the direct, miraculous intervention of God secures the victory for His Redeemer.

The warlike mood permeating these legends comes as a surprise to those who know how weak was the position, how peaceable the character, and how humble the behavior of the Jews in the Diaspora. However, these two facets are not contradictory; they are, rather, complementary. The long centuries of oppression and persecution drove home a bitter lesson to all Jews, who lived as a defenseless minority in the midst of an often hostile and brutal Gentile majority. The lesson was that in order to be left alone, to be allowed to eke out a living, to be enabled to stay put in the places in which God's inscrutable will implanted them, they had to learn how to react with humility to insult, with resignation to injustice, and with patient endurance to hurt. Yet the suppressed reaction of rage had to find some sort of outlet, if not in overt behavior, at least in imaginary action. Since they could not take revenge on their tormentors, they fantasized about a divine retribution that would be meted out by God to the Gentiles in the days of the Messiah. Thus the Messianic legends of great wars against the Gentiles, and of a global victory over them, served as something of an emotional safety-valve through which pent-up rage could be let off and psychological satisfaction achieved.

This is the psychogenesis of a book like the medieval *Sefer haYashar* (not to be confused with the lost *Sefer haYashar* mentioned in the Bible, cf. chapter 14, note 5), a Hebrew legendary chronicle which depicts Biblical figures, such as the sons of Jacob, Moses, Joshua, as greater-than-life heroes who excel in fighting and wreak havoc among the enemies of Israel. And this is the origin of the many legends telling about the global wars in which Israel, led by the Messiah and aided by divine miracles, will destroy the infernal hosts of Gog and Magog, of Armilus, and of all the nations of the world. Chapters 15 through 18 present this legendary material, grouped, as far as the nature of the narratives allows, according to its constituent themes.

Two men remained in the camp. The name of one of them was Eldad, and the name of the other Medad. And the Holy Spirit descended upon them... and both prophesied as one and said: "In the End of Days, Gog and Magog and their armies will fall into the hands of King Messiah, and for seven years the Children of Israel will light fire from the shares of their weapons; they will not go out to the forest and will not cut down a [single] tree....

(Targ. Yer. to Num. 11:26)

R. Akiba said: "Five things will have a duration of twelve months:... the punishment of Gog and Magog will last twelve months."

(M. 'Eduyot 2:10)

The Holy One, blessed be He, showed Moses [before his death]... the Plain of Jericho on which Gog and all his masses will fall.

(Sifre Deut., p. 149b)

The sages said: "The exodus from Egypt will be remembered *all the days of thy life* (Deut. 16:3)—this refers to the future, to the days of the Messiah." Ben Zoma said to the sages: "Will, indeed, the exodus from Egypt be remembered in the days of the Messiah? Is it not written, *Behold, days will come, saith the Lord, that they shall no more say, As the Lord liveth who brought up the Children of Israel out of the Land of Egypt, but, As the Lord liveth who brought up and who led the seed of the House of Israel out of the north country and from all the countries whither I had driven them (Jer. 23:7 −8)."* They said to him: "Not that the exodus from Egypt will be uprooted from its place, but that the subjugation by the kingdoms will be the main thing [remembered] and the exodus from Egypt will be secondary... " *Behold, I will do a new thing, now shall it spring forth* (Isa. 43:19). R. Yosef taught: "This is the War of Gog and Magog. To what can this be likened? To a man who was walking on the road and met a wolf and escaped from it. He went on and on telling the story of [his encounter with] the wolf. Then he met a lion and escaped from it, and went on and on telling the story of the lion. Then he met a snake and escaped from it, whereupon he forgot the two previous events and went on and on telling the story of the snake." Thus Israel: the later troubles make them forget the earlier ones.

(B. Ber. 12b-13a)

R. Yose said: "In the future to come, the nations of the world will come and become proselytes." Will they be accepted? Is it not taught that in the days of the Messiah no proselytes will be accepted?... [However,] they will become self-made proselytes, not formally admitted. They will put *Tefillin* [phylacteries] on their foreheads and on their arms, and *Tzitzit* [fringes] on their garments, and *Mezuzot* [capsules with Biblical texts] on their doorposts. [But] when they see the war of Gog and Magog, they will ask them against whom they are coming, and they will answer, "Against the Lord and His Messiah...." Thereupon the proselytes will tear [those appurtenances of] the commandments from them, and will go away.... But the Holy One, blessed be He, will sit and laugh at them.... To this R. Yitzhaq added that on that day alone is there laughter for the Holy One, blessed be He....

(B. 'Av. Zar. 3b)

Behold, tomorrow about this time I will cause it to rain a very grievous hail such as hath not been in Egypt since the day it was founded even until now (Ex. 9:18).... However, there will be like it in the time to come. When? In the days of Gog and Magog....

(Ex. Rab. 12:2)

R. Levi said: "In the Future to Come, Gog and Magog will say: 'The first ones were fools, for they occupied themselves with plans against Israel, and did not know that they have a Patron in Heaven. I shall not act like them, but first of all shall attack their Patron, and thereafter attack them....' But the Only One, blessed be He, says to him: 'You wicked one! Me you want to attack? By your life, I shall wage war against you....'"

(Lev. Rab. 27:11)

At that time the angels of heaven will say to one another: "We have a nation on earth, and her merits are small, and she has neither kings nor dominions to go forth and wage war against the camps of Gog. What shall we do to our sister on the day on which the nations plan to march forth against her in battle?" Michael, the [heavenly] prince of Israel, will say: "If she is like a fortress among the nations, and will give money for the glorification of the oneness of the name of the Master of the World, we and you with her teachers will surround her like layers of silver and the nations will have no permission to subdue her, just as the worm has no permission to subdue the silver. And even if she should be poor in the commandments, we shall ask mercy for her before the Lord and He will remember her for the merit of the Tora with which the children occupy themselves, and which is written on the tablet of the heart, and she will stand up against the nations like a cedar."

(Targum Song of Songs 8:8—9)

The Holy One, blessed be He, said to Gog: "Say not that I do not know what you are thinking in your heart.... I, the Lord, scrutinize the heart. And say not that from the time I created you I do not know your heart, for even before I created you I knew what you were going to think in the future. . . ."

The Holy One, blessed be He, said to Gog: "Say not that I do not know what you planned to do. See, many generations ago I said to Eldad and Medad that they should prophesy about you, as it is said, *But there remained two men in the camp, the name of the one was Eldad and the name of the other Medad . . . and they prophesied in the camp* (Num. 11:26). What does it mean, *And they prophesied, but they did so no more* (ibid., v. 25)? They prophesied and said that after Gog and Magog there will be no more exile nor enslavement. See, how many generations ago they prophesied about you!"

(Aggadat B'reshit, ed. Buber, p. 5)

And what did Gog think? He said: "Pharaoh who went forth against Israel was a fool, for he let their Patron [i.e., God] be and went against them, and likewise Amalek and Sisera, and all those who arose against them. They let the Holy One, blessed be He, be; they were fools. But I, what will I do? I shall go forth first against the Patron of Israel, [since] if I first slay the Messiah, he will cause other Messiahs to arise. Therefore I shall go against the Holy One, blessed be He. . . ." What did they [the hosts of Gog] do? They stood on their feet and looked up toward the Holy One, blessed be He, and said: "*Come, let us cut them off from being a nation, that the name of Israel may be no more in remembrance* (Ps. 83:5)." What does "the Name[1] of Israel" mean? They said: "Let us uproot Him who wrote, *Blessed be the Lord, the God of Israel* (Ps. 41:14)." And what does the Holy One, blessed be He, do to them from Above? They stand on their feet, and He punishes them. . . . [He says:] "Those feet which wanted to stand up against Me, *Their flesh shall consume away while they stand upon their feet* (Zech. 14:12). And those eyes which looked up, *And their eyes shall consume away in their sockets* (ibid.). And that tongue which spoke against the Lord, *And their tongue shall consume away in their mouth* (ibid.)."

The Holy One, blessed be He, says to them: "At first you were not at peace with one another. . . . And now you made peace with one another so as to come against Me. . . . I, too, shall do likewise. I shall call the birds and the beasts who were not at peace with one another, and I shall cause them to be at peace with one

---

1. The legend interprets the word "Name" as referring to God. In Rabbinic literature "the Name" is often used instead of "God."

another in order to go forth against you. And because you said, *That the name of Israel may be no more in remembrance* (Ps. 83:5), by your life, you will die and they will bury you and will take a name [i.e., become famous] in the world."

(Aggadat B'reshit, ed. Buber, pp. 5—7)

R. Y'huda haLevi bar Shalom, and R. Pinhas haKohen, and Rav Huna, all the three of them said that Gog and Magog would come against Israel in the future to come three times, and the third time they would come up against Jerusalem and go to Judah, and dictate to them, for they are mighty men. . . .

Behold I will make Jerusalem a cup of staggering unto all the peoples round about (Zech. 12:2). What is "cup of staggering"? [It means] that He will in the future make peoples drink the cup of staggering of blood. . . . When they [Gog and Magog] go up there, what do they do? They assign two warriors to every one of the Children of Israel. Why? So that they should not escape. When the heroes of Judah ascend and reach Jerusalem, they pray in their heart. . . . In that hour the Holy One, blessed be He, gives heroism to Judah and they draw their weapons and smite those men on their right and on their left, and slay them.

(Mid. Tehillim, Ps. 119, ed. Buber, pp. 488—89)

Michael, the Great [celestial] Prince of Israel, divulged a secret to the Prophet Elijah on Mount Carmel, [about] the end and the time which will come to pass in the future days, at the end of four kingdoms, in the days of the fourth king who will be in the future: The spirit of God carried me and took me to the south of the world, and I saw there a high place, burning in fire, and no creature could enter it. And again the spirit carried me and took me to the east of the world, and I saw there stars battling one another and resting not. Again the spirit carried me and took me to the west of the world, and there I saw souls being punished with great pain, each according to his deeds. And then Michael said to me: "The end of the future will be at the end of days, in the days of the king who will be in the future, and Harmalet is his name." And some say, Tarmila is his name. R. El'azar says, Hartahshasta is his name. R. Y'huda ben B'tera says, Cyrus is his name. R. Shim'on ben Yohai says, Hakashra is his name. And the Halakha [decision] is according to R. Shim'on, who said Hakashra is his name.

The last king in Persia will go up to Rome for three years, year after year, until he rebels against her for twelve months. And three mighty warriors will come up from the sea to meet him, and they will be delivered into his hand. . . .

And these will be the signs which Daniel foresaw in him [King Hakashra]: His face is elongated, between his eyes is haughtiness, his stature is very tall, the soles of his feet are arched, and his thighs are thin. And he will stretch forth his hand on that day against the faithful nation [Israel], and he will shake it on that day three times. And all the constellations will gather and go to one place. They [the king's men] will oppress houses and rob fields, and slay the orphan and the widow in the marketplace. . . .

On the twentieth of Nissan, a king will rise from the sea and destroy and shake the world, and he will come to the holy mountain of the gazelle [i.e., the Temple Mount in Jerusalem] and will burn it. Accursed be among the Women she who will bear him! [This is] that horn which Daniel saw. And on that day there will be suffering and war against Israel.

The second war will be waged by Demetrus son of Poriphus and Anphilipus son of Panapos. And with them will be 100,000 horsemen and 100,000 foot soldiers, and hidden in ships will be 300,000.

On the twentieth of Elul, Messiah will come, and his name is Yinnon. And on that day Gabriel will descend for nine to ten hours, and will devastate the world [and slay] 92,000 men. On the twentieth of Teveth, the third war will put an end to Qirtalus and all the countries with them, a very great multitude, from the Great Plain to Jaffa and to Ashkelon.

And on the twentieth of Shevat, Messiah will come and angels of destruction descend and wreak havoc in all that multitude, and not a soul will be left.

In that hour the Holy One, blessed be He, will say to Abraham: "Your children will in the future sink down to the lowest rung. . . . But thereafter they will be exalted over all nations. . . . And all the nations will come and prostrate themselves before each and every one of Israel, and lick the dust of their feet. . . ."

On the twentieth of Adar, Messiah will come, and with him 30,000 saintly men. . . . And when the nations of the world see this, instantly each one of them will be crushed, they and their horses. . . . In that hour the Holy One, blessed be He, will say to the nations of the world: "Woe to you, you evil ones, for at the end of the four kingdoms all of you will be ejected from the world!"

And one kor [measure] of wheat will make nine hundred kors, and the wine and the oil likewise. And each tree will be loaded with delicacies and fruits. . . . And Israel will eat and rejoice for four years. And thereafter the Holy One, blessed be He, will bring up Gog and Magog and all its legions. And then all the peoples of the earth will gather and surround Jerusalem to fight it. And the Holy One, blessed be He, will go up and fight them, and Messiah will come, and the Holy One, blessed be He, will help him, and wage war against them. . . . On that day the mountains will tremble and the hills dance, and the walls and towers collapse. And the Holy One, blessed be He, will gather all the fowl of heaven and the beasts of the earth to eat of their flesh and to drink of their blood. . . . And for seven years Israel will use their weapons for fuel. . . .

And these are the cities which will be destroyed: Jericho, Beerot, Bet Horon, Susin, Malka and Arad, Shalom and Shimron, Bet Magdiel, Tyre and Bet Halafot and Lod, Buz and Bet 'Enam, Hamat, Sefar, Harsha, Antiochia, Alexandria, and Edom. And all the cities of Israel will be surrounded by fire and by ministering angels. . . .

(Sefer Eliyahu, BhM 3:65−67)

We have learned: The seventy guardians [of the nations of the world] will in the future gather the armies of the whole world from all sides to wage war against Jerusalem, the holy city, and to take counsel against the Holy One, blessed be He. And what do they say? "Let us first attack the Patron, and then his people and his Temple." Then the Holy One, blessed be He, laughs. . . . At that time the Holy One, blessed be He, clothes Himself in grandeur and uproots them from the world. . . .

R. Abba in the name of old R. Yesa said, and thus also did R. Shim'on say: "In the future the Holy One, blessed be He, will bring back to life all those kings who afflicted Israel and Jerusalem: Andrianus [Hadrian], Lupinus, and Nebuchadnezzar and Sanherib, and the other kings of the nations who destroyed His House. And He will let them rule as before, and the other nations will gather with them. And the Holy One, blessed be He, will take vengeance on them in a revelation in the environs of Jerusalem . . . as it is written, *In the greatness of Thine excellency Thou overthrowest them that rise up against Thee* (Exod. 15:7). This refers to the time when the Messiah comes, so that this song is a song for all eternity."

(Zohar 2:58b)

[God says:] "Ephraim, My firstborn, you sit on My right until I subdue the army of the hosts of Gog and Magog, your enemies, under your footstool...."

The Messiah will arise over Israel, will gather the exiles of Israel in Jerusalem, and will rebuild Jerusalem.... And all the kings of the nations of the world will come to the door of the Messiah and will serve before him and bring him presents.... And all the nations of the world will come and seek out the Children of Israel to be tutors and wet nurses for them.... And more than that: they will lick the dust from under the feet of Israel and will kiss them, like this snake which licks dust with its mouth and tongue.... And Israel will dwell in safety in its land, the Land of Israel, in peace and quiet and in security for forty years.

And after forty years Gog and Magog will come upon the Land of Israel and will launch three wars against the Messiah and the People of Israel, in the month of Teveth.... And how will Gog and Magog come into the country? We are taught that the Holy One, blessed be He, will arouse the spirit of Gog and Magog, and will cause [evil] inclinations and [a desire for] riches and honor and silver and gold and precious stones and pearls and property and booty and spoils to rule them.... And for seven years there will gather great hosts and many peoples, officers and charioteers, and riders on horses, and holders of shields and bucklers and spears, and shooters of bows and throwers of arrows without end and without number. And at the end of seven years up will go a great company and a huge army, with horses and chariots, with bows and arrows, with shields and bucklers, with shield and spear, to the Land of Israel from the ends of the North, like a devastation, and they will cover the whole Land of Israel, four hundred parasangs, like a cloud which comes to cover the land.... And in one hour the earth will jump [and they will advance] five hundred parasangs. ... And when they reach the Land of Israel, the nations of the world will hear it, and many peoples will come up with them, and a great multitude, and they will conquer all Israel.

In the first ten days they will take much booty and capture

many spoils, and gather riches and herds of sheep and cattle, camels and donkeys, horses and mules, and men and women captives. During the next ten days they will capture and conquer cities and towns, districts and villages, in the Land of Israel, and will collect silver and gold, precious stones and pearls without measure and without number. And in the last ten days they will come and sit in the gates of Jerusalem and drive half of the city into exile . . . but the remainder of the people will not be cut off from the city.

In that hour the Messiah will come forth from Jerusalem to make war with them, and all the pious will be with him, a great multitude. And the Messiah will issue decrees over them, and in that hour a thousand thousands and a myriad myriads of them will die. . . . In that hour the Holy One, blessed be He, will descend from the highest heaven above, and the ministering angels with Him. . . . And they will make war against Gog and Magog. . . .

And how will be the wars of Gog and Magog? The Holy One, blessed be He, will wage war against them with six measures of war, and they are: pestilence, blood, pouring rain, hailstones, fire, and brimstone. . . . Pestilence is none other than the Angel of Death to whom He will give power over their souls in that hour. . . . Blood is their heavenly prince who is like unto blood, and whom God casts down from heaven. . . . In that hour the Holy One, blessed be He, will grab a handful of fire from the River of Fire and hurl it at them, at Gog and Magog and their hosts, and the fire will turn into torches which will enter their nostrils, and their souls will be consumed by the fire, but their bodies will not, for all the beasts of the fields and all the fowl of heaven will be ordered to come there that day to eat their flesh and to drink their blood. And all those who walk on earth will see it and will ask about it and say: "What is the nature of this fire which has been burning in the West for seven days and seven nights?" And they will be told: "It is Gog and Magog, who have come against Ephraim, the righteous Messiah of the Holy One, blessed be He, and against His people Israel, to make war against them. And the Holy One, blessed be He, fights for them, and He caused fire and brimstone to rain upon them and burned their souls in their places. . . ."

In that hour the whole world becomes affrighted and they tremble because they hear the power and the greatness of the Holy One, blessed be He. . . .

Thereafter the inhabitants of Jerusalem, by permission of the Messiah, go out, company by company and group by group, and plunder their plunderers and despoil their despoilers. And for three months they will gather all their belongings and all the weapons they had with them, buckler and shield, bow and arrows, armor and helmet, lance and spear and hand stick, and bring all of it into Jerusalem, and they will fill Jerusalem like a pomegranate with the riches of Gog and Magog. And for seven years they will not take wood from the fields and from the vineyards, and will not cut trees from the forests and from [the shores of] the lakes, nor [branches] from all the trees, but all the inhabitants of the Land of Israel will make fire with the weapons.... And for seven months all the winged birds and all the fowl of heaven and all the beasts of the field will eat their flesh and drink their blood, and lick their fat, until they sate and fatten their bones to such an extent that they will be unable to flee and to run because of the abundance of their fat....

In that hour all the winged birds and all the fowl of heaven and all the beasts of the field will open their mouths in praise of their Creator and will say: *The truth of the Lord endureth forever, Hallelujah!* (Ps. 117:2).

At the end of seven months all Israel will arise and bury them in the Valley of Aravim to the east of the sea in the Land of Israel, and they will cleanse the whole land of the bones of Gog and Magog....

(Mid. Alpha Betot, 2:438—42)

16

Armilus

In the preceding chapter we got acquainted with the evil king of many names who will lead the armies of the nations against God, Israel, and the Messiah. In a group of medieval texts this king is called Armilus, which name is reflected in the forms Harmalet and Tarmila (see chapter 15). The earliest reference to Armilus dates from the seventh century. It is found in the Targum to Isaiah 11:4, which reads in the original, *And with the breath of his lips he* [i.e. the Shoot out of the stock of Jesse] *shall slay the wicked*, but which it renders, "And with the speech of his lips he shall slay the wicked Armilus." From about the same time dates the Targum Jonathan which, in its rendering of Deut. 34:3, adds to the list of places God showed Moses before his death the following: "...and the cataclysm [*pur'anut*] of the wicked Armaglus [or Armalgus, i.e. Armilus], and the battle orders of Gog; and in that time of great suffering, Michael will arise with an arm for the Redeemer."[1]

Armilus is a Satanic creature, born of a stone statue of a woman which had been impregnated either by "worthless people" or by Satan himself. Myths of this type were current in several places, among them in Italy, and it is quite possible

---

1. Cf. M. Ginsburger, *Pseudo-Jonathan*, p.365.

that the Jewish Armilus legend reflects some such foreign influence.[2] In the Midrash, the eschatological role of Armilus is to slay Messiah ben Joseph, and to be slain in turn by Messiah ben David. Many attempts have been made to explain the Midrashic name of this mysterious satanic king. Some derive Armilus from Romulus, others from Heremolaos (i.e., "Destroyer of peoples"), or from Suetonius' description of Caligula who, he says, *armillatus in publicum processit* (chs. 50 and 52), and was tall, bald, had thin legs, and a crooked eye—all features reminiscent of the Midrashic portraiture of Armilus. Still others connect the name with the Persian Ahriman, the god of evil. Remarkable is the statement in one version of the Midrash that he is called "Antichrist."

And after all this, Satan will descend and go to Rome to the stone statue and have connection with it in the manner of the sexual act, and the stone will become pregnant and give birth to Armilus. He will rule for forty days. And his hand will be heavier than forty *se'ah* (measures). And he will issue evil decrees against Israel, and men of good deeds will cease while men of plunder will multiply. If Israel is worthy, Messiah ben David will sprout up in Upper Galilee, and will go up to Jerusalem, and will build the Temple and offer sacrifices. And fire will descend and consume his sacrifices, and Israel will dwell in safety all his days....

> (Mid. 'Aseret haSh'vatim, OM, 466)

They say that there is in Rome a stone of marble, and it has the shape of a beautiful girl. She was created in the six days of the Beginning. And worthless people from the nations of the world come and lie with her, and she becomes pregnant, and at the end of nine months she bursts open, and a male child emerges, in the shape of a man whose height is twelve cubits and whose breadth is two cubits. His eyes are red and crooked, the hair of his head is red like gold, and the steps of his feet are green, and he has two skulls.

---

2. Cf. R. Patai, *Adam w'Adama* 2:14ff.

They call him Armilus. And he will go to Edom [Rome] and say to them: "I am your Messiah, I am your god!" And he will mislead them and they will instantly believe in him, and make him their king. And all the Children of Esau [i.e. the Romans] will gather and come to him. And he will go and announce to all cities saying to the Children of Esau: "Bring me my Tora ['Law'] which I gave you!" And the nations of the world will come and bring the book...and he will say to them: "This is the book which I gave you." And he will [further] say to them: "I am your god, I am your Messiah and your god!"

In that hour he will send [a messenger] to Nehemiah [i.e. Messiah ben Joseph] and to all Israel, and say to them: "Bring me your Tora and testify that I am god." Instantly all Israel becomes confused and frightened. And in that hour Nehemiah will rise, and three men with him from among the Children of Ephraim, and they will go with him, and the Tora scroll will be with them, and they read before him: "*I am the Lord*" and "*Thou shalt have no other gods*" (Exod. 20:2–3). And he will say: "There is nothing of this in your Tora, and I shall not let go of you until you believe that I am god in the manner in which the nations of the world believe in me."

Instantly Nehemiah stands up against him and says to him: "You are not God, but Satan." And he says to them: "Why do you deny me? I shall command that you be killed!" And he says to his servants: "Seize Nehemiah!" Instantly thirty thousand warriors rise from Israel and make war against him, and slay two hundred thousand of the camp of Armilus. And the wrath of Armilus is kindled, and he gathers all the armies of the nations of the world, and makes war against the Children of Israel, and he slays of Israel a thousand thousands. And he also slays Nehemiah at noontime.... And those who are left of Israel will flee to the desert of the nations and will dwell there for forty-five days without bread and without water; only the grass of the field will be their food. And after forty-five days Armilus will come and wage war against Egypt and capture it.... And then he will turn and put this face toward Jerusalem to destroy it a second time....

At that time Michael the Great Prince will rise and blow the shofar three times.... That shofar is the right horn of the ram of Isaac, and the Holy One, blessed be He, increases its length to a thousand cubits. And he will blow *T'qi'a*, and Messiah ben David and Elijah will be revealed, and both will go to Israel who are in the desert. And Elijah will tell them: "This is the Messiah!" And he will revive their hearts and strengthen their hands....And all Israel will know the sound of the shofar and will hear that He has redeemed Israel....

And those lost in the Land of Assyria will come. And instantly the fear of the Lord will fall among the peoples and upon all the nations. And Israel will return with the Messiah until they reach the Desert of Judah, and they will meet together with all the Children of Israel, and come to Jerusalem, and ascend the steps of the House of David which will be left from the destruction. And the Messiah will sit there.

And Armilus will hear that a king arose for Israel, and he will gather the armies of all the nations of the world, and they will come to King Messiah and to Israel. And the Holy One, blessed be He, will fight for Israel and will say to the Messiah: "Sit at my right." And the Messiah will say to Israel: "Gather together and stand and see the salvation of the Lord." And instantly the Holy One, blessed be He, will go forth and fight against them....May that time and that period be near!

(T'fillat R. Shim'on ben Yohai, BhM 4:124−26)

And when the days of the Messiah arrive, Gog and Magog will come up against the Land of Israel, because they will hear that Israel is without a king and sits in safety. Instantly they will take with them seventy-one nations and go up to Jerusalem, and they will say: "Pharaoh was a fool to command that the males [of the Israelites] be killed and to let the females live. Balaam was an idiot that he wanted to curse them and did not know that their God had blessed them. Haman was insane in that he wanted to kill them, and he did not know that their God can save them. I shall not do as they did, but shall fight against their God first, and thereafter I shall slay them...." And the Holy One, blessed be He, will say to him: "You wicked one! You want to wage war against Me? By your life, I shall wage war against you!" Instantly the Holy One, blessed be He, will cause hailstones, which are hidden in the firmament, to descend upon him, and will bring upon him a great plague....

And after him will arise another king, wicked and insolent, and he will wage war against Israel for three months, and his name is Armilus. And these are his marks: he will be bald, one of his eyes will be small, the other big. His right arm will be only as long as a hand, and his left arm will be two and one half cubits long. And he will be leprous on his forehead. And his right ear will be stopped up and the other open. And when somebody will come to him to say something good to him, he will bend to him his stopped-up ear, but if a man will want to tell him something evil, he will bend to him his open ear. And he will go up to Jerusalem and will slay Messiah ben Joseph....

    And thereafter will come Messiah ben David.... And he will kill the wicked Armilus.... And thereafter the Holy One, blessed be He, will gather all Israel who are dispersed here and there.

(Mid. waYosha', BhM 1:56)

    And He lets Messiah ben Joseph sprout up for them, and he will bring them up to Jerusalem and rebuild the Temple and offer up sacrifices. And fire will descend from heaven and consume their sacrifices.... If they have not acquired merits, Messiah ben Ephraim will come; and if they have acquired merits, Messiah ben David will come. And a wicked king will arise, and his name is Armilus. He is bald, and his eyes are small, and his forehead is leprous, and his right ear plugged up, and his left ear is open.... And he is a creature of Satan and of stone, and he goes up against Jerusalem and wages war there with Messiah ben Ephraim, in the eastern gate.... And Israel will be exiled to a desert of marshes, to graze in the salty flats and the roots of broom bushes, for forty-five days. And then they will be tested and purified. ...And Messiah ben Ephraim will die there, and Israel will mourn him. And thereafter the Holy One, blessed be He, will reveal to them Messiah ben David, and Israel will want to stone him and they will say to him: "You spoke lies, for already the Messiah was killed and no other Messiah will arise." And they will despise him.... And he will retire and hide himself from them....

    And when Israel suffers, they will again cry out because of hunger and thirst, and instantly the Holy One, blessed be He, will reveal Himself to them in His glory.... And King Messiah will sprout up there.... And he will blow upon that wicked Armilus and slay him....

    And the Holy One, blessed be He, will whistle and gather all Israel and bring them up to Jerusalem.... And fire will descend from heaven and devour Jerusalem down to three cubits. And He will evict the foreigner, the uncircumcised, and the impure from

her midst. And from heaven will descend built-up and embellished Jerusalem, and in her will be seventy-two pearls which will shine from one end of the world to the other. And all the nations will walk in the light.... And a built-up Temple will descend from heaven, and it will be tied to the *Z'vul* [one of the heavens], as Moses, peace be upon him, saw it through the Holy Spirit....
(Nistarot R. Shim'on ben Yohai, BhM 3:80)

And the tenth kind will be Armilus son of the stone, which is in the winter house of the frivolous. And all the nations from all the places will come and stand before the stone, and will burn incense. And they will not be able to look at her because of her beauty, and all those whose heart will rise to look at her will not be able to. And these are the distinguishing marks of Armilus son of stone: The hair of his head is dyed, and his hands [hang down] until the steps of his feet, and the length of his face is a span, and his stature is twelve cubits high, and his eyes are deep, and he has two skulls. And he will ascend and rule in Imus [Emmaus?], the countries of Satan which his father took. And all those who see him will be frightened by him. And thereafter Menahem ben Amiel [the Messiah] will come before him from the Valley of Shittim, and will blow into his face and kill him....
(Sefer Zerubbabel, Wertheimer, *Bate Midrashot* 2:502)

...the land of the enemy...and to bring low all those who raised themselves above them, and their thought will not prevail, and the earth will shake and quake.... And the Children of Gomer will fight against the Japhetites.... After these things a man will go forth from the Desert of San'a,[3] from among the Children of Yoqtan,[4] tall of stature and comely of visage, and a thinker of thoughts, and a teller of the end. And the land of his birth is Gilgal, and through him all the Children of al-Galb[5] will be cut off and no man will remain of them to sit on the royal throne, for rumors will

---

3. The capital city of Yemen.

4. The Biblical Yoqtan (Gen. 10:25–29), in Arabic Qahtan, is considered by Arab genealogists the ancestor of the South Arabian tribes. This ancestry makes the "man of San'a" an Arab, but in the sequel he appears to be a Jew intent on making the religion of the Lord of Hosts supreme.

5. The reference possibly is to the Beni Kalb, one of the most important Yemeni or Qahtani tribes.

frighten them, from the voice of a great tumult. And they will go out in a hurry, and will flee to the Land of the East. At that time he of San'a will come with a great host, very numerous, like unto the sand which is on the shore of the sea, to the great land of Qamonia Afriqia.... [6] And he will find it in confusion, perplexity, and complete defeat, and its people like a flock which has no shepherd. And they will go against it to take the whole land of the East and Edom and the Mountain of Esau and the whole land of Cush. And he will break the languages of all religions and laws, for he will say that there will be one law and one religion, that of the Lord of Hosts. And he will slay the warriors of the Children of Ishmael and the Children of the East, and also the inhabitants of Tyre. And he will gather the gold and the silver into the city of Jerusalem. Then his name will become great, and his heart will be lifted up....

And in his days will rise up a false Messiah, a speaker of lies and emptiness and deceit. And his name will grow great and his heart become haughty, and many people will go astray after him and will die. His feet will be like the feet of a bear, and his hands like the paws of a panther. He will be beautiful of eyes, and will break jaws, will roar like a young lion and growl like a lion. He will make the dead come alive, and will set free the prisoners of the pit, and open the eyes of the blind. And he will bring manna down from heaven for them, and will make rivers of honey flow in the valleys. And all the Children of Kedar [7] will go after him. And he will reign forty days....

> (Manuscript from Yemen in the Cambridge University
> Library, no. 890, Add. 3381)

Ninth sign... Armilus will go to the city of Emmaus in the country of his father and set up his throne there....

> (Midrash fragment, Marmorstein,
> REJ 52 [1906], p. 183)

And another [king, i.e. Armilus] will rise in the Maghreb [the West], more wicked and evil than the one who preceded him. And these will be his signs: His height will be one hundred cubits and eleven spans; his width, ten spans; his mouth, one span; and he will

---

6. It is not clear which African country is meant by this designation.

7. The Children of Kedar are the Arabs.

have much hair on his face. He will capture the West. And many wicked men, lovers of war, will be in those days, and they will gather around him from the whole earth, and will tell him that he is the Messiah, and this rumor will spread all over the world. And the whole earth will submit to him, and he will slay those who do not submit. There will be suffering in the whole world, and they will go up the mountains and reach their summits. And the army of Gog and Magog will join the king and go with him, and those who see them will recognize them from this: all will have four eyes, two in the front and two in the back. And the people will have to bear and suffer distress and much trouble, and the Children of Israel more than all the others....

He will bring up a fish from the sea and will give him the flesh of Israel to eat....

Then a man will appear in that place, and all Israel will leave their places and gather around him. That man will be of the Children of Ephraim. And together they will go to that wicked man [Armilus] who says, "I am the Messiah your king and your prince." And the Children of Israel will say to him: "We ask of you three signs so that we know your truth." He will say: "What are the signs you request? Let me hear!" They will say to him: "We ask of you these signs: The first, that you too do with this staff which Moses our Master, peace be upon him, turned into a snake before Pharaoh, as he did. The second, that the staff of Aaron, peace be upon him, which was dry wood, should bring forth new leaves and should bear fruit in our sight. And the last sign which we ask is that you bring forth the flask of manna which Aaron left to be preserved, and show it to us. Perform therefore these three signs, and we shall know that you speak the truth." And that evil one will be unable to perform even one sign....

Then all Israel and their chieftains will join together and go to the desert of Ephraim, and clothe themselves in sackcloth, and sit down on the earth, and call upon God.... And he [the evil king] will become angry and will command that they be killed, and Messiah ben Joseph will be slain. And the Children of Israel will flee with their wives and children, together they will go to the desert, and will raise their voices in weeping and mourning, and will sit on the earth, and will cry to God, and will make a great mourning for forty days. Then God will send them His mercy and will open the windows of heaven. A month will be like a week, a week like a day, and a day like an hour....

Then they will rise up against the man who said that he was the Messiah and will kill him. And the Lord, His name be blessed, will appear from the heaven. And a great tremor will go forth from Zion and from the Temple, and a mighty voice will be heard. And all Israel will find favor in the eyes of God. In place of destroyed Jerusalem He will bring down for them a built-up Jerusalem from heaven. And a shoot from the stem of Jesse will appear, and the banner of Messiah ben David will fly high. He will slay the army of Gog and Magog....

(Ma'ase Daniel, pp. 222–25)

And a spirit carried me and brought me to the Land of Kasdim [Chaldea], and there were the emissaries with a writing from our Lord the King, and in it it was said: "... Now go and gather the whole congregation and tell them all the things, and go out with them to the fields where there is a great cave, and in the entrance to the cave stands the great accuser Armael [Armilus?], the prince of Edom. And bind him with these chains which are in the hands of the emissaries.... And then rise up with the companions [and go] to Rome, and before the city you will find a great abomination, a great stone in the form of a female, as you know, and utter the declaration of the oneness of God which I put in your hands. And be very careful with her, for a great host supports her, but let them not frighten you, although, as you know, the Side of the Female is more dangerous than the Side of the Male. And know that she has seven heads, and they support her. And when these heads of hers fall, a great fear and trembling will seize her, and she of her own will be delivered into your hand, and all her hosts will fall slain before you...."

(Doenmeh notebook)

17

Messiah ben Joseph

It is time now to have a closer look at Messiah the son of Joseph, to whom reference has repeatedly been made in the preceding chapters. He is the warrior-Messiah whose coming was predicted to his first ancestress, Rachel. When, after years of barrenness, Rachel finally gave birth to a son, she called his name Yosef, saying, *May the Lord add [yosef] to me another son* (Gen. 30:24). A Midrash fragment explains: "Hence [we know] that the Anointed of War will arise in the future from Joseph.... [And Rachel said:] *God hath taken away [asaf] my reproach* (ibid. v. 23)—because it was prophesied to her that the Messiah would arise from her" (BhM 6:81). In another Midrash fragment the two Messiahs are compared: "In the Future to Come, the Anointed of War will arise from Joseph. And the Messiah who will arise from Judah [i.e., Messiah ben David] will be stronger than he" (BhM 6:96).

Messiah ben Joseph, also called Messiah ben Ephraim, referring to his ancestor Ephraim, the son of Joseph, is imagined as the first commander of the army of Israel in the Messianic wars. He will achieve many signal victories, but his fate is to die at the hands of Armilus in a great battle in which Israel is defeated by Gog and Magog. His corpse is left unburied in the streets of Jerusalem for forty days, but neither beast nor bird of prey dares to touch it. Then, Messiah ben David comes, and his first act is to bring about the resurrection of his tragic forerunner.

Scholars have repeatedly speculated about the origin of the Messiah ben Joseph legend and the curious fact that the Messiah figure has thus been split in two. It would seem that in the early legend, the death of the Messiah was envisaged, perhaps as a development of the Suffering Servant motif. A prophecy of Daniel, written about 164 B.C.E., is the earliest source speaking of the death of a *Mashiah* ("Anointed") sixty-two (prophetic) weeks after his coming and after the return and the rebuilding of Jerusalem (Dan. 9:24–26; see chapter 1). While it appears that Daniel had a temporal ruler in mind, whom he calls *Mashiah Nagid* ("Anointed Prince"), some two centuries later, the author of 4 Ezra unmistakably refers to the Messiah, belief in whom had developed in the meantime, when he puts words in the mouth of God to the effect that after four hundred years (counted from when?), *My son the Messiah shall die* (see first excerpt below).

When the death of the Messiah became an established tenet in Talmudic times, this was felt to be irreconcilable with the belief in the Messiah as the Redeemer who would usher in the blissful millennium of the Messianic age. The dilemma was solved by splitting the person of the Messiah in two: one of them, called Messiah ben Joseph, was to raise the armies of Israel against their enemies, and, after many victories and miracles, would fall victim to Gog and Magog. The other, Messiah ben David, will come after him (in some legends will bring him back to life, which psychologically hints at the identity of the two), and will lead Israel to the ultimate victory, the triumph, and the Messianic era of bliss.

This splitting of the Messiah in two persons, which took place in the Talmudic period, achieved another purpose besides resolving the dilemma of the slain Messiah. According to an old tradition, the Messiah was perfectly prefigured in Moses. But Moses died before he could lead the Children of Israel into the Land of Promise. Consequently, for the parallel to be complete, the Messiah, too, had to die before accomplishing his great task of ultimate Redemption. Since, however, the Messiah would not be the True Redeemer of God if he did not fulfill that ultimate task, the only solution was to let one Messiah, like Moses, die, and then assign the completion of the work of Redemption to a second Messiah (see Introduction, section VI).

And whosoever is delivered from the predicted evil shall see My wonders. For My son, the Messiah, shall be revealed, together with those who are with him, and shall gladden the survivors four hundred years. And it shall be, after those years, that My son, the Messiah, shall die, and all in whom there is human breath. Then shall the world be turned into the primeval silence seven days, as it was at the first beginnings....

(4 Ezra 7:27−30)

And the land shall mourn, every family apart (Zech. 12:12). Two have interpreted this verse. One said: "This is the mourning over the Messiah," and the other said: "This is the mourning over the Evil Inclination" [which will be killed by God in the Messianic days].

(Y. Suk. 55b)

And the land shall mourn (Zech. 12:12). What is the reason of this mourning? R. Dosa and the rabbis differ about it. R. Dosa says: "[They will mourn] over the Messiah who will be slain," and the rabbis say: "[They will mourn] over the Evil Inclination which will be killed [in the days of the Messiah]...."

(B. Suk. 52a)

The rabbis have taught: The Holy One, blessed be He, will say to Messiah ben David, may he be revealed soon in our days!: "Ask of Me anything, and I shall give it to you, for it is written, *The Lord said unto me, Thou art My son, this day have I begotten thee, ask of Me and I will give thee the nations for thy inheritance* (Ps. 2:7−8)." And when he will see that Messiah ben Joseph will be slain, he will say before Him: "Master of the World! I ask nothing of you except life!" God will say to him: "Even before you said, 'life,' your father David prophesied about you, as it is written, *He asked life of Thee, Thou gavest it him* (Ps. 21:5)."

(B. Suk. 52a)

R. Yishma'el said: Metatron said to me: "Come and I shall show you the Curtain of the Place which is spread out before the Holy One, blessed be He, on which are engraved all the generations of the world and their deeds, whether they did them or will do them until the end of all generations." And I went and he showed me with the fingers of his hand like a father who teaches his son the letters of the Tora....

And I saw Messiah ben Joseph and his generation, and all the deeds which the nations of the world will do there. And I saw Messiah ben David and his generation, and all the battles and wars of their deeds, and their acts which they will perform with Israel, whether for good or for bad. And I saw all the battles and wars which Gog and Magog will do in the days of the Messiah, and all that the Holy One, blessed be He, will do with them in the Future to Come. And there were the chiefs of the generation, whether among Israel or among the nations of the world, whether they did or will do in the Future to Come, until all generations, all was engraved there on the Curtain of the Place. And I saw them all with my own eyes, and at the end when I had seen I opened my mouth and spoke in praise of the Place....

(Sefer Hekhalot, BhM 5:187–88)

When eight years will be left of the years of the end, which are the years of the beginning of the redemption...a man will rule over Israel for not less than nine months and not more than three years. And at that time a man will arise from among the Children of Joseph...and he will be called Messiah of God. And many people will gather around him in Upper Galilee, and he will be their king.... But most of Israel will be in their exile, for it will not become clear to them that the end has come. And then Messiah ben Joseph, with the men who rally around him, will go up from the Galilee to Jerusalem, and they will slay the procurator of the king of Edom, and the people who will be with him.... And when all the nations hear that a king has arisen among the Children of Israel in Jerusalem, they will rise up against them in the other countries and will expel them, saying: "Until now you were with us in faith, and so that you should have neither king nor prince; but now that you have a king you must not dwell in our land."

And many of Israel will go out into the desert... and will dwell there in tents, and many of them will lack bread and water...and they will suffer in accordance with their deeds. And many of them will leave the covenant of Israel, for they will become weary of their lives....

And when Messiah ben Joseph and all the people with him will dwell in Jerusalem, Armilus will hear their tiding and will come and make magic and sorcery to lead many astray with them, and he will go up and wage war against Jerusalem, and will defeat Messiah ben Joseph and his people, and will kill many of them, and will capture [many] others, and divide their booty.... And he will slay Messiah ben Joseph and it will be a great calamity for Israel.... Why will permission be granted to Armilus to slay Messiah ben Joseph? In order that the heart of those of Israel who have no faith should break, and so that they say: "This is the man for whom we have hoped; now he came and was killed and no redemption is left for us." And they will leave the covenant of Israel, and attach themselves to the nations, and the latter will kill them.

And to those who are left in the Land of Pathros, Messiah ben David will reveal himself....

And most of the slain will be [scattered] in the land for forty days. When Messiah ben Joseph is killed, his body will remain cast out [in the streets] for forty days, but no unclean thing will touch him, until Messiah ben David comes and brings him back to life, as commanded by the Lord. And this will be the beginning of the signs which he will perform, and this is the resurrection of the dead which will come to pass. And then Messiah ben David and Elijah and Israel, who come from the deserts to Jerusalem, will sit in safety and peace for many days, and will build houses and plant vineyards, and they will succeed in herds and property, until Gog will hear their tiding.... And the Land of Gog and Magog is of the Land of Edom.... And they will come to fight and they will wage war against Jerusalem, and Messiah ben David, and Elijah and all the people who are in it....

(Hai Gaon, Responsum)

The sages said: "R. Hiyya commanded his generation: 'When

you hear that an insolent king has arisen, do not dwell there, for he will decree, All those who say the God of the Hebrews is One, should be killed. And he will command and abolish the Tora from Israel....' They said to him: 'My master, where shall we flee?' He said to them: 'To Upper Galilee....'"

R. Huna in the name of R. Levi said: "This teaches [us] that Israel will be gathered in Upper Galilee; and there Messiah ben Joseph will look for them from the Galilee. And they will go up from there, and all Israel with him, to Jerusalem.... And he will go up and rebuild the Temple, and offer up sacrifices. And the fire will descend from heaven. And he will smite all the Canaanites. And he will go up against the Land of Moab and slay half of it and capture the other half. And they will pay tribute to him. And at the end he will make peace with Moab...and they will dwell in safety for forty years, and will eat and drink, and foreigners will be your cultivators and your vintners....

"And after all this, Gog and Magog will hear and go up against them...and will enter and kill him [Messiah ben Joseph] in the streets of Jerusalem.... And Israel will see it and say: 'The Messiah is lost to us, and no other Messiah will come.' And they will mourn him in four family groups.... And the Holy One, blessed be He, will go forth and fight them [Gog and Magog]...and the mountains will move and the hills will shake, and the Mount of Olives split asunder from His arrows. And the Holy One, blessed be He, will descend upon it, and Israel will flee and escape.... And thereafter Israel will be exiled to a desert of reeds, to graze among the saltwort and the roots of broom bushes for forty-five days. And Clouds of Glory will surround them. And there Israel will be hidden. And all those who will have in their heart a bad thought against the Holy One, blessed be He, the clouds will cast them out and the Canaanites will slay them. And many of Israel will go out to the Canaanites, and those [who do this] will have no share with Israel in the World to Come...."

(Mid. Leqah Tov, pp. 258–59)

18

Wars and Victories

Under the charismatic leadership of the second Messiah, Messiah ben David, the great wars will continue. God fights the battles of His Messiah and the ultimate victory comes to pass. The final confrontation takes place on two planes: in heaven, where God chastises and subdues the celestial princes of the nations of the world, thereby weakening the earthly armies under their protection; and down on earth where God intimidates and devastates those armies with fearsome portents. Thus the small nation of Israel, led by Messiah ben David, can overcome its enemies despite their vast superiority in numbers.

While almost all the texts presented here are medieval, we begin with two curious passages from Philo of Alexandria (c. 20 B.C.E. − 50 C.E.), the Jewish philosopher who wrote in Greek and whose thinking was influenced by Greek philosophy at least as much as by the Bible and Jewish tradition. Philo does not mention the Messiah by this name, but speaks of the "Shoot" (rather infelicitously rendered in the Loeb Classical Library edition as the "rising"), the well-known Biblical symbolic designation of the earthly leader who was expected to usher in the era of salvation (cf. Zech. 6:12 and Isa. 11:1). But Philo reinterprets this old Biblical concept and defines the "Shoot" as an entirely spiritual, noncorporeal being who—remarkable words in the mouth of a Jewish thinker—"differs not a whit from the divine image," and is the Divine Father's "eldest son" (see first quote below). In the second selection, Philo gives a psychological picture of a Messiah-like warrior, and it is rather doubtful whether he has the same image in mind in both passages.

About a century after Philo, lived Onkelos the proselyte who translated the Bible into Aramaic. In his rendering, quoted below, of the eschatological prediction of Num. 24:17-18 (see above, Chapter 1), he substituted "Messiah" for the original "scepter," and thereby transformed this passage into an explicitly Messianic prophecy.

I have heard also an oracle from the lips of one of the disciples of Moses which runs thus: *Behold a man whose name is the rising* (Zech. 6:12), strangest of titles, surely, if you suppose that a being composed of soul and body is here described. But if you suppose that it is that Incorporeal One, who differs not a whit from the divine image, you will agree that the name "rising" assigned to him quite truly describes him. For that man is the eldest son, whom the Father of all raised up, and elsewhere calls him his first-born, and indeed the Son thus begotten followed the ways of his Father, and shaped the different kinds, looking to the archetypal patterns which that Father supplied.

(Philo, *De confusione linguarum* 4:45)

For "there shall come forth a man" says the oracle, and leading his host to war he will subdue great and populous nations, because God has sent to his aid the reinforcement which befits the godly, and that is dauntless courage of soul and all-powerful strength of body, either of which strikes fear into the enemy, and the two if united are quite irresistible.

(Philo, *De praemiis et poenis* 16)

Now I will tell you a very evident sign that you may under-stand when the end of all things is coming on earth. When swords in the starlit heaven appear by night towards dusk and towards dawn, and straightway dust is carried from heaven to earth, and all the brightness of the sun fails at midday from the heaven, and the moon's rays shine forth and come back to earth, and a sign comes from the rocks with dripping streams of blood; and in a cloud you shall see a battle of foot and horse, as a hunt of wild beasts, like unto misty clouds. This is the consummation of war which God, whose dwelling is in heaven, is bringing to pass.

(Sibylline Books 3:796—807)

I see him, but not now,
I behold him, but he is not nigh:
A king shall arise from Jacob,
And the Messiah shall be anointed from Israel,
And he shall slay the lords of Moab
And shall rule over all sons of man,
And Edom shall become his possession,
And Seir a possession of those that hate him,
And Israel shall succeed in prosperity.

(Targum Onkelos ad Num. 24:17–18)

R. Yitzhaq said: "In the year in which King Messiah will be revealed, all the kings of the nations of the world will provoke each other. The king of Persia will provoke the king of Arabia, and the king of Arabia will go to Aram [Syria] to take counsel from them. And he will drive back the king of Persia and devastate the whole world, and all the nations of the world will tremble and fear and fall upon their faces. And pangs will take hold of them like unto the pangs of a woman in childbirth. And Israel will tremble and fear, and they will say: 'Where shall we come and go, where shall we come and go?'

"And He will say to them: 'My children, fear not! Everything I did, I did only for you! Why then should you be afraid? Fear not, the time of your redemption is come. And this last redemption will not be like the first redemption, for after the first redemption you suffered pain and enslavement by kingdoms, but after this last redemption you will suffer no pain nor enslavement by kingdoms.'"

(Pes. Rab. ch. 35)

In the generation in which the Son of David will come, Seraphim of fire will be sent into the [holy] Hall, and the stars will appear like fire in every place. And there will be pestilence for three years, year after year, and that is an emissary of the Holy One, blessed be He.... In the third year of the pestilence, the exiles will make atonement, and at the end of the year the king will be killed, and the people will flee into the deserts. And the earth will cry out from her place, and the sages will die.... And in the fifth year... all kings will incite each other, the king of Persia [will fight] with the king of Arabia and destroy him.... And in the hour when Edom falls, heaven and earth will shake from the sound of her fall, and half the world will be captured.... And the Holy One, blessed be He, will gather their multitudes and deliver them into the hands of Israel.... And in the future the Holy One, blessed be He, will bring the [celestial] prince of Edom and flog him. And the prince of Edom will say: "Where shall I flee? If I go to Egypt, the Shekhina is there.... If I flee to Edom, the Shekhina is there.... If I flee to Babylon, the Shekhina is there.... If I flee to Elam, the Shekhina is there...."

This can be likened to [the tale of] the fox, to whom the lion said: "Give me a share!" Thereupon the fox arose and fled to a distance of three days' journey. Nevertheless the lion caught him and said to him: "Give me a share even in this place!" The fox said to him: "It is you from whom I fled!" But the lion said: "And still you are in my territory!" Thus the Holy One, blessed be He, will say in the future to the prince of Edom: "Can you hide from Me?" And He will deliver him into the hands of Israel.

And the Holy One, blessed be He, will in the future don clothes of vengeance to avenge Himself on the seventy nations. ... And He will dress in ten garments, as against the ten times that Israel was called [in Scripture] the Bride of God.... [The garments were put on by God] when He created the world, when He revealed the Tora, [and will be put on] when he delivers the nations of the world to Israel, on the day of Edom's downfall, on the day when He wages war against the nations, on the day of Gog and Magog, [when He destroys] the kingdom of Italy, and he will don two garments on the day of the resurrection of the dead.

Before the fall of Edom [i.e., Rome], ten places will be destroyed, ten places overturned, ten shofars blown, ten evils come to pass, ten evils originate, and an insolent king will arise and decree evil decrees in his kingdom. And a great king will march forth against Alexandria in a camp, and a great evil will be in the world, and he will rebel and rule for three and a half years. And the princes of Edom will fall, and there will be ten battles, and then Israel will prevail over all the nations.... Ships from the Land of Israel will in the future sail to Edom.... And Israel will go up and encamp against Tyre for forty days. And at the end of forty days they will rise at the time of the reciting of the *Sh'ma'* and say: *"Hear, O Israel, the Lord our God, the Lord is One!"* And the walls of the city will fall, and the city will be conquered by them, and [its inhabitants] will flee from it. And all the silver and gold and the rest will be plundered. And from there they will go up to Rome, and from there bring the vessels of the Temple. And King Nehemiah the Messiah will go out with them and they will come to Jerusalem.

And Israel will say to the king of the Arabs: "The Temple is ours. Take silver and gold and leave the Temple." And the king of the Arabs will answer: "You have no rights in this Temple. But, choose yourselves a sacrifice as you used to in ancient times, and we too shall sacrifice, and he whose sacrifice will be accepted [will be the Chosen People]. And we shall become one nation." And Israel will sacrifice and will not be accepted because Satan will accuse them before the Holy One, blessed be He, and the Children of Kedar [the Arabs] will sacrifice and be accepted.... In that hour the Arabs will say to Israel: "Come and accept our faith!" And Israel answers them: "We shall rather slay and be slain, but we shall not deny the Essence!"

In that hour swords will be drawn, and bows bents, and arrows shot, and they will fell many men from the Gate of Ephraim until the Gate of the Corner. And Nehemiah will be killed with them. And those of them who survive will flee to the Desert of Moab and to the Land of the Children of Ammon, and the remnant of Israel will stay there. And God will work miracles for them there, and a well will spring up for them from the abyss.... And they will eat there the roots of broom bushes for forty-five days. ...And when they see these miracles, they send messages to all the princes who are despoiling Jerusalem: "Come and fight us!" They will come in full armor against Israel.

And Israel will say to King Messiah: "It is not good for us to sit here. Why have you come? To provoke war against us as before?" And King Messiah will say to them: "Stand up and see the salvation of the Lord!" And he will blow upon them with the breath of his mouth, and all of them will fall dead before him....

And Gog and Magog will come up that day and encamp against Jerusalem for seven days and a half day, and will capture Jerusalem. And the Community of Israel will say before the Holy One, blessed be He: "Master of the World! All the nations who have despoiled me, I am ashamed to go around to them and to take what is mine from their hands." And the Holy One, blessed be He, will answer her: "I shall bring them all into your midst.... And I shall gather all the nations to Jerusalem for war." And they are these: Gomer, Agapia, Turkey, Africa, Garmit, Garmamia, Cappadocia, Barbary, Italia, Ethiopia, Andalusia and Saba, Harman and Dulaym, Aharsan, Sasonia, Galicia, Gotzia, Lombardia, Calvaria, Pentapolis, Tripoli, Tyre, Macedonia, England, Monaqakh, Tzipari, Niro, Gozan, Daronia, Osia, Talqi, Alemania, Tarsus, 'Elam, and all the rest. And the men of these countries will march out with lances and swords and bows, and each one of them will hold on to a door fortified with nails....

And they will divide into three groups. The first group will drink all the waters of the Sea of Tiberias. The second will drink the dregs. The third will cross over on foot, and they will say to each other: "To whom does this place belong?" And they will grind the stones of the mountains of Israel with their horses, and Jerusalem will be delivered into their hands, and they will capture the city but kill no one.... And they will violate in the city two women of two families.

Rabbi Yohanan said: "This can be likened to a king whose palace was entered by thieves. The king said: 'If I catch them now in my house, they will say, "The king has power only in his house." Therefore I shall wait until they go outside [and catch them there].' Thus the Holy One, blessed be He, will say: 'If I kill them now in Jerusalem, they will say, "He has power only in Jerusalem." Therefore I shall wait until they go out to the Mount of Olives.' And there the Holy One, blessed be He, will reveal Himself to them in His glory, and wage war against them until none is left of them...." And the Holy One, blessed be He, will gather all the beasts of the field and birds to eat their flesh.... And for seven years Israel will burn the wood of their bows and their shields and their lances.

(Pirqe Mashiah, BhM 3:70−73)

It was taught in the name of the rabbis: In the septenary in which the Son of David comes, in the first year there will be insufficient food; in the second, arrows of famine are sent out; in the third, great famine; in the fourth, neither famine nor abundance; in the fifth, great abundance, and a star will sprout up from the east. This is the star of the Messiah, and it will abide in the east fifteen days, and if it tarries longer, it will be to the good of Israel; in the sixth, sounds and rumors; in the seventh, wars. And at the end of the seventh the Messiah will be expected, and the Children of the West will become overbearing and will come and will maintain a reign with insolence, and they will come unto Egypt and capture all the captivity. And in those days will arise an insolent king over a poor and destitute people....

And Israel will be exiled to the desert of marshes to graze in the salt plants and roots of broom bushes for forty-five days. And Clouds of Glory will surround them, and there Israel will hide. And all those who have evil thoughts in their hearts about the Holy One, blessed be He, the clouds will eject them, and the nations of the world will slay them. And many from Israel will go out to the nations of the world, and they will have no share with Israel in the World to Come. But those who will suffer from [eating] salt plants for forty-five days will be addressed by a Divine Voice saying: "Go down to Babylonia, for there you will be saved!" And the Divine Voice rings out again: "Go to Edom, and perform My vengeance!" And Israel will come to Rome, and the Divine Voice issues a third time saying: "Do to her as Joshua did to Jericho!" And they will march around the city and blow the shofars, and at the seventh time they blow a *T'ru'a*: *"Hear, O Israel, the Lord our God, the Lord is one!"* And the walls of the city will crumble, and they enter it and find its young men dead in its streets.... Thereafter they gather all its booty, and Israel will seek their God and David their king. And instantly King Messiah reveals himself and says to them: "I am he, King Messiah, for whom you were waiting!"...

(Aggadat Mashiah, BhM 3:141–43)

In the days of the Messiah he will begin [to address the nations] in peace... and they will subject themselves to him... and will bring him presents.... They will hurry and come with their offerings.... [But then] a spirit of madness enters them and they will revolt against King Messiah, and instantly he will slay them... and only Israel will be left....

In the Future to Come they will say to King Messiah: "A certain country has rebelled against you." And he will say: "Let locusts come and devastate it.... [And they will again say to him:] "A certain country has rebelled against you." And he will say: "Let the Angel of Death go and destroy it...." When they see that they are in serious trouble, they will come and prostrate themselves before King Messiah....

(Yalqut haMakhiri ad Isa. 11:4, p. 86)

A lion's whelp is Judah (Gen. 49:9) who is not afraid of anything. *The lion hath roared, who will not fear?* (Amos 3:8). This is King Messiah.... In the Future to Come, *behold a people that riseth up as a lioness, and as a lion doth he lift himself up* (Num. 23:24)—in the days of the Messiah the nations will bow down to him....

(Mid. Leqah Tov, ed. Buber, 1:235)

A Medieval Apocalypse

At that time I, Berekhyahu ben Shalwiel, servant of the Lord God of Israel, put my soul into my hand and beseeched Him to let me know what will be the end of our people as a result of these wars. And I lifted up my eyes and saw, and behold, three heroes pursuing one another and running one after the other. Each was as far from the other as a bowshot, and each said to the other: "Run and fight me!" And I saw, and behold, the first ran toward the second, and the second fled from before him, and while fleeing he shot at him a sharpened arrow. And the arrow fell before his feet and hit a creeping stone and overturned it, and then hit his foot and remained stuck in it. And the man let loose an exceedingly great and bitter cry, and said: "Woe to me, Lord God of my fathers, for the arrow which hit me will kill me because of the poison which is in it!" And he was still speaking when his foot swelled up like a skin full of wind, and within a moment the pain increased and all his body felt it, until his limbs and flesh swelled like yeast.

And when I heard the sound of his cry, I was filled with compassion for him and I ran and approached him and whispered into his ear, and his pain fled from all his body because of my whisper. And when the first hero, who had shot him in his foot with his arrow, saw that his wound was healed through my whisper, he ran to him with his spear and struck him in his navel and pierced his belly, and his guts spilled out upon the earth and he fell down there and died. And when the third one saw that the first one killed the second one, he ran after the first one with his sword drawn in his hand, and struck him once, and a second time, and a third time, until ten strokes, and he died from the tenth.

And I approached the swordsman and greeted him and said to him: "The Lord be with you, hero of war! Please, my Lord, tell me the meaning of this war which I saw in a vision!" And he showed me an old man with a hoary head sitting on the chair of judgment, and his garments were violet and purple. And he said: "Go, ask that man who sits on the mount of judgment, and he will tell you and let you know what are these wars and what is their end, since he is from the children of your people."

And I ascended the mount of judgment and approached the old man and knelt down and fell on my face upon the earth before his feet. And he placed his two hands upon me and raised me up on my feet before him. And he said to me:

"My son, peace be your coming, peace, peace be unto you and unto all those who love you, for you were saved from the wars, and in all my wars you became victorious. And now, know and understand that for many days and years I have sat here hoping you would come. And now, behold, I shall tell you the meaning of the wars which you saw.

"The three heroes who pursued one another are three kings who will arise in three corners of the earth, the adherents of three contrary views. And they will wage war against one another, and when they muster their camps, army against army, the first, the southern one, will send word to the second, the northern one, and the second will flee from before his words. And the messenger of the first one, who caused him to flee with his words at first, will run after him and will tell him a second thing which will enter his heart like an arrow. And the creeping stone that you saw is a frightening, terrifying thought which creeps and attracts the word as the [lode] stone attracts iron with its inherent power. And the word will touch the essence of the kingdom, and because of it the heart of the second king will die in him. And when his heart dies, the sages of his people will arise to advise him, and their advice will cause his heart to rest for a time from his anguish. And this is the whisper which you whispered into his ear, and through it he was healed from the poison of the arrow of the thought which struck him.

"And that which you then saw, that the first hero struck him a second time, that means that he will add bitter words to his words, and with them he will prevail and will take away his kingdom from him and [the second king] will die.

"And that which you saw, that the third struck the first one who defeated the second, and that he struck him a second and a third time, and went on to strike him four and five times until the end of ten strokes—that is the eastern king who will defeat the southern one who slew the northern one, according to the word of the Lord who strikes the tenth blow always in accordance with our deserts. This is why you said to him, 'The Lord be with you,' when you asked him to tell you the meaning of the war. And as for him sending you to me, [that was done] because we are of the Children of Israel, and he is not of the children of our people, but merely one whom the Lord sent to fight for us against all our enemies.

"The three kings have three heroic names, like the names of their supernal [i.e., heavenly] patrons. The name of the first is Qadriel, and the name of the second is Magdiel, and the name of the third is Alfiel. And the name of the hero whom you saw in a vision in the beginning [i.e., prior to the fight of the three] is Turiel. And my name is Yehoel, for I deigned to speak to you for many years. Therefore your name shall be called from now on in Israel, Roiel the Seer son of M'qoriel, who lives because you were hewn from the source of life and you have chosen life, and with life shall you live. And alive are the children of Abraham and Isaac and Israel our fathers, and all those who adhere to them will adhere to the God of Truth and will live with us.

"And behold there is a fifth hero, he is my Messiah who will rule after the war of the four kingdoms. This is the meaning which is revealed to all, but the hidden meaning will be understood only by him whose mind understands. . . ."

(Abraham Abulafia, *Sefer haOt*)

19

The Ingathering and the
Return of the Shekhina

One of the great themes of the Messianic legend cycle is that of the *Qibbutz Galuyot*, the Ingathering of the Exiles, from the four corners of the earth. Ever since the destruction of Jerusalem and the Temple by the Romans in 70 C.E., the Jews have prayed three times a day for the Ingathering (cf. Appendix I), which was for them synonymous with Redemption. Closely connected with it are the colorful legends about the Ten Lost Tribes of Israel, exiled by the Assyrians in 721 B.C.E. and believed to dwell beyond the magic river Sambatyon, to which brief reference has been made in the Introduction. These tribes, the legend has it, will be ingathered by the Messiah in the Land of Israel together with the Diaspora of the West.

To make the Ingathering complete, it also has to be a restoration of the Community of Israel to God. Therefore, not only all the tribes of Israel have to return to their ancestral land, but also the exiled Shekhina has to come back with them. The Shekhina ("Dwelling") is the personified Presence of God. In the Talmudic period, the Shekhina was identified with the "Holy Spirit." These concepts, originally imagined as hypostatic aspects of the Deity, gradually assumed an independent character and came to be conceived as something like a feminine divine entity. (Both Hebrew terms are of the feminine gender.) Still in Talmudic times, the Shekhina became identified with the "Community of Israel" (also a feminine term), and as such represented Israel in its relationship with God.

When the Temple was destroyed and Israel went into exile, the Shekhina went with them and lamented the fate of her children and of her desecrated sanctuary—this is a favorite Midrashic theme. These ideas, well attested in Talmudic literature, were further elaborated and amplified in the Kabbala, where the Shekhina was given a new epithet, Matronit ("Matron"), and considered the spouse of God the King. The passage describing the Matronit's misery as she laments over her desolate bedchamber, the Holy of Holies of the Jerusalem Temple, is one of the most moving scenes contained in the entire Kabbalistic literature.[1]

With these antecedents it was inevitable that the Shekhina should play an important part in the Messiah legend. The divine Matronit, who went into exile with her children when the Temple was destroyed, will lead the great return. At the third blast of the Great Shofar by the prophet Elijah, the Shekhina will appear (see chapter 14). Again it is in Kabbalistic literature that the return of the Shekhina is dealt with in greatest detail. In the Zohar is found the striking idea that after the exile, when the Matronit and her divine Husband were separated, God had union with Lilith, the slave-woman, and she ruled over the Holy Land.[2] But with the advent of the Redemption, God will bring back the Matronit, she will reunite with Him in joy, and will again rule over the Land of Israel and her ingathered children, the people of Israel.

> Happy are they who will live in those days
> To see the good fortune of Israel
> Which God shall bring to pass

---

1. Cf. R. Patai, *The Hebrew Goddess*, pp. 137–56, 194–95.
2. *Ibid.*, pp. 207–45.

In the ingathering of the tribes.
May God hasten His mercy upon Israel,
May He deliver us from the impurity of the unholy foe!
The Lord is our king for ever and ever.
                              (Psalms of Solomon 17:44–46)

On the twentieth of the month of Marheshvan the world will tremble, and heaven and earth will shake. On the twentieth of Kislev all Israel will stand in prayer and in crying before their Father in heaven, and on the same day a sword will descend and fall among the nations of the world, for it is written, *For the sword devoureth in one manner or another* (2 Sam. 11:25).

On the twenty-second of Nissan the First Exile will come forth from Babylon with eighteen thousand men and women, and not one of them will be lost. On the twenty-fifth of Tishri will come forth the Second Exile which is on the River Sabbation, with seventeen thousand, and of them twenty men and fifteen women will be killed. On the twenty-fifth of the eighth month [Heshvan], the Third Exile will come forth, and they will weep and cry over their brethren who were killed, and they will cry in the desert for twenty-five days, and they will carry nothing along but will live on that which issues from the mouth of God. The first Exile does not leave Babylon until the Second reaches Babylon....
                              (Sefer Eliyahu, BhM 3:65–66)

Our sages said: King Messiah is subjected to sufferings in every generation according to the sins of that generation. The Holy One, blessed be He, said: "In that hour [of the Redemption] I shall create him anew and he will no longer suffer...."

The ten tribes underwent three exiles. The first: they were exiled to the Sambatyon; the second: they were exiled beyond the Sambatyon; and the third: they were exiled to the slopes of Rivlata, and *swallowed up there* (Hos. 8:8). [In the days of the Messiah, God will] *say to the prisoners, "Go forth"* (Isa. 49:9)—to those who are on the Sambatyon; *and to them that are in darkness, "Show yourselves"* (ibid.)—to those who are beyond the Sambatyon. And as for those who were swallowed up in Rivlata, the Holy One, blessed be He, will make for them underground channels, and they will be tunneled in them until they come under the Mount of Olives in Jerusalem. And the Holy One, blessed be He, will stand on top of it, and it will split open, and they will come up from it.... And those three exiles will not come alone, but from every place in which Israel is found they will come and gather. *Behold, these shall come from far, and, lo, these from the north and from the west.* (ibid. v. 12)—these are those who are in the far places of Aspamia. *And these from the land of Sinim* (ibid.)—these are the sons of Jonadav ben Rechab. As a rule, he who walks on the road is hungry and thirsty; but not so they: *They shall not hunger nor thirst, neither shall the heat nor sun smite them* (ibid. v. 10). And more than that: the Holy one, Blessed be He, will flatten out the mountains before them, and make them roads before them. And likewise all the deep places He will raise up before them, and make them a plain before them, as it is written, *And I will make all My mountains a way, and My highways shall be raised on high* (ibid. v. 11). The Holy One, blessed be He, will say to the heavens and the earth: "Why are you standing [in silence]? When there was mourning you mourned with them, as it is written, *I clothe the heavens with blackness, and I make sackcloth their covering* (ibid. 50:3). Now that the joy has come, rise and rejoice with them, *Sing, O heavens, and be joyful, O earth, and break forth into singing, O mountains.* Why? *For the Lord hath comforted His people* (ibid. 49:13).

(Pes. Rab., ed. Friedmann, 146b–147a)

When the exiles who abide in the north awaken, they will come and camp in the south. When Gog who dwells in the north awakens, he will come and fall in the south.... When King Messiah who abides in the north awakens, he will come and build the Temple which is in the south.... And the winds will in the future become envious of one another. The south wind will say: "I bring the exile of Yemen and the exile of Hagra and all the south!" And the north wind will say: "I bring the exile of the north!" And God will make peace between them and they will enter one gate.... R. Honya in the name of R. Binyamin bar Levi said: "In This World, when the north wind blows, the south wind blows not; but in the Future to Come, the Holy One, blessed be He, will say: 'I will bring an *argastes* [Greek for northwestern] wind upon the world, and both winds will serve simultaneously.'"

(Num. Rab. 13:2)

When Israel are dispersed, the Shekhina is with them, as it is said, *The Lord shall return your captivity* (Deut. 30:3). It is not said, "Will bring back" but "will come back" [that is, He will come back with you].

(Deut. Rab. 7:10)

The Holy One, blessed be He, said: "In This World, because of their sins, they were exiled and dispersed in the gates of the earth, but in the Future to Come, *If thy dispersed be in the ends of heaven, from thence the Lord thy God shall gather thee* (Deut. 30:1); *And He shall gather the scattered of Judah from the four winds of the earth* (Isa. 11:12).

(Deut. Rab. 23:14; Mid. Tanh. Buber, p. 168)

The day on which the exiles will be ingathered is as great as the day on which the Tora was given to Israel on Mount Sinai. And what will be the order of their coming? The Shekhina will walk at their head . . . and the nations of the world after them, and the prophets at their sides, and the Ark and the Tora will be with them. And all Israel will be clothed in splendor and wrapped in great honor, and their radiance will shine from one end of the world to the other. And in that hour the hands of the nations of the world will become weak, and there will be not a single warrior able to stretch forth his hand to take up his weapons . . . and there will be no weapon which will not be damaged. . . . And there will no image or shape [idols] which will not be devoured. . . . And the nations of the world will come and take their deities and cast them away. . . . And why will all this happen? In order to remove all idolatry from the world before the Holy One, blessed be He. . . . And the Blessed One will rule from one end of the world to the other. . . .

(Pes. diR. Kahana, ed. Mandelbaum, 2:463–64)

Come, see: All the time that Israel are in exile, the Shekhina is in exile with them. . . . And since the Shekhina is with them, the Holy One, blessed be He, remembers them, to do good to them and bring them out of the exile. . . . It is written, *And God remembered His covenant* (Ex. 2:24)—this refers to the Shekhina; *with Abraham*—this refers to the southwest [of the exile], *with Isaac*—this refers to the northwest; *and with Jacob*—this refers to the one total coupling [between God and the Shekhina], the full coupling, as is proper.

(Zohar 1:120b)

In the hour when the Holy One, blessed be He, remembers His people, the Community of Israel, the Shekhina, will return from the exile first and go to the House, because the Temple will be rebuilt first. And the Holy One, blessed be He, will say to her: "Arise from the dust!" She will answer and say: "To what place shall I go, since my House is destroyed, my Sanctuary is burnt in fire?" But then the Holy One, blessed be He, will rebuild the Temple first, and reestablish the Sanctuary, and rebuild the city of Jerusalem, and thereafter He will raise her from the dust.... And the exiles of Israel will gather....

(Zohar 1:134a)

R. El'azar and R. Abba were on their way from Tiberias to Sepphoris, and as they were walking, a Jew met them and began [to expound]: "...*Behold, the Lord rideth upon a swift cloud and cometh unto Egypt, and the idols of Egypt shall tremble at His presence* (Isa. 19:1)...." The King [God] went to bring out the Matronit [the Shekhina] who was there.... The Holy One, blessed be He, wanted to honor her, and came to raise her up and to take her by the hand and straighten her up, as will the Holy One, blessed be He, do at the end of the exile of Edom [Rome].... In the exile of Edom the Holy One, blessed be He, will want to be honored in the world and will raise the Matronit, and let her shake off the dust....

(Zohar 2:7a)

Time will come when a voice will announce to the Matronit [Shekhina] and say: "*Rejoice greatly, O daughter of Zion, shout, O daughter of Jerusalem, for behold, thy King cometh unto thee. He is righteous and victorious, lowly, and riding upon an ass* (Zech. 9:9)." ...For he would be hiding until that time in a place which is not his, in an alien place.... For until that time he was righteous without righteousness, but now, when they [the King and the Matronit] couple, he will be *righteous and victorious,* for He will no longer dwell in the Other [Evil] Side.... For He was lost to the Matronit and adhered to the Other Place, which is called Slave-woman [i.e., Lilith].... We have learned that this Slave-woman was appointed to rule over the Holy Land as the Matronit had ruled over it previously.... But the Holy One, blessed be He, will bring back the Matronit to her place as in the beginning. And then, what will the rejoicing be? Say, the joy of the King and the joy of the Matronit. The joy of the King over having returned to her and having parted from the Slave-woman, as we have said, and the joy of the Matronit over having returned to couple with the King.

(Zohar 3:69a)

Come, see the supernal love the Holy One, blessed be He, has for Israel. It is like that of a king who had an only son. That son committed offenses against the king. One day he misbehaved before the king, whereupon the king said to him: "All these days I have disciplined you, but you have not improved [your ways]. Now, see, what shall I do to you? If I banish you from the country, and deprive you of your royal rank, perhaps bears of the field or wolves of the field or robbers will cause you to perish from the earth. What shall I do? I and you together will leave the country and be together in exile."

Likewise the Holy One, blessed be He, said to Israel: "What shall I do to you? Lo, I have chastised you but you have not lent your ears. I have brought upon you bearers of shields, masters of destruction, to beat you, but you did not listen. If I make you leave the land by yourselves, I fear for you, because many bears, many wolves will arise against you and cause you to perish from the world. Therefore, what will I do to you? I and you together shall leave the land and go into exile.... And do not say that I have abandoned you, for I, too, shall be there with you...."

It is written, *Behold, for your iniquities were ye sold, and for your transgressions was your mother put away* (Isa. 50:1). The Holy One, blessed be He, said: "You have brought it about that I and you shall wander[3] in the world. Lo, the Matronit will leave her Hall[4] with you. Lo, the whole Hall, Mine and yours, has been destroyed, for the Hall is not worthy of the King except when He enters it with the Matronit. And the joy of the King is found only in the hour in which He enters the Hall of the Matronit, and her son[5] is found there with her. [Then] all of them rejoice together. Now that the son and the Matronit are not found [there], the Hall is desolate from all. But I, what will I do? I, too, will be with you." Now, although Israel are in exile, the Holy One, blessed be He, is found

---

3. Reading *nidod* for the *nidor* of the printed text, which makes no good sense.

4. The Temple.

5. The people of Israel personified as the son of the Matronit and of God.

with them and has not abandoned them. And when Israel comes out from the exile, the Holy One, blessed be He, will return with them, as it is written, *And the Lord thy God will return* (Deut. 30:3), He Himself will surely return.

(Zohar 3:115a)

20

The Triumph of the Lord

With the victory over Armilus and the defeat of Gog and Magog, followed by the ingathering of the exiles of Israel led by the divine Shekhina, the Messiah will have accomplished the greater part of the tasks for which he was created in the six days of the Beginning. Then comes the time of triumph, in which all the nations of the world recognize him as their spiritual leader and ruler, and he becomes a veritable *pantocrator*, world ruler—always, of course, in his capacity as the faithful servant of God.

Thus the victorious conclusion of the Messianic wars is a triumph, not so much of the Messiah who acts merely as an agent of the Lord, but of God Himself. The Messiah plays a rather subordinate role in apocalyptic and Aggadic visions of the ultimate triumph. The First Book of Enoch merely alludes to him by the name "Son of Man" (see below, first excerpt); in the Testament of Levi he is termed "new priest," the Testament of Judah refers to him even more enigmatically as "a star." In the Midrash we hear about the rich presents the nations of the world will bring to King Messiah, but his very first decision as to whether to accept or reject them is corrected by God. Another legend states, on the basis of Biblical quotations, that King Messiah will rule over the whole world, but no single act performed by him in his capacity as global sovereign is specified (see below, first excerpt from Numbers Rabba).

The only explanation I have for this remarkable Aggadic reduction of the Messiah to insignificance after his great wars and victories is that the era of Messianic rule was conceived as a rule of God over the whole world, and that the attention of the Aggadists was focused on what God would say and do, and on what the nations of the world would say and do when, defeated in the Messianic wars, they finally recognize God as the Master of the World. In this great triumph of the Lord over idolatrous mankind, the Messiah—the human agent whose heroic valor brought it about—becomes almost superfluous. Once the kingdom of heaven over the earth is established, his active role has come to an end, and nothing more is left for him than to sit on David's throne in Jerusalem and be the visible but passive representative of God in the world of man.

And the Lord of spirits will abide over them,
And with that Son of Man shall they eat,
And lie down, and rise up forever and ever.
And the righteous and elect shall rise from earth
And cease to be of downcast countenance,
And they shall be clothed with garments of glory.
And these shall be their garments:
Garments of life from the Lord of Spirits.
And your garments shall not grow old,
Nor your glory pass away before the Lord of Spirits.
                              (1 Enoch 62:14–16)

Then shall the Lord raise up a new priest,
To whom all the words of the Lord shall be revealed;
And he shall execute true judgment. . . .
And his star shall arise in heaven as the star of a king,
Lighting up the light of knowledge as the sun the day.
And he shall be magnified in the world,
And shine forth as the sun on the earth,
And remove all darkness from under heaven.

And there shall be peace in all the earth.
The heavens shall exult in his days,
And the earth shall be glad,
And the clouds shall rejoice.
And the knowledge of the Lord shall pour forth
Upon the earth, as the water of the seas.
And the angels of glory before the Lord
Shall rejoice in him.
The heavens shall be opened,
And from the temple of glory shall come upon him
      holiness,
With the Father's voice, as from Abraham to Isaac.
And the glory of the Most High shall pour forth over him,
And the spirit of understanding and holiness shall rest
      upon him.
For he shall give the majesty of the Lord to His sons in
      truth for ever,
And none shall succeed him for all generations.
And at the time of his priesthood the nations shall increase
In knowledge upon the earth.
And in his priesthood shall sin come to an end,
And the lawless shall cease to do evil,
And the just shall rest in him.
And he shall open the gates of paradise,
And shall remove the sword which threatens Man,
And give to the saints to eat from the Tree of Life,
And the spirit of holiness shall be upon them.
And he shall bound Belial [Satan],
And give strength to his children to tread upon evil spirits.
And the Lord shall rejoice in His children,
And be well pleased in His loved ones forever....
                              (Testament of Levi, 18)

And a star shall rise for you from Jacob in peace,
And a man shall arise from my seed,
Like unto the sun of righteousness:
Walking with the sons of man in meekness,
And no sin shall be found in him.
And the heavens shall open unto him,
To pour upon him the spirit of blessing.
And he shall pour upon you the spirit of grace,
And ye shall in truth be sons unto him,
And ye shall walk in his commandments....
Then shall the scepter of My kingdom shine forth,

> And from your root shall arise a stem,
> And from it shall grow a rod of righteousness to the
>   nations,
> To judge and save all that call upon the Lord.
>
> (Testament of Judah 24)

In the future to come you will find that all nations will bring presents to King Messiah, and Egypt will bring first. And the Messiah will be disinclined to accept [gifts] from them. But the Holy One, blessed be He, will say to him: "Egypt served as a lodging place to My children...." Instantly he will accept [gifts] from them. Thereupon Ethiopia will draw an inference: "If the Messiah accepts [gifts] from Egypt which enslaved them, then how much more [will he accept gifts from] us who have never enslaved them!" ... Instantly all the other kingdoms will hear this, and they also will bring [gifts].... Thereafter the kingdom of Edom [Rome] will draw an inference for herself and will say: "If these, who are not Israel's brothers, [had presents] accepted from them, then how much more will they be accepted from us [who are their brothers]." But when she will be about to bring her presents to King Messiah, the Holy One, blessed be He, will say to him: "*Rebuke the wild beast of the reeds* (Ps. 137:31), which lives on robbery...."

> (Ex. Rab. 35:5)

There was a tradition in the hands of the tribe of Judah, their wise men and their great ones, from our Father Jacob, concerning all that would come to pass in the future to every tribe until the days of the Messiah....[This is why Nahshon, the prince of Judah] offered a silver dish and a silver basin [to the Sanctuary], corresponding to the kings of the House of David who were to arise from him in the future and would rule over the world, the sea, and the dry land, such as Solomon and King Messiah.... From whence do we know this about King Messiah? For it is written, *He shall have dominion from sea to sea, and from the River to the ends of the world* (Ps. 72:8). From whence [do we know that he will rule] over the earth? For it is written, *All kings shall prostrate themselves before him, all nations shall serve him* (ibid., v. 11). And it says, *And, behold, with the clouds of heaven came one like unto a son of man*, etc., *and there was given him dominion, and glory, and a kingdom, that all the peoples, nations, and languages should serve him* (Dan. 7:13–14).

And the stone that smote the image became a great mountain and filled the earth (Dan. 2:35). Therefore he [Nahshon] offered a dish, corresponding to the sea which surrounds the whole world and is like a dish...and a silver basin [*mizraq*], corresponding to the world which is fashioned like a ball, and which is thrown [*nizraq*] from hand to hand....

The nations of the world brought presents to Solomon, and so they will bring in the future to King Messiah, as it is said, *The kings of Tarshish and of the isles shall render tribute, the kings of Sheba and Seba shall offer gifts.* (Ps. 72:10).

(Num. Rab. 13:14)

And the staff of Aaron (Num. 17:21). Some say: "It was the staff which had been in the hands of Judah...." And some say: "It was the staff that had been in the hands of Moses...." That same staff was in the hands of every king [of Judah] until the Temple was destroyed, and then it was hidden away. That same staff will in the future be in the hands of King Messiah—[may it be] speedily in our days!

(Num. Rab. 18:23)

Our master taught: "In the hour in which King Messiah reveals himself, he will come and stand on the roof of the Temple and will let Israel hear, and will say: 'O you meek ones! The time of your Redemption is come. And if you do not believe it, see my light which shines upon you....' And it will shine only upon them, but not on the idolaters..... In that hour the Holy One, blessed be He, lets shine the light of the Messiah and of Israel, and all the nations of the world will be in darkness and blackness, and all will walk in the light of the Messiah and of Israel...and they will come and will lick the dust under the feet of King Messiah....And all will come and fall upon their faces before the Messiah and before Israel, and will say to him: 'Let us be servants to you and to Israel!' And each one of Israel will have 2,800 servants...."

(Pes. Rab. pp. 162a—b)

The Holy One, blessed be He, will cause Ephraim, His True Messiah, to put on a garment whose radiance will reach from one end of the world to the other. And Israel will use its light and will say: "Happy the hour in which he was created! Happy the womb from which he issued! Happy the generation whose eyes see him! Happy the eye which waited for him! For the opening of his lips is blessing and peace, and his speech is a pleasure of the spirit, and the thoughts of his heart are safety and security. Happy is the eye which was worthy to see him, for the words of his tongue are forgiveness and pardon for Israel. His prayer is sweet savor; his supplication—purity and holiness. Happy are his fathers who deserved the goodness of the world which is preserved for eternity and which is like a bride who adorns herself with her garments...."

(Pes. Rab. ch. 36)

Ten kings ruled from one end of the world to the other. The first king is the Holy One, blessed be He, who rules in heaven and earth. And it came up in His thought to raise up kings on earth, as it is said, *And He changeth the times and the seasons, He removeth kings and setteth up kings* (Dan. 2:21). The second king was Nimrod...the third, Joseph...the fourth, Solomon...the fifth, Ahab...the sixth, Nebuchadnezzar...the seventh, Cyrus...the eighth, Alexander of Macedonia...the ninth is King Messiah who will rule from one end of the world to the other, as it is said, *And the stone that smote the image became a great mountain and filled the whole earth* (Dan. 2:35). The tenth king: Kingship will return to its owner: He who was the first king, He is the last king....

(Pirqe R. Eliezer, ch. 11)

A king of flesh and blood does not allow others to wear his crown, but the Holy One, blessed be He, will give His crown to King Messiah, as it is written, *Thou setteth a crown of fine gold on his head* (Ps. 21:4). A king of flesh and blood does not allow others to wear his purple, but the Holy One, blessed be He, will give His purple to King Messiah, as it is written, *Honor and majesty dost Thou lay upon him* (ibid. v. 6).

(Mid. Tehillim, p. 173)

R. Aha said: "As long as Israel are in exile, the right hand of the Holy One, blessed be He, is, as it were, in subjection. But when Israel will be redeemed, see what is written: *His right hand and His holy arm hath wrought salvation for Him* (Ps. 98:1); *The Lord hath made bare His holy arm*, redeemed His servant Jacob, *and all the ends of the earth shall see the salvation of our God* (Isa. 52:10); *He hath remembered His mercy and His faithfulness toward the House of Israel* (Ps. 98:3).

Shout unto the Lord all the earth, break forth and sing for joy, yea, sing praises. Sing praises unto the Lord with the harp, with the harp and the voice of melody, with trumpets and the sound of the shofar, shout before the King, the Lord. Let the sea and its fulness roar (Ps. 98:4–7). All this because of the redemption[1] of Israel: to teach you that there is no complete joy until Israel are redeemed.

(Mid. Tehillim, p. 422)

R. Y'huda in the name of R. Sh'muel said: "As long as Israel are in exile the kingdom of heaven is not complete, and the nations of the world dwell in tranquillity. But when Israel is redeemed, the kingdom of heaven will be complete, and all the nations of the world will tremble. This is meant by *The Lord reigneth, let the peoples tremble* (Ps. 99:1)."

What does it mean, *The Lord is great in Zion and He is high above all the peoples* (ibid. v. 2)? R. Yohanan said: "*The Lord is great in Zion*—because of what he did in Zion: He had no mercy on His own house; when he comes to take revenge on those who destroyed it, how much more so!" R. Hanina said: "*The Lord is great in Zion*—when He returns His Shekhina to Zion, in that hour He will be great in Zion."

(Mid. Tehillim, p. 423)

In the hour in which the Song of the Sea (Exod. 15:1–18) is recited, the Community of Israel is crowned with the crown which the Holy One, blessed be He, has prepared for the crowning of King Messiah—and that crown bears the impress of the engravings of Holy Names—as the Holy One, blessed be He, was crowned on the day on which Israel crossed the sea, and all the armies and chariots of Pharaoh were drowned. Therefore one must recite that Song with great devoutness. And he who merits [to do so] in This World will merit to see King Messiah crowned with that crown and girded with his weapons, and will merit to praise [him] with this Song there.

(Zohar 2:132a)

---

1. Reading *g'ulatan* for *galutan* ("exile of").

The Messiah is coming
From the high heavens,
A golden shofar in his hand
He comes ablowing.
   When you see, mother,
   That good day
   With what a joy (will you see it)!

The Messiah is coming
From the heavens high
A golden shofar in his hand
He comes singing.
   When you see, etc.

A golden shofar in his hand
He comes ablowing,
To the Turks and the Christians
He brings death.
   When you see, etc.

To the Turks and the Christians
He brings death,
And to our Jews
He brings salvation.
   When you see, etc.

A golden shofar in his hand
He comes ablowing,
The Turks and Christians
He comes smiting,
And our Jews
He comes ruling.
   When you see, etc.
      (Sephardi song, from Attias, *Romancero*.)

21

Resurrection

Next follows the great universal miracle of Resurrection.[1] The idea, of course, goes back to Ezekiel's grandiose vision of the dry bones (see chapter 1), which prophecy of Resurrection is contemporary with the destruction of the First Temple of Jerusalem (586 B.C.E.). Ezekiel, however, had no Messianic idea in mind; the purpose of his prophecy was theological-political-psychological: he wanted to implant the belief in a speedy return to their own land into the hearts of the despairing Judean exiles in Babylonia. In the rabbinic version, Resurrection becomes a Messianic miracle, the diachronic counterpart of the synchronic ingathering of the exiles. What it achieves is a bringing together of all the people from the whole world, whether they lived in the past or will live at the time of the Messiah's advent.

The earliest mention of a future Resurrection is found in the Apocrypha. In 2 Maccabees—an abridgment of a lost book originally written in Greek by a certain Jason of Cyrene in about 150 B.C.E.—the hope for Resurrection forms an integral part of the story of the woman and her seven sons who suffered martyrdom for the sanctification of the Name

---

1. The best study of resurrection in Jewish tradition is still that of Löwinger, "Die Auferstehung in der jüdischen Tradition," in Grünwald, *Jahrbuch für jüdische Volkskunde*, 1:23–122.

of God (6:18ff.). In 2 Baruch (written in the early first century C.E.), Resurrection is tied to the appearance of the Messiah. In rabbinic literature the belief in Resurrection in the Messianic days became a basic tenet, and on that basis it was included among the Thirteen Articles of Faith of Maimonides.

The question of who will and who will not be resurrected in the Messianic days, and the related question of who will and who will not have to be tried on the great day of the Last Judgment (see chapter 22), have occupied the minds of the rabbis for whom these issues were of concrete import. A collection of opinions on the subject is contained in a Mishna which (omitting the Biblical quotations the sages adduced in order to indicate the existence of a Biblical basis for their opinions) reads:

> All Israel have a share in the World to Come. . . . And these have no share in the World to Come: He who says, "There is no Resurrection of the dead from the Tora, and the Tora is not from heaven," and the Epikuros [disbeliever]. . . . The generation of the deluge has no share in the World to Come and it will not stand in judgment. . . . The generation of the dispersion [who built the Tower of Babel] has no share in the World to Come. . . . The People of Sodom have no share in the World to Come . . . but they will stand in judgment. . . . They will not stand in the community of the righteous but will stand in the community of the wicked.

About the Israelite spies who brought back an evil report from Canaan, the generation of the desert, the community of Korah who rebelled against Moses, and the ten tribes of Israel who were exiled by the Assyrians (cf. 2 Kings 18:9ff.), there is a difference of opinion between R. Akiba, who holds that they will not have any share in the World to Come, and R. Eliezer, who opines that they will (M. Sanh. 10:1–3).

[One of the seven martyr brothers says:] "It is meet that those who perish at man's hands cherish hope divine that they shall be raised up by God again...."

[Their mother says:] "It is the Creator of the world who fashions man and devises the generating of all things, and He it is who in mercy will restore you to the breath of life...."

(2 Macc. 7:14, 23)

And it shall come to pass after these things, when the time of the advent of the Messiah is fulfilled, that he shall return in glory. Then all who have fallen asleep in hope of him shall rise again. And it shall come to pass at that time that the treasuries will be opened in which is preserved the number of the souls of the righteous, and they shall come forth, and a multitude of souls shall be seen together in one assemblage of one thought, and the first shall rejoice and the last shall not be grieved....

(2 [Syriac] Baruch 30:1–5)

R. Yohanan said: "Three keys are in the hand of the Holy One, blessed be He, and they have not been entrusted to the hand of an emissary, and they are: the key of rains, and the key of birth, and the key of the resurrection of the dead."

(B. Ta'an. 2a)

R. Hiyya bar Yosef said: "In the future the pious will sprout up and emerge in Jerusalem, as it is said, *They will blossom out of the city like grass of the earth* (Ps. 72:16).... And they will rise up in their garments, as can be concluded from the wheat: If the wheat, which is buried naked, rises in several clothes, how much more so the pious who are buried in their clothes."

(B. Ket. 111b)

R. El'azar said: "The dead of foreign lands will not be resurrected...." R. Abbahu said: "Even a Canaanite slave-woman in the Land of Israel is assured of having a share in the World to Come...." R. Yirm'ya bar Abba said in the name of R. Yohanan: "All those who walk as little as four cubits in the Land of Israel are assured of a share in the World to Come...." Will, then, the righteous who live in foreign lands not be resurrected? R. Ila'a said: "[They will:] Their bones will roll over to the Land of Israel." To this R. Abba Sala the Great objected: "[Such] rolling is painful for the righteous." Abbaye said: "[Not so, because] channels will be made for them in the soil."

(B. Ket. 111a)

The prophet [*sic*] Solomon said: When the dead come back to life, the Mount of Olives will be cleft, and all the dead of Israel will rise from beneath it, and even the righteous who died in exile will come, by way of channels under the earth, and will emerge from beneath the Mount of Olives. And the wicked who died and were buried in the Land of Israel will be hurled forth as a stone a man hurls with a sling. Then all the inhabitants of the earth will say: "What was the merit of this people which the earth sends up by myriad myriads, like on the day when it emerged from the desert to the Land of Israel? And that it is pampered by the compassion of its Master as on the day when it appeared under Mount Sinai to receive the Tora?" And in that hour Zion, which is the mother of Israel, will give birth to her children, and Jerusalem will receive the children of the exile.

(Targum Songs 8:5)

Hadrian (may his bones be ground) asked R. Y'hoshu'a ben Hanania: "From what will the Holy One, blessed be He, rebuild the bodies of the dead in the future to come?" He said to him: "From the *luz* [a bone] of the spine." He said to him: "How do you know?" He said to him: "Give me one, and I shall show you." He cast it into fire, and it did not burn. He put it into water, and it did not dissolve. He ground it between millstones, and it could not be ground. He put it on an anvil and hit it with a hammer—the anvil split in two and the hammer broke, but the *luz* was not damaged.

(Gen. Rab. 28:3)

Our master said two things in the name of R. Helbo: Why did the Fathers love to be buried in the Land of Israel? Because the dead of the land of Israel will be the first to come to life in the days of the Messiah, and they will eat [i.e., enjoy] the years of the Messiah. And R. Hama bar R. Hanina said: "He who dies abroad and is buried there, two deaths are in his hand. . . ." R. Simon said: "If so, the righteous who are buried abroad will be the losers? [Not so,] for what does the Holy One, blessed be He, do? He hollows out the earth before them, and makes them into something like a skin bottle, and they will roll and come until they reach the Land of Israel. And when they reach the Land of Israel He puts the spirit of life into them and they stand up."

(Mid. Tan. Buber, 1:214)

Each saintly person will come back to life as he was when he passed from the world. He who was blind, will come back blind in his resurrection; and he who was lame, comes back lame; and thus all the afflicted, so that each of them should recognize his fellow man, and that they should not say, "These are different creatures." And thereafter, the Holy One, blessed be He, will heal them. . . .

(Milhamot Melekh haMashiah, BhM 6:119)

And then will come the last day, which will be about forty days long, and the mountains and hills will tremble and shake, and the earth will shout at the wicked and say: "In such and such a place a certain man murdered a certain man. . . ."

Elijah of blessed memory said: "I see dead bodies sunk in the river, and their dust is gathered, and they become as they were in the beginning, to give praise to God. . . . And the ministering angels open their graves and cast their souls back into them, so that they live, and they make them stand up on their feet. And they push all those who are guilty into a big ditch two thousand cubits long and fifty cubits wide. And all those who did not love the Tora of the Holy One, blessed be He, the eyes of the pious will see their downfall. . . ."

(Sefer Eliyahu, BhM 3:67)

R. Hanina said: "All Israel who die abroad, their souls will be gathered in the Land [of Israel]. . . . And those of the idolaters who die in the Land of Israel, their souls will be hurled in a sling out of the Land of the Living. . . . In the future to come, the Holy One, blessed be He, will get hold of the wings of the Land [of Israel] and shake all the uncleanness from it (cf. Job 38:13), like a man who shakes out a garment, and He will shake out everything that is in it, and cast it outside. . . ."

R. Shim'on said: "All the bodies touch the dust of the earth until nothing remains of them except a spoonful of decay, and mixes with the dust of the earth like the leaven mixes with the dough. And in the future to come, when the Holy One, blessed be

He, calls upon the earth that it should return the deposit of those bodies, [that spoonful of decay] mixes with the dust of the earth and beautifies and increases the dough. Instantly the earth shakes and the mountains tremble and the graves open and the grave-stones scatter one from the other. . . ." R. 'Azaria said: "The Holy One, blessed be He, opens the graves and opens the storehouses of the souls and puts back each soul into its own body. . . ."

(Pirqe R. Eliezer, ch. 34)

In that hour the Holy One, blessed be He, will crown the Messiah and place a helmet of salvation on his head, and give him splendor and radiance, and adorn him with clothes of honor, and stand him up on top of a high mountain in order to bring glad tidings to Israel. And he will let it hear with his voice: "Salvation is near!" And Israel will say: "Who are you?" And he will say: "I am Ephraim." And Israel will say: "Are you the one whom the Holy One, blessed be He, called 'Ephraim My firstborn, Ephraim is a darling son to Me'?" and he will say, "Yes." And Israel will say to him: "Go and bring glad tidings to them that sleep in [the Cave of] Machpela, that they should rise first."

In that hour he goes up and brings glad tidings to those who sleep in Machpela, and says to them: "Abraham, Isaac, and Jacob, rise! Enough have you slept!" And they reply and say: "Who is this who removes the dust from over us?" And he says to them: "I am the Messiah of the Lord. Salvation is near, the hour is near." And they answer: "If it is really so, go and bring the tidings to Adam the first man, so that he should rise first." In that hour they say to Adam the first man: "Enough have you slept." And he says: "Who is this who drives the slumber from my eyes?" And he says: "I am the Messiah of God, from among the children of your children." Instantly Adam the first man and all his generation, and Abraham, Isaac, and Jacob, and all the pious and all the tribes and all the generations from one end of the world to the other rise and utter sounds of jubilation and song. . . . And how beautiful are Moses and his generation coming from the desert!

This can be likened to a king who had two sons, and one of them died, and all the people in the country put on black garments. The king said: "You put on black garments now when my first son died; I shall dress you in white for the rejoicing [the wedding] of my second son." Similarly the Holy One, blessed be He, said to all the mountains: "Since you wept over my sons when they were exiled from their land . . . I shall bring the rejoicing of my sons to the mountains. . . ."

(Pirqe Mashiah, BhM 3:73-74)

In the future the Holy One, blessed be He, will resurrect the dead. How will He do it? He takes the Great Shofar and blows it seven times. At the first blast, the whole world shakes and suffers pangs like a woman in childbirth. At the second, the dust is scattered and the graves open. At the third, the bones gather together. At the fourth, the limbs are stretched out. At the fifth, skin comes into being. At the sixth, spirits and souls enter the bodies. At the seventh, they live and stand up on their feet in their clothes.

And the Holy One, blessed be He, stands and arranges the order of those who walk in the world: of the righteous, and of the kings, and of the generous ones, and of each and every soul. And He causes Enoch, who is Metatron, to descend, and also the Holy Beasts who are under the Throne of Glory. And He brings up Korah and all his community, and makes them stand on their feet, and says to them: "Have you seen any other God except Me in the heavens above and in the earth below?" And they say: *"Who is God save the Lord? (Ps. 18:32)"*

(Pes. Hadta, BhM 6:58)

In the future to come, the Holy One, blessed be He, will bring dust of the earth and dust of the dead, and mixes them together, and puts into it skin and flesh and sinews and bones. And the angel in charge of the souls comes and infuses souls into them. And then they enter the House of Study where Abraham, Isaac, and Jacob sit before Him, the kings of Israel and Judah behind Him, and David at the head. . . .

(Pes. Hadta, BhM 6:47)

And when all the exiles come, He will divide for them the Sea of Egypt and the River of Egypt into seven rivers, and no one of Israel who will be alive will remain in any place, until they all come to Jerusalem. And only the dead will remain. And then He will blow the Great Shofar. And it is said that Zerubbabel will blow that Shofar. . . .

And why will then be such a great earthquake? So that the bones which were trampled into the earth and built into buildings and burnt into bricks and buried under the ruins should come up, so that bone go to its bone.... And the Holy One, blessed be He, will stretch sinews upon them and cover them with flesh and envelop them with skin, but there will be no spirit in them. And then the Holy One, blessed be He, will cause the dew of life to descend from heaven, in which there is the light of the life of the soul.... And they will recognize that they had lived and died and then have risen to life.... And all those who had a blemish will at first rise with their blemish, and if he was old he will come back with his old age and the weakness of his flesh, so that they should not say, "These are other creatures." And then the Holy One, blessed be He, will heal them....

And for whom is this resurrection of the dead? For all those who were pious in Israel at first, and also for those who sinned and repented. But those whose sins were more numerous than their merits and who did not repent, will not rise in the days of the Messiah.... And Israel will marvel and say: "From whence did all these come suddenly?".... And the nations of the world will also marvel....

And the nations which remain will become proselytes. ...And when they come before King Messiah, he will command them to cause swords and wars to cease.... And then Sodom and Gomorrah will be settled, their towns and all the surroundings, so that the Land of Israel should not be left blemished by a destruction in her midst.... And he will also cause all evil animals to cease from the land.... And those people whom King Messiah will find alive will live long lives and then will die.... And no man will die as a youth or a young man.... And he will uproot death from the world.... And those who will die in the days of the Messiah will live in the life of the World to Come, because of the merits of the totally saintly....

(Hai Gaon, *Responsum*, pp. 60a–b)

The resurrection of the dead will be brought about by the Holy One, blessed be He, in this world in order to sanctify His great name in the days of the Messiah, and in order to give rewards to those who love Him and fear Him in the World to Come.... The Holy One, blessed be He, will bring upon them a dew of lights and

will seat them between His knees, and pet them and embrace them and kiss them and bring them to the life of the World to Come. . . .
(Seder Eliyahu Rabba, 5, p. 22)

The Holy One, blessed be He, calls the ministering angels and says to them: "My children I created you only for the sake of this hour, so that you cause Me satisfaction." The ministering angels answer Him and say before Him: "Master of the World! Behold, we stand before You in everything you want." The Holy One, blessed be He, answers and says: "Go and roam about in the four winds of the world, and lift up the four corners of the earth, and prepare channels in the soil for each and every pious man who is in foreign countries to the Land of Israel, and bring Me each and every pious man, the pious and the saintly and the sages who gave up their lives for the sanctification of My name day after day, so that they should not suffer and should come to the Land of Israel, and [there] I shall resuscitate them."

Instantly they set out, every angel and every seraph, and every heavenly prince, and every host. And they roam about in the four winds of the world and lift up the four corners of the earth, and shake the wicked off it. . . . And they make channels in the soil of the earth for all the pious men who are in foreign countries, and bring them through the channels to the Land of Israel, to the Holy One, blessed be He, to Jerusalem. And the Holy One, blessed be He, Himself rises and resuscitates them and makes them stand on their feet.

And how does the Holy One, blessed be He, resuscitate the dead in the World to Come? We are taught that the Holy One, blessed be He, takes in His hand a Great Shofar, which is a thousand cubits of the cubits of the Holy One, blessed be He, and blows it, and its sound goes from one end of the world to the other. At the first blow the whole world shakes. At the second blow the dust breaks up. At the third blow their bones gather. At the fourth blow the members become warm. At the fifth blow their skins are stretched over them. At the sixth blow spirits and souls enter their bodies. At the seventh blow they become alive and stand up on their feet in their clothes. . . .
(Mid. Alpha Beta diR. Akiba, BhM 3:31)

It appears to us from these sayings [of the Prophet Ezekiel] that those people whose souls will return into their bodies [at resurrection] will eat and drink and copulate and give birth and die after a very long life, just like those who will be found [alive] in the days of the Messiah.

However, the life after which there is no death is the life of the World to Come, in which there is no body. For we believe it, and it is the truth [held] by all those who have a mind, that the World to Come is souls without bodies, like the angels.

(Maimonides, *Treatise on Resurrection*, p. 17)

I believe with a perfect faith that there will be resurrection of the dead at a time when the will shall arise from the Creator, may His Name be blessed and His remembrance exalted for all eternity.

(Maimonides, *Thirteen Articles of the Faith*, Article 13)

Come and see: Whatever the Holy One, blessed be He, has smitten in This World, will be healed in the World to Come. The blind will be healed . . . the halt will be healed . . . all will be healed. But, as a man goes [i.e. dies], so he will come [i.e. rise]. If he went blind, he will come blind; if he went deaf, he will come deaf; if he went halt, he will come halt; if he went dumb, he will come dumb. Just so, if he went clothed, he will come clothed. . . . And why will everyone come as he went? So that the wicked of the world should not say: "When they died the Holy One, blessed be He, healed them, and then He brought them [back to life]." [Or, so that they should not say:] "It seems that these are other persons." [Therefore] the Holy One, blessed be He, said: "Let them rise as they went, and thereafter I shall heal them. . . ." And thereafter even the wild beasts will be healed. . . . But he who brought suffering upon all [i.e. the Serpent] will not be healed. . . .

(Mid. Tanh. Buber, Gen., pp. 104b–105a)

In the hour when the Holy One, blessed be He, resurrects the dead, He shakes His locks, and the dew descends from His head, and the dust becomes kneaded [together with it]. . . .

(Yalqut Shim'oni, Songs, no. 988)

At the time when the Holy One, blessed be He, is about to resuscitate the dead, he causes dew from His head to come down upon the earth, and by means of that dew all will rise from the dust. This is what is written, *For a dew of light is Thy dew* (Isa. 26:19). What is *dew of light?* It is actually lights from those supernal lights by means of which He gives eternal life to the earth.

(Zohar 1:130b)

In the Gulgalta sit thirteen thousand myriads of worlds which move on feet and lean on them. And from that Gulgalta dew drips upon Him who is outside, and fills his head every day, as it is written, *My head is filled with dew* (Songs 5:2). And from that dew which He who sits outside shakes from His head, the dead will awaken in the World to Come, as it is written, *For a dew of light is Thy dew, and the earth shall bring forth the shades* (Isa. 26:19). That dew is the light of the pale glow of the Ancient One. And from that dew exist the supernal saints, and it is the manna which they grind for the righteous in the World to Come. And that dew drips down to the field of Sacred Apples. . . .[2]

(Idra Rabba, Zohar 3:128b)

Come, see: At that time, when the Holy One, blessed be He, prepares to resurrect the dead, He will create bodies for all those dead who will be found abroad, in the other foreign lands, as it is suitable. For one bone remains of man under the earth. That bone will become like the leaven in the dough, and upon it the Holy One, blessed be He, will build the whole body. But the Holy One, blessed be He, will not give them souls, except in the Land of Israel, where all of them will receive souls, except for those who

---

2. The language of this passage is difficult in the original. *Gulgalta*, lit. "skull" or "head," refers to the aspect of God termed *Arikh Anpin*, while "He who is outside" refers to God as the *Z'ir Anpin*. These two Aramaic terms are ambiguous. *Arikh Anpin*, which means both "long suffering" and, in a more literal sense, "long of face," refers to God in His merciful, long-suffering aspect. *Z'ir Anpin* can mean either "the impatient" (as Scholem maintains in his *Major Trends*, p. 270), or "small of face," and refers to God as comprising the qualities of mercy and compassion plus justice and stern judgment, i.e., the potencies of the lower Sefirot. In several passages of the Zohar the differences between these two aspects of God are explained as differences in size or comprehensiveness, due to divine emanations which resulted in a diminishing of the remaining substance of God. Cf., e.g., Idra Rabba, Zohar 3:135b and Idra Zutta, Zohar 3:292b, and Y'huda Ashlag's Zohar commentary (*Sullam*) to those passages in vol. 15, p. 113, and vol. 18, pp. 47ff. "Ancient One," or more fully the "Holy Ancient One," is often conceived as identical with the Long-Suffering, indicating a state of the deity prior to the onset of Creation.

had defiled themselves and defiled the earth.

(Zohar 1:69a)

R. Yosef said: "Are not the days of the Messiah and the resurrection of the dead one and the same?" R. Nahman said to him: "No. For we have learned that [the rebuilding of] the Temple will precede the ingathering of the exiles; the ingathering of the exiles will precede the resurrection of the dead; and the resurrection of the dead is the last of all of them...." We have learned: "The ingathering of the exiles will precede the resurrection of the dead by forty years...." Rav Kahana said in the name of R. B'roqa: "From the ingathering of the exiles until the resurrection of the dead many sufferings, many wars, will arise against Israel, and happy is he who escapes them...." And in those days there will be days [about which] they will say: "I want them not!" And from the end of the sufferings until the resurrection of the dead there will be forty years.... And from the time of the resurrection of the dead on, the world will be fully populated....

(Zohar 1:139a–b; Mid. haNe'elam)

In the time to come, *The flocks shall again pass under the hands of him that counteth them* (Jer. 33:13). And we do not know who he is. But since at that time all will be in union without separation, there will be One who will count [and say]: "Arise, old man, bestir yourself and become strong in your power and sail the sea.".... When the Holy One, blessed be He, arises to resuscitate the dead, those who had gone through repeated transmigrations and [therefore possessed at least] two bodies with one soul, two fathers, two mothers, how many transmigrations will they have to experience?... However, *Who hath counted the dust of Jacob* (Num. 23:10), that is, He will put everything right, nothing will be lost, and all of them will rise....

(Zohar 2:105b)

R. Yishma'el said: "Zaganzagel, the Prince of the Face [i.e., the highest-ranking angel] said to me: 'The first generations were not worthy of having it revealed to them, but you weigh in your generation as did Aharon the priest.

"'In the second generation, in which the Son of David will come, the whole world will be like a woman in childbirth. They will eat and drink, but their heart will not be upon them. And there will be wailing among the holy ones and crying in the families of the mighty, and a trembling will arise in the cities and a terror in the countries. And the vine will not give its fruit, and the wine will be dear, and the olives will be smitten, and the oil will be expensive. And when the nations of the world see this, they will give permission that every idol should be uprooted...and as soon as you see these signs, know that it is the Messianic End.

"'And thereafter four nations will come from the four winds of the world—and they are: the Children of Masqariya from one wind, the Children of Shabur from one wind, the Children of Patros from one wind, and the Children of Ethiopia and Maragesh from one wind. And they will wage war one against the other, and will slay one another, and there will fall of them more than two hundred thousand slain. In that hour they will say to one another: "Why should we wage war? Come, let us be reconciled, and he who is victorious let him be king over us, and let all of us serve him."

"'In that hour Messiah will come out of the jail-house with his staff and his bag, and he will come to them and say to them: "Let me meet you face to face." In that hour they will say one to the other: "With what will this one defeat us? His appearance is not like other people, and his looks are not like other people, and he has no army like other people; while we have riches, have armies, are warriors, are sons of kings—and this one, with what will he defeat us?" And they will say to him: "If you defeat me, I and all Israel will be your servants." When they hear this, because of their great desire to subjugate Israel, each of them says: "Say what you have to say!" The Messiah then says to them: "I have but a small thing to say, not a big one: he who brings all these slain men back to life, let him be king over us!" Instantly they fall silent and have no mouth to speak.

"'In that hour the Messiah stands up and wraps himself in prayer and girds himself like a hero before Him who spoke and the world was, and says before Him: "Master of all the worlds! Remember my sorrow and my sighs, the darkness and the gloom in which I dwelt, my two eyes which saw no light, and my ears which heard great disgrace. I cried over myself and my heart broke in me and my strength became feeble in sorrow and sighs. It is revealed and known before You that I did not do all this for my honor, nor for the honor of my father's house, but I did it for Your honor, for the sake of Your nation and Your sanctuary, and Your children who are caught in suffering among the nations of the world!"

"'In that hour those two hundred thousand men rise up on their feet and say: "We are of Israel! We are of Israel!"...In that hour the Messiah says to them: "Go and gather all your brethren from all the nations!" And they go and gather all Israel and bring them and set them before the Messiah....'"

R. Yishma'el said: "Zanganzagel, the Prince of the Face, said to me: 'In the future all the nations of the world will come to the Messiah and say to him: "Have we not heard about you that it is in your power to slay and to bring back to life? If you will, speak before the Holy One, blessed be He, that He should accept a present from us." He says to them: "And what present will you bring Him?" They say to him: "His dwelling house. We destroyed it; we shall rebuild it!" And He says to them: "You wicked ones! He does not need your building!..." They say to him: "If so, we shall fill it with precious stones...."'"

(Yemenite Apocalypse, pp. 326–27.)

The ignorant will be resuscitated by the Holy One, blessed be He, by means of the dews of sleep. For when the scholars study and fall asleep over their books, the Holy One, blessed be He, preserves the spittle which flows out of their mouths and makes dew out of it, and with it He resuscitates the ignorant dead.

(Yalqut Hadash, Messiah, par. 25.)

Little ribbon, little pearl, golden banner,
Messiah ben David sits on high
Dressed in gold and silver,
In his right hand he holds a cup,
Pronounces a blessing over the whole land,
Amen and Amen. This is true.
The Messiah will come this very year,
If he comes a-riding,
We shall have good times.
If he come in a carriage,
We shall have good years.
If he comes on foot,
All the dead will rise.

(Yiddish Folksong, from Ruth
Rubin, *Voices of a People*, p. 140.)

22

The Last Judgment

In the Bible, beginning with the prophetic writings of the eighth century B.C.E., the belief in a "Day of the Lord" is attested as an old popular tenet. The people expected and hoped that a day would come in which God would execute judgment over the nations of the world. Amos cautioned that the Day of the Lord would be *darkness and no light* (5:18–20), meaning that also Israel itself would have to undergo the stern scrutiny of God and receive its punishment for injustice. Thereafter the Day of the Lord was expected to be a day of national calamity. When, less than two centuries after Amos, Jerusalem was destroyed by the Babylonians, this was interpreted as the fulfillment of those expectations (see, for instance, Lamentations). Following the Babylonian exile, the hope arose that the Day of the Lord would be a day of rejuvenation, restoration, and Redemption, on which the enemies of Israel would, in turn, receive retribution.

Toward the end of the Biblical period, the Day of the Lord assumed a more and more supranatural coloring and an eschatological character. This appears fully developed in the Book of Enoch, written in the second century B.C.E., from which is taken the first excerpt below. The leitmotiv in it is that God will deliver the kings and the mighty of the nations to the angels for punishment. In the Sibylline Books, only a few decades later, the Day of the Lord is connected to the appearance of "a king" who has definitely Messianic features (see second excerpt below). By the time of the Psalms of Solomon (c. 63 B.C.E.), the "Son of David," that is, the Messiah, had definitely become the agent carrying out God's vengeance on the "godless nations."

Talmudic teachers elaborate the idea. They treat us to lively arguments taking place between God and the wicked nations, who try to plead a fraudulent defense of their evil deeds, but, of course, to no avail. In these texts the punishment of the idolatrous nations and of the wicked of Israel, their sentencing to Gehenna, is repeated in many variations. Typically, however, while the Last Judgment is projected into the Messianic era, the Messiah himself has no role in the proceedings. It is God, sitting on His exalted Throne of Judgment, who hears the cases, examines the culprits, and sentences them.

In connection with the Last Judgment, the question is raised, what is responsible for the sins a person commits during his lifetime? Is it the body or the soul? The answer, given in the form of a fine parable, is attributed to R. Y'huda haNasi (the Prince), the head of the Jewish community in Roman Palestine toward the end of the second century C.E. and the redactor of the Mishna (see below). The same parable also explains, although it does not say so explicitly, why, to the highly developed sense of justice of the Jews, the Resurrection was a logical prerequisite of the Last Judgment.

The Lord of Spirits will so press them
[The kings and the mighty of the nations]
That they shall hastily go forth from His presence,
And their faces shall be filled with shame,
And the darkness grow deep on their faces.
And He will deliver them to the angels for punishment,
To execute vengeance on them,

Because they have oppressed His children and His elect.
And they shall be a spectacle for the righteous and for His
    elect;
They shall rejoice over them,
For the wrath of the Lord of Spirits shall rest upon them,
And His sword shall be drunk with their blood.
And the righteous and elect shall be saved on that day,
And never again see the sinners and the wicked.

(1 Enoch 62:10—13)

And then from the sunrise God shall send a king who shall
give every land relief from the bane of war. Some he shall slay, and
to others he shall consecrate faithful vows. Nor shall he do all these
things by his own will, but in obedience to the good ordinances of
the mighty God.

And again the Hall of the mighty God shall be laden with
great wealth, with gold and silver and purple adornment; the land
shall bear her fruit, and the sea shall be full of good things. And
then with a mighty voice God shall speak unto all the foolish and
empty-minded people, and judgment shall come upon them from
the mighty God, and all shall perish at the hands of the Eternal. . . .

(Sibylline Books 3:652—72)

Behold, O Lord, and raise up unto them their king, the
    Son of David,
At the time which thou seest, O God, that he reign over
    Israel Thy servant.
And gird him with strength that he may shatter
    unrighteous rulers,
And purge Jerusalem from nations that trample her down
    to destruction.
Wisely, righteously, he shall thrust out sinners from the
    inheritance,
And break the pride of the sinner as a potter's vessel.
With a rod of iron shall he shatter all their substance,
And destroy the godless nations with the word of his
    mouth.
At his rebuke nations shall flee before him,
And he shall reprove sinners for the thoughts of their

heart.

And he shall gather the holy people to lead them in
    righteousness,

And judge the tribes of the people sanctified by the Lord.

And he shall suffer no unrighteousness to lodge in their
    midst,

Nor shall there dwell with them any man that knoweth
    wickedness,

For he shall know them, that they all are sons of their God,

And shall divide them according to their tribes upon the
    land,

And neither stranger nor alien shall dwell with them
    anymore.

He shall judge peoples and nations in the wisdom of his
    righteousness. *Selah.*

Him heathen nations shall serve, under his yoke,

He shall honor the Lord before the whole earth,

And shall purify Jerusalem in holiness as of old.

All nations shall come from the ends of the earth to see his
    glory,

Her tired children shall come carrying gifts,

To see the majesty of the Lord with which God adorned
    her.

And he shall be a righteous king, taught of God, over
    them,

And in his days no iniquity shall be in their midst,

For all shall be holy, and the Messiah of the Lord their
    king.

For he shall not trust in horse, and chariot, and bow . . .

(Psalms of Solomon 17:21–36)

R. Hanina bar Papa, and according to others R. Simlai, expounded: "In the Future to Come, the Holy One, blessed be He, will bring a Tora scroll and put it in His lap and say: 'Those who occupied themselves with this, let them come and get their reward.' Instantly all the nations of the world will gather and come in confusion. . . . But the Holy One, blessed be He, will say to them: 'Do not gather in confusion before Me, but rather let each nation and its scribes approach [separately]. . . .' Thereupon the kingdom of Edom [Rome] will enter first before Him. . . . The Holy One, blessed be He, will speak to them: 'With what did you occupy yourselves?' They will answer: 'Master of the World! We have built many roads, set up marketplaces, built many bathhouses, collected much gold and silver, and did all this only for Israel, so that they [should be able to] occupy themselves with the Tora.' But the Holy One, blessed be He, will answer them: 'You fools in the world! Everything you did you did only for yourselves. You set up marketplaces in order to seat whores in them; bathhouses in order to find pleasures in them; and as for the silver and gold, it belongs to Me.... Is there any one among you who studied the Tora?' Thereupon they will leave abashed. As soon as the kingdom of Rome leaves, the kingdom of Persia will enter.... The Holy One, blessed be He, will speak to them: 'With what did you occupy yourselves?' They will say: 'Lord of the World! We have built many bridges, conquered many cities, waged many wars, and we did all this only for Israel, so that they should occupy themselves with the Tora.' But the Holy One, blessed be He, will answer them: 'Everything you did you did only for yourselves. You built bridges in order to collect tolls on them; conquered cities in order to levy forced labor from them; and as for the wars, I Myself waged them.... Is there anybody among you who studied the Tora?' Thereupon they too leave abashed.... And likewise all the other nations. Why do those two kingdoms count as important and the others do not? Because their rule will continue until the coming of the Messiah."

(B. 'Av. Zar. 2a–b)

R. Pinhas in the name of R. Reuben: "A parable. A king gave a banquet and invited guests, and issued instructions saying: 'Everyone should bring along with him that on which he will sit.' Some brought rugs, and some brought mats, and some brought mattresses, and some brought covers, and some brought chairs, and some brought wood, and some brought stones. The king observed [it] and said: 'Everyone should sit on what he brought.' Those who sat on the wood and the stones complained against the king and said: 'Is this [according to] the honor of the king that we should sit on the wood and the stones?' When the king heard this he said to them: 'Is it not enough that you defaced the palace with stones and wood which stood in my way in several exits; must you add insolence and band together to accuse me? It is not I who gives you honor, but you yourselves!'

"Thus in the Future to Come, the wicked will be sentenced to Gehenna, and they will complain against the Holy One, blessed be He: 'We were waiting for the salvation of the Holy One, blessed be He, and now is this what happens to us?' The Holy One, blessed be He, says to them: 'In the world in which you were, were you not men of quarrels and of evil tongue, and of all kinds of iniquity? Were you not people of strife and violence?... Therefore, now walk in the light of your fire and in the sparks which you lit! And say not that this came upon you from My hands; no, but you did it for yourselves. Therefore you will lie down in anguish, for it came from your own hands.'"

(Eccl. Rab. 3:9)

For thirteen hundred years they will rejoice in the joy of the Messiah, and the Temple will be completed.... The thirteen hundred years of the days of the Messiah will be for Israel holidays and feasts and happiness and greatness and honor, until the great Day of Judgment. But that day will be a day of darkness and dread, lighted up [only] by the light of the burning torch. Then the Holy One, blessed be He, will reveal the Garden of Eden and Gehenna which He created prior to the creation of the world.... And God will give to Abraham all those who came from the true seed, and all Israel will go to Eden. And the sinners will say to them: "Woe, prophets [i.e., Fathers]! Is it not that you are our descendants,[1] and now you push us away?" But they [Abraham, Isaac, and Jacob] will answer them nothing, and at once they all will be sent to Gehenna.

(Ma'ase Daniel, pp. 226–27)

Elijah of blessed memory said: "I see fire and brimstone descend from heaven upon the wicked.... And the Holy One, blessed be He, will remove the Sanctuary far away from the destruction of the world so that the pious will not hear the cries of the wicked and will not ask mercy for them. And the wicked will become as if they had never been."

(Sefer Eliahu, BhM 3:67)

And at the end of two thousand years, the Holy One, blessed

---

1. The Midrash here refers to the idolatrous ancestors of Abraham.

be He, will sit on the Throne of Judgment in the Valley of Yehoshaphat. And instantly the heaven and the earth will decay, and the sun will become ashamed, and the moon and the mountains will shake, and the hills tremble so as not to remind Israel of its sins. And the gates of Gehenna will open in the Valley of Yehoshaphat, and the gates of the Garden of Eden in the east, on the third day....

The third day is the Day of Judgment, and woe to all those who die on it! And the Holy One, blessed be He, will cause every nation to pass before Him, and He will say to them: "You who worship gods of silver and gold, see whether they can save you!" Instantly they pass, and are burned.... And Israel will come after them, and the Holy One, blessed be He, will say to them: "Whom do you worship?" And they will say: "[We worship You,] for You are our Father...."

And the nations of the world will say in Gehenna: "Let us see whether He judges Israel, His people, as He judged us." Instantly the Holy One, blessed be He, passes through the middle of Gehenna with the People of Israel, and it becomes before them like cool water.... In that hour the sinners of Israel will be shaken into Gehenna for twelve months, and thereafter the Holy One, blessed be He, will bring them up, and they will sit in the Garden of Eden and enjoy its fruits....

(Nistarot R. Shim'on ben Yohai, BhM 3:80−81)

And from the Temple will open the gates of the Garden of Eden.... And Gehenna, too, will open from there, and there the Holy One, blessed be He, will bring down His throne and set it up in the Valley of Yehoshaphat, and there He will cause each nation and its idols to pass before Him. And when the nations of the world pass there, they will fall into Gehenna.... And what brings this about for them? Because they stretched forth their hand against the Sanctuary.... And the sinners and rebellious of Israel will cry so much that they will cool down Gehenna with their tears.... And when the sinners and the rebellious fall into Gehenna, the fire of the Lord will burn their bodies, and their teeth will fall out of their mouths....

(Pirqe Mashiah, BhM 3:74−75)

And seventy-two pearls will be hung in Jerusalem, and they

will shed light from one end of the world to the other, and all the
nations of the world will walk in that light. . . . And the Holy One,
blessed be He, will make the Sanctuary descend from heaven, as
He showed it to Moses. . . . And Israel will dwell there two
thousand years, and they will eat Leviathan. And at the end of two
thousand years, the Holy One, blessed be He, will sit on the
Throne of Judgment in the Valley of Yehoshaphat. Instantly the
heaven and the earth will pass away, and the sun and the moon will
be ashamed. . . . And on the third day will be the Judgment. . . . The
Holy One, blessed be He, will bring every nation and language
and say to them: "What did you worship in the world that has
passed, and to whom did you prostrate yourselves?" And they will
say: "To idols of silver and idols of gold." And the Holy One,
blessed be He, will say to them: "Pass through the fire. If your gods
can save you, let them!" Instantly they pass and are burned.
. . . Thereafter Israel will come, and the Holy One, blessed be He,
will say to them: "And you, whom did you worship?" Instantly
they will answer: "For You are our Father . . . our Redeemer,
everlasting is Your name." Instantly the Holy One, blessed be He,
will save them from the punishment of Gehenna. And they will sit
in the Garden of Eden and enjoy its fruits. . . . And then the Holy
One, blessed be He, will renew for them the heavens and the
earth. . . . And when He renews the world, He will arrange the
order of the pious and the order of the saintly, and thus for every
generation and every creature and every soul. And the earth which
He will renew will produce trees and all kinds of delicacies and all
will live forever and ever. He who wrought miracles and portents
in those days and at that time, may He work for us miracles and
portents in these days and in this time, and gather us from the four
winds of the world and lead us to Jerusalem, and make us rejoice in
her, and let us say Amen, *Selah!*

(Mid. waYosha', BhM 1:56–57)

A parable. Some people had a lawsuit at court and they were
afraid of the judgment. The judge said to them: "Speak and fear not
the judgment, be daring in your heart!" Thus the Holy One,
blessed be He, will speak to the angels when Israel will stand in
judgment before Him and they will be afraid of the judgment. And
the ministering angels will say: "Fear not. Do you not know Him?
He is one of your city. . . . He is one of your relatives. . . . He is your

brother, and, most of all, He is your father...."

(Mid. Hallel, BhM 5:107)

Antoninus said to Rabbi [Y'huda haNasi]: "The body and the soul can avoid punishment. How? The body can say: 'The soul sinned, for from the day that it departed from me I have been lying in the grave like a dumb stone.' And the soul can say: 'The body sinned, for ever since I departed from it, I have been flying about in the air like a bird.'"

Rabbi said to him: "I shall tell you a parable: To what can this be likened? To a flesh-and-blood king who had a beautiful orchard full of fine fruit. He placed into it two watchmen, one lame and one blind. The lame said to the blind: 'I see fine fruits in the orchard. Come, let me ride on your back and we shall fetch them and eat them.' The lame rode on the back of the blind, and they took the fruit and ate it.

"Days later the owner of the orchard came and said to them: 'The fine fruits, where are they?' The lame said: 'Do I have feet to walk on them?' The blind said: 'Do I have eyes to see with them?' What did the king do? He made the lame ride on the back of the blind and judged them as one. Thus the Holy One, blessed be He, too, will bring the soul, cast it into the body, and judge them as one."

(B. Sanh. 91a–b)

23

Messianic Jerusalem

The earliest indication of the idea of a new Jerusalem is found in the apocryphal First Book of Enoch (written about 150 B.C.E.) in which it is referred to as "a new house" brought by "the Lord of the sheep" for his "flock", that is, the Jewish people. By the early first century C.E. this concept had developed into the expectation that a new "building" (i.e. Temple) would be built in Zion, "renewed in glory and perfected for evermore" (2 Baruch, see below). About the time of the destruction of Jerusalem (70 C.E.) the author of 4 Ezra expected a new city, "now invisible, [to] appear."

Entirely within the spirit of these Jewish apocalypses is the vision of the heavenly Jerusalem contained in Revelation (the last book of the New Testament), chapter 21. The Book of Revelation was written—in Hebrew, Aramaic, or Greek—late in the first century C.E. Its author was a Judeo-Christian, well versed in the Scriptures, who, while he believed in the Messiahship of Jesus (whom he calls "the Lamb"), expected his return in the Future to Come, and described the heavenly Jerusalem in Jewish apocalyptic-Aggadic terms.

In the Talmud and Midrash, the heavenly Jerusalem is a standard Aggadic notion, presented in great detail and in many variants. In them, the undying love of the Jewish people for Jerusalem, the Holy City, the city of the Temple and the royal seat of David, finds eloquent expression in limitless flights of fantasy describing the glories of the future Jerusalem in the days of the Messiah. This Messianic Jerusalem, which will descend in its entirety from heaven, will comprise a thousand towers, fortresses, street corners, pools, and cisterns, it will extend as far as Damascus, its height will increase by miles, its gates will be huge precious stones, jewels and pearls will be scattered all over its streets and environs like pebbles, and its radiance will light up the whole world and will rise up to God's Throne of Glory.

And I saw till the Lord of the sheep brought a new house, greater and loftier than the first, and set it up in the place of the first which had been folded up: all its pillars were new, and its ornaments were new and larger than those of the first, the old one which He had taken away, and all the sheep were within it.

(1Enoch 90:29)

After a little time the building of Zion will be shaken in order that it may be built again. But that building will not remain, but will again after a time be rooted out, and will remain desolate until the time. And afterwards it must be renewed in glory, and perfected for evermore.

(2 [Syriac] Baruch 32:2—4)

For behold the days come, and it shall be when the signs which I have foretold unto you shall come to pass. Then shall the city that is now invisible appear, and the land which is now concealed be seen. And whosoever is delivered from the predicted evils shall see my wonders.

(4 Ezra 7:26—27)

And I saw a new heaven and a new earth: for the first heaven and the first earth were passed away; and there was no more sea. And I John saw the holy city, new Jerusalem, coming down from God out of heaven, prepared as a bride adorned for her husband.

And I heard a great voice out of heaven saying, Behold, the tabernacle of God is with men, and He will dwell with them, and they shall be His people, and God himself shall be with them, and be their God. And God shall wipe away all tears from their eyes; and there shall be no more death, neither sorrow, nor crying, neither shall there be any more pain: for the former things are passed away.

And he that sat upon the throne said, Behold, I make all things new. And he said unto me, Write: for these words are true and faithful. And he said unto me, It is done. I am Alpha and Omega, the beginning and the end. I will give unto him that is athirst of the fountain of the water of life freely. But the fearful, and unbelieving, and the abominable, and murderers, and whoremongers, and sorcerers, and idolaters, and all liars, shall have their part in the lake which burneth with fire and brimstone: which is the second death.

And there came unto me one of the seven angels which had the seven vials full of the seven last plagues, and talked to me, saying, Come hither, I will show thee the bride, the Lamb's wife. And he carried me away in the spirit to a great and high mountain, and showed me that great city, the holy Jerusalem, descending out of heaven from God, having the glory of God: and her light was like unto a stone most precious, even like a jasper stone, clear as crystal; and had a wall great and high, and had twelve gates, and at the gates twelve angels, and names written thereon, which are the names of the twelve tribes of the Children of Israel. On the east three gates, on the north three gates, on the south three gates, and on the west three gates. And the wall of the city had twelve foundations, and in them the names of the twelve apostles of the Lamb.

And he that talked with me had a golden reed to measure the city, and the gates thereof, and the walls thereof. And the city lieth foursquare, and the length is as large as the breadth: and he measured the city with the reed, twelve thousand furlongs. The length and the breadth and the height of it are equal. And he measured the wall thereof, an hundred and forty and four cubits, according to the measure of a man, that is, of the angel. And the building of the wall of it was of jasper: and the city was pure gold, like unto clear glass. And the foundations of the wall of the city were garnished with all manner of precious stones. The first foundation was jasper; the second, sapphire; the third, a chalcedony; the fourth, an emerald; the fifth, sardonyx; the sixth, sardius; the seventh, chrysolyte; the eighth, beryl; the ninth, a topaz; the tenth, a chrysoprasus; the eleventh, a jacinth; the twelfth, an amethyst. And the twelve gates were twelve pearls; every several gate was of one pearl: and the street of the city was pure gold, as it were transparent glass. And I saw no temple therein: for the Lord God Almighty and the Lamb are the temple of it.

And the city had no need of the sun, neither of the moon, to shine in it: for the glory of God did lighten it, and the Lamb is the light thereof. And the nations of them which are saved shall walk in the light of it: and the kings of the earth do bring their glory and honor into it. And the gates of it shall not be shut at all by day: for there shall be no night there. And they shall bring the glory and honor of the nations into it. And there shall in no wise enter into it anything that defileth, neither whatsoever worketh abomination, or maketh a lie: but they which are written in the Lamb's book of life.

(Revelation 21)

Rabba said in the name of R. Yohanan: "Jerusalem of This World is not like Jerusalem of the World to Come. Jerusalem of This World—anybody who wants to go up to visit her, can do so; but to Jerusalem of the World to Come only those can go up who are invited to come...."

And Rabba said in the name of R. Yohanan: "In the future, the Holy One, blessed be He, will elevate Jerusalem by three parasangs...."

Resh Laqish said: "In the future the Holy One, blessed be He, will add to Jerusalem a thousand gardens, a thousand towers, a thousand fortresses, and a thousand passages, and each of them will be like Sepphoris in its tranquil days." R. Yose said: "I saw Sepphoris in its tranquil days, and there were in it 180,000 marketplaces of merchants of pot dishes."

(B. Bab. Bath. 75b)

Once R. Yohanan sat and expounded: "In the future the Holy One, blessed be He, will bring precious stones and pearls of thirty by thirty cubits in size, and will hew out in them openings of ten by twenty, and place them in the gates of Jerusalem." A disciple mocked at him: "At present we cannot find precious stones even as big as an egg of a dove, how could there be jewels of that size?" Days later this disciple was sailing in a ship in the sea, and he saw ministering angels sit and saw precious stones and pearls which were thirty by thirty, cutting into them openings of ten by twenty. He said to them: "For whom are these?" They said to him that the Holy One, blessed be He, will in the future set them in the gates of Jerusalem. [Upon his return the disciple] went before R. Yohanan and said to him: "Expound, O Master, it behooves you to expound. As you said so I saw." R. Yohanan said to him: "You good-for-nothing! Had you not seen it you would not have believed it. You mocked the words of sages!" And he directed his eyes at him, and he became a heap of bones.

(B. Bab. Bath. 75a)

R. Binyamin ben Levi said: "In the future the environs of Jerusalem will be full of precious stones and pearls, and all Israel will come and take of them as many as they like. In this world Israel sets boundaries with stones and bushes, but in the future to come it will set boundaries with precious stones and pearls. . . ."

R. Levi said: "In the future, the area of Jerusalem, measuring twelve by eighteen miles, will be full of precious stones and pearls. For in this world, if a man owes his neighbor something and he says to him, 'Let us go and be judged by the judge,' at times the judge makes peace between them and at times he does not make peace between them, and the two do not come out satisfied. But in the future to come, if a man owes his neighbor something, and he says to him, 'Let us go and be judged by King Messiah in Jerusalem,' as soon as they reach the outskirts of Jerusalem they will find them full of precious stones and pearls, and he will take two of them and say to him, 'Do I owe you more than these?' And the other will answer him, 'Not even this much! Let it be forgiven to you, let it be left to you!'"

(Pes. diR. Kahana, ed. Mandelbaum, pp. 299–300)

How beautiful upon the mountains are the feet of the messenger of good tidings (Isa. 52:7)—this teaches you that in the future the Holy One, blessed be He, will cause built-up Jerusalem to descend from heaven, and will set her upon the tops of four mountains: Upon

Sinai, and upon Tabor, and upon Hermon, and upon Carmel. And she will stand on the tops of mountains and give good tidings to Israel about the End, the Redemption.
(Pes. diR. Kahana, ed. Mandelbaum, p. 466)

The ministering angels expect the rebuilding of Jerusalem, for in the hour when Jerusalem was destroyed they wept and mourned over her.... It is like a flesh-and-blood king who abandoned his house and went to a lodging place, and the members of the household were saddened, and the servants became exhausted on the way, and all were mourning because they had to leave the house of the king. Likewise the Holy One, blessed be He.... Who are the servants who are saddened? They are the Holy Beasts who carry the Throne of Glory. And the members of the household who are exhausted are the ministering angels who mourned when the King of Kings of Kings, the Holy One, blessed be He, abandoned the Temple. And it is to this that Isaiah refers: *Rejoice ye with Jerusalem, and be glad with her all ye that love her, rejoice for joy with her all ye that mourn for her* (Isa. 66:10).
(Pes. diR. Kahana, ed. Mandelbaum, p. 466)

Elijah said: "I see a beautiful and great city descend from heaven, built up, as it is written, *Jerusalem that art builded as a city that is compact together* (Ps. 122:3). Built up and embellished, and her people dwell in her midst, and she rests on three thousand towers, and between each two towers there is a distance of twenty *ris* [2/15 of a mile], and every *ris* comprises twenty-five thousand cubits of smaragds and precious stones and pearls...."
(Sefer Eliahu, BhM 3:67)

Elijah of blessed memory said: "I see the houses and gates of the pious. Their lintels and sideposts are of precious stones, and the treasuries of the Sanctuary open right unto their doors. And Tora and peace are among them...."
(Sefer Eliahu, BhM 3:68)

R. Hanina said: "In the future the Holy One, blessed be He, will show His glory to all those who walk on earth, and will let His throne descend to the middle of the firmament, and then let it rest in the place in which the sun shines in the *T'qufa* of Teveth [i.e. in midwinter]...."

(Mid. Tanh. Buber, V:31)

How many fortresses will there be in the future Jerusalem? 1,184. How many towers will there be in her in the future? 1,485. How many street corners? 1,496. How many pools? 1,876. And where will the water flow out? Into 900 cisterns.

(Mid. Tehillim 275–76)

It is said in praise of Jerusalem that she will be built in the future of precious stones and pearls.... And also the territories of Israel will in the future be full of precious stones.... And if a Gentile or a sectarian asks you saying: "Can such a thing be?" tell him that it was already like this in the days of Solomon....

Let us now praise the House of Holiness which will be built in the future of twelve onyx stones.... The entire world will be lighted up by the radiance of the House of Holiness, which will spread about and ascend until the firmament and until heaven and until the Holy Beasts and until the Divine Chariot and until the Throne of Glory....

(Pirqe Mashiah, BhM 3:69)

In the future there will be found in Jerusalem ten kinds of precious stones, and they are: ruby, topaz, emerald, beryl, onyx, jasper, carbuncle, sapphire, diamond, and gold—these are ten. And the Holy One, blessed be He, will add to them two at the building of the Temple, and they are: *kodkod* and *eqdah* [different varieties of rubies and carbuncles].

(Milhamot Melekh haMashiah, BhM 6:118)

In Jerusalem there will be in the future, three thousand towers, each tower with seven thousand stories, standing on top of three mountains: on Sinai, and on Tabor, and on Carmel. And in each story there will be seven thousand portals, and each portal will measure sixty-two cubits, and will stand on top of thirty-three sides, and the Temple will be on top of all. How will people be able to go up to them? Like clouds and like doves, they will fly and flutter.... And the Temple will extend until Damascus....

And seven walls will surround Jerusalem, of silver, of gold, of precious stones, ot stibium, of sapphire, of chalcedony, and of fire.

And its glow will light up the world from one end to the other. And the Temple will be built on four mountains, of purified gold, of clear gold, of drawn gold, and of Parwayim gold, which last one is like gold that produces fruits. And it will be set in sapphires and capped in greatness. Its height will reach heaven and until the stars and until the wheels of the Divine Chariot. . . . And the Shekhina of God will fill it, and His Glory will fill its Hall, and each angel will be busy there with his work: Gabriel with his thousands, and Michael with his myriads. And he will make multitudes and more multitudes enter it, and some he will separate for eternal life, and others for shame and eternal perdition.

(Pirqe Mashiah, BhM 3:74–75)

Our Masters said: "On the day on which the death of Moses our Master drew near, the Holy One, blessed be He, took him up to heaven on high and showed him the reward he would get, and what will be in the future. The Divine Quality of Mercy stood before Moses our Master, peace be upon him, and said to him: 'I bring you good tidings which will make you rejoice. Turn your face toward the Throne of Mercy and see.' He turned his face toward the Throne of Mercy and saw the Holy One, blessed be He, building the Temple of precious stones and pearls. And between stone and stone there was the radiance of the Shekhina which was better than pearls. And Messiah ben David was standing inside it, and Moses' brother Aaron was standing on his feet and his priestly robe was upon him.

"Aaron spoke to Moses: 'The time is come. Touch me not, for I am afraid of you because of the Shekhina, for no man can enter here until he has tasted the taste of death and has given his soul to the Angel of Death.' When Moses heard the words of Aaron, he fell upon his face before the Holy One, blessed be He, and said to him: 'Master of the World! Give me permission to speak with Your Messiah before I die!' The Holy One, blessed be He, said to him: 'Go!' and He taught him His Great Name so that the flame of the Shekhina should not consume him.

"When Messiah ben David and Aaron saw him, they understood that the Lord had taught him His Great Name, and both of them stood before him and said to him: 'Blessed is he who comes with the Name of the Lord!' Messiah ben David then asked Moses: 'The Holy One, blessed be He, told me that He would build the Temple on earth, the Temple for Israel, yet I saw Him here building the Temple in heaven with His own hands.' And the Messiah said to Moses: 'Moses, your father Jacob saw the Temple which was to be built on earth, and also saw the Temple which the Holy One, blessed be He, would build with His own hands in heaven. And he understood with all his being that the Temple which the Holy One, blessed be He, would build with His own hands in heaven, of precious stones and pearls, and with the radiance of the Shekhina, would be the Temple which would stand for Israel forever and ever until the end of all generations. And so he said that night when he slept upon the stone and saw built-up Jerusalem and Jerusalem built in heaven.'

"And Moses saw our father Jacob standing, and heard the Holy One, blessed be He, say to him: 'My son Jacob! At this time I stand over you until your children will stand before Me....' And when Jacob saw one Jerusalem on earth, and another in heaven, he said: 'This one which is on earth is nothing.... This is not a house which will stand for my children for all generations; but that House of God which He builds with His own hands will....'

"When Moses our Master heard these words in the presence of Messiah ben David, he rejoiced with great joy, and turned back his face to the Holy One, blessed be He, and said to Him: 'Master of the World! When will this built-up Jerusalem descend?' The Holy One, blessed be He, said: 'I have not revealed the time to anybody, neither to the first ones nor to the last ones. How could I tell it to you?' Moses said to him: 'Master of the World! Give me a hint of the events!' The Holy One, blessed be He, said to him: 'I shall first scatter Israel with a winnowing fork in the gates of the earth, and they will be dispersed in the four corners of the world among all the nations.... Then I shall stretch forth My hand a second time and shall gather those who went with Jonah ben Amitai to the Land of the Pathrusim [Upper Egypt], and those who will be in the Land of Shinar [Babylonia], and in Hamath and in Elam, and in Ethiopia....'

"In that hour Moses descended from heaven rejoicing, and the Angel of Death descended after him, but he did not give his spirit and his soul to the angel until the Holy One, blessed be He, showed him His face. And he gave his soul to the Holy One, blessed be He, with a whole heart and a willing soul."

(B'reshit Rabbati, pp. 136–37)

24

Miraculous Fertility

The miracles of the Messianic days will not be confined to the descent from heaven of a jewel-studded Jerusalem. They will, in the Aggadic fantasy whose first traces can be found in the Book of Enoch (second century B.C.E.; see below), also comprise a fabulous fertility encompassing men, beasts, and plants. A deep-seated desire and a pious hope for fertility, a firm belief in its bestowal by God as a reward for merits and its withholding as a punishment of sin—these were features of the Hebrew psyche from earliest Biblical days.[1] If fruitfulness is a blessing, a miraculously rich fruitfulness must, of course, be considered as a supreme boon. Hence the Messianic era, which is a period of blessings in overabundance, had to be characterized, among other things, by miraculous fertility.

Aggadic imagination, once let loose, knows no bounds. The wildly exaggerated statements about the miraculous fertility in Messianic days of women, animals, and vegetation are not meant to be taken literally, or even seriously. They are mental games in which the sages, otherwise so serious and ponderous, playfully try to outdo one another.

---

1. Cf. R. Patai, *Sex and Family*, pp. 71–91; *idem*, *Man and Temple*, pp. 146, 149–50, 156–61.

The dialogue between Rabban Gamliel and an unnamed disciple is a case in point. Rabban Gamliel asserts that in the Messianic era women will bear children every day like a hen which lays eggs every day, and loaves of bread and ready-made woolen garments will grow out of the earth. The disciple "mocks him" after each pronouncement (see below). In matters of serious doctrine no disciple would have dared to mock the highly respected head of the Sanhedrin. But in response to sayings which were not meant to be taken seriously, a disciple could allow himself to mock the master by quoting, *There is nothing new under the sun* (Eccles. 1:9), meaning that the Bible had long ago ruled against the possibility of such new miraculous phenomena as those Rabban Gamliel predicted for the Messianic age. Had this been a serious discussion, the master could have easily countered the disciple's argument by quoting another Biblical verse, such as, *I will give you a new heart and I will put within you a new spirit* (Ezek. 36:26), which, in the spirit of Aggadic exegesis, would have proved that new phenomena were indeed possible in the Future to Come. Instead, he chose to squelch the disciple's objection by referring to something in This World which showed that the miraculous Messianic fertility he was speaking about would not be a truly new thing because it had its counterpart in the present.

Be that as it may, the whole tenor of the statements about the miraculous fertility in the days of the Messiah shows that they are playful Aggadic fantasies. The sages indulged in them because they derived a psychological satisfaction from thinking up and uttering such grossly exaggerated descriptions of the blissful conditions in which Israel would live in the Future to Come.

> And then shall all the righteous escape,
> And live till they beget thousands of children,
> And all the days of their youth and old age
> Shall they complete in peace.

And then shall the whole earth be tilled in righteousness,
And shall all be planted with trees and be full of blessing.
And all desirable trees shall be planted on it,
And they shall plant vines on it
Which shall yield wine in abundance,
And as for all the seed which is sown thereon,
Each measure [of it] shall bear a thousand,
And each measure of olives shall yield ten presses of oil.

(l Enoch 10:17—19)

And it shall come to pass when all is accomplished that was to come to pass in those parts, that the Messiah shall begin to be revealed. And Behemoth shall be revealed from his place, and Leviathan shall ascend from the sea, those two great monsters which I created on the fifth day of creation, and shall have kept until that time; and then they shall be for food for all that are left. The earth also shall yield its fruit ten thousandfold, and on each vine there shall be a thousand branches, and each branch shall produce a thousand clusters, and each cluster a thousand grapes, and each grape a *kor* of wine. And those who have hungered shall rejoice. Moreover, they shall behold marvels every day. And morning after morning winds shall go forth from before Me to bring the fragrance of fruits to make the hearts rejoice; and at the close of the day clouds shall distill health-giving dew. And it shall come to pass at that time that the treasury of manna shall again descend from on high, and they will eat of it in those years, because these are they who have come to the end of time.

(2 Baruch 29)

Why was it [one of the Temple gates] called Water Gate? R. Eliezer ben Ya'aqov said: "Because in it water bubbled forth." This teaches us that the waters were bubbling forth and rising as if coming out of a flask. In the future they will come forth from under the threshold of the Temple.... All the waters of Creation will in the future come forth as if coming from the mouth of a flask.

(M. Middot 2:6; T. Suk. 3:3, 10;
B. Yoma 77b—78a)

R. Y'huda said: "In This World the crops ripen in six months, and a tree yields fruit in twelve months, but in the Future to Come the crops will ripen every month, and the trees will yield fruit every two months...." R. Yose said: "...In the Future to Come the crops will ripen in fifteen days, and the trees yield fruit every month."

(Y. Sheqalim 50a mid.)

Once Rabban Gamliel sat and taught: "In the future a woman will bear every day...." A disciple mocked him and said: "*There is nothing new under the sun*" (Eccles. 1:9). He said to him: "Come and I shall show you something like it in This World." He went out and showed him a hen. And again once Rabban Gamliel sat and taught: "In the future the trees will bear fruit every day...." That disciple mocked him and said: "But it is written, *There is nothing new under the sun!*" He said to him: "Come and I shall show you something like it in This World." He went out and showed him a caper bush. And again Rabban Gamliel sat and taught: "In the future the Land of Israel will bring forth loaves of bread and woolen garments...." That disciple mocked him and said: "*There is nothing new under the sun.*" He said to him: "Come and I shall show you something like it in This World." He went out and showed him mushrooms and truffles, and regarding the woolen garments he showed him the bark of a young palm shoot.

(B. Shab. 30b)

The rabbis taught: "[In the Future to Come] the wheat will shoot up like a date palm and be higher than the peaks of the mountains. And should you think that it will be hard to reap it—no, for the Holy One, blessed be He, will bring a wind from His storehouses, and it will blow at it and it will shake loose its fine flour, and people will go out into the field and bring home full hand-plates, and from it they and their families will have livelihood...." They said: "In the future a grain of wheat will be like two kidneys of a big ox. And be not astonished at this, for once a fox made its nest in a turnip, and when they weighed it they found that it weighed sixty pounds...." They said: "The World to Come will not be like This World. In This World there is much trouble in harvesting the grapes and pressing them; in the World to Come a man will bring one grape in a wagon or a boat and put it in a corner of his house, and take from it wine as from a big cask, and its wood will serve as fuel under the pot, and in each grape there will be thirty kegs of wine...." When Rav Dimi came he said: "...There will be no vinestock in the Land of Israel which will not require a whole city to harvest it... and there will be no shade tree in the Land of Israel which will not produce a load of fruit for two asses... and think not that the fruits will have no wine in them, or that it will not be red, or that it will not refresh, or that it will have no taste, or that it will not be equally suited for youths and for old men...."

(B. Ket. 111b)

How beautiful is King Messiah bringing glad tidings to Israel! The mountains will dance like calves before him, and the trees of the field will clap their hands seeing the salvation of Israel.... How beautiful are the mountains of Israel, flowing with milk and honey like streams of water, and also rivers of wine.... And from where will they issue? From the House of the Lord, and they will water the Valley of Shittim. What will its source be like? As it issues from the Holy of Holies until it reaches the threshold of the House, it will at first be like a thread of the weft; then, until the Hall, it will be like a thread of the warp; until the Courtyard it will be like the horn of a ram; until the Altar it will be like the horns of Locusts; until the Outer Court it will be like a small jar...; and from there it will flow down like a strong stream, suitable [*kasher*] for pilgrims, menstruating women, and sin-offerings to submerge in it. And the Angel of Death will not be able to cross it... and even a boat cannot cross it. And it will flow down until the Sea of the Plain in order to increase the fish for Israel. And they will have salt from that place.... And on its banks will grow all the trees of pleasure of Lebanon.... And every month the ethrog will ripen there, and its wood will be eaten just as its fruit.... How beautiful is the Temple which will descend from heaven and will be built on its hill....

(Pirqe Mashiah, BhM 3:74)

And Israel will sit and eat and drink and be fruitful and multiply and enjoy the radiance of the Shekhina. And the Holy One, blessed be He, will make the stature of each of them two hundred cubits tall....

And each one in Israel will beget children every day.... And each vinestock in the days of the Messiah will have grapes no less than the load of a foal... and all the shade trees which never bore fruit will bear fruit....

In the World to Come a man will bring his grape in a cart or in a boat and place it in a corner, and it will suffice for a big jar, for him and the members of his family.... And in the future the vinestock will stretch out and ascend on top of the mountains like a staff.... And the Holy One, blessed be He, will cause a wind to blow upon it and make its fruit fall to earth, and each one of Israel will take of it and thus find his livelihood and that of his family.

And in the future the Holy One, blessed be He, will make seven canopies for each pious man: a canopy of clouds, a canopy of smoke, a canopy of day, a canopy of fire, a canopy of light, a canopy of flame, and a canopy of night.

And the Holy One, blessed be He, will make all the prophets of Israel stand before Him, from the first generation to the last generation, and will say to them: "Come and see the good I have preserved for you. Come and eat and enjoy the blessings I have reserved for you...."

(Pirqe Mashiah, BhM 3:77–78)

25

The Banquet

The same playful Aggadistic fantasy that we discerned in the preceding chapter's description of the miraculous fertility in the Messianic days is evident in the statements about the equally fantastic Messianic banquet. The idea that after the wars and victories, following the Resurrection and the Day of Judgment, the pious will be entertained by God at a great banquet has no Biblical basis, nor is it present in the Apocrypha. What the Talmudic Aggadists did in this case was to take certain mythical animals mentioned in the Bible, such as the gigantic sea-dragon Leviathan (Isa. 21:1, etc.), and its dry-land counterpart, the mountainous Behemoth (Ps. 50:11, etc.), and build a new legend upon them. The meat of these monstrous animals, we are told, will be served by God at a great banquet to the pious of Israel. Those who prefer fowl to either fish or beef can enjoy the meat of Ziz Sadai (Ps. 50:11, etc.), which, since the days of the Psalmist, has grown into a wading bird of cosmic proportions. The beverage to complement the meal will be the legendary "wine preserved in its grapes" ever since the days of Creation. A paradisiac fragrance, wafted by the wind, will add to the pleasures of the pious, and incense will be burnt before them.

To cap the enjoyment of the righteous, their heavenly host, the Holy One, blessed be He, himself will come down and join them at the table. And not only that, but He will dance for them, flanked by two of the pious, and accompanied by the sun, the moon, and the stars dancing with Him.

The banquet is the high moment of the Messianic days. God will fulfill all the wishes the pious express before Him. David will say the benediction over the cup of wine. All the great leaders of Israel, the Fathers, Moses, Isaiah, and many others, will keep them company at the table, while the wicked will stand outside the walls of Paradise, their necks elongated unnaturally, so that they can gaze over the tall ramparts at the sight that will fill their hearts with envy and shame. And, finally, to render the banquet free of all worry about the future, on that occasion God will slay the Angel of Death.

Near the end of this chapter we append a brief description of the Messiah-banquet introduced by Shabbatai Zevi and celebrated by him in the company of his followers at the outgoing of the Sabbath, close to midnight. While such a meal was not as antinomian as many of the other innovations of Shabbatai Zevi, its introduction by the false Messiah is a testimony to the hold exercised by the concept of the Messianic banquet over the Jews of Turkey (and undoubtedly of other countries as well) as late as in the seventeenth century.

A different kind of Messianic banquet, strictly within the limits of the traditionally permissible, was introduced in 1977 by the Lubavicher Hasidim in Israel. This is celebrated on the last day of Passover, which is the traditional expected time of the arrival of the Messiah (see last item in this chapter).

God created a male and a female Leviathan, and had they copulated they [that is, their offspring] would have destroyed the whole world. What did the Holy One, blessed be He, do? He castrated the male and killed the female and preserved her in salt for the pious in the Future to Come. And also the Behemoth in the

Thousand Mountains He created male and female, and had they copulated they would have destroyed the whole world. What did the Holy One, blessed be He, do? He castrated the male and cooled the female and preserved her for the pious in the Future to Come.

When Rav Dimi came, R. Yohanan said: "In the future Gabriel will go out to hunt for Leviathan . . . and would the Holy One, blessed be He, not help him he would be unable to overcome him. . . ." When Rav Dimi came, R. Yohanan said: "In the hour when Leviathan is hungry he emits a breath from his mouth and brings to a boil all the waters which are in the deeps. . . . And would he not stick his head into the Garden of Eden, no creature would be able to stand his stench. . . . And when he is thirsty, he makes furrows in the sea. . . ." Rav Aha bar Ya'aqov said: "The abyss does not return to its place [after Leviathan drinks] for seventy years. . . ."

Rabba said in the name of R. Yohanan: "The Holy One, blessed be He, will in the future prepare a banquet for the pious from the meat of Leviathan. . . . And they will divide the leftovers and make of them merchandise in the marketplaces of Jerusalem. . . ."

And Rabba said in the name of R. Yohanan: "The Holy One, blessed be He, will in the future make a booth for the pious out of the skin of Leviathan . . . and the leftovers He will spread out over the walls of Jerusalem, and their radiance will shine from one end of the world to the other. . . ."

(B. Bab. Bath. 74b–75a)

In the Future to Come the Holy One, blessed be He, will make a banquet for the pious in the Garden of Eden, and they will need neither balsam nor spices, for the north wind and the south wind will sweep the Garden of Eden and bring them all kinds of spices which will give off their fragrance. . . . And Israel will say before the Holy One, blessed be He: "Is there a host who makes a banquet for the guests and does not sit down with them? And is there a bridegroom who makes a banquet for those invited and does not sit down with them?" The Holy One, blessed be He, will say to them: "Behold, I shall do as you wish." In that hour the Holy One, blessed be He, will come to the Garden of Eden. . . .

Because they became embittered in the exile, and because

they perfumed themselves with the Sanctification of the Name of Heaven, therefore in the future the Holy One, blessed be He, will give them pleasures in the Garden of Eden and will burn before them all kinds of incense.... Because they bared their souls unto death in the exile... and occupied themselves with the Tora which is sweeter than honey, therefore in the future the Holy One, blessed be He, will give them to drink wine preserved in its grapes since the six days of creation, and will let them bathe in streams of milk.

(Num. Rab. 13:2)

R. Berekhya and R. Helbo said: "The Holy One, blessed be He, will act as the head dancer for the righteous in the Future to Come.... Righteous on this side and righteous on that side, and the Holy One, blessed be He, in the middle...."

(Cant. Rab. 1, 3:3, on Songs 1:3)

In the day of his espousals (Songs 3:11)—this refers to the days of the Messiah, for [then] the Holy One, blessed be He, will be like a bridegroom. *And in the day of the gladness of his heart* [ibid.]—over the rebuilding of the Temple.

(Yalqut Shim'oni, Songs, no. 988)

Elijah of blessed memory said: "I see Abraham, Isaac, and Jacob, and all the pious sit, and the earth before them is strewn with all kinds of delicacies. That tree which the Holy One, blessed be He, prepared, stands in the middle of the Garden.... And ships come from 'En Gedi to 'Eglayim, laden with riches and honors for the pious."

(Sefer Eliahu, BhM 3:67)

And Israel will dwell in safety for two thousand years, and they will eat Behemoth and Leviathan and Ziz. They will slaughter Behemoth, and Ziz will tear Leviathan apart with its claws, and Moses will come and slaughter Ziz Sadai.

(Nistarot R. Shim'on ben Yohai, BhM 3:80)

In that hour the Holy One, blessed be He, will set tables and slaughter Behemoth and Leviathan and Ziz Sadai, and prepare a great banquet for the pious. And He will seat each one of them according to his honor, and say to them: "Do you want to drink apple wine, or pomegranate wine, or grape wine?" And the pious will say: "The choice is Yours to do what You wish." And the Holy One, blessed be He, will bring them wine that was preserved in its grapes since the six days of creation. . . . And He fulfills the wishes of the pious, rises from the Throne of Glory, and sits with them. . . . And He brings all the fine things of the Garden of Eden. . . .

And each pious man will see His Glory, and each of them will point with his finger and say: "This is God, our God, for ever and ever!" And they will eat and drink and rejoice, until the Holy One, blessed be He, commands that the cup of benediction be filled, and the pious say to Abraham: "Arise, and say the benediction!" But Abraham will reply: "Ishmael accuses me!" They say to Isaac, and he replies: "Esau accuses me!" They say to Jacob, and he replies: "The two sisters [my two wives] accuse me!" They say to the [twelve patriarchs of] the tribes, and they reply: "The testimony of Joseph accuses me!" Finally they reach David and place four cups into his hands. . . . And the cup of benediction will hold a hundred and twenty *logs*. And how much is a *log*? One and a half eggs. And David will say: "It behooves me to say the benediction, it behooves me to praise God." And he will rise and bless and praise and exalt with all kinds of songs. . . .

In that hour the Holy One, blessed be He, will take His crown and place it on the head of David and on the head of Messiah ben David, and speak their praise and their piety until all generations. And He will let Israel dwell in safety and security, and make a canopy for each pious man, and a dwelling according to his honor, and He will walk with the pious and raise His hand like a man who taps in his merriment. . . .

Then the Holy One, blessed be He, says: "I have said, *They shall see with shame* (Isa. 26:11)." And Israel says: "Master of the World! Let it be as You say: let them see and be ashamed." And the Holy One, blessed be He, increases the stature of the nations of the world, making them taller than the walls of the Garden of Eden, and they see the rejoicing of Israel, and they are ashamed. And fire issues from the mouths of the pious and burns them. . . .

And in the future the Holy One, blessed be He, will make the light of the sun and of the moon pale, and will bring the skin of Leviathan and make of it booths for the pious. . . . He who deserves a booth, they make him a booth; —a necklace, they make him a necklace; he who deserves a crown, they make him a crown. And what is left over of it they stretch over the Temple, and its light will shine from one end of the world to the other.

(Pirqe Mashiah, BhM 3:76–77)

In the Future to Come, the Holy One, blessed be He, will bring the pious to the Garden of Eden and say to Gabriel: "Go, and greet the pious in My name!" Instantly Michael and Gabriel, the [celestial] princes of Israel, go and stand at the gates of the Garden of Eden and say to the pious: "Be greeted in the name of the King of Kings of Kings, the Holy One, blessed be He!"

In that hour the pious respond and say: "Michael and Gabriel! Go and say to the Holy One, blessed be He, that if it is His will, let Him come and celebrate with us at the banquet which is prepared for us in the Garden of Eden."

Then Michael and Gabriel go and say to the Holy One, blessed be He: "Master of the World! Thus say the pious, that You come and feast with them."

Instantly the Holy One, blessed be He, hearkens unto them, and enters with them into the Garden of Eden. And as soon as the Holy One, blessed be He, comes there, the pious stand up on their feet, and the whole world becomes filled with light. . . . And He says to them: "Peace be unto you, O pious men! Why are you standing on your feet? Sit down, each of you!" And He Himself seats them at their places, and says to them: "Drink well and eat, and I, too, have come only to feast with you. . . ." And He says to them: "My sons, from the day that I created My world, I never withheld anything from you except My Throne of Glory. . . . But now I give you a share even in My Throne of Glory. . . ."

Then the Holy One, blessed be He, announces the names of the good chieftains of Israel, and brings them inside, before Him, and they play before Him, with Him, like a man who plays with his friend, as it is written, *I shall raise up among them seven shepherds and eight princes* (Mic. 5:4). And these are the seven shepherds: Adam, Seth, Enosh, and Methushelah on His right, Abraham, Isaac, and Jacob, on His left. And these are the eight princes: Jesse, Saul, Samuel, Amos, Zephaniah, Hezekiah, Elijah, and the Messiah. And David sits opposite the Shekhina at a distance of six handbreadths; and our Master Moses sits at a distance of six handbreadths from the Shekhina corresponding to the size of the Two Tablets of the Law.

In that hour Saul stands on his feet and he has no place to sit. Thereupon David stands up and says: "Master of the World! Saul was king of Israel before me, and he is a totally pious man, give him a place to sit." Instantly the Holy One, blessed be He, gives him a place to sit. And Solomon stands in front of his father and says: "You asked for mercy for Saul and asked for him a place to sit. Should you not even more ask mercy for me to seat me?"

In that hour the Holy One, blessed be He, begins to praise Solomon and honors him in front of all the pious, and says to them: "What did Solomon do? He built a house for himself in thirteen years, and a house for Me in seven. And more than that: he gave preference to My reign over his reign...." And He gives him a place to sit.

After each one of them is seated in his place, our Master Moses prepares a banquet for the pious.... In that hour Melchizedek stands up and gives the due reward to each pious man, and says: "This one and that one will eat at the banquet tomorrow...."

In that hour the Holy One, blessed be He, stands up on His feet and gives a draft to each one of the pious and says to them: "What kind of wine do you prefer? Of apples or of pomegranates, or of wine that has been preserved in its grapes since the six days of creation? And I Myself shall rejoice with you."

In that hour all the wicked come and see all the pious, each one in his honor and high regard, headed by Abraham, Isaac, and Jacob. And lightnings of fire issue from their mouths, and rays of glory on their heads, and their radiance shines from one end of the world to the other. And the evil ones says: "Who are these to whom the Holy One, blessed be He, gives all this honor?" And they say to them: "These are the pious of Israel!" In that hour they say: "*Happy is the people that is in such a case, yea, happy is the people whose God is the Lord* (Ps. 144:15). Happy is he whose King is this, happy is the King whose people are these, and happy is the whole people to whom the Holy One, blessed be He, gives this honor!"

In that hour the Holy One, blessed be He, sends away the Angel of Death who had brought accusations against Israel, and the Evil Inclination which pulled the heart of man to sin, and removes him from them and slays him with the fire of the River of Flames, and burns him and causes him to be swallowed up from the world, as it is written, *He will swallow up death forever* (Isa. 25:8), and it will no longer be found. And the Holy One, blessed be He, will be salvation and comfort and joy to the pious....

(S'udat Livyatan, BhM 6:150–51)

The letter *kaf* [whose name means "palm of the hand,"] indicates that at the banquet of the pious in the World to Come, He will clap His hands in great joy, and will rise and dance before them at the banquet. And each pious man will be accompanied by the Shekhina with a myriad myriads of ministering angels, with pillars of lightning round about them, and sparks of splendor will surround them, and fireworks of radiance will make their faces glow, and sparks of light will make their eyelids shine. And winds will gather before them, and clouds drip before their faces, and mountains dance before them....

In the future Isaiah will say before the Holy One, blessed be He, at the banquet of the pious in the Garden of Eden, in the hour when He dances before them: "Master of the World! Your hand is exalted. Let not the wicked come and see the happiness of the pious." But the Holy One, blessed be He, answers and says: "Isaiah, My son, let them come and see the joy and the happiness of the pious, and let them be covered with shame and disgrace...." Isaiah answers and says before the Holy One, blessed be He: "Let them not come and not see!" The Holy One, blessed be He, says: "Who should decide between us so that we do as he says?" Isaiah answers and says before Him: "Master of the World! Let the Great Community of Israel come and decide between us, and we shall do [accordingly]." Instantly the Holy One, blessed be He, calls Metatron, the Prince of the Face, and says: "My servant, go and fetch the Community of Israel, so that she decide between us." Instantly Metatron goes and brings the Community of Israel before the Holy One, blessed be He, and before Isaiah. And when the Community of Israel sees the Holy One, blessed be He, she says before Him: "Why did You summon us?" The Holy One, blessed be He, answers and says to her: "My daughter, because I say let the wicked come and see the happiness of the pious [and Isaiah says let them not come]." She answers: "Let them come and be shamed...."

In that hour the wicked come to the door of the Garden of Eden, and stand and watch the happiness of the pious. And they see all the pious, each one with the face of his glory, in royal robes, and with a royal crown, and with jewels of kingly pearls. And each one sits like a king on his golden throne, and before each one is a table of pearls, and in the hands of each is a golden goblet emblazoned with precious stones and pearls and filled with the elixir of life. And all the delicacies of the Garden of Eden are placed before them on the table, and before each one stand three ministering angels to serve them. And rays of majesty are on their heads, and sparks and lightnings issue from their mouths, and the radiance of their faces goes from one end of the world to the other like the radiance of the sun. . . . And the heaven and the heaven of heavens open their doors, and let rain upon them fragrant dews of pure balsam whose scent goes from one end of the world to the other. And a thousand thousands of ministering angels stand before them, holding in their hands pipes and harps and cymbals and every instrument of song, and they sing before them at the banquet. And the Holy One, blessed be He, Himself stands and dances at the banquet, and the sun and the moon and the stars and the constellations are on His right and left, and dance with Him before them.

And when the wicked see all that greatness and royalty, and all that splendor and glory, they stretch their height to one hundred cubits so as to be able to see the honor of the pious in the Hall, and they ask about them, saying: "Who are these to whom the Holy One, blessed be He, has given all this honor and all this greatness?" And the ministering angels will answer and say to them: "These are the people of the Holy One, blessed be He, who occupied themselves with His Tora and with His commandments, and they were brought to the Garden of Eden to receive a goodly reward and a good portion." Instantly the wicked fall upon their faces and open their mouths in praise of the Holy One, blessed be He, and of the pious, and say: *Happy is the people that is in such a case; yea, happy is the people whose God is the Lord* (Ps. 144:15).
(Mid. Alpha Beta diR. Akiba, BhM 3:33–34)

R. Y'huda said to R. Hiyya: "That which we have learned, namely that the Holy One, blessed be He, will in the Future to Come give a banquet to the righteous, how will it be?" He said to him: "I have not yet come before the holy angels to know how it will be. . . ."

R. El'azar said: "The banquet of the righteous in the Future to

Come will be as it is written, *And they beheld God, and did eat and drink* (Exod. 24:11); this is what we have learned, that they will be fed." And R. El'azar said: "In one place we learned that they enjoyed, and in another place that they fed. What is the difference between these? [It is this:] The righteous who have no supreme merits will enjoy that splendor but will not completely achieve [or: understand] it. But those righteous who have [achieved supreme] merits will be fed until they achieve complete understanding. And the eating and drinking [quoted above] refer to nothing else but this, and this is the banquet and the eating. And how do we know this? From Moses. For it is written, *And he was with the Lord forty days and forty nights; he did neither eat bread nor drink water* (Exod. 34:28). What does it mean that *he did neither eat bread nor drink water?* Because he was fed another meal, from that splendor of the Above. And the same will be the case at the banquet of the pious in the Future to Come."

R. Y'huda said: "The banquet of the pious in the Future to Come will be to rejoice in His joy...."

R. Yose said: "The wine preserved in its grapes from the six days of Creation [which the righteous will drink at the Messianic banquet]—these are ancient words which were not revealed to man ever since the world was created, and they will be revealed to the righteous in the Future to Come. And this is the drinking; and the eating is certainly this."

R. Y'huda ben R. Shalom said: "If so, what is Leviathan and what is the ox [which the righteous will eat at the Messianic banquet]?" R. Yose said: "... They are merely allusions to the kingdoms [which God will destroy]...."

R. Y'hoshu'a said: "This belief which the rabbis expressed, [they directed it] to the majority of the people: that they will be invited to that banquet of Leviathan and that ox, and that they will drink good wine which has been preserved from the creation of the world. They found a verse for it and expounded it, namely, *Ye shall eat your bread until ye have enough* (Lev. 26:5)." For R. Zera said: "The Holy One, blessed be He, persuaded Israel with all kinds of enticements to make them turn back to good. And the greatest of those enticements is this, that He said to them, *Ye shall eat your bread until ye have enough....* The Holy One, blessed be He, said to them: 'If you will listen to the voice of the commandments, *ye shall eat until ye have enough.*' In a like manner, when the rabbis saw that the exile is long, they relied on the verses of the Tora and said [to them] that they are destined to eat and be merry at the great banquet which the Holy One, blessed be He, will arrange for them. And because of this most people were able to stand the sufferings of the exile, because of [the promise of] that banquet."

R. Yohanan said: "We must not destroy that which all believe, but must uphold it, for the Tora testified about it. . . ."

(Mid. haNe'elam, Zohar 1:135b, 136a)

Our masters said that the harp of the Sanctuary was of seven strings, of the Messiah of eight, and of the World to Come of ten.

(Yohanan Alemanno [1435– c. 1504], *Sefer Sha'ar haHesheq*, Livorno, 1790, p. 56a)

The Fourth Meal of the outgoing of the Sabbath was taken by Shabbatai Zevi close to midnight, and he used to say, "This is the Banquet of King Messiah," and he used to make of it a very important affair, and would eat only a little at the [traditional] Third Meal so that he should have appetite for this Banquet.

(*Iny'ne Shabbatai Zevi*, p. 94)

O our Rebbenyu, tiram tiram tam, our Rebbenyu
What will we eat at the banquet, ay?
What will we eat at the banquet?
The wild ox with Leviathan, the wild ox with Leviathan,
The wild ox with Leviathan will we eat at the banquet, ay!

. . . .

O Rebbenyu, tiram tiram tam, Rebbenyu!
What will be there at the banquet, ay?
God Himself with His glory will be there,
In the Garden of Eden will we sit,
Aaron the priest will bless us,
Moses our master will teach us Tora,
Miriam the prophetess will dance,
King David will play for us,
King Solomon will sing for us,
The preserved wine will we drink,
The wild ox with Leviathan will we eat,
At the banquet, ay!

(Yiddish Folksong, M. Bassin, *Antologi*, 1:101–3)

For thirteen hundred years Israel will enjoy the banquet of the Messiah, and the Temple will be completed.... And they will have wellbeing, feasts, joy, and honor, until the Great Day of Judgment....

(Persian Jewish legend)

Habad Hasidim are organizing "Messiah-banquets" on the seventh day of Passover, towards evening, following the instructions of their leader, the Rabbi of Lubavich.

The instructions are based on the Hasidic tradition according to which the Ba'al Shem, the founder of Hasidism, used to have a festive meal on the last day of Passover, towards evening. He called this meal "Banquet of the Messiah," for on that day it was possible to receive divine inspiration about the revelation of the light [i.e., the coming] of the Messiah.

The Rabbi therefore suggested that an effort be made that every Jew should hold a "Messiah Banquet," and should try to have also others participate in it, in order to bring about a strengthening of the faith in the coming of the Messiah soon.

According to a Habad custom, which was introduced by Rabbi Shalom Dover, the fifth leader of the Habad sect, one must drink four glasses of wine during this banquet.

Organized Messiah Banquets will be held by Habad Hasidim in many places in the country.

(*HaAretz* of Apr. 8, 1977, p. 12.)

26

New Worlds and a New Tora

With the banquet the chain of events of the Messianic era reaches its end. What remains thereafter, to endure for centuries, for millennia, or forever, is the new order of a world ruled by King Messiah. When this stage is reached in the legendary narrative of the future, the Messiah texts, with their imagination exhausted, lapse into generalities. We are told, but without any particulars, that new worlds would be created, that the pious would do the will of God, that God would teach them a new Tora, and that the Messiah would give them thirty new commandments. However, not a word is said about what will be new in that new Tora, compared, that is, to the old Tora of Moses. This silence on so crucial an issue is due to the fear that any concrete indication of new teachings or new commandments would be an infringement on the sanctity and immutability of the Tora of Moses. Even the notion of a new Tora in the abstract may have been a daring proposition in view of the established doctrine, codified by Maimonides in his *Thirteen Principles of the Faith*, the ninth of which reads: "I believe with a complete faith that this Tora will not be exchanged and there will be no other Tora from the Creator, blessed be His name."

There is one exception to the general silence about the contents of the Messianic dispensation. In Leviticus Rabba, it is stated that all sacrifices and prayers will be abolished in the Messianic days, except for the thanks offerings and thanksgiving prayers, because, as Isaac ben Judah Abrabanel (1437−1508) explains, in those happy days there will be no Evil Inclination and thus no sin, so that no offerings or prayers to atone for transgressions will be needed. Of course, Leviticus Rabba was written in the fifth century, that is, about four hundred years after the destruction of the Temple and the cessation of the sacrificial ritual, which made it relatively easy for the authors to contemplate such a contingency.

The later Kabbalists, less restrained in many respects than their traditional predecessors, let their fantasy dwell freely on what the new Tora would be like. For the Rabbinic tenet that the Tora as a whole was immutable, they substituted the daring innovation that only the totality of all the letters contained in the Tora has been fixed for all eternity, and that the same complement of hundreds of thousands of letters can be and will be rearranged into different words expressing different instructions. This is what will happen in the Messianic days, and this is the new Tora which God will expound in His Messianic House of Study.

The legend of the new Tora is exceptional within the whole legend complex of the Redemption in quite a different, and rather significant, aspect. In all the other legends, nothing is said about what will happen to the women in the days of the Messiah. A reading of all the legends clearly shows that the Israel which figures in them was imagined as a community of men only. The sufferings, the wars, the victories, the banquet, and all the rest, are in these legends purely masculine affairs. Even the legend of the mother of the Messiah (chapter 13) is no exception, because its speaks, not of the Messianic days, but of the birth of a child in past times who was destined to be the Messiah after many millennia will have passed. Again, in the whimsical statements of Rabban Gamliel about the miraculous fertility (chapter 24), women appear as mere childbearing machines and not as human beings in their own right.

All this is, of course, understandable in view of the historically conditioned masculine prerogative of fulfilling the great commandment of Tora study, which was the soil nourishing the Messiah legend. It appears that the feminine element in mystical Jewish thinking was confined to the figure of the Matronit, the divine Matron, God's spouse, who was the embodiment of the Community of Israel and was reflected in such an undying superhuman figure as Rachel, Israel's *mater dolorosa*. This supernal Female was very much present in the male consciousness—present, in fact, to such an extent that no room was left for thought about the role, tasks, functions, and feelings of mere flesh-and-blood women in the Messianic ambience.

Thus it is the more remarkable that at least one legend tells of the pious women of Israel sitting before God in His Messianic House of Study and listening with radiant faces to the new Tora expounded by God (see below, Midrash fragment). True, this great reward and joy are given to them because, while alive, they saw to it that their sons were taught Tora. But the fact remains that this legend—the only one in the Messianic legend cycle—assigns an equal place to women with their menfolk in the matter that counts above all else, the study of the Tora in the presence of God.

In those days...
...there shall be bestowed upon the elect wisdom,
And they shall live and never again sin,
Either through ungodliness or through pride:
But they who are wise shall be humble,
And they shall not again transgress,
Nor shall they sin all the days of their life.
Nor shall they die of [the divine] anger or wrath,
But they shall complete the number of days of their life.
(1Enoch 5:8—9)

When he, about whom it is written, *Lowly and riding upon an ass* (Zech. 9:9) will come... he will elucidate for them the words of the Tora... and elucidate for them their errors. R. Hanina said; "Israel will not need the teachings of King Messiah in the Future to Come, for it is said, *Unto him the nations shall seek* (Isa. 11:10)—[the nations, but] not Israel." If so, why will King Messiah come, and to do what will he come? To gather the exiles of Israel, and to give them thirty *mitzvot* [commandments]....

(Gen. Rab. 98:9)

R. Pinhas and R. Levi and R. Yohanan in the name of R. Menahem of Galya: "In the Future to Come all the sacrifices will be abolished, but the thanks offerings will not be abolished. All the prayers will be abolished, but the thanksgiving prayers will not be abolished...."[1]

(Lev. Rab. 9:7)

R. Hizqiya in the name of R. Simon bar Zibdi said: "The whole Tora which you learn in This World is vanity as against the Tora of the World to Come. For in This World a man learns Tora and forgets, but in the Future to Come [he will not forget], as it is written, *I will put My Tora in their inward parts and in their heart will I write it* (Jer. 31:33).

(Eccl. Rab. 11:1)

If you listened [to the Tora] in This World, you will listen [to it] in the World to Come from the mouth of the Holy One, blessed be He. R. Yona... said: "It is not necessary that Israel should receive the Tora in This World, since all of them will learn Tora from the mouth of the Holy One, blessed be He, in the World to Come. Why then was it given to them in This World? So that when the Holy One, blessed be He, will come to teach them in the World to Come all of them should know which section He deals with."

(Mid. Tanh., Ki Tavo, par. 4)

---

1. Because there will be no Evil Inclination, hence no sin, no deprivations, etc., the only rituals which will continue will serve the expression of thanks to God. Cf. Abrabanel, *Y'shu'ot M'shiho*, 'Iyyun R'vi'i, end of chapter 1.

Zerubbabel and Elijah will come [in the Messianic age] and explain and expound all the secrets of the Tora and all that which is crooked and distorted....

(*Halakhot G'dolot*, p. 223 top)

The Holy One, blessed be He, will in the future call all of the pious by their names, and give them a cup of elixir of life in their hands so that they should live and endure forever.... And the Holy One, blessed be He, will in the future reveal to all the pious in the World to Come the Ineffable Name with which new heavens and a new earth can be created, so that all of them should be able to create new worlds.... The Holy One, blessed be He, will give every pious three hundred and forty worlds in inheritance in the World to Come.... To all the pious the Holy One, blessed be He, will give a sign and a part in the goodly reward, and everlasting renown, glory and greatness and praise, a crown encompassed in holiness, and royalty, equal to those of all the pious in the World to Come. The sign will be the cup of life which the Holy One, blessed be He, will give to the Messiah and to the pious in the Future to Come.

(Mid. Alpha Beta diR. Akiba, BhM 3:32)

And He will take away the spirit, the soul, the rule, and the holy ghost from every angel and every seraph, so that they should come to an end all at once. In that hour none will be left of the generations of heaven nor of the generations of the earth, nor of the ministering angels, nor of the children of the creatures whom the Holy One, blessed be He, created in the world, but He alone.... [And He, too, will remain] without His throne, without His glory, without servants, without slaves, without a palace, without anything, except for the pious who will carry the Holy One, blessed be He, by His pinions.... And He will say [to them]: "Fear not!" And when He renews the World to Come, He will renew His throne and His glory and His canopy and His precious seat, and raise the pious in the world [to be] like ministering angels, and give them six wings like the ministering angels. And some of them will stand facing the Throne of Glory like the ministering angels, and some will stand in the world to do His will in the world, going from one end of the world to the other, like clouds and like eagles, and they will not tire. They will run like sparks and lightnings to serve the glory of their Creator, and will not be weary....

(Mid. Alpha Betot, Wertheimer,
Bate Midrashot 2:442)

In the future the Holy One, blessed be He, will sit in the Garden of Eden and expound [the Tora]. And all the pious will sit before Him, and all the Supernal Family will stand on its feet. On the right of the Holy One, blessed be He, will be the sun with the constellations, and on His left the moon and all the stars. And the Holy One, blessed be He, will expound to them the meanings of a new Tora which He will give them through the Messiah. And when He reaches the Aggada [legends], Zerubbabel ben Shealtiel will rise to his feet and will say: "Yitgadal w'yitqadash, may the Great Name of the Lord be exalted and sanctified [the Kaddish prayer]. . . ." And his voice will go from one end of the world to the other, and those who walk on earth will answer, "Amen." And even the wicked of Israel and the pious of the nations of the world who will have remained in Gehenna will answer and say, "Amen," from the depths of Gehenna, until the whole world reverberates and their voice is heard before the Holy One, blessed be He, and He asks about them and says: "What is this great reverberation which I hear?"

The ministering angels answer and say before Him: "Master of the World! These are the wicked of Israel and the pious of the nations of the world who have been left in Gehenna, who answer 'Amen' from Gehenna."

Instantly the compassion of the Holy One, blessed be He, is greatly aroused toward them and He says: "What can I do for them about this punishment which the Evil Inclination had brought upon them?"

In that hour the Holy One, blessed be He, takes the keys of Gehenna and, in front of all the pious, gives them to Michael and Gabriel, and says to them: "Go and open the gates of Gehenna, and bring them up from Gehenna. . . ."

Instantly Michael and Gabriel go and open the forty thousand gates of Gehenna, and bring them up from Gehenna. And how do they bring them up from Gehenna? It teaches us that each Gehenna has a length of three hundred parasangs and a width of three hundred parasangs, and its thickness is a thousand parasangs, and its depth is a thousand parasangs, and none of the wicked who fall into it can get out of it. What, then, do Michael and Gabriel do? In that hour they get hold of the hand of each one of the wicked and pull them up, like a man who raises his fellow man and pulls him up from a pit.... And Gabriel and Michael stand over them in that hour, and wash them, and anoint them with oil, and heal them of the wounds of Gehenna, and clothe them in beautiful and good garments, and take them by their hand, and bring them before the Holy One, blessed be He, and before all the pious, all spruced and cleaned up....

And when they reach the gate of the Garden of Eden, first Gabriel and Michael enter and take counsel with the Holy One, blessed be He. The Holy One, blessed be He, answers them and says: "Let them enter and see My glory." As soon as they enter they fall upon their faces and prostrate themselves before Him and bless and praise the name of the Holy One, blessed be He. Instantly the totally pious and honest who sit before the Holy One, blessed be He, give praise and exalt the Holy One, blessed be He....

As soon as the wicked are brought up and repent before the Holy One, blessed be He, they are accepted before the Shekhina like the pious and the saintly who never sinned.... And more than that: they are brought up and seated in the Yeshiva next to the Shekhina because they broke their heart in repentance before the Holy One, blessed be He....

(Mid. Alpha Beta diR. Akiba, BhM 3:27−29)

When the Holy One, blessed be He, sees David and the Messiah, he calls David and says to him; "My son, sit on My right, for I have brought sufferings upon him [the Messiah], and praise Me...." And the Holy One, blessed be He, sits and reveals the meanings of the Tora to them: Why he prohibited us pork, and blood, and lard, and meat with milk, etc.

(Pes. Hadta, BhM 6:47)

The house of study of the Holy One, blessed be He, in the Future to Come will be eighteen thousand times ten thousand parasangs by eighteen thousand times ten thousand parasangs. And the Holy One, blessed be He, sits on the Throne of Judgment, and the throne of David is opposite Him. And all the peaceable women who have given fees to have their sons taught

Tora and Scripture and Talmud and proper manners, and all the honest women, come and take their reward from the Holy One, blessed be He, and sit in His presence.[2] And all the men see their faces, and their faces shine like the radiance of the Shekhina, and they hear a new Tora from the mouth of God. And Zerubbabel ben Shealtiel stands and translates and explains every word from the mouth of the Holy One, blessed be He.

(Midrash fragment, BhM 6:151–52)

[R. Hiyya in a dream] heard a voice which said: "Make room, make room, for King Messiah is coming to the academy of R. Shim'on [ben Yohai]!" For all the righteous who are there were heads of academies [on earth], and those academies are recorded there. And all those scholars who were in all the academies, went from the academy of this place to the academy of the firmament. And the Messiah comes to all those academies and sets his seal [of approval] on the Tora [which issues] from the mouth of the teachers. And in that hour the Messiah came and was crowned by the heads of the academies with supernal crowns. In that hour all the scholars rose, and R. Shim'on rose, and his light shone forth to the height of the firmament. He [the Messiah] said to him: "Rabbi, happy are you for your Tora issues forth in three hundred and seventy lights, and each light branches out into six hundred and thirteen meanings which issue forth and bathe in rivers of pure balsam. And the Holy One, blessed be He, Himself seals the Tora of your academy, and of the academy of Hezekiah king of Judah and of Ahija the Shilonite. And I am not come to seal [the Tora of] your academy, for the Master of Wings [i.e. Metatron] is about to come here, and we know that he comes to no other academy but yours." In that hour R. Shim'on told him what the Master of Wings had said, whereupon the Messiah was seized with trembling and lifted up his voice, and the firmaments trembled, and the great sea trembled, and Leviathan trembled, and the world seemed to collapse.

While this went on, he [the Messiah] noticed R. Hiyya at the

---

2. In another version of this legend, the women "stand in a partition of reeds made like a fence, and hear the words of Zerubbabel ben Shealtiel translating before the Holy One, blessed be He, and answer after him 'May His great Name be blessed and hallowed for ever and ever,' and the pious say, 'Amen,' and the wicked in Gehenna say, 'Amen.'" (Pirqe Mashiah, BhM 3:75)

feet of R. Shim'on, and he said: "Who let this man, clothed in the garments of that world, come here?" R. Shim'on said: "This is R. Hiyya, the shining light of the Tora." The Messiah said to him: "Let him and his sons be gathered in [i.e., let them die], and let them be of your academy." R. Shim'on said to him: "Please, give him time!" He was given time, and he went out from thence, all trembling, with tears running from his eyes.

Then R. Hiyya [awoke], trembled and wept and said: "Happy is the portion of the righteous in That World, and happy is the portion of Bar Yohai who has merited this!"

(Zohar 1:4b)

This is the secret of the Tora which the Holy One, blessed be He, will renew for Israel.... The Tora will remain in her place. But at present her words are combined in physical combinations, as they were needed for this physical world. But in the future, when the Children of Adam will divest themselves of this physical body and will ascend and attain to the mystery of the body which Adam the first man had before he sinned, then they will become adepts in the mystery of the Tora, when that which is hidden will be revealed. And after the sixth millennium, when they will ascend even higher, they will understand even more the mystery of the Tora in the hidden reality, and every man will be able to understand the miraculous teachings of the Tora, and the hidden combinations....

Just as the children of man will divest themselves of the body, so the Tora will be divested of her bodily aspect, and her hidden face will radiate, and the righteous will occupy themselves with her. But the Tora herself is one for all eternity, she will always remain what she was, and will stand for ever, and will not change, God forbid!

(Abraham Azulai, *Hesed l'Avraham*, 13c–14a)

In the Future to Come, in the generation of the Messiah, Moses, peace be upon him, will come in a transmigrated form, and will teach Israel the Tora. But even then he will be *of uncircumcised lips* (Exod. 6:12), and his interpreter will be Elijah of blessed memory, who lives and endures, and who is Pinhas the son of Aaron, the brother of Moses our Master.

(Hayyim Vital, *Sefer haHezyonot*, p. 160)

Look and see what rank the pious will attain at the time they hear the teaching from the mouth of the Holy One, blessed be He. For, although nobody sits in heaven except Metatron, the Prince of the Face, nevertheless the rank of Metatron will be given to them in the hour of the teaching, and they will sit, and all the Supernal Family will stand on their feet. And the Holy One, blessed be He, will sit and expound the new Tora which He will give through the Messiah. "New Tora" means the secrets and the mysteries of the Tora which have remained hidden until now. It does not refer to another Tora, heaven forfend, for surely the Tora which He gave us through Moses our Master, peace be upon him, is the eternal Tora; but the revelation of her hidden secrets is called "new Tora."... The Tora was before the Holy One, blessed be He, containing six hundred thousand letters, in disarray. And when Adam the first man sinned, [God] arranged the letters into words, such as, *When a man dieth in the tent* (Num. 19:14), or the section about inheritance, and the section about levirate, and many more the like. For had Adam not sinned, the letters would have arranged themselves into other words. Therefore, in the Future to Come, when the sin of Adam will have been forgiven, the words will return to their primordial state, and the very Tora of Moses will contain the full complement of letters, neither fewer nor more, arranged into other words, as it would have been had Adam not sinned. And this is the new Tora which the Holy One, blessed be He, will expound to the pious. But it will be the same Tora of Moses. Or, it is possible that the order of the words into which the Tora is arranged now, such as, *When a man dieth in the tent*, and the like [will remain, but] the Holy One, blessed be He, will reveal their [secret] intention, since in those days there will be no death, no inheritance, no levirate, no leprosy in the flesh and in the skin and in the garments. He will explain them in a different way, and this is the truly new Tora, a hidden and deep thing which will be a new teaching for those who hear it.

(Mid. Talpiyot, 58a)

In the future the Holy One, blessed be He, will seat the Messiah in the supernal Yeshiva [House of Study], and they will call him "the Lord," just as they call the Creator....

And the Messiah will sit in the Yeshiva, and all those who walk on earth will come and sit before him to hear a new Tora and new commandments and the deep wisdom which he teaches Israel.... And Elijah of blessed memory will stand before him as translator, and when he teaches, his voice goes from one end of the world to the other....

And the House of Study of the Messiah will be eighteen thousand parasangs... and the Holy One, blessed be He, will reveal them, through the mouth of Elijah of blessed memory, rules of life, rules of peace, rules of alertness, rules of purity, rules of abstinence, rules of piety, rules of charity.... And no person who hears a teaching from the mouth of the Messiah will ever forget it, for the Holy One, blessed be He, will reveal Himself in the House of Study of the Messiah, and will pour His Holy Spirit upon all those who walk on earth, and His Holy Spirit will be upon each and every one. And each one in His House of Study will understand the *Halakhot* on his own, the *Midrashot* on his own, the *Tosafot* on his own, the *Aggadot* on his own, the traditions on his own, and each one of them will know on his own.... And even the slaves and the slave-women of Israel who were bought for money from the nations of the world, the Holy Spirit will rest upon them, and they will expound on their own... and each one of them will have a House of Study in his house, the House of the Shekhina.

(Yemenite Midrash, pp. 349–50)

In the Future to Come, the Name [i.e. God], blessed be He, will reveal to us even the [meaning of the] blank spaces in the Tora, so that we should understand the blank letters in our Tora. And this is the meaning of *For* [a new] *Tora shall go forth from Me* (Isa. 51:4), so that all Israel should understand even the letters which are blank in our Tora which was given to Moses. But at present those letters of whiteness are concealed from us.... And when our Righteous Messiah comes, we shall understand also the blank spaces in the Tora, quickly in our days, Amen!

(Levi Yitzhaq of Berdichev, *Imre Tzaddiqim*, p. 10 [5b]

27

Universal Blessings

Popular imagination knew no bounds in describing the various blessings which will be enjoyed by the pious in the days of the Messiah. Some of the features attributed to that blessed era reflect universal human yearnings for peace, prosperity, happiness, beauty, health, longevity, or even immortality. Others project into the future the fear of ritual transgressions, a constant threat in observant Jewish existence. Still others testify to the male's desire to be wooed and courted by women instead of having to engage in efforts to win them.

R. Berekhya in the name of R. Sh'muel bar Nahman said: "Although all things were created in their full measure, when Adam the first man sinned they became spoiled. And they will not be restored to their former completeness until the coming of the [Messiah] son of Peretz.... Six things will be restored, and they are: Man's splendor, life, and stature; the fruits of the earth and the fruits of the tree, and the luminaries...."
R. Hiyya taught: "Man will walk with an upright stature, unafraid of any creature." R. Yudan said: "His height will be one hundred cubits, like Adam the first man."

(Gen. Rab. 12:6)

A Psalm of Solomon about the Messiah of God....
May God purify Israel in the day of mercy with a blessing,
In the day of choosing the kingship of His Messiah.
Happy are they who shall live in those days
To see the goodness the Lord shall perform for the generation
    to come
Under the rod of chastening of the Lord's Messiah,
In the fear of his God,
In the spirit of wisdom and justice and might,
To straighten man with acts of justice,
With the fear of God, that He may
Establish them all before the Lord,
A good generation, in the fear of God,
In the days of mercy. Selah!

> (Psalms of Solomon 18:1, 5–9)

[In the days of the Messiah] *I will cause evil beasts to cease out of the land* (Lev. 26:6). R. Y'huda said: "He [God] will calm them so that they should do no damage." R. Shim'on said: "When is the praise of God [greater]: When there are none to cause injury, or when there are such but do not cause any injury? I say, at a time when there are such but cause no injury.... Thus God will calm those who cause injury in the world, so that they will cause no injury. To this refers the verse, *And the wolf shall dwell with the lamb, and the leopard shall lie down with the kid...and the cow and the bear...and the suckling child shall play on the hole of the asp* (Isa. 11:6–8). This teaches us that in the future a babe from Israel will stick his finger into the eyeball of a basilisk and will extract gall from its mouth...."

> (Sifra b'Huqotai 2:1; Yalqut haMakhiri, p. 86)

Some say: "All the animals which have been declared impure in This World, the Holy One, blessed be He, will declare them pure in the Future to Come."

> (Mid. Tehillim, p. 268a)

R. Sh'muel bar Nahmani said: "In This World the male courts the female, but in the Future to Come the female will court the male...."
R. Simon in the name of R. Shim'on the pious said: "In This

World if a man goes to gather figs on a Sabbath, the fig tree says nothing; but in the Future to Come if a man will go to gather figs on the Sabbath the fig tree will cry out and say: 'Today is Sabbath!'"

(Mid. Tehillim, p. 168a)

R. Yona in the name of R. Simon bar Zabid: "All the prosperity which man sees in This World is vanity as against the prosperity of the World to Come. For in This World a man dies and leaves his prosperity in inheritance to another, but in the World to Come it is written, *They shall not build and another inhabit* (Isa. 65:22)."

(Eccl. Rab. 2:1)

Come, let us go down and there confound their language (Gen. 11:7). He [God] confounded their languages so that they could not understand each other's language. For the first language which they spoke was the Holy Language, and in that language was the world created. The Holy One, blessed be He, said: "In This World, through the Evil Inclination, My creatures became divided into seventy languages, but in the World to Come all will become equal, and shoulder to shoulder they will call upon My Name and will serve Me, as it is said, *For then will I turn to peoples a pure language, that they may call upon the name of the Lord to serve him with one shoulder* (Zeph. 3:9)."

(Mid. Tanh., Noah, par. 19)

In This World He worked for them a miracle in the night [of the Exodus], which was of a brief duration; but in the Future to Come the night will become day, as it is said, *The light of the moon shall be as the light of the sun, and the light of the sun shall be sevenfold, as the light of the seven days* (Isa. 30:26)—as the light which the Holy One, blessed be He, created in the beginning and hid in the Garden of Eden.

(Ex. Rab. 18:11)

We find that in the Future to Come, the Holy One, blessed be He, will create ten new things. The first is that He will light up the world. . . . But can a man look at the Holy One, blessed be He? No. What then will the Holy One, blessed be He, do? He will give the sun forty-nine parts of light . . . and even a sick person, the Holy One, blessed be He, will command the sun to heal him. . . . The second: He will cause living waters to come out of Jerusalem, and with them He will heal all those afflicted by a disease.... The third: He will make the trees give their fruits every month, and people will eat of them and become healed.... The fourth: The ruined cities will be rebuilt, and there will be no ruined place in the world, and even Sodom and Gomorrah will be rebuilt in the Future to Come.... The fifth: He will rebuild Jerusalem with sapphire stones...and those stones will shine like the sun, and those who worship stars will come and see the honor of Israel.... The sixth: *Cow and bear shall graze together* (Isa. 11:7). The seventh: He will bring all the wild beasts and all the birds and all the creeping things, and will conclude a covenant with them and with Israel.... The eighth: There will be no more weeping and wailing in the world.... The ninth: There will be no more death in the world.... The tenth: There will be no more sigh, no more groan, no more sorrow, but all will rejoice....

(Ex. Rab. 15:21)

Moses said to Israel: "You have seen all the miracles and great deeds and marvels which the Holy One, blessed be He, performed for you. Much more than that will He do for you in the Future to Come. For not like This World is the World to Come. In This World there are wars and sufferings and Evil Inclination and Satan and the Angel of Death, and they have permission to rule the World. But in the World to Come there will be no sufferings, no hatred, no Satan, no Angel of Death, no sighs, no enslavement, no Evil Inclination, as it is written, *He will swallow up death forever, and the Lord God will wipe away tears from off all* (Isa. 25:8)."

(Mid. waYosha', BhM 1:55)

When King Messiah comes—may he be revealed quickly in our days and save us, as it is said, *For ye shall go out with joy, and be led forth with peace; the mountains and the hills shall break forth before you into singing* (Isa. 55:12); and as it is written, *I will make thy officers peace* (ibid. 60:17)—then the blessing of the earth will be peace, as it is said, *For as the seed of peace, the vine shall give her fruit, and the earth shall give her increase* (Zech. 8:12). And the Land of Israel will be elevated in peace, as it is said, *He maketh thy borders peace* (Ps. 147:14). And for the sake of peace the Holy One, blessed be He, will establish the throne of David, as it is said, *In his days shall the righteous flourish and abundance of peace* (Ps. 72:7). And so, in peace He will prepare his throne and the throne of his seed after him, and will build him a faithful house forever, as it is said, *Great is the salvation of His king, and He showeth mercy to His Messiah, to David, and to his seed for evermore* (Ps. 18:51).

(Mid. Gadol uG'dola, BhM 3:130)

Blessed be the name of the Holy One, blessed be He, who chose Israel from among seventy nations.... And He wished to justify them and to give them merits, and gave them many laws ...and allotted His sayings to them, and let them hear Ten Commandments which are the body of the Tora and the essence of the laws.... And as against the Ten Commandments, the Holy One, blessed be He, will in the future make ten signs prior to the coming of the Redeemer—may the Holy One, blessed be He, hasten to redeem His children and save them from the enslavement, in our lifetime, soon, in our days....

The Holy One, blessed be He, will restore to Israel ten things which He took from them so that they were absent from the building of the Second Temple...and they are: the Ark and the Cherubim, the anointing oil, the wood of the altar fire, the Urim and Thummim, and the Holy Spirit...and the crowns which were lost at Sinai...and the blessing of the field crops, and the fatness of the fruits—these are ten. And as against them there are ten consolations and promises which the Holy One, blessed be He, promised Israel.... The first, the coming of the Redeemer; the second, the ingathering of the exiles; the third, the resurrection of the dead; the fourth, the building of the Temple which will be as Ezekiel saw it; the fifth, that Israel will rule over the whole world, from end to end, and the whole world will return to the judgment of the Holy One, blessed be He, and His Tora; the sixth, that the Holy One, blessed be He, will cause all enemies of His people to perish and will wreak vengeance upon them; the seventh, that the Holy One, blessed be He, will remove all illness and all affliction from Israel; the eighth, that the Holy One, blessed be He, will lengthen the days of Israel like a tree; the ninth, that the Holy One, blessed be He, will reveal Himself to Israel eye to eye, and also that He will make all Israel prophets; the tenth, that the Holy One, blessed be He, will remove the Evil Inclination and all evil things from Israel.

(Milhamot Melekh haMashiah, BhM 6:117−20)

R.Pinhas said: "In the future time to come, the Holy One, blessed be He, will render the bodies of the pious beautiful like the beauty of Adam the first man when he entered the Garden of Eden."

(Zohar 1:113b, Mid. haNe'elam)

The impurity ceased at the Revelation of the Tora. But the Throne was not completed, and will remain uncompleted until all the idolaters return to the worship of our Creator, blessed be He, and convert, so as to be gathered under the wings of the Shekhina, to observe His Tora, and to worship Him shoulder to shoulder and with a complete heart.... And all the Sephirot [the emanations of the divinity] will be united in one single adhesion, so that all receive one effluence from the Lord who is One over all....

(Yalqut R'uveni, waYishlah, p. 147b)

There were twenty-four good qualities in the world, and the sins caused all of them to disappear. And in the future the Holy One, blessed be He, will restore them to Israel at the End of the Days. And they are: The image[1] and the stature[2] and the Garden of Eden and the Tree of Life and the heroism[3] and the years[4] and many children and the peace[5] and the Holy Language[6] and the

---

1. After the enumeration of the twenty-four features, the text of the Midrash haGadol adduces Biblical passages in order to show that each of them actually existed in the history of man and Israel, and that they were taken away by God because of their sins, and, finally, that they will be restored in the Future to Come. Since these quotations have no real connection with the features enumerated, but are forcibly reinterpreted so as to find in them the requisite allusions, there would be no point in translating and presenting them. However, several of the features enumerated in the text require some elucidation.

The "image" refers to Gen. 1:26, which says, *In the likeness of God He created him*.

2. According to the Aggada, originally Adam's body was gigantic: "*Thou hast created me back and front* (Ps. 138:5)—this teaches that the stature of Adam the first man reached from east ('front') to west ('back')," p. 136.

3. The reference is to the heroism of the antediluvian giants, cf. Gen. 6:4.

4. I.e. the long life, such as the 930 years of Adam, cf. Gen 5:5.

5. I.e., safety from harmful demons, and the absence of suffering, p. 137.

6. The Aggadic view is that until the Generation of the Dispersion (the tower of Babel), the whole world spoke Hebrew. This is inferred from Gen. 11:l; p. 137.

richness[7] and the fruits[8] and the manna and the well[9] and the pillar of fire[10] and the pillar of smoke and the Ineffable Name[11] and the Shekhina[12] and the joy[13] and the Gihon[14] and the Sanhedrin and the kingship of the House of David and the High Priesthood and the Temple and the Holy Spirit. And of all these, none was left except the Tora and Charity....

(Mid. haGadol, Gen. pp. 135—36)

---

7. The ubiquity of precious stones, as inferred from Job. 28:6; p. 137.

8. General fertility of the earth, inferred from Gen. 13:10 and Job 28:5; pp. 137—38.

9. The miraculous Well of Miriam (inferred from Num. 11:28) which, according to the Aggada, provided water for all the tribes and irrigated their camps, and caused fruit trees to grow; p. 138.

10. On the basis of Exod. 40:37, our Midrash, on p. 138, states that "The pillar of fire went before them and beat down the snakes and scorpions and thistles, and lighted up the whole camp by night."

11. The Ineffable Name was *A crown of glory on your head* (Ezek. 16:12); p.139.

12. "They saw the Shekhina every day in the shape of a *Pillar of smoke standing at the door of the Tent (of Meeting)* (Exod. 33:10); p. 139.

13. The joy: "There was among them neither sorrow nor sigh"; p. 139.

14. "The Gihon issued forth from Jerusalem and irrigated the whole country"; p. 140.

28

Messiah Dreams

Throughout their history, from the earliest Biblical times on, the Jews believed that dreams contained revelations, or at least indications, of future events. Among the numerous disparate Talmudic views on the genesis of dreams, that of R. Jonathan (second century C.E.) is noteworthy for its resemblance to Freudian theory: "R. Sh'muel bar Nahmani said in the name of R. Jonathan: A man is shown [in his dreams] only that which is in the thoughts of his heart" (B. Ber. 55b). This psychological explanation of the origin of dreams was a thousand years later elaborated by Maimonides.[1]

While these views remained unknown to the people in general, it is in them that we must seek the genesis of Jewish dreams about the Messiah. An idea that preoccupied the people with such intensity was bound to agitate the subconscious and appear in dreams. The apocalyptic literature (especially Daniel, 4 Ezra, and Baruch) is replete with dream visions whose meaning is interpreted as presaging what was to happen in the End of Days.

In this chapter a very few selections of Messianic dreams

---

1. Cf. Maimonides, *Guide of the Perplexed* 2:36–38; *Sh'mona P'raqim*1; *Yad haHazaqa*, Y'sode Tora 7:2.

are assembled. The prophecies of Daniel about the Messiah are stated in the text to have been "dreams and visions" (Dan. 7:1), or "visions by night" (7:2; cf. 9:21), or simply "visions" (10:7, 8, etc.). Since we are already familiar with these earliest Messianic dreams (cf. chapter 1), we begin here with the apocryphal apocalypses. These are followed by recorded dreams of sixteenth-century Kabbalists and of the Ba'al Shem Tov. To them is added, as a curiosity, a childhood Messiah dream of Theodor Herzl, founder of modern political Zionism.

And I saw that a white bull [the Messiah] was born, with large horns, and all the beasts of the field and all the birds of the air feared him and made petition to him all the time.... This is the vision which I saw while I slept....

(1 Enoch 90:37)

In a night vision Ezra sees an angel and hears him say to him:

Whosoever is delivered from the predicted evils shall see my wonders. For my Son the Messiah shall be revealed, together with those who are with him, and shall rejoice the survivors four hundred years. And it shall be, after these years, that my Son the Messiah shall die, and all in whom there is human breath. Then shall the world be turned into the primeval silence seven days, like as at the first beginnings; so that no man is left.

And it shall be after seven days that the Age which is not yet awake shall be roused, and that which is corruptible shall perish.

And the earth shall restore those that sleep in her,
And the dust those that are at rest therein...
And the Most High shall be revealed upon the throne of
   judgment....

The angel then explains the dream Ezra saw:

As for the lion whom thou didst see roused from the wood and roaring, and speaking to the eagle and reproving him for his unrighteousness and all his deeds, as thou hast heard: This is the Messiah whom the Most High hath kept unto the end of the days, who shall spring from the seed of David, and shall come and speak unto them; he shall reprove them for their ungodliness, rebuke them for their unrighteousness, reproach them to their faces with their treacheries. For at first he shall set them alive for judgment; and when he hath rebuked them he shall destroy them.... This is the dream that thou didst see and this is its interpretation.

(4 Ezra 7:28–33; 12:31–35)

In the year 487 of the Hegira (c. 1123 C.E.), in the month of Rabi'a, several Jews saw in their dream that they would fly in the air. They told this to their brethren, and all of them scattered their fortune and their property, expecting the coming flight. And the end was that they did not fly at all but became the object of ridicule among the people.

(Ibn al-Athir, *al-Kamil*, p. 15)

Hayyim Vital (1542–1620), one of the greatest Kabbalists, lived in Safed, Palestine, where he was a disciple of Yitzhaq Luria and the interpreter of his teachings. The following dreams are described in Vital's *Sefer haHezyonot* ("Book of Visions").

I dreamt: I was standing on top of the great mountain to the west of Safed, at the beginning of the mountain. In the middle it has two great peaks which are toward the village of Meron. And I heard a voice proclaim and say: "Behold, the Messiah is come!" And behold, the Messiah stood before me, and he blew the shofar, and thousands and myriads from Israel gathered around him.

And he said to me: "Come with me, and you will see the vengeance of the destruction of the Temple." And we went there. And he fought there, and smote all the Christians who were there. And he entered the Temple and killed also those who were in it. And he commanded all the Jews and said to them: "My brethren, cleanse yourselves and our Temple of the defilement of the blood of the bodies of the uncircumcised and the defilement of the idolatry which is in it."

And we cleansed ourselves and rebuilt the Temple on its site, and offered up the daily sacrifice through the hands of the High Priest who had the likeness of my neighbor R. Israel haLevi. And I asked the Messiah: "How can a Levite be a priest?" And he said to me: "You were in error when you thought that he was a Levite; in fact, he is a Kohanite." Thereafter he brought out the Tora scroll from the sanctuary of the Temple and read from it. And I woke up.

(Hayyim Vital, *Sefer haHezyonot*, p. 41)

On the twenty-sixth of Heshvan I dreamt a great dream but I remember only this small part of it:

I saw a certain man, a good friend of mine, bringing me a letter of the size of one-half of our usual papers, written in large Assyrian [Hebrew] characters, similar to the letters of the script of our Tora scrolls. And he put it into my hand and said to me: "You have always been desirous to see the handwriting of the Messiah, king of Israel. Behold, I brought it to you from a land more distant than two years [journey], from the place where the [lost] tribes live. But I brought it to you in a hurry, in a short time, and it is written by the hand of the Messiah himself, and he sent it to you."

Then I made him swear three times that it was true that it was the handwriting of the Messiah himself, and that he himself had sent it to me especially. And he swore to me that it was absolutely true. And I opened it and, behold, in its beginning he wrote many greetings as is usual in letters, and after that he wrote at length and in a general way to let me know that he was already preparing to come to the Land of Israel, and that therefore I must make efforts to turn Israel to repentance so that this should be a help for him when he will come soon.

(*Ibid.*, pp. 71–72)

In my dream...in the night of the Sabbath, the twenty-seventh of the month of Av, in the year 5368 of the Creation [1608 C.E.], I saw that I was going to Jubr [a town in Syria, near Damascus], to the synagogue, to observe the eve of the New Moon. And as I was walking on the road, I met a man, most splendid in appearance, and he asked me whether we have made peace with the sage, our master, the divine rabbi, may the Merciful One preserve him. And I answered him that we have agreed to make peace with him. And then he said to me: "If you only knew who that sage is, you would go to his house early in the morning and late in the evening to kiss his hands and feet, to shelter under his wings." I answered him: "Do I not know that he is very great in wisdom?" He said to me: "The whole world knows that he is great in wisdom, but you do not know who he is." Then I importuned him to tell me who he is. He said: "He is the Messiah...."

(*Ibid.*, p. 241)

Samuel Vital (1598–c. 1678), whose dream follows, was the youngest son of Hayyim Vital. He edited and annotated his father's writings.

On the twenty-fourth of Shevat my son Samuel dreamt that two Turks came to my house, and I locked the door. But then one panel of the door opened by itself, and they entered the house through it and sat down with me and said to me: "Fear not, for we are pious Jews, and we came in the shape of Turks so that you should receive our words with joy and follow them." And one of them had a white turban, and the other a turban like the color of parsley. And I recognized that they had come in order to hear words of Tora from my mouth, and I expounded to them. And in the course of my exposition I spoke of the superiority of the firstborn, and of his superiority in the eyes of the Holy One, blessed be He.

My son said to me [in his dream]: "What is this superiority?" I said to him: "Behold, the Messiah is a firstborn, and on his father's side he is of the tribe of Judah, but on his mother's side of the tribe of Reuben the firstborn, although a little of the birthright was given to Joseph. And all this is [merely] from his bodily aspect, but from the aspect of his soul he is a descendant of Joseph who took the essence of the birthright from Reuben; and, also, he was the firstborn of his mother Rachel."

Then my son turned his face to the man with the parsley-colored turban and said to him: "See, I am the firstborn of my mother. Can it be that the Messiah will come from me?" And he said to me: "It can be that either you or one who will issue from your seed will be the Messiah." Then he spoke to me and said: "Be it known to you that we have come to you on a mission from the old sage who always dwells in Jerusalem and who loves you dearly. And behold, take this writing which he sent you." I said: "When I knew him, he, my dear friend, was very old. Can it be that he is still alive?" And he said to me: "Why should you be amazed at this, and why should he not be alive?"

And I took the writing and read it, and there were many things in it said at length, but what he remembers was in brief: "You, R. Hayyim, you are aware that they esteem you in heaven beyond imagination. You also know that the Redemption will not come but through you. Therefore you will do well to hurry, of your own, to bring the Redemption near, and you will receive a great reward. And should you tarry, the end will be that they will compel you from heaven to do it, and then you will perforce have to do it and you will not receive a great reward. And, in truth, it is not possible that the Redemption should come except through you, either of your own will or by being coerced." These were the words of the writing.

And after I finished reading it, the man with the parsley-colored turban repeated the performance of his mission orally, everything that was written in the writing. And his friend said to him: "Why do you have to say all this? Does he not know all this well?" And then I gave them to eat and to drink. And he awoke.

(*Ibid.*, pp. 106–7)

A Dream-Vision of the Ba'al Shem

On New Year's day of 5507 [1746 C.E.], I performed an adjuration for the ascent of [my] soul, as it is known to you, and I saw wondrous things in a vision the like of which I had never before seen since I have known my mind. And what I saw and learned when I ascended there cannot be told and related even from mouth to mouth. But when I returned to the terrestrial Garden of Eden, I saw many souls of the living and of the dead who were known to me and who were not known to me, without measure and number. And they strove to ascend from world to world, through the pillar which is known to those familiar with the Hidden Wisdom, [and they did this] with great and exceeding joy which the mouth would tire to relate and the bodily ear would weary to hear. And also [I saw that] many of the wicked repented and their sins were forgiven to them, because it was a time of great grace, and it was very amazing to my eyes, for many of them were accepted in their repentence, and you too know them.

And all of them as one begged me and importuned me saying: "Your exalted honor, your greatness in Tora, God graced you with great understanding to grasp and to know these things. Ascend with us to be a help and an aid for us!" And because of the great rejoicing I saw among them I resolved to ascend with them. And I saw in the vision that Samael ascended to accuse, and he was full of joy the like of which had never existed, and he performed his acts—decreeing forced conversion upon many souls, [and] that they die a violent death.

And great fear seized me and I almost gave up my soul, and I begged my Teacher and Master[2] that he come with me, because the danger was great in going and ascending to the supernal worlds, [and] because ever since I could stand up I had never ascended in such great ascents. And I ascended, step after step, until I entered the Hall of the Messiah where the Messiah was studying the Tora with all the Tannaites and the righteous, and also with the Seven Shepherds.[3] And there I saw a very great rejoicing, and I did not know the reason for it, and I thought that that rejoicing was, heaven forfend, over my passing from this world. But they informed me thereafter that I was not to die yet, because they took pleasure above when I engaged in mystical unifications[4] below by means of their Holy Tora. But the nature of that rejoicing has remained unknown to me to this day.

And I asked the mouth of the Messiah: "When will the Master come?" And he answered me: "This is how you will know: when your teaching will spread and be revealed in the world—*and let thy springs be dispersed abroad* (Prov. 5:16)—[and when all will know] what I have taught you and what you have understood, so that they too will be able to make unifications and ascents like you, then all the husks will perish, and that will be the time of grace and salvation."

---

2. The prophet Ahijah of Shiloh (1 Kings 11:29ff.) whom the Baʻal Shem considered his teacher and master.

3. The seven shepherds, cf. Micah 5:4, are identified in B. Suk. 52b, as Adam, Seth, Methuselah, Abraham, Jacob, Moses, and David.

4. In Hebrew *Yihudim*, Kabbalistic technical term for the procedure of concentrating on combining various divine names and thus bringing about a unification of God with the Shekhina.

And I was amazed at this, and it was for me a great anguish because of the length of time, for when can this happen? But since while I was there I learned three charms and three holy names which one can easily learn and explain, my mind was set at rest. And I thought that through them, perhaps, also others of my age could reach the grade and the quality which I had reached, that is, that they too would be able to [achieve] ascents of souls and would learn and understand like me. But I was not given permission to reveal this for the rest of my life....

(Ba'al Shem Tov, letter to his brother-in-law, ed. A. Kahana, *Sefer haHasidut*, pp. 73–74)

Theodor Herzl (1860-1904), the founder of political Zionism and father of the State of Israel, grew up in Budapest in an assimilant Jewish family. The Jewish education he received was rudimentary. However, one of the presents he received on the occasion of his Bar Mitzva, at the age of thirteen, was a book of Jewish legends. Many years later he remembered:

I read in it about the coming of the Messiah whose arrival is awaited daily by many Jews even in this generation. And he comes as a pauper riding on an ass. The words of the legend I read were fragmentary, and in many places I could not understand their meaning. It seemed to me that something was missing. But even those fragments of the Messiah legend kindled my imagination. My heart filled with pain and vague longings.... One night, as I was going to sleep, I suddenly remembered the story of the Exodus from Egypt. The story of the historical exodus and the legend of the future redemption which will be brought about by King Messiah became confused in my mind. The past and the future, all became for me one beautiful, magic legend, a kind of exalted and wondrous song. And in my mind the idea took shape of writing a poem about King Messiah. For several nights this thought kept me awake. I was ashamed to tell anybody about them. I knew they would mock me and say to me, "Behold the man of dreams!" The days of examinations in the school arrived: also new books came (in those days I regarded the poems of Heinrich Heine as new discoveries), and diverted my thoughts from the suffering of the Messiah. But in the depth of my soul, it seems, the legend continued to expand though I was unaware of it. One night I had a wonderful dream: King Messiah came, and he was old and glorious. He lifted me in his arms, and he soared with me on the wings of the wind. On one of the clouds, full of splendor, we met the figure of Moses (his appearance was like that of Moses hewn in marble by Michelangelo; from my early childhood I like to look at the photographs of that statue), and the Messiah called to Moses: "For this child I have prayed!" Then he turned to me: "Go and announce to the Jews that I will soon come and perform great miracles for my people and for the whole world!" I woke up, and it was a dream. I kept this dream a secret and did not dare to tell it to anybody.

(Reuben Brainin, *Hayye Herzl*, pp. 17–18;
Joseph Patai, "Herzl's School Years," pp. 58–59.)

29

The Modern Postlude

While the Enlightenment has done much to dampen the Messianic fervor and even to extinguish the Messianic faith in widening circles of assimilated and modernized Jews, the Messiah theme has continued to reverberate in the writings of modern Jewish authors. In the preceding chapter we have met with one manifestation of this continued preoccupation with the Messianic idea in the childhood dream of Herzl. Understandably, most of the modern authors who evinced an interest in the concept did so not in writings about the Messianic hopes in general, but in novels, stories, or plays dealing with one or the other of the false Messiahs whose appearance had shaken the Jewish community time and again. Well past the middle of the twentieth century, dozens of novels, short stories, plays and biographies were written about Shabbatai Zevi, and several more about false Messiahs of lesser fame, such as David Reubeni and Solomon Molcho. This rich literary crop is either historical fiction or scholarly historiography, and thus does not belong in the present book. Only a few authors tried to recreate the legend which was woven around these false Messiahs in their lifetime. Such writings have a place among our Messiah texts, and a representative sample of them, written by the noted German-Jewish novelist Jakob Wassermann (1873–)1933) is presented below.

Larger is the number of those modern Jewish authors who wrote stories depicting the meaning of the Messiah for his believers and devotees. These writers make serious attempts to enter into the minds and souls of groups or individuals who lived in a past era and whom the Messianic idea filled with faith, trust, expectation, and occasionally despair. They create legends in the old mold but in a modern style, the characters in their stories represent traditional attitudes, their descriptions conjure up the mood of waiting for the Messiah or imagined events attendant on his coming which can occur only in an ambience of belief, in an atmosphere in which the myth of the Messiah is an undoubted truth, a living reality, a moving force. To this category of writing belong the stories and excerpts from the pens of Martin Buber, Shalom Asch, Joseph Patai, Efraim Frisch, Rachel Berdach.

Another type of writing presents a stark contrast to the above. It consists of the work of those authors who express, in a more or less veiled form, their own unbelieving, critical, sophisticated attitude, occasionally indulging in an ostentatious display of their cerebral superiority over the old, pious, unquestioning belief in the Messiah and his impending advent. Their disillusionment with traditional religion and its values prompts them to engage in a literary debunking of the Messiah, of the belief in him, of his psychohistorical significance. They wish to show that the great expectation of centuries had been naïve and childish, and that the time has come to grow out of it. Had Sigmund Freud been a novelist he could have written such a story, showing that for modern, self-relying, rational man the Messiah has become superfluous. An attitude of this type underlies the brief vignettes by Franz Kafka and Elie Wiesel, and the story by William Zuckerman presented below.

This chapter concludes with two modern poems written one generation apart. The first is by Hayyim Nahman Bialik (1873–1934), considered unanimously the greatest Hebrew poet of modern times; the second by Uri Zevi Greenberg (1894–   ), one of the most original and forceful among the new Israeli poets. No collection of Jewish writings about the Messiah would be complete without these two powerful poems.

JAKOB WASSERMANN

The Legend of Shabbatai Zevi

One day a strange old Jew, Zacharias Naar, appears in the city of Fürth and proclaims the Messiah, Shabbatai Zevi.

Zacharias Naar walked through the dark lanes of the town towards the synagogue. The service was still in progress there, for it was the eve of the Day of Atonement. Soon he was standing unnoticed among the crowd of men, who murmured their prayers. His Tallith was around his shoulders, his shining eyes were fixed upon the Ark. There was no peaceful, festive atmosphere here. Each man seemed to serve his God alone, for himself. Now and then a vague sound of uproar arose, from which a voice, screaming or chiding, would detach itself. The house of God was filled with the musty odor of a cave; it smelled of old leather, old clothes, smoke, and rotting wood. Children stood about and stared with dull reverence at the pages of their books grown brown with age. The room seemed like an underground chamber of conspirators, a cell for ascetic scourgings of the flesh. Nothing of the joy of life, and nothing of the joy of God could be found in it. The lamps smoked, and a person coming in from the fresh air would have felt as if he were sinking into a sultry, steaming gorge.

When the last Kaddish was ended, and all were preparing to leave, Zacharias Naar went up to the Ark and raised his hand: a sign that he wished to speak. Silence fell, and all eyes were turned to the stranger. He began to speak in a low voice, almost as though talking to himself. At first he spoke brief, hurriedly uttered words, about the wretched and pitiable condition of the Jewish people, about the oppression they suffered, about their dispersal in all parts of the world. Then, once he was sure that all were listening attentively, his voice grew louder, it lost its casual tone, and his eyes began to flash. He called upon the Ancient God of the Jews, the God who had piled up promises upon promises, and poured poverty upon His Chosen People, with torments and tribulations worse than the Egyptian plagues. There was deadly silence. The very walls seemed to be listening, to be eagerly absorbing his words. The speaker went on:

"The anger of the Lord is kindled against His people, and He stretches forth His hand to smite them till the mountains shake and their corpses lie in the streets like garbage. Have they not accused us: You poisoned our wells? Have they not slaughtered our brethren by the thousands? Have they not cried: You use the blood of our children as sacrifice on the Passover? You use it for your pregnant woman? Have they not robbed us of our possessions? Are we not condemned to wander as outcasts, so that many of us are without shelter like Cain who slew his brother? Have they not broken us upon the wheel, and delivered us into the hands of the executioners like diseased cattle? Have they not burned our children, violated our women, and when the plague came, did they not rage more terribly among us than the pestilence itself? Yet, with all this, the Lord has not turned His wrath away from us.

"But now, now He will raise up a banner as a sign to the heathen in far countries, and will whistle to them from the ends of the earth. And, behold, they will come in hurried flight. And none of them shall be weak and none stumble, neither will they give themselves up to rest or to sleep. The girdles of their loins will not break, nor will the straps of their shoes be torn. The hoofs of their horses will be hard like rocks, and their wheels will be like the storm wind. They shall roar like a lioness and like young lions, and will growl and seize their prey and carry it off, and none shall rob them of it. And there will be a roaring over Judah like unto the roaring of the sea, and whosoever will look upon the land will see a fearsome darkness, and the light of the firmament above will be turned into night. Approach, you heathens and hearken, and you peoples look up and listen! For the earth hears what fills it, the universe and all that springs therefrom. For the Lord is wroth with all the heathens, He has marked them for slaughter. Their corpses will be thrown down, and their dead bodies will stink, and the hills will run with their blood. The stars will crumble and the sky be rolled up like a parchment. But our meadows will be full of joy, the plains will rejoice before us and flourish like the rose. They will flourish, yea, flourish and rejoice, rejoice and exult! The splendor of Lebanon will be given unto them, and the glory of the Carmel. Make firm your trembling joints and strengthen your weak knees! Say unto them that are afflicted of heart: Be strong! The eyes of the blind will be opened, and the ears of the deaf will hear! Then the lame and the halt will leap as the hart, and the tongue of the dumb will sing praises!

"For, behold, a man has arisen in the city of Smyrna, in Asia Minor, and he is the True Messiah of God, and the Kingdom of Heaven is near! Yea, I can see your eyes shine and your hands tremble! Have you not heard the call of his voice from the shores of the Mediterranean Sea? A new work of Redemption goes before him, and the *Olam haTikkun* [the World Restored] will arise. For he alone has perceived the Divine Being, he, Shabbatai Zevi! Gather together, O my brethren, arise, raise up your wives, teach your children to speak his name, and comfort the orphans with his words! The age of Redemption began in the year 5408 of the creation of the world, for in that year Shabbatai Zevi revealed himself unto us. Miracle upon miracle has he performed, and the Jews of the East cry unto him with jubilation!"

A terrible uproar interrupted the speaker. News of the event had long since reached Franconia, but only in the form of vague rumors, mysterious hints, brought by wandering monks, by wandering Jews, or by gypsies. It had been no more than the dull echo of distant thunder, which would stir the mind in the silence of the night and in dreams. But the light of the day would bring doubts and unbelief. Now, for the first time, it penetrated the ears like a trumpet blast, like a clear clarion call to battle, like the clash of a thousand shields and swords, a cry of resurrection. Their eyes were set on fire, the day dawned before them, the age of gloom and oppression seemed near its end. Here was sunshine, freedom, a God-sent and divine chosenness for great things, splendor and joy and ecstatic yearnings, the reward of serving God for centuries in unshakable faith. It entered their unhappy souls like the call to a new life. Boys saw themselves as grown men, men clenched their fists, and hot and cold shivers ran down their spines. And when the first intoxication had passed, they thronged around the stranger, assaulted him with requests for particulars, and listened, listened. Forgotten was the hour of departure, forgotten the commandments of the day of fasting. The women streamed out of their enclosures and listened with flushed cheeks. In their imagination they saw him come to life, that mysterious prophet from Smyrna, moving through the bright daylight of history like a glowing meteor, filled with Lurianic mysticism, convinced that he was bringing the end of all time.

Zacharias Naar went on speaking, absorbed, like a man in a dream. He told them how Shabbatai Zevi would mortify his flesh, bathe summer and winter, by day or by night, in the sea, how his body had acquired a sweet fragrance from the water of the ocean and his eyes a clear light. He had never touched a woman, and, although he had twice taken a wife, he had avoided and soon repudiated both of them. His bearing was grave, his being solitary, and he had a beautiful voice with which he sang Kabbalistic verses or poems of his own composition. He proclaimed the year 5426 [1666 C.E.] as the Messianic year which would bring a new grandeur to the Jews, and lead them back to Jerusalem. His soul gave itself joyfully up to the sweet intoxication with the consciousness of God. He had been driven out of Smyrna, but thereupon the smoldering fire burst into a consuming flame—his humiliation had become his greatness and glorification. At Salonica he held a festival and was solemnly wedded, in the presence of his friends, to the Holy Scripture: the Tora, Daughter of Heaven, was united with the Son of Heaven in an indivisible union. Fifty Talmudists ate at his table, and no beggar was turned away from his door. At prayer he shed streams of tears, and all night long he sang the Psalms by bright candlelight. Love songs he sang also. He sang the song of Meliselda, the beautiful daughter of the emperor:

> Ascending a mountain
> And descending a valley
> I came to fair Meliselda,
> In the emperor's coronation hall.
> Gently she came forth
> With flowing hair,
> And her face was gentle,
> Her voice was sweet.
> Her face shone like a sword,
> Her eyelids were like a steel bow,
> Her lips were corals,
> Her flesh pale like milk.[1]

---

1. This is part of a poem which actually was a favorite of Shabbatai Zevi. It was originally an old Spanish love-song to which he gave a mystical interpretation. In order to render the poem in rhyme, Wassermann took considerable liberties with

Children would follow him through the streets while their mothers sang praises to his name. He announced that he would lead the ten tribes of Israel from the River Sambation to the Holy Land, riding upon a lion which would have a seven-headed dragon in its mouth....[2]

(From *Die Juden von Zirndorf*, pp. 17–23)

MARTIN   BUBER

"The world of the nations [said R. Jacob Yitzhaq, the "Seer" of Lublin] is in an uproar and we cannot wish that it cease, because only when the world breaks up in convulsion do the pangs of the Messiah begin. Redemption is not a complete gift of God which is sent down from heaven to earth. The world-body must be in labor, must suffer great pain, must come to the brink of death, before Redemption can be born. For its sake God permits the earthly powers to rise up against Him more and more. But as yet it has not been inscribed upon any tablet in heaven when the struggle between light and darkness will pass into the last great combat. Here there is something God has delivered into the power of His Tzad-

the original. The gentleness of Meliselda's walk and face (both Wassermann's inventions) are not consonant with the imagery of her face shining like a sword and eyelids like a steel bow, which are part of the original. The following is a literal translation of the corresponding lines in the original Ladino folk-poem as it was sung by Shabbatai Zevi and as it is still known among Sephardi Jews:

> As I went down to the river,
> As I went up the valley,
> I encountered Meliselda,
> Daughter of the emperor.
> She was coming from the bath,
> From the bath in which she washed.
> . . . .
> Her body emerged
> Like a rose from the rosebush,
> Her forehead was shining
> Like a polished sword,
> Her cheeks were white and clear
> Like milk and blood,
> Her eyebrows arched
> Like the hunter's bow.

Two versions in Ladino with Hebrew translation were published by Moshe Attias, in his *Romancero S'faradi*, pp. 82–84.

2. Cf. chapter 3, "Early Messiahs."

diqim, and this it is about which it is said, 'The Tzaddiq decides and God fulfills.' And why should it be so? Because God wants the Redemption to be our own Redemption. We ourselves must bring it about that the struggle be intensified into the pangs of the Messiah. As yet the smoke clouds around the mountain of the nations' world are small and passing. Bigger and more persistent ones will come. We must await the hour in which the sign will be given us, we must influence it in the depths of the mystery. We must keep the power in us awake until the hour appears in which the dark fire fails to challenge the light one. We then are charged not with extinguishing but with stirring up the flame."

(From *Gog und Magog*, pp. 84–85)

"It is written [said the "Jew" of Przysucha], *Thou art clothed with glory and majesty* (Ps. 104:1). All glory and majesty, which we consider the essence of God, is nothing but His garment. He clothes Himself in it in order to approach His creature. Even the outermost of the divine majesty, which we are able to perceive, is nothing but a self-abasement of God for our sake.

"But in two instances He clothed Himself in a veritable servant's garb. One was that He allotted His Shekhina, His 'Indwelling,' to the world, and let her, His Shekhina, enter into the history of the world and partake in the contradictions and sufferings of the world, and sent her along into the exile of man and the exile of Israel. She is not proof against blows and wounds, she totally betook herself into our fate, into our misery, yea, into our guilt, and when we sin she experiences our sinfulness as something that happens to her. She not only shares our degradation but also that which we do not want to recognize as shame she tastes in all its shamefulness.

"The other instance was that He put the responsibility for the Redemption of His world into the power of our returning. It is written, *Return, ye backsliding children, I will heal your backsliding* (Jer. 3:22). God wants to complete His creation in no other way except with our help. He does not want to reveal His kingdom before we have founded it. He does not want to put the crown of the King of the World on His head except if He accepts it from our hands. He does not want to unite with His Shekhina until we lead her to Him. He lets her wander along the highway of the world with dusty and bleeding feet until we take pity on her.

"Therefore, all calculations of the end of time are false, and all efforts to bring the Messiah must miscarry. Yes, all this diverts us from the one and only thing which truly matters: to lead the Shekhina back to Him through our returning.

"Surely, there is a secret here. But he who knows it cannot make it known, and he who pretends to make it known proves that he knows it not.

"And surely, there is a miracle here. But he who wants to bring it about causes it to fail. Only he who does not attempt it can hope to have a share in it. Redemption is near. It only depends on our returning."

(From *Gog und Magog*, pp. 173—74)

SHALOM ASCH

Jesus and the Messiah

The heavy gates of St. Peter's swung open, and the Jew of the city of Nazareth, which is in Galilee, climbed down from his cross on the eastern wall and went out of the church. The wound in his side was covered by the sheet of Joseph of Arimathea. So clad, he wandered through the streets of Rome. He did not wear on his back the yellow badge, the sign of his people, and therefore the watchmen of the city did not molest him, though the gates of the ghetto had long been closed and he, a Jew, had no right to be outside the gates after the ringing of the bell. Nor were there many to mark his passing, for those Romans who were awake were busy putting the last touches on the masks and costumes which they would wear at the Carnival. They were not aware of the presence of the Man-God in their midst; they did not know he had left his accustomed place on the eastern wall of the church. His sheet glimmered palely as he slipped through the great columns of the Square of St. Peter. Unnoticed he passed by the ancient synagogue over against the Colosseum, and heard the lamentations from within. He caught the words of their prayer, in which they suppli-cated the Almighty to be with them on the next day, the first Carnival Sunday, so that their humiliations might be fewer; and above all they implored their Father in heaven that the Holy Father might be gracious to them, and, when he put his foot on the head of the elder of the Jews, might not kick the Scrolls of the Law to the ground. The moon hung over the vast, ancient ruin, as if it could not find the way out. It seemed to the Jew of Nazareth that here, under the shattered walls of the Colosseum, he could still catch the last cries of those who, long ago, dying in the jaws of the wild beasts, had called upon him.

The Man-God crossed the city and reached the Augustus Gate which led into the country. On the other side of the gate, curtained by the night, he came upon the figure of the Messiah, seated on a stone, and chained with both feet to the wall of the city. He held a trumpet in one hand; the cruse of oil was at his side; and, so sitting, he waited for the word of God to sound the call to the liberation. His eyes were fixed on the ground and the high, steely forehead glimmered down the length of the Via Appia. To him the Man-God said:

"I have come to thee, O Messiah. Forgive me for that which they do in my name."

The eyes of the Messiah remained fixed on the earth.

"Did I not come to you? Would I not have gathered you under my wings as a hen gathereth her brood? Did I not shed my blood for you in the presence of my Father? To whom else did I go? Was I not always to be found in your prayer houses, and did I not spread my word in your courts? And when you turned from me strangers came; they tore the sheet from my body and made themselves banners. They dipped the banners in my blood, and with these before them, and my name on their lips, they spread desolation among my brothers. My word of peace they have distorted into a war cry; the forgiveness I proclaimed they have turned into vengeance. The young men of my people have been harnessed to chariots, and their brides, my sisters, shamed unto death."

The eyes of the Messiah remained fixed on the earth.

"They have seated themselves upon my chair, to gorge and swill and rule over the earth. See, they utter in my name words which I did not speak; they have not comforted the lowly; they have not wiped away the tears of those that suffer. They add their oppression to those that are oppressed, and they crawl at the feet of the mighty. O ye strangers, who has given you the right to enter into judgment between brother and brother? You knew not and know not my pain, you understood not and understand not now my sorrow."

Still the eyes of the Messiah remained fixed on the earth.

"Here, by thy side, I will take my place upon a stone. Let my limbs, like thine, be chained to the wall of the city. Let my eyes, too, be fixed on the earth. With my brothers and sisters I will bear all suffering and humiliation, for my soul is weary of their songs of praise. For they bow down to my image, and have forgotten my word. Here I will sit with thee and wait for the day which God has appointed, and thou wilt blow thy trumpet to assemble the peoples under the hill of God. Then, like the shepherd who brings water to his sheep in the heat of the day, I will bring together my flock, I will warm those that are frozen, and I will make whole those whom the lions have rent and the dogs bitten. I will wipe away the tears of the unhappy, and lift up the broken of spirit, for then I will be with them and my words will live in them."·

(From *From Many Countries* pp. 348–50)

Eretz Israel

In the darkness of the night, at the sea's edge, in Israel, a small group of young men concealed themselves in the cleft of a ravine that gave on the Mediterranean. The heavy darkness lay like a great dead form upon the sea and on the shore. The sea was stormy, releasing its fury in high waves that beat upon rocks along the shore. The backlash wet the cold shivering feet of the young people who waited there.

The immigration center had made contact with a ship filled with survivors from German concentration camps that had managed to get through the English blockade and was nearing the shore of Eretz Israel. They had sent out an advance guard to a point along the shore that was hidden and protected by high rocky cliffs. From there the land party would signal the ship's captain in code, instructing him where to land. And they would await the lifeboats filled with immigrants that would come from the ship.

A little farther inland, hidden in a thick orange grove, there were trucks waiting for the immigrants—trucks with armed guards ready to distribute the newcomers among various villages in Israel.

The young people on the beach had been especially trained for this work. Among them were first-aid girls, whose equipment of medicines, blankets, and field cots lay hidden in the cleft of the ravine. They waited impatiently for the arrival of the lifeboats. Though they had purposely chosen this stormy night, they had not been prepared for the torrent of rain that came down upon them in full force. This would seriously interfere in their work. The fact that they themselves were soaked to the bone did not matter to them. Their real worry was for the blankets and the cots, which were wet through. These had been prepared for the sick among the immigrants so that they might be cared for as soon as they reached the shore.

A light in the window of an isolated little house some distance inland guided the ship in its approach. But the disembarkment of the immigrants could take place only in lifeboats because of the perils of the rocky shore. The group on the beach was forbidden to use lights as signals. In the storm it would be impossible for them to hear the sound of the oars; they had no way to tell whether the boats were approaching, for in the pitch-dark night it was impossible to see more than a few feet. There was no choice but to try to pierce the darkness somehow, and to sharpen their ears in order to catch the signal of their lookout on the rocky point that projected into the sea. The lookout would try to direct the lifeboats to this landing place.

They waited and listened for hours on end. It was already far into the night. The damp cold congealed the marrow in their bones, and they had no way to warm themselves.

They were hungry for cigarettes but did not dare strike a light. Mostly young people who had been born in this land, they had only heard of the bitterness of exile without ever knowing its taste; they waited in silence. The only one who kept up a stream of talk from the very beginning of their watch was "Lady Hadassah." She was called Hadassah because she was in charge of the first-aid girls on these occasions. And she was called lady because she was a mature woman who had been one of the head nurses of the Hadassah Hospital. Also she seemed to them all a kind of symbol of the Hadassah. Whenever anyone thought of that great institution they thought also of Lady Hadassah.

Actually it was some time since she had been a nurse in the hospital. But wherever there was a misfortune, an accident, wherever an ambulance was needed, there Lady Hadassah was to be found. She was a chubby, homey woman with a bright motherly face, healthy red cheeks, and constantly smiling eyes. Young men said that one could tell she was an old maid, and there was a good deal of truth in this. There was something perennially healthy and serene in her face that was untouched by time; for, as sometimes happens with the faces of elderly spinsters who live under the mantle of their dreams, time seemed to have no effect upon her. On the face of Lady Hadassah, too, there was the romantic radiance of idealism.

If one did not look too closely to discover her age, one saw in her a young and energetic woman. Though there was no danger to which she would not expose herself, mostly she was to be found among the children of the Youth Aliyah. She was possessed of an extraordinary patience, which somehow had its effect on children who could not be controlled or quieted by anyone else. Whenever there were difficulties with the youthful immigrants in the various colonies, she was called, and with the magic of her motherly gift for harmony she would straighten out the difficulties.

Because of her gift with children she was made the leader of a group of Hadassah nurses whose task was to receive illegal immigrants, take care of the children, quiet them after their upsetting experiences, and make them feel at home in Israel. She it was who accompanied the immigrants in the trucks and wagons to the villages. Yet she insisted on taking her place on the beach so as to be among the first to receive the newcomers. It was she who relieved the tired mothers of their crying children.

On this dark night she clambered over the jagged rocks, holding on against the heavy waves that might have washed her into the sea. Soaked through by the rain, she waited cheerfully with her comrades for the arrival of the little ships, keeping up a continual chatter and enlivening the spirits of the others with her talk.

"When we sit like this on the shore in the darkness waiting for the newcomers, there is no way of telling what sort of people will emerge from the sea. Sometimes it seems to me that a little boat will appear out of the darkness of the night, and from it will descend our fathers, Abraham, Isaac, and Jacob—to remain and live with us."

A chuckle was heard from the youngsters about her. The older generation, they seemed to say, the older generation and their romantic dreams!

"Why does it have to be Abraham, Isaac, and Jacob?" a young voice asked.

"Doesn't this sea remind you of the sea of Jewish sorrows, with its stormy waves howling over our pain and suffering, over martyrdom and pogroms? Then wouldn't it be fitting that out of this roaring sea and this black night a ship should approach our shore and that out of that ship should come our ancient patriarchs, returning to be with us as witnesses before the whole world that we are the true inheritors of this land that God promised us! Just imagine what sort of impression this would make upon the whole world, upon all of our enemies in the world, and upon our friends."

"An old maid's dream," one lad whispered to another.

"Not only the dream of an old maid, but the dream of an old generation, of the old world from which she comes," the other one answered. "They all go about with these dreams."

"If we really must dream about a little boat coming to us out of the night, sent by heaven, then I know something better it might bring, something that will have more effect on our enemies."

"What's that?"

"Let our father Moses send us that magic rod of his, by the little boat that will come to our shore out of the night."

This came from Ben Arye, the leader of the group, whom the English had more than once dropped by parachute behind the German lines, into the Jewish ghettos, where he had organized resistance and partisan units.

"The rod of Moses?" some of them repeated, wonderingly.

"The rod that brought down the plagues on Pharaoh. We ought to have a rod like that for the new Pharaoh that spits out fire and dynamite and bombs. That's what the enemy will understand," someone added, in agreement with Ben Arye.

"A rod has two ends. If it shoots fire out of one end, it might send back bombs out of the other. But if someone were really to drift toward us out of the night, from among our people in exile, then I have a more important wish—let the ship of Messiah himself come to us out of the darkness, not only for us but for the entire world which is on the point of death and longing for salvation—a little boat that will bring the sanctified spirit that we and the entire world are waiting for."

They all knew the voice of the orthodox worker, Aaronchik, who had been rescued from Hitler's hell by a series of miracles and wonders and whose faith had not been weakened but actually strengthened by all of the horrors through which he had passed. Since his recent arrival in Israel, he had volunteered to serve among those who went into every sort of danger in order to rescue whomever they could from Europe and bring them to the motherland. Tonight he had been sent on this mission, for it was thought that he would find others like himself among the immigrants, and because of their common experiences in the past, he would best be able to help them on their way to the new life.

"Another dreamer," his companions whispered among themselves.

"It's not to be wondered. He has nothing left but his faith. Hitler made a bachelor out of him," the leader said quietly to the others. He reminded them again to respect the religious sentiments of their comrade and not enter into disputes with him. And after this, the group became quiet.

But soon after they fell silent, the voice of the lookout was heard, "Ready! Be ready!"

As though sparked into action, they all leaped up, and four young men, one after another, jumped from the rocks into the sea, swimming through the angry waves. The others stood ready to catch the boat's line and drag it to the shore.

And then a tiny lifeboat appeared out of the stormy night. It was pulled and pushed by the youngsters, who guided it between the rocks. Silently, with practised hands, they flung the line to the outstretched hands of their comrades on shore, and, all pulling in unison, dragged the little boat up on the rocky beach.

They stood as though turned into stone when, instead of a load of immigrants, they found only an aged, sick Jew lying on the bottom of the boat and, close to him, a crying child of about three.

"This is all they let down from the ship," said the Jewish sailor who was rowing the lifeboat. "The old man is nearly dead, so they had to get him ashore. And he wouldn't be separated from the child. Because of the storm, they are going to try to find another place along the shore where it will be easier to land the rest of the immigrants. Better take him now—I'm afraid he might be dead by now."

Lady Hadassah set to work. She put her ear against his chest. The old Jew was still alive; she could hear him gasping. "Eretz Israel?" he asked, with his last strength.

"Yes, you are in Eretz Israel," Lady Hadassah answered.

She tried to quiet him while bringing her flask of brandy to his lips. But the Jew's lips were closed. From between them his feeble voice came, "Now I can die. Father in heaven, I am thankful."

"You will live and not die. Here, take this in your lips," Hadassah insisted.

"I don't need anything any more. All that I wanted was to bring the child into Eretz Israel and fulfil my vow to his mother."

"From where have you come?"

"Do not ask. Take the child. I give him into your hands. I thank Thee, Lord of the World, that Thou hast permitted me to fulfil my vow." And the Jew closed his eyes and was silent.

Lady Hadassah took the child in her arms and said, "Even so has our dream been fulfilled. A ship came, bringing our forefathers to our shore."

"Not only her prayer, but mine, too, has been heard," remarked the orthodox young man from Poland. "For the ship has brought Messiah to our shore."

"Our forefathers? Messiah?" the young people repeated wonderingly.

"Yes, our forefathers, and Messiah. Don't you realize, don't you understand? The past and the future lives in every child; the beginning and the end—our forefathers and the Messiah."

"Is that what you mean? Come, comrade, we have work waiting for us," said the leader.

And they carried on to the shore a dead Jew, and after him the living child.

(From *From Many Countries*, pp. 304—9)

JOSEPH PATAI

The Messiah-Dreamer of Ujhely

Every midnight, when the great clock on the wall struck twelve, Rabbi Moses son of Hanna, the Tzaddiq of Ujhely, gave a start, raised his head from the large folio, and looked around sadly.

"Has he not come yet?"

None of the followers who were standing about him answered his question. The Tzaddiq suddenly got up from his armchair, went to the window, leaned out, and let his large, sorrowful eyes sink into the dark, silent night. Then he gropingly moved over to the door, opened it, looked out, and then closed it again.

"He is not yet coming!" he repeated sadly.

For a moment he remained waiting at the door, then, as if reconciled to the will of the Almighty, he touched with his lips the name of God which shone toward him from the capsule of the holy writing nailed to the doorpost. Then he approached the stove, scooped up a handful of ashes, and strewed it upon his head, covering the spot on which every morning he would place the holy Tefillin before the morning prayers. Meanwhile he murmured the words of the prophet:

> *"To appoint unto them that mourn in Zion,*
> *To give them a garland for ashes"* (Isa. 61:3).

Disheartened, he took off his slippers, washed his hands, and sat down on the floor next to the doorpost. He took the wax candle that flickered mystically in the dark corner, and put it next to himself on the wooden stool. He bent his head deep down to his knees and, beating his breast, he recited the *Ashamnu* ["We have sinned"], word after word, and then intoned the lament of the midnight prayer:

> *"By the rivers of Babylon, there we sat down, yea, we wept,*
> *When we remembered Zion"* (Ps. 137:1).

Sobbing, he recited the midnight dirges to their end, about the murderous Edom, the suffering of Jerusalem, about the blood which cries from the depth of earth to heaven, about the unburied bodies of the precious children scattered about the Holy City and devoured by birds of prey, and about the dolorous mother Rachel who wanders upon the heights of Rama, inconsolable, lamenting her lost, erring children.

> *"Gather, O children of Jacob, and hearken,*
> *Rend your hearts and not your garments,*
> *Because of your sins was your mother put away"* (Joel 2:13; Isa. 50:1).

And the laments sing about the Shekhina, the Light of the Lord, who herself is wandering in exile, mourning the loss of her Spouse, for she has none for whom she could shine; and about the Matronit, the soul of Israel, who was the radiant eternal Bride, under the baldachin of the Lord's Clouds of Glory on Mount Zion, and now must drag herself along alien streets like a beggar woman: the enemy tore off her gown and she is miserable and forsaken. . . .

And the lamentations sing about the Tora, who is in mourning ever since her splendor was humiliated, and whose crown fell into the dust when her Holy Hall became the prey of flames. . . .

For more than an hour the Tzaddiq of Ujhely sat on the floor weeping and sobbing. And when he reached the words of consolation, he suddenly arose, and as if his soul had been filled anew with hope, he sang jubilantly:

> *"Shake thyself from the dust, O prisoner of Jerusalem,*
> *Loose thyself of the bands of thy neck, O captive Daughter of Zion"*
> (Isa. 52:2).

And he paced joyfully back and forth in his room, and concluded the midnight prayer clapping his hands as if beating its rhythm:

> *"The Lord doth build up Jerusalem,*
> *He gathereth together the dispersed of Israel"* (Ps. 147:2).

His disciples, who until then sat in silent reverence around the table, now broke into singing and clapping. All of them felt the great truth of what the Tzaddiq of Kálló had said: that the soul of the Prophet Jeremiah had risen anew in their Rabbi, this is why he can mourn over the destruction of Jerusalem with all his heart, as if he had seen it with his own eyes, and this is why he awaits day and night the coming of the Messiah and the rebuilding of Zion.

Only a few hours were left of the night for resting, and the Tzaddiq retired to his sleeping alcove.

"But be sure to pay attention; if you hear any noise during the night, wake me immediately, for surely it is the Messiah!"

The followers took turns keeping the vigil in the adjoining room. The Tzaddiq rested on his couch with half-closed eyes, and sat up at the slightest noise.

"Is he come?" he asked as if half in sleep, and then fell back upon his bed.

As soon as the dawn broke, the Tzaddiq rose, washed his hands and face, and then hurried to the window and opened it.

The rays of the morning slipped into the room, which was heavy with steam. They were like sparkling little angels and filled the room with light and glow.

The Tzaddiq spread his arms toward the open sky and recited the greeting of the dawn in his sweet singing voice. Then with a radiant face he turned to his followers.

"He has not yet come. But my right ear can all the time hear the sound of the Messiah's trumpet, while the music of the celestial hosts sings into my left ear. He has not yet come, but he will come! If not today, certainly tomorrow!"

All day long the Tzaddiq was kept busy by his followers, who made the pilgrimage to him from near and far, some with complaints, others with requests, some for advice, others for help. And Rabbi Moses listened to all of them, patiently, gently. He gave advice, he comforted, encouraged, strengthened failing hands, and poured new life into broken hearts. And in between he sighed from time to time.

"Master of the World! My Father! Lift the earthly troubles from the shoulders of Your children, and all of them will be pure like the angels of heaven, and then the Redemption can come!"

When Passover, the Feast of Freedom, approached, the Tzaddiq could no longer restrain his impatient expectation of the Messiah. In the early afternoon he put on his white festive clothes, placed six Matzot in a basket and next to them a bottle of wine and a big silver cup. He tied the basket to his staff, flung it over his shoulder, and stood in front of the open window and listened: can the sound of the Messiah's trumpet be heard? Thus he remained standing until nightfall, gazing in the distance. And when his followers gently reminded him that it was time for the evening prayers of the feast, and that the congregation was waiting for him in the synagogue, the Tzaddiq sadly lowered the basket from his shoulder and said with resignation:

"He is still not coming. But perhaps there still are souls which must first cleanse themselves, so that they can go along with the Redeemer and stay not behind in eternal damnation. Let us therefore wait a little longer for them, for, after all, they too are our brothers!"

And so passed day after day, year after year. And the Tzaddiq of Ujhely awaited the Messiah every moment of his life. His hair, his beard turned white, his eyes became troubled and sad, time plowed deep furrows into his forehead and face, his back became bent, his limbs weak. Only by leaning upon the shoulders of two young disciples was he able to walk a few steps in his room. And Rabbi Moses was very worried: Perhaps the Messiah will come now, how will he be able to follow his speeding triumphal chariot? But then he found comfort in the words of the ancient sages who said that at the time when the Messiah comes the Lord will lift the sun out of its sheath so that it can freely irradiate the earth; the wicked will be destroyed by its force, but the righteous will be healed and rejuvenated by it. . . . And for a moment the Tzaddiq felt as if the holy words had already taken effect for him, and as if he had regained the strength of his youth. He rose from his chair, but barely did he walk one or two steps when he fell exhausted upon his couch.

And Rabbi Moses son of Hanna felt that his last hour was approaching. A deadly disease gnawed at his weak body which was near collapse. But all the pains of the body were overshadowed by the limitless anguish of his soul that he would not live to see the coming of the Messiah. And the agitation, the longing, inflamed his eyes, and a sweat of fever broke out on his wrinkled brow. His followers stood with bent heads and sorrowful hearts around the snow-white sickbed, silently murmuring psalms, and throwing timid, worried glances at the dying, holy old man. . . .

Suddenly the murmuring of the psalms was interrupted. The Tzaddiq raised his head, sat up, and, lifting his two arms toward heaven, he cried:

"Master of the World! My Creator, my Father! I am the least of Your servants, but You know that never did an untrue word issue from from my lips. Now, too, I cannot lie. I must tell You that which burns in my heart. My Creator, my Father! Had Your servant, Moses son of Hanna, known that he would grow hoary and the Messiah would not come, he surely could not have endured it. But You, O Master of the World, You baited and enticed him with cunning, from day to day, until the poor man grew white with age. Surely it was an easy thing for the Master of the World to mislead such a poor fool. . . . But, at least now, let the Messiah Come! Not for my sake, but for the sake of Your name, so that You be sanctified on earth . . . I am not thinking of myself, You can see my soul. But let me be the sacrifice of atonement for all Israel. . . . Let me never reach heaven, the glorious Hall of the Saints. . . . Only the Messiah should come, and I shall sacrifice my salvation for the glory of Your holy name. . . ."

And Rabbi Moses fell back on his couch, and breathed out his pure soul.

And for a very long time the pure soul wandered in the endless heights of heaven. For Rabbi Moses did not want to enter the Supernal Realm until the Messiah appeared on earth and the time of the Redemption of all souls arrived. The soul of the Tzaddiq fluttered in the endless void, and could not be brought up into the Hall of Souls, where the prophets, Moses and Jeremiah, awaited him with yearning.

And then the Supernals again resorted to a ruse. They sent down King David from his heavenly throne to approach the erring soul of the Tzaddiq. And King David descended to the lower heavens, with sounds of harp and songs of psaltery. The soul of the Tzaddiq flew after the sweet sound of the harp, the soothing, enchanting song of the psalms, and, intoxicated by the music of the spheres, it rose higher and higher, attracted by the heavenly sounds. Until finally, when it awakened from its rapture, it found itself in the Hall of Souls, where the souls of the saints sing songs of comfort to the Lord, who rises every night from the secret hiding places and mourns over His unredeemed, suffering children, and lets two teardrops fall into the endless ocean....

(From *Lelkek és Titkok*, pp. 82–88)

EFRAIM FRISCH

The Legend of Kuty

The miserable settlement, nothing more than a heap of tightly packed mud huts, cowered in the flat defile under the autumn sky heavy with rain, and seemed to cling with its ruinous roofs to the black, soaking earth. At its upper end, along the road leading from the great forests which glowered in the distance, it was enclosed by the remains of a low brick wall, part of some ancient fortification. But the people, an amalgam of Jewish families who escaped the fire and the sword of the Cossacks, haunted by the memory of their spilled blood, have long lost all confidence in walls and ramparts. The sky, which bent down so deep over the wide, sad plain, was nearer to them, and to it their hearts were open. In the minds of the community elders, who themselves had seen murder and arson, the horrible events have gradually been transformed into ghostlike happenings, into struggles between the unearthly forces of good and evil, which, as foretold, were to take place before the appearance of the Redeemer, the Messiah. The gold-helmeted cavalry of Prince Wisnowiecki, whom they had glimpsed through the dust of a hot summer day sweeping by in a storm to relieve the city of Kameniecz, appeared in their stories as a shining host of angels come down from heaven. The nations wage wars and rage against one another, and know not why. But the Jews know. What else is death and martyrdom and all the suffering of the body, they say, than a testing and a strengthening of the hope that God will carry out His plan and send the Redeemer? The dead always become more and more numerous, the living fewer and fewer. But they are one people, and there is one God for whom they live and die. . . . The smaller the miserable remnant of Israel, the nearer the Promised End. . . .

In the world round about, life had resumed its busy course. The horrors of the war were forgotten, the merchants, safeguarded by armed escorts, again made their rounds, the noblemen assembled in their noisy diets, and a new day rose over the graves and the ruins. Every Thursday the weekly market was held, with horses, oxen, cows and calves, with drunken peasants, with much shouting and haggling under the wooden booths—ordained by God so that the Jews could eke out a living and grab a few pennies for the sanctification of the Sabbath. Occasionally a foreign wanderer would arrive. Then, next morning, at the door of the synagogue, near the wash barrel, they would find a long table full of books spread out in rows, from large tomes of the Talmud printed in Lublin or Vilna, edifying stories and tales of martyrs who sanctified God's name, to the latest pamphlets which tell about the big communities and the doings of the world. Once in a blue moon a pious preacher would show up in the townlet, and make people smile at his strange dialect and peculiar singsong. One would listen willingly, because it is always God's word, one would nod or shake one's head. People here are not very eager to hear teachings which come from afar; this is the place where the great Rabbi Moshe teaches. Night after night, in the synagogue and house of study, with heads bent over the holy books and with eyes hollow from fasting and vigil, they would discuss what is written and what transmitted in tradition, and interpret the words of the teacher, Rabbi Moshe, the man who can penetrate all obscurity and knows the end of all things.

Something unusual, mysteriously great, something that will shake the balance of the world, is in preparation. One must not touch upon it with profane words, one must not let one's thoughts run away, heaven forfend.... Only composure, looking inward, purification. Everyone can quietly help to untie the secret powers which are about to gather in the supernal sphere. For weeks Rabbi Moshe has been visibly preoccupied with the secret work. Ever since the first day of the month of Elul, the beginning of the annual time of repentance, his face has been veiled, his mouth shut to the world. No disciple dares approach him with a question, even those nearest to him speak only in whispers in his presence. Only the young, merry Israel, his attendant, is allowed to be about him. He divines his wishes, he stands at his side like a young tree, slender and untiring. Today, on the eve of the great day, the Day of Atonement, when in the course of the predawn penitential prayers the passage "The soul is Yours and the body is Yours" was reached, Rabbi Moshe, absorbed in meditation, suddenly cried out so wildly that the whole congregation shook with fright, and the Hazan began to sob and was unable to continue.

At that moment Israel turned with shining eyes toward the silent community, lifted up his hand as if he were greeting an honored guest, and called out in his clear boy's voice: "Enter, redeem us!" At these words, and even more at the sight of him, something like a storm of joy passed through the hearts. But Rabbi Moshe, his bent figure turned away, impatiently struck the prayer-desk with his flat hand so that it resounded, signaling that they should continue.

The afternoon prayer is finished. The big, nail-studded gates of the old wooden synagogue are wide open. Inside there is a scent of fresh hay and warm wax. The last preparations for the evening and the great day must be hastily completed, before the people can sit down to the pre-fast meal, the last one until the evening of the following day, after the first stars appear. How many and how weighty are the things one must think of and do in one's restless heart in order to be ready to stand before the Judge, to be weighed by the angels of judgment who cannot be bribed, to merit atonement and be accepted, or to be rejected. The men hurry home, their hair and sidelocks still wet from the ritual bath. Before the steps of the Holy Ark, one man kneels on the fresh heap of hay, his face pressed to the floor, beating his chest, murmuring the confession of sins, while a spare old man counts out thirty stripes as he beats his back with a leather slipper. A few latecomers stand in the corners, shaking in fervent prayer. Boys clad in long black caftans, with a rope around the midriff, fill boxes and earthenware jars with sand to steady the yellow tapers. Big and thick wax candles and poor little lights made of tallow stand helter-skelter on the cornice of the east wall, form dense wreaths in the brass chandeliers hanging from the ceiling, crowd the tables and the stairs in tight bunches. More and more candles are being brought in. Everyone carries his own carefully in his arms, like a treasure, and timidly tries to find a place for it. It would be a bad omen, a sign of shortened life, if it went out prematurely.

When two men meet, they grasp each other's hands, look with tear-filled eyes at each other, and with a humble heart ask forgiveness for all slights or wrongs they committed in deed, or only in thought. Enemies face each other for a while, ashamed and uncertain, with bowed heads, then throw themselves crying into each other's arms, acknowledging that they were in the wrong. The crooked alleyways leading to the house of prayer become filled. Men, women, children, stream forward, all dressed in white, pale, suffering. A good-bye as before a great voyage, as before death. For everyone will have today his sentence and judgment in heaven.

"The Rabbi! Make room!" is suddenly heard. They press to the side, a passage is cleared. Rabbi Moshe has stepped out of his house, diagonally across the street from the synagogue. With one hand he leans on Israel, who towers over him, the other he stretches forward as if groping. His Tallith hangs billowing from his head and shoulders, stuck on the left side into his belt, whose silver buckle sparkles. His black beard, criss-crossed by white hair, is sunk deep onto his chest. One cannot see his face. Quickly, with short steps, he crosses the street. Those who want to approach him are kept away by Israel with brief headshakes and silent gestures. Behind him walks, straight and tall, a gray-bearded man, one of the community elders.

The long, gloomy dusk is over. Men in white shrouds stand before the open doors of the synagogue and send searching glances toward the sky: it is heavily overcast, no star can be seen. A whisper ripples through the crowd gathered inside, waiting for the beginning of the Kol Nidre prayer. Why did Rabbi Moshe keep silent? What did Israel mean? What great thing will come to pass today? Their hearts tremble in fear and hope.

All the lights are burning. Their flames flicker and bend as if buffeted by an invisible wind. Three dull beats sound from the platform. Those who stand outside hurry in, the gates close. The people is alone with its God.

Silent and thin, like the twitter of a bird, rise the first notes from the mouth of the Hazan. The shriveled, eighty-year-old man, whose name is almost unknown to the young people—he is simply called "the Old One"—slowly emerges from the depth of his silent prayer, his face still soaked in tears. Although he has been standing on this spot for fifty years and more, year after year, on the high holy days of repentance, each time he must intone the Kol Nidre his heart dies in him of fear and hesitation. He feels near collapse under the weight of the call: how dare he, the unworthy, approach heaven on behalf of the whole congregation, carry the prayer before the Highest One as the "messenger of the community"? Yet, as soon as he hears his voice rise, pure and clear, over the silence, he feels a strength grow in him, which makes the poor broken body forget its pain, and fills his heart with so much childish confidence and reliance on God that next day, after the closing prayer, he feels stronger than at the beginning. A sign that his prayer was not rejected.

But today the Old One feels a resistance. He has had his experiences with the supernal carriers of the prayers along the road to the Source of Grace. . . . He becomes frightened. Was his mind not pure? Has he overlooked something that the angels of prayer do not open the right gate, and that the Adversary is encamped before it like a black shadow? He increases his efforts, his voice rises with difficulty, woe-laden from a distressed heart. . . . He folds back the Tallith that covers his head. Rabbi Moshe stands motionless on his right, with the Tora scroll in his arm. His face is stony. The Old One can see only the whites of his inward-rolled eyes.

Twice the Kol Nidre has risen. The third time the Old One intones it with increased force. Israel leans over the shoulder of the Rabbi and whispers in his ear. He does not move.

It is hot and sticky in the wide, low-ceilinged hall. The white, wrapped-up figures of the supplicants filling the pews are enveloped in a red mist. The smoking flames of the candles flicker, their light spins moving shadows cobweblike over the congregation. They stand tightly packed, but barely feel it in their absorption. But now the pressure increases. Here and there someone involuntarily frees his arm, another pushes the Tallith back from his face bathed in sweat. It does not help. There is a confinement that bears in equally from both sides. Disconcerted, one or another tries to step out of the pews into the aisle. But that, too, is packed full of white figures, which slowly flow forward like a tenacious mass. Unease grips the startled men. What is this? The gates are surely closed. From whence this crowd?

Suddenly there is a cry. Who dares to disturb the prayer? The voice of the Hazan falters in distress and is smothered. Then, again a cry. In the pews men and children swoon and sink to the floor, and cannot be helped up. Panic seizes the people. They do not yet dare to speak. In confusion, whispering, they point at the platform in the middle, empty as a rule, but now barely able to contain the mass of white figures. The benches crack, the edges of the iron railings cut into the flesh. It is as if the walls had closed in, as if the black ceiling from above and floor from below would press together. The whimpering, weeping, and crying grow to a tumult. The voice of the Hazan is extinguished like a strangled light. The Old One sinks down under his reader's desk. Nobody can get near him.

Again Israel bends over the shoulder of the Rabbi. And, suddenly awaking, the Rabbi turns, his eyes sweep the room. With a terrible voice, which, like the roar of a lion, drowns out the tumult, he cries: "Throw down your Talliths, all you who live, and move not!" Quickly, rustling, the Talliths glide down from the heads and the shoulders, and lay bare faces, beards, and wildly fluttering eyes. But not all of those present follow the order. A pulling and quivering passes through the tightly packed rows of people. The tenacious stream of white figures on the platform, in the aisles, is checked, comes to a halt, and turns. The shuffling and scraping of a thousand feet can be heard in the sudden soundless quiet. With the Talliths, many of them of an ancient design no longer seen, drawn tightly around their invisible faces as if abashed, the figures move voicelessly toward the locked doors and windows. Many of the men who are grazed by the departing see with horror that the shewfringes are missing from one corner of their trailing coats. In such garments are the dead buried. Did the graves burst, did the dead rise?

The living shudder and hide the heads of the children under their cloaks. For a long time, gray, rolling clouds continue to cast their shadow over the steps of the entrance hall, over the black, curtainless windows.... Then it becomes lighter. The flames of the candles rise up high, almost white....

Three dull beats sound again from the platform. Rabbi Moshe had ascended it, the elders with the Tora scrolls in their arms surrounded him.

"Woe, woe!" he cries, and a groan escapes his breast. "Woe to this generation, which is too weak to receive Your Redeemer! Strengthen it, O Lord, and forgive them and me!" And sobbing he intones again the Kol Nidre, which was interrupted at the third time.

Ever since that night it has been the custom in Kuty not to wear white garb on the eve of Yom Kippur.

("Die Legende von Kuty")

RACHEL   BERDACH

The Sage and the Rabbi

"In my family [said Rabbi Jacob Charif BenAron to Emperor Frederick II] we have this tradition which I received from my grandfather. A young rabbi from the school of Hillel—it was he who insisted that one should love one's neighbor like oneself—one of the many to revolt against the Romans, was taken to the judge. His trial showed that he stood higher than the others, a man endowed with God's own spirit. The judge might have acquitted the fanatic, but his disciples did not want it so. Blinded by the prophecies of Scriptures and by the wish to free their homeland, they said he was the King and Israel's Saviour. Since he behaved so strangely, and did not deny the accusation, he was condemned to die on the cross, as was Roman custom. Stumbling under his cross to the place of execution, he stopped at the house of one of my forefathers, an old man called the Sage. The Rabbi had quite often been his guest. He then stood by the door; his clothes were torn as if in mourning, and he was crying bitterly. His little grandchild hugged him. The Rabbi with the cross looked at the old man and at the child. He beckoned them to come to him. The Sage went to the prisoner and asked him tremblingly: 'Sir, won't you rest a little?'

The Rabbi said in comfort: 'Not yet, but soon. I must not rest now while I'm on the way to my goal. Come close to me; I want to tell you something. You must not rest either, nor must the child. No Jew should rest, but you shall wander until the Messiah comes to the world. Say't to your friends, carry it to the people: that they shall wander, that they shall teach, when all men are united shall Israel find its peace. Tell them—God be with you.' For a short moment he took his right hand off the burden of his cross. He placed it on the boy's head, blessing him."

(From *The Emperor, the Sages, and Death*, pp. 152–53.)

FRANZ KAFKA

The Coming of the Messiah

The Messiah will come as soon as the most unbridled individualism is possible—when nobody destroys this possibility, nobody tolerates the destruction, hence the graves open. This, possibly, is also the Christian doctrine, both in the actual presentation of the example which should be followed—an individualistic example—as well as in the symbolic presentation of the resurrection of the Mediator in the single individual.

The Messiah will only come when he is no longer needed. He will only come one day after his advent, he will not come on the last day but on the very last one.

(From *Parables and Paradoxes*, p. 80)

ELIE WIESEL

The True Waiting

Having concluded that human suffering was beyond endurance, a certain Rebbe went up to heaven and knocked at the Messiah's gate.

"Why are you taking so long?" he asked him. "Don't you know mankind is expecting you?"

"It's not me they are expecting," answered the Messiah. "Some are waiting for good health and riches. Others for serenity and knowledge. Or peace in the home and happiness. No, it's not me they are awaiting."

At this point, they say, the Rebbe lost patience and cried: "So be it! If you have but one face, may it remain in shadow! If you cannot help men, all men, resolve their problems, even the most insignificant, then stay where you are, as you are. If you still have not guessed that you are bread for the hungry, a voice for the old man without heirs, sleep for those who dread night, if you have not understood all this and more: that every wait is a wait for you, then you are telling the truth: indeed, it is not you that mankind is waiting for."

The Rebbe came back to earth, gathered his disciples and forbade them to despair:

"And now the true waiting begins."

(From *One Generation After*)

WILLIAM   ZUKERMAN

The Messiah Who Was Late

All through the night we sat at the crossing of the roads waiting for the coming of the Messiah. The night was dark and cold; the dew was heavy on the ground; we were chilled; the stars winked at us brightly and roguishly. The silence of the night beat upon the darkness like a hammer upon an anvil.

We sat and waited silently, but without fear and anxiety, without that inner, burning restlessness which had shriveled our bodies and dried up the marrow of our bones throughout those many years we had waited before. For this time we were sure of His coming and there was not the slightest doubt in our minds about it. The ancient prophecy had been fulfilled in every detail. The cup of our suffering had at last overflowed and was foaming and seething all over the world as a heavy, mountainous sea. The white steed of the Messiah had been seen over the hills. His trumpet had already sounded throughout the world, and we, the small remnant of the faithful who, in spite of failure and frustration had clung piteously to the forgotten belief in Him, were now gathered from all corners of the earth to meet our Redeemer at the parting of the roads and bring Him to a world steeped in pain, suffering, and degradation.

We were waiting at the roadside in the dark, chilly night, straining every nerve to hear the thudding of the hoofs of His steed, we the remnant of the faithful who had clung to the last shred of hope. If a messenger had come out of the night just then and had told us that He for whom we had been waiting so long and so ardently, was again delayed, our hearts would have burst with grief. Yet, when that messenger did not appear, and the wind brought us the vague sounds of faraway thudding of hoofs on the wet ground, we were strangely calm. Why did not our hearts beat wildly in expectation? Was not the hour at hand? Was not our Messiah near? He in whom we had gathered all our hopes as thirsty ones in the desert collect the dew of the night? Why were we almost indifferent? And why did the stars above wink so roguishly at us?

Suddenly as we were sitting thus, silent like mourners in the dark and chilly night, a thought instead of a messenger came galloping out of the dark and spoke loudly as if it were knocking at the gates of our hearts, and said:

"Suppose you who have been martyred by your waiting, you whose lives have been one long torture of tremulous expectation, should at this moment of fulfillment suddenly turn your backs on him for whom you have been waiting so long and so passionately? Suppose you, the last remnant of the faithful, who clung to your belief in His coming when it was no more than a dull spark in cold ashes, should now, at the moment when your faith is about to be vindicated and to blaze forth in a conflagration, suddenly decide that you had waited in vain, and should retreat silently into the loneliness from whence you came, without greeting, or even seeing Him?"

The thought fluttered wildly in the dark void like a bird caught in a mysterious trap. But even from its trap it continued to shriek into the night and awaken an echo in our hearts:

"Why not?" something in us responded to the strange call. "Why not, indeed? Have we no justification for such an act? Nay, is it not the only honest and dignified thing to do? For years we have waited, years which have been drawn out into centuries and aeons of time. We have waited until life has been emptied of every other content, and we have become like marble monuments of waiting. Can any other human suffering compare with the long torture of indefinite waiting? What greater mental pain is there than the torment of daily, hourly expectation? The tremulous start with each knock at the door; the straining of every nerve to hear the approaching footsteps; the hungry scanning of the passing faces; the fears, the doubts, the anxieties, the slow passing of time; the pitiful struggle of faint hope fighting extinction like a small candlelight struggling with the wind in a dark night. Is there any fulfillment that can atone for such a long, hopeless, and forlorn waiting? What happiness, riches, and bounty that our Redeemer is bringing us now, can make up for the loneliness and despair of the empty days and dreadful nights?

"But the long and dreary years of waiting have not passed altogether in vain for us. We have grown wise through our sorrow and big through our pain. We have outgrown our redemption and become bigger than our Redeemer. The fulfillment He is bringing is a child's toy which might have thrilled our hearts years ago, but will leave us cold and indifferent now. Our pain is bigger than His salvation; our grief is nobler than His happiness; our poor martyrdom is richer than His great promise.

"For He is a Redeemer who has delayed His Redemption until there is nothing left of it but a dry memory. He is a messenger who delivers a flower of spring late in the autumn, when the fire has gone out of life and there is a cold, heavy dew on the ground. A salvation that is delayed too long grows over-ripe and rotten; a fulfillment paid for too dearly in suffering is but another pain. For it is not only fulfillment that matters; the hour of redemption is as important as the act itself. Time is one of the greatest realities in life; it transforms great truths into lies, beauty into ugliness, and promise into disillusionment. A Messiah who is late is, therefore, a false Messiah; a Redeemer who delays His redemption brings only emptiness and cold bitter ashes instead of a flame.

"And so, why should not we, who have grown lean and bitter, but also wise and big through the long years of waiting and suffering, at the last moment not turn our backs upon Him for whom we have been waiting so long and so passionately? What else can we do, but reject the useless treasures which he brings us so late? For we are stronger in our misery than we can ever be in the poor little joys that He is bringing us. We are richer in our poverty than we can ever be in the wealth that He is offering us. Why not admit the truth which we all know in the secrecy of our hearts, that we have waited in vain all these years and that our Messiah brings us nothing that we did not have long ago?"

The night is dark and cold; the dew is heavy on the ground; the wind brings clearly the heavy thudding of hoofs on the wet ground. The silence of the night beats upon the darkness like a hammer upon an anvil. The lonely thought beats its wings wildly like a bird caught in some invisible trap, and its shrieks resound clearly in our hearts, but we continue to wait as we have waited for centuries. And the stars wink brightly and roguishly at us from above.

(From *Refugee from Judea*, pp. 124–28)

HAYYIM NAHMAN BIALIK

And When the Days Grow Long

And it will come to pass when the days grow long, and will be
  like all the days of the world,
One shape will they have, like yesterday and the days before,
Days of no feature, of little rest, much toil,
And weariness will befall every man,
And the wilderness seizes man and beast.
At dusk man goes to the sea to take a stroll,
And looks, and, behold, the sea does not flee,
And he yawns.
And he goes to the Jordan, and, behold, it turns not back,
And he yawns.
And he looks at the Orion and the Pleiades, and they have not
  moved away from their places,
And he yawns.
And man and beast together sit in weariness,
And heavy upon them is the burden of their life.
Each man tears out his hair from weariness,
And the cat loses its whiskers.

Then the yearning will arise.
Of itself it will rise, as the wild mushroom rises
On the rotting wooden beam.
And the yearning fills all the holes and cracks
As lice fill rags.
And when man returns home to eat his evening meal,
And dips in vinegar his bread and salted fish,
He yearns.
And when he drinks his muddy, lukewarm beverage,
He yearns.
And when he takes off his shoes and socks on the edge of the bed,
He yearns.
And man and beast will sit together and yearn.
Each man in his dream howls from the overflow of yearning,
And on the tin roof the cat claws and caterwauls.

Then the hunger will come.
And the hunger will peak and spread as never before,
Not a hunger for bread and for vision, but for the Messiah!
And each morning, as the sun rises,
And each man gets up from his bed and from the depth of his
    chamber,
Broken by sleeplessness, sated with dreams, and empty of soul,
And while the webs of a wrathful sleep cover his eyelids,
And the dread of night is in his bones,
And while the wailing of the cat and the scratching of its claws
Dig into his brain and his bowels,
He hurries to his window and wipes the steam from the pane,
Or to the threshold and shades his eyes with his hand,
And lifts up a bleary eye, a feverish eye, hungry for succor,
To the narrow path beyond his yard
And to the dungheap opposite his house—
And seeks the Messiah!
And the woman awakes and folds back her blanket,
And her hair is disheveled, her flesh crushed, and she is gloomy
    of spirit,
And pulls out her shriveled breast from the mouth of her child,
And bends an ear and listens eagerly:
Is the Messiah coming yet?
Can one hear the braying of his ass?
And the child from its cradle raises its head,
And the mouse peeps out of its hole:
Is the Messiah coming yet?
Is the bell of his she-ass ringing?
And the servant-girl blows into the fire under the kettle,
And turns her sooty face toward the door:
Is the Messiah coming yet?
Can one hear the blast of his trumpet?

(From: *Kol Kitve H. N. Bialik*, pp. 46–47)

URI ZEVI GREENBERG

I Shall Tell It to a Child

A Hebrew child in my house, in humiliated Zion. Evening.
   Twilight. I speak—and you on my knees.
To you, my dear, I shall tell the story about the good Messiah
   who has not come.
I shall not tell it to those older than you, my dear. The grownups
   don't have such eyes, nor such a glow as there is in your
   eyes.
The grownups will not listen, like you; the fate in Zion has sealed
   them up, and their soul is like an earthenware lamp in a
   village.
And their sorrow does not shine forth in two wondrous tears, as
   in your eyes.
And I cannot kiss their forehead as I can yours while I am telling
   the story of the Messiah's disaster.

He has not come, the Messiah . . . Like an eagle he soars above the
   abysses of blood.
Day and night I heard the beating of his wings.
And he reached the shore of Jaffa in the shape of a man with a bag
   on his shoulders: a pauper, a beggar, with a vision and a sword.
And then I recognized him in the plowman walking in the furrow
   under the flaming sun,
And in the stonecutter who crushes the rocks of Jerusalem.
And he was so near . . . Here he was, like the bubbling of wine from
   cruse to cup I heard the bubbling of his blood.
I heard him leaping from mountain to mountain like a deer, and his
   steps like a gazelle's on towering crags.
But he came not to the Temple Mount: this is the only mountain
   his feet have not trod.
He reached only the approach, only the threshold of kingship—
   and there the hawkers found him. His wrath flared up,
A burning mane of horns around his head,
And in his hand the fiery key to the gates of the Temple,
As is the way of the Messiah.
And there they received him . . . with scorn and denial in their
   Hebrew tongue—the hawkers.
What did they tell him? I heard what they said:

   You erred, O wanderer. In every generation there is such an
      errant who sees vain visions: the kingdom of Jerusalem,
      ha-ha! . . .

And in every generation we thus stand at the threshold to impart understanding to erring visionaries.

Jerusalem needs a rich generation, a sackful of produce and goods, to build with it houses, and to trade, to eat, and to drink,

With a Temple of God on the mountain, but without a throne for David our king, and without warriors' shields.

Jerusalem needs a golden calf and not the image of Bar Giora: a pauper, a beggar, with vision and sword...

Jerusalem needs calm and gold and calm...

And nothing is wrong with Araby being on the top of the mountain and we in the valley—

Did you understand, O wanderer?

And it came to pass when they ended their words, after which they laughed, ha, ha, that the Messiah staggered, like one who was cut with a knife.

I too staggered like one who was cut with a knife.

Had they risen against him with a knife and thrust it into his heart—he would have leapt, with the knife in his heart, away from their bodies.

But since they wounded him with derision—they vanquished him,

They, the hawkers.

And I heard him ask with blood in his mouth: And where are the generations which awaited my coming?

Which called me from Rome, from the Arch of Titus, to the threshold of the kingdom?

And I heard him conclude: the generations are not with me... woe and woe to me!

And woe to you my land on both sides of the Jordan!

And the Messiah turned aside; where he went I know not, I, the narrator, know not.

Perhaps he is the jackal which wails here in Canaan's vineyards...

And perhaps he sought solitude in the loneliest of all fortresses on earth,

The fortress of Masada... And there he sits, ungarbed, roasting in the burning heat, his body pockmarked... he sits

And a flock of flies licks his blood... he sits.

And the night commands the winds of the wilderness to bring up water from the Dead Sea and to sprinkle it with their breath

Upon the wounds of the strange man who sits—

And perhaps not so...perhaps he entered into me: he sits amidst
my ribs, and flames and rages and roars like the dibbuk of a
lion.
And I tell nobody about his hiding place in my ribs.
And I feed him flesh from my living body, and let him drink blood
better than wine.
And deep inside me I play for him on a cello
Dirges and penitential songs, and prayers come down from my
fathers,
And when the moon rises, like the face of prophecy, among the
olive trees, I play for him deep inside me on an organ:

Beautiful is she, beautiful, your Jerusalem, the eternal,
In the glory of moonlight, as in the nights of the kingdom of
David's house,
And Israel's generations, wrapped in Talliths, with a fearsome
halo on their heads,
I can see, are waiting for the Gatherer—

Until thin shudders pass through my thighs, and my cheeks and
temples sink in, and the eyes burn.
And he moans inside my ribs.

Perhaps not so...perhaps he was the one who rose up in the shape
of an eagle from the Kidron Valley,
And soared and circled over the Temple Mount, and cried.
I saw him circle and heard him cry. A crying bird...And then I
said: O crying bird, is this the end of hope, the circle of
parting, the conclusion?
Israel's Messiahship in the shape of a bird takes leave of the Temple
Mount...
And the eagle completed its circle and flew to the sea.
It flew without a wing beat, and it was so dark.
Perhaps it returned to the city of Titus, to the Triumphal Arch,
Again a body, invisible, in his chains for two thousand years, with
his head in the depths of the Hebrew well of blood,
As is the way of the Messiah—

Again for two thousand years...who knows.
                                        (Jerusalem, Elul, 1930)

(From *Sefer haQitrug w'haEmuna*, pp. 37–38)

30

Recapitulation

In conclusion we present two comprehensive statements about the Messianic times, which contain a sequential
enumeration of the main features of that hoped-for age. Most
of the details contained in them are by now familiar from
earlier chapters in this book. Nevertheless, these summary
statements are interesting because they show the medieval
Jewish tendency to collect and systematize the many legend
fragments scattered in a great many sources spanning almost
two millennia.

One is an apocalyptic Midrash entitled *Otot haMashiah*
(Signs of the Messiah), which dates probably from the
twelfth century. It describes ten "signs" which will come to
pass. It is remarkable that, in speaking of Armilus, this
Midrash identifies him with Satan on the one hand, and with
the "Antichrist" of the nations of the world, on the other.

The second is from the pen of Sa'adya Gaon (882–942),
the great Jewish philosopher, scholar, and head of the
academy of Sura in Babylonia. The fact that a scholar of his
stature unquestioningly accepts all the fantasies about the
Messiah indicates that these beliefs were a heritage common
to the simple folk and the most learned in medieval Jewry.

As a comparison of the two texts shows, there were no
basic differences between the Aggadist and the philosopher.

Beliefs which began as legendary embellishments of the Messiah idea became, in the course of time, solidly entrenched religious tenets which philosophers of religion, such as Sa'adya Gaon, or Hai Gaon, or even the strict rationalist Maimonides (see appendix II) considered as part of the system of true belief. Although Sa'adya Gaon presents the Messianic credo not as his own but as a tradition of "our ancestors," it is clear from the tenor of his presentation that he found nothing exceptionable in it. As for Maimonides, although he protests that the Messiah must not be expected to perform signs and portents, or to resuscitate the dead, or to change the customary order of the world, he nevertheless believes in the Ingathering, the rebuilding of the Temple, the rule of peace, and universal goodness and delights. Incidentally, his denial of the Resurrection of the dead by the Messiah must not be taken to mean a denial of Resurrection in general, which was a Talmudic tenet. As we have seen in chapter 21, the contrary is true. Maimonides believed in bodily Resurrection, devoted to it an entire treatise, and included it among his *Thirteen Articles of Faith*, but he considered it an apocalyptic event to be brought about by God Himself, and not by the Messiah.

The Aggadist

The First Sign. The Holy One, blessed be He, will raise up three kings who will deny and lie, and show themselves to people as if they were serving the Holy One, blessed be He, but they will not, and they will lead astray and confuse all the creatures. And the nations of the world will deny their own laws, and even the sinners of Israel, who will have lost hope in the Redemption, will deny the Holy One, blessed be He, and cease to fear Him.... And the adherents to the truth will become like herds, and will go and flee and hide in caves and crevices of dust. And all the strong men of the generation will gather. And people of trust will cease, and the gates of wisdom become hidden, and the world will stand in a peculiar fashion. And at that time there will be neither king nor prince in

Israel...nor heads of *yeshivot*, nor a leader in Jacob, nor faithful shepherds, nor pious men, nor men of renown. And the gates of heaven will become closed, and the doors of livelihood and sustenance locked. And at the time when Messiah is revealed in his power, his generation will pass and fall in his lifetime, because of the cruel and peculiar and frightening decrees issued by those three kings. And they will also decree that the Lord must be denied in the Temple, and the Tora must be denied. And the Holy One, blessed be He, has decreed that this rule of evil should last nine months.... And they will decree cruel decrees and impose a double tax on Israel: ten to one. He who used to give ten must give a hundred, and he who used to give eight must give eighty, and those who have not, their heads will be cut off. And all those nine months the decrees will be constantly renewed, one harder than the other. And people will come forth from the end of the world, people who are exceedingly ugly, and all those who see them will die of fright. And they will not have to wage war, but will slay all with the fear they inspire. Each of them will have two heads and seven eyes, and they will burn like fire, and will be light in their walk like gazelles. In that hour Israel will cry and say: "Woe, woe!" And the little ones of Israel will be affrighted and will go and hide, each one under his father and under his mother and say: "Woe, woe! Father, what shall we do?" And their fathers will answer them: "Now we are close to the Redemption of Israel."

The Second Sign. The Holy One, blessed be He, will bring into the world heat from the sun, with consumption and fever, and many dangerous diseases, and pestilence and epidemics, which will kill a thousand times thousands of the nations of the world every day. And all the wicked of Israel will also die. Until the nations of the world will weep and cry: "Woe to us, where shall we go, where shall we flee?" And they will dig graves, every man for himself, in his lifetime, and they will wish they were dead. And they will hide in crevices and caverns and hollows to cool themselves, and they will seek out caves and holes of dust. And if you ask, how will the pious be saved from the heat of the sun— the Holy One, blessed be He, will give them a remedy in that heat....

The Third Sign. The Holy One, blessed be He, will cause a dew of blood to descend, and it will seem to the nations of the world like water and they will drink of it and will die. And also the wicked of Israel, who will have despaired of the Redemption, will drink of it and die, but the pious, who hold fast to the belief in the Holy One, blessed be He, will not be damaged at all.... And the whole world will be blood throughout those three days....

The Fourth Sign. The Holy One, blessed be He, will cause a dew of healing to descend, to heal the blood, and the mediocre people will drink of it and be healed of their illness....

The Fifth Sign. The Holy One, blessed be He, will cause the sun to return to darkness for thirty days.... And after thirty days the Holy One, blessed be He, will restore it as it was before.... And the nations of the world will be sore afraid and will be ashamed, and they will know that all these signs have come for the sake of Israel, and many of them will become Jewish in secret....

The Sixth Sign. The Holy One, blessed be He, will make wicked Edom ruler of the whole world.... And another king will arise in Rome and will rule over the whole world for nine months, and will destroy many countries. And his wrath will be kindled against Israel, and he will impose upon them heavy taxes. And Israel will be in great distress in that hour because of the many decrees and disturbances which will become renewed over them every day. And Israel will diminish and perish in that time, and will have no helper.... And at the end of nine months Messiah ben Joseph will be revealed, and his name is Nehemiah son of Hushiel, with the tribes of Ephraim and Manasseh and Benjamin and some of the Children of Gad. And Israel will hear in all the countries that the Messiah of God has come, and they will gather to him, a few from each country and from each city.... And Messiah ben Joseph will come and wage his war with the king of Edom, and will defeat Edom, and will slay of them heaps and heaps, and will slay the king of Edom and will devastate the city of Rome, and will recover a few of the vessels of the Temple which are kept hidden in the house of Julianus Caesar. And he will come to Jerusalem, and Israel will hear and gather to him. And the king of Egypt will make peace with him and will slay all the men of the countries which are around Jerusalem until Damascus and Ashkelon, and all the people of the world will hear and great fear will fall upon them.

The Seventh Sign. The Holy One, blessed be He, the Master of Miracles, will work a portent in the world. They say that there is in Rome a stone of marble in the shape of a beautiful maiden, and she was not made by the hand of man but the Holy One, blessed be He, created her, such is His power. And the wicked of the world, worthless people, will come and warm her and lie with her, and the Holy One, blessed be He, preserves their drop in the stone and creates in it a creature, and fashions in it a child, and the statue bursts and the shape of a man emerges from it, and his name is Armilus the Satan. This is the one whom the nations of the world call Antichrist. His height is ten cubits and his breadth two, and between his two eyes there is a span, and they are deep and red. The steps of his feet are green, and he has two skulls. And he will go to Edom the wicked and say to them: "I am Messiah, I am your god!" Instantly they believe in him, and make him king over them, and all the Children of Esau join themselves to him and come to him. And he goes forth and conquers all the countries, and says to the Children of Esau: "Bring me my Tora which I gave you!" And they bring him their obscenity, and he says to them: "Is it true what I gave you?" And he tells the nations of the world: "Believe in me, for I am your Messiah." And instantly they believe in him.

In that hour he sends to Nehemiah son of Hushiel and to all Israel and says to them: "Bring me your Tora and testify to me that I am god." Instantly they are afraid and confused. In that hour Nehemiah son of Hushiel arises, and thirty thousand warriors from among the Children of Ephraim, and they take the Tora scroll and read before him: *I am the Lord thy God, thou shalt have no other gods before Me* (Exod. 20:2–3). And he says to them: "There is nothing in this Tora of yours; come and testify to me that I am god, as did all the nations." Instantly Nehemiah rises against him. And Armilus says to his servants: "Catch him and force him!" Instantly Nehemiah son of Hushiel arises and the thirty thousand who are with him, and wage war against him and slay two hundred thousand of his men. Instantly the wicked Armilus becomes wroth, and gathers all the armies of the nations of the world to the Valley of Harutz, and fights Israel, and heaps and heaps are killed of them, and Israel will be smitten a little, and the Messiah of God will be slain. And the ministering angels come and take him and inter him with the Fathers of the World. Instantly the heart of Israel melts, and their strength is weakened. And the wicked Armilus will not know that the Messiah died, for would he know it he would leave neither a survivor nor a remnant of Israel.

In that hour all the nations of the world will expel Israel from their countries and will not allow them to dwell with them in their countries, and will say: "Have you seen this despised and lowly people who rebelled against us and chose a king?" And it will be a suffering for Israel the like of which has not been ever since the world exists and to that time.

And in that hour Michael will rise to sort out the wicked from Israel.... Instantly all Israel will flee to the deserts, and those whose heart will doubt his judgment will return to the nations of the world and will say: "This is the Redemption for which we have been waiting, for the Messiah has been killed." And all those who do not expect the Redemption will be ashamed of it and return to the nations of the world.

In that hour the Holy One, blessed be He, will examine Israel and purify them like silver and like gold.... And all the rest of Israel, the saintly ones and the pure ones, will be in the desert of Judah for forty-five days and they will pasture and eat salt plants and gather leaves of bushes.... In that hour all the wicked of Israel will die, all those who are not deserving of Redemption.

And Armilus will come and wage war against Egypt and will capture it...and then he will turn his face toward Jerusalem to devastate her a second time....

The Eighth Sign. Michael will rise and blow the shofar three times.... The first blast will reveal Messiah ben David and the prophet Elijah to those pious people who have been selected from Israel, who fled to the desert of Judah. At the end of the forty-five days they will return their hearts and strengthen their weak hands, and their faltering knees will become strong. And all Israel who will be left in the whole world will hear the sound of the shofar and will know that the Lord has remembered them and that the full Redemption has come. And they will gather and come as it is written, *And it shall come to pass in that day that a great shofar shall be blown, and they shall come that were lost in the land of Assyria and they that were dispersed in the land of Egypt* (Isa. 27:13). And from that sound fear and trembling will fall upon the nations of the world, and evil illnesses will seize them. And Israel will gird to march out, and Messiah ben David will come, and the prophet Elijah, with the pious who have returned from the desert of Judah and with all Israel who have gathered, and he will come to Jerusalem, and will ascend the steps of the House which have remained, and will sit there. And Armilus will hear that a king arose in Israel and will say: "How far will this despised and lowly nation do this?" Instantly he will gather all the armies of the nations of the world, and will come to fight the Messiah of the Lord. And then the Holy One, blessed be He, will not require the Messiah to fight, but will say to him: "Sit on My right!" And He will say to Israel: "Stay and see the salvation of the Lord which He will perform for you today!" Instantly the Holy One, blessed be He, fights them, as it is written, *Then shall the Lord go forth, and fight against those nations, as when He fighteth in the day of battle* (Zech. 14:3). And the Holy One, blessed be He, will cause fire and brimstone to descend from heaven.... Instantly the wicked Armilus will die, he and all his army, and the wicked Edom which destroyed the house of our God and exiled us from our land. In that hour Israel will wreak great vengeance upon them....

The Ninth Sign. Michael will blow a great blast, and the crevices of the dead will burst open in Jerusalem, and the Holy One, blessed be He, will revive them. And Messiah ben David and the prophet Elijah will go and revive Messiah ben Joseph, who has been gathered into the gates of Jerusalem. And they will send Messiah ben David to the remnant of Israel who are scattered in all the lands. Instantly all the kings of the nations of the world will lift them up on their shoulders and bring them to the Lord.

The Tenth Sign. Michael will blow a great blast, and the Holy One, blessed be He, will bring out all the tribes of Israel from the River Gozan and from Halah and Habor, and from the cities of Media, and they will come with the Children of Moses, in countless numbers and in endless measure. The land before them will be like the Garden of Eden, and after them flame will burn, and they will leave behind no sustenance for the nations of the world. And in the hour in which the tribes will come forth, Clouds of Glory will surround them, and the Holy One, blessed be He, will go before them.... And He will open for them the sources of the Tree of Life, and will give them to drink on the way....

May the Holy One, blessed be He, allow us to see the Redemption quickly, and allow us to see the Chosen House, and fulfill upon us the verse which says, *Behold, I will turn the captivity of Jacob's tents, and have compassion on his dwelling-places, and the city shall be builded upon her own mound and the palace shall be inhabited upon its wonted place* (Jer. 30:18). And may He fulfill upon us all His comfortings and all His promises, as is written by the hands of His prophets, *At that time will I bring you in, and at that time will I gather you, for I will make you to be a name and a praise* (Zeph. 3:10).

(Otot haMashiah, BhM 2:58—63)

The Philosopher

Our ancestors of blessed memory had the tradition that we will be overtaken by many sufferings and evils because of which we shall choose to repent, and then we shall be worthy of Redemption. And this is what they said:

If Israel repents, it will be redeemed, and if not, the Holy One, blessed be He, will raise against them a king whose edicts will be cruel like those of Haman, and thereupon they will repent and will be redeemed. And they said that for this reason there will arise a man from among the Children of Joseph in the mountain of Galilee, and men of the children of our people will gather around him. And he will go to the Temple which will be in the power of Edom, and will stand there with them for a while. And then up will come against them a king whose name is Armilus, and he will wage war against Jerusalem and will conquer her, and he will kill and enslave and torture, and the man from the tribe of Joseph will be among the slain. And our people will be in great distress...and they will be driven into the deserts until they suffer hunger and thirst. And because of the great sufferings, many of them will abandon their Tora, and only the select and the purified will be left.

And then Elijah will appear to them and he will come to judge the Mountain of Esau.... And a few people from the nation of Israel will gather around him, not many....

If we do not repent, the events of Ben Joseph will come to pass. But if we repent, they will not, and Messiah ben David will appear to us suddenly. And if Messiah ben Joseph precedes him he will be as a messenger of Messiah ben David, as one who prepares the nation and clears the road of stones...and as one who cleanses in fire those guilty of great sins, and as one who washes with lye those guilty of small sins.... And if he does not come, and Ben David comes suddenly..., he will bring with him the people until he reaches Jerusalem...and he will capture Armilus and slay him....

Then the men of Gog will hear the tidings about Ben David and his people, and about the goodness of their land and the riches of their property, and that they dwell in safety without fortresses and without walls and similar things, and it will arise in their hearts to capture them.... And he will gather a great multitude from many nations, and will pass through many lands until he will reach them. . . . And those who gather around him will be of two kinds: one of them totally evil who will be delivered to death, and the other people who will consider entering into the Tora of Israel. . . .

And four kinds of afflictions will come upon the wicked in that day. Some of them will die in a rain of fire and brimstone and rocks. . . . Some of them will die by the sword, or they will kill each other. . . . Some of them will die because their flesh will rot and their limbs will fall apart . . . so that if one should come to clasp the hand of his fellow, the hand will come loose. . . . And the rest will exhibit signs of afflictions which will come upon them, such as the gouging of the eyes, the slicing off of the nose, and the cutting off of the finger. And they will go to the ends of the lands and will recount that which they saw. . . .

And the repentant, too, will be of four kinds. Some of them will serve the Children of Israel in their homes, and these will be the great ones among them. . . . And some will serve them in the work of the cities and the villages. . . . And some will serve them in the fields and the deserts. . . . And the rest will return to their land, and they will be under the hand of Israel. And Ben David will decree upon them every year that they must observe the Feast of Sukkot. . . . And any nation which will not celebrate this feast, no rain will fall upon it. . . .

And then the nations will understand that the greatest thing they can do in order to approach Ben David is to carry to him someone of his people as a gift. . . . Each nation will do as best it can: their wealthy ones will carry the Children of Israel on horses and mules and in litters and carriages, displaying largess and honor. . . . And the poor among them will carry them on their shoulders, and their sons in their bosom. . . . And those of them who will be on the isles of the sea will bring them on ships with silver and gold. . . . And those of them who will be in the Land of Cush [Ethiopia], they will bring them in reed boats until they reach Egypt, for in the high place there is a mountain which enters the water [i.e., a cataract], and the boats cannot pass there without being wrecked, but the reed boats, since they are made with wax, when they reach the mountain they bend and break not. And those of Israel who will be left in the deserts or in places where there are none of the nations to bring them, our God will bring them quickly, as if the clouds would carry them . . . or as if He were a bird . . . or as if the winds were carrying them.

And when all the living of Israel who believe will be in-gathered, as I mentioned, then will be the resurrection of the dead.... And Ben Joseph will be at their head, for he is a saintly and much-tried man, and the Creator will recompense him in good measure. Then the Creator will renew the building of His Temple... with precious stones....

And all the land will be settled until no desolate place will be left in it. Then the light of the Shekhina will shine on the Temple until the luminaries will be dimmed by its light... so that those who do not know the way to the Temple will go toward that light, because it will be from heaven to earth. Then prophecy will spread in our people until even our children and our servants will proph-esy.... Until if one of the Children of Israel will go to one of the lands and will say that "I am of Israel," they will say to him, "Tell us what will be tomorrow?" or, "What was yesterday?" of the things which were secret among them. And when he tells them, it will be clear to them that he is from Israel....

And they will have a world which will be all joy and rejoicing, as if their heaven and their earth had been renewed for them....

(Sa'adya Gaon, *Emunot w'De'ot*, ch. 8, pp. 152–57)

Appendix I

Prayers for the Coming
of the Messiah

The requests for Redemption and the coming of the Messiah, addressed to God, are part of the 'Amidah prayer—popularly referred to as "The Eighteen Benedictions"—which, together with the Sh'ma' ("Hear, O Israel") is the most important Jewish daily prayer recited three times every day. This prayer was edited by Rabban Gamaliel II soon after the destruction of the Jerusalem Temple by the Romans in 70 C.E. The full text of the seventh, tenth, fourteenth, and fifteenth benedictions reads as follows:

7. Consider our suffering and fight our cause, and redeem us quickly for the sake of Thy name, for Thou art a powerful Redeemer. Blessed art Thou, O Lord, the Redeemer of Israel.

10. Blow the Great Shofar for our freedom, and lift up a banner to gather our exiles, and gather us from the four corners of the earth. Blessed art Thou, O Lord, who gatherest the banished of Thy people Israel.

14. And to Jerusalem Thy city return in compassion and dwell therein as Thou hast spoken and build her soon in our days to stand for all eternity, and reestablish in her the throne of David quickly. Blessed art Thou, O Lord, the builder of Jerusalem.

15 Let the Shoot of David Thy servant sprout up quickly,

and raise up his horn with Thy salvation, for all day long we hope for Thy succor. Blessed art Thou, O Lord, who makest the horn of salvation grow.

(Seder 'Avodat Yisrael, pp. 92, 96–97)

Appendix II

Maimonides on the Messiah

Moses Maimonides (1135–1204), the great rationalistic Jewish philosopher and codifier of the Halakhic law, considered belief in the coming of the Messiah a basic principle of Jewish faith. The twelfth of his *Thirteen Principles of the Faith* deals with the Messiah, and the thirteenth with resurrection:

12. I believe with a complete faith in the coming of the Messiah; and even though he tarry, nevertheless I await him every day that he should come.

13. I believe with a complete faith that there will be resurrection of the dead at a time when the will will arise from the Creator, blessed be His name, and may His remembrance be exalted for all eternity.

In his great Halakhic code, the *Yad haHazaqa* ("The Strong Hand"), also known as *Mishne Tora* ("The Second Tora"), Maimonides explicates in detail what must be considered the authoritative view of the Redemption:

King Messiah will arise in the future and will restore the kingship of David to its ancient condition, to its rule as it was at first. And he will rebuild the Temple and gather the exiled of Israel. And in his days all the laws will return as they were in the past. They will offer up sacrifices, and will observe the Sabbatical years and the jubilee years with regard to all the commandments stated in the Tora. And he who does not believe in him, or he who does not await his coming, denies not only the [other] prophets, but also the Tora and Moses our Master. For, behold, the Tora testifies about him [the Messiah], as it is written, *The Lord will return your captivity and have compassion upon thee, and will return and gather thee from all the peoples whither the Lord thy God hath scattered thee. If any of thine that are dispersed be in the uttermost parts of heaven, from thence will the Lord thy God gather thee, and from thence will He fetch thee. And the Lord thy God will bring thee into the land which thy fathers possessed, and thou shalt possess it* (Deut. 30:3–5).

And these are things which are explicitly stated in the Tora, and they comprise all the things which were said by the prophets. Even in the section "Balaam" it is said and there he prophesied about the two Messiahs: about the first Messiah who was David, who saved Israel from the hands of its enemies, and about the last Messiah, who will arise from among David's children and who will save Israel at the End. And there he says: *I see him but not now* ((Num. 24:17), this refers to David; *I behold him but not nigh* (ibid.), this refers to King Messiah; *A star shall step forth out of Jacob* (ibid.), this refers to David; *and a scepter shall rise out of Israel* (ibid.), this refers to King Messiah....

And think not that the Messiah must perform signs and portents and bring about new things in the world, or that he will resuscitate the dead, or the like. Not so. For, behold, R. Akiba was one of the greatest of the sages of the Mishna, and he was a follower of King Ben Koziba [Bar Kokhba], and he said about him that he was King Messiah. And he and the sages of his generation thought that he was King Messiah, until he was slain because of the sins. As soon as he was slain it became evident to them that he was not the Messiah. And the sages had asked of him neither a sign nor a portent. And the essence of the matter is that the laws and ordinances of this Tora are forever and ever, and one must neither add to them nor subtract from them.

And if there should arise from the House of David a king who studies the Tora and occupies himself with the commandments as his father David had, according to the written and the oral Tora;

and if he forces all Israel to follow the Tora and observe its rules; and if he fights the wars of the Lord—then he must be presumed to be the Messiah. And if he succeeds in his acts, and rebuilds the Temple in its place, and gathers the exiled of Israel—then he certainly is the Messiah. And he will repair the whole world to serve the Lord together, as it is written, *For then will I turn to the peoples a pure language that they may all call upon the name of the Lord to serve Him with one consent* (Zeph. 3:9).

It should not come to one's mind that in the days of the Messiah anything in the customary order of the world will be annulled, or that there will be something new in the order of Creation. For the world will continue in its path. And that which Isaiah said, *The wolf shall dwell with the lamb, and the leopard shall lie down with the kid* (Isa. 11:6), is but an allegory and a riddle. The true meaning of it is that Israel will dwell in safety with the wicked of the idolaters who are likened to a wolf and a leopard. . . . And all of them will return to the faith of truth, and they will neither rob nor despoil, but will eat the things which are permitted, in pleasure, together with Israel, as it is written, *The lion shall eat straw like the ox* (Isa. 11:7). And likewise, all the similar things said about the Messiah are but allegories. And in the days of the Messiah it will become known to everybody what thing the allegory signified and to what thing it alluded.

The sages said that the only difference between this world and the days of the Messiah will be with regard to the enslavement to the kingdoms. It appears from the plain meaning of the words of the prophets that at the beginning of the days of the Messiah, there will be the war of Gog and Magog. And that prior to the war of Gog and Magog, a prophet will arise to straighten Israel and to prepare their hearts, as it is written, *Behold, I will send to you Elijah the prophet before the coming of the great and terrible day of the Lord* (Mal. 3:23). And he will come not to declare the pure impure, or the impure pure; nor to declare unfit those who are presumed to be fit, nor to declare fit those who are held to be unfit; but for the sake of peace in the world. . . . And there are those among the sages who say that prior to the coming of the Messiah will come Elijah. But all these things and their likes, no man can know how they will be until they will be. For they are indistinct in the writings of the prophets. Neither do the sages have a tradition about these things. It is, rather, a matter of interpretation of the Biblical verses. Therefore there is a disagreement among them regarding these matters. And in any case, these things are mere details which are not of the essence of the faith. And one should definitely not occupy oneself with the matter of legends, and should not expatiate about the *midrashim* that deal with these and similar things. And one should not make essentials out of them. For they lead neither to fear nor to love [of God]. Neither should one calculate the End. The sages said, "May the spirit of those who calculate the End be blown away." But let him wait and believe in the matter generally, as we have explained.

In the days of King Messiah, when his kingdom is established and all Israel are gathered into it, the descent of all of them will be confirmed by him through the Holy Spirit which will rest upon him, as it is written, *And he shall sit as a refiner and purifier of silver, and he shall purify the sons of Levi, and purge them as gold and silver* (Mal. 3:3). And he will first purify the Children of Levi and will say: "This is of priestly descent, and this is of Levitic descent." And he will reject those who are not descended of Israel, as it is written, *And the Tirshatha* [governor] *said to them that they should not eat the most holy things till there stood up a priest with Urim and Thummim* (Ezra 2:63). From this you learn that the presumption of descent will be confirmed, and those with established descent will be announced by the Holy Spirit. And he will establish the descent not from Israel [in general] but from each tribe and tribe. For he will announce that this one is from such and such a tribe, and this one from such and such a tribe. . . .

The sages and the prophets yearned for the days of the Messiah not in order that they should rule over the whole world, and not in order that they should lord it over the idolaters, and not in order that the nations should elevate them, and not in order that they should eat and drink and rejoice; but in order that they should devote themselves to the Tora and its wisdom, and that there be nobody to oppress them and to negate, so that they should merit life in the World to Come. . . .

And in that time there will be neither hunger nor war, neither jealousy nor competition, but goodness will spread over everything. And all the delights will be as common as dust. And the whole world will have no other occupation but only to know the

Lord. And therefore Israel will be great sages, and knowers of secret things, and they will attain a knowledge of their Creator as far as the power of man allows, as it is written, *For the earth shall be full of the knowledge of the Lord, as the waters cover the sea* (Isa. 11:9).

(Maimonides, *Yad haHazaqa*, Shoftim,
Hilkhot M'lakhim 11–12)

Appendix III

A Messiah Catechism

The following material is taken from a Hebrew manuscript dated 1466 (no. 1048, Harley 5686, in the British Library, London, fol. 128a-134a). In the original manuscript, each paragraph is the heading of a section in which are assembled assortments of Biblical quotations proving the truth of the statements contained in the heading. In their totality these headings amount to a veritable catechism about the Messianic events.

These are the glad tidings of the Messiah ben David, that is, Ben Adam [the Son of Man].

At the coming of the Messiah there will be one faith in the world, the faith of all, and knowledge will multiply, and the Lord will be one and His name will be one.

These are the glad tidings of the reign of Messiah ben David: some he will bring low, and others he will elevate.

Behold the true proof that the Messiah will reign forever over the whole world.

At the coming of the Messiah there will be general peace and eternal peace, and even the wild animals will cause no harm.

At the coming of the Messiah there will be general and eternal salvation for Israel.

At the coming of the Messiah Jerusalem will be settled.

At the coming of the Messiah the air will be healed and nature strengthened, and men will live long.

The salvation of the Messiah will be accompanied by the resurrection of the dead.

At the coming of the Messiah all Israel will be together as they have not been since the days of Rehoboam.

Soon after the coming of the Messiah will follow the war of Gog and Magog.

In the war of Gog the victory will belong to Israel and Israel will be avenged on all their enemies.

The Tora of Moses or Master will be preserved, and the glad tiding of our knowledge of the Tora and of the truth of her commandments will spread abroad.

The commandment of circumcision which God gave us will be observed for all generations.

God has not exchanged us and will not exchange us for another nation forever.

Jerusalem and the Temple are called "the Footstool of the Lord."

Where the Bible says "Hebrew," it refers to Israel.

These are the glad tidings of joy in the days of the Messiah.

These are the glad tidings of eternal salvation and the good purpose of Israel.

As promised in the prophecies, the Merciful One will save us from the punishment of Gehenna.

Appendix IV

The Pope's Letter

Following the Biblical quotations described in the introductory paragraph of Appendix III, the same manuscript, on fol. 134a–b, contains a remarkable piece of writing purporting to be the Hebrew translation of an "answer" sent by an unidentified pope to a likewise unidentified king of France, and containing a justification of the killing of Jesus by the Jews. The pope's argument, exonerating the Jews of the responsibility of killing Jesus, is cast in the favorite Midrashic form of a parable.

The answer sent by the pope to the king of France [advising him] that he should safeguard the Jews who are guiltless in the slaying of that man [i.e., Jesus].

"A parable. This is like unto a king who entrusted his orchard to his friend that he should watch over it, and commanded him that anyone who wanted to enter the orchard should be killed. Many days later the king wished to test his friend by entering the orchard himself. He disguised himself and put on other clothes, and made himself unrecognizable, and went to the gate of the orchard and tried to enter by force. And he said that he was the king, but his friend the gatekeeper said: 'You will not enter here, for the king warned me that nobody must enter it. You are not the king.' The king wanted to show his power, but his friend came and killed him. Thus the Holy One, blessed be He, gave a commandment to Israel and said, *I am the Lord thy God . . . thou shalt have no other gods before Me* (Exod. 20:2–3), and you shall guard your souls very much, for you have seen no likeness [of Me at Mount Sinai], lest you lift up your eyes to heaven [and make] a likeness of a male or of a female, or a likeness of any creeping thing. And I have said, *For man shall not see Me and live* (Exod. 33:20). When Jesus came into the world, he came in the likeness of a man, and he made himself a deity, and they killed him. Had they known that he was the deity, they would not have raised a hand against him."

Our Savior will save us and will send us our true Messiah quickly in our days. In his days Judah and Israel will be saved, and the people of Israel will dwell in safety. Amen.

Appendix V

A Messianic Disputation

On December 26, 1375, a disputation took place in Pamplona, capital of the Kingdom of Navarre in northern Spain, between R. Shem Tov ben Isaac Ibn Shaprut and the Cardinal Pietro (Pedro) de Luna, who later (in 1394) became the antipope Benedict XIII. The subject of the disputation was whether or not Jesus was the Messiah whose coming was foretold in the Hebrew Bible. Subsequently R. Shem Tov returned to this subject and presented it in an amplified and greatly elaborated form in his book *Even Bohan* ("Touchstone"), which he completed in 1385, and two manuscripts of which are found in the library of the Jewish Theological Seminary of America, New York. The account R. Shem Tov gives of his disputation with the cardinal (manuscript no. 831 in the Bibliothèque Nationale, Paris) opens with a compilation and literal interpretation of numerous Biblical Messianic prophecies, including two quotations from the New Testament. R. Shem Tov evidently quotes from memory, and occasionally becomes guilty of minor inaccuracies. This introductory part, which is twice as long as the report of the disputation itself, is of interest to us in the present context because the many proof-verses quoted give, in their totality, a detailed picture of the events which were expected to occur upon the advent of the Messiah. They thus amount to a list of the belief items which formed the basis of the Messiah legends collected in this volume.

The Book of Disputation

Proofs from [Scriptural] verses about the Messiah, that he has not come yet but will come in the future.

It is written, *I will gather them unto their own land, and I will leave none of them there* (Ezek. 39:28)—This has not yet been fulfilled, for in the [time of the] Second Temple only forty [two] thousand three hundred and sixty returned, as explained in the Book of Ezra (Ezra 2:64).

Also it is written, *For the nation and the kingdom that will not serve thee shall perish* (Isa. 60:12); however, in the Second Temple they [the Children of Israel] were subject to [other] kingdoms.

Also it is written, in connection with the downfall of Gog, *And I will call him to judgment with pestilence and with blood, and I will cause to rain upon him and upon his followers overflowing rain and great hailstones, fire and brimstone* (Ezek. 38:22)—and this has not yet been fulfilled.

Also it is written, *And the Lord will utterly destroy the tongue of the Egyptian sea*, etc., *and there shall be a path for the remnant of His people*, etc. (Isa. 11:15 – 16)—and this has not yet been fulfilled.

Also it is written, *And the Mount of Olives shall be cleft in half toward the east and toward the west* (Zech. 14:4), *And living waters shall go out from Jerusalem, half of them toward the eastern sea*, etc. (ibid., v.8)—and this has not yet been fulfilled.

Also it is written *And they shall beat their swords into plowshares*, etc. (Isa. 2:4)—this points to the multiplication of peace which will be in the world, and in the Second Temple, and thereafter as well, there was the opposite.

Also it is written, *And the Lord shall be King over all the earth, in that day the Lord shall be one and His name one* (Zech. 14:8), and in the Second Temple, and to this day, most of the world practices idolatry, a great part of the world.

Also it is written that the land of Sodom will be rebuilt and reestablished (cf. Ezek. 16:53,55)—and this has not been fulfilled.

Another strong proof is in the portion *B'Huqqotai* where He says that if you do not listen to Me, *I will scatter you among the nations*, etc. (Lev. 26:33), *because, even because they rejected My ordinances* (ibid., v. 43). And at the end of the portion *Q'doshim* He said, *Ye shall therefore keep all My statutes*, etc., *so that the land whither I bring you to dwell therein, vomit you not out* (Lev. 20:22). And in the portion *Ki Tavo, But it shall come to pass, if thou wilt not hearken unto the voice of the Lord thy God*, etc., *that the Lord shall scatter thee among all peoples*, etc. (Deut. 28:15, 64). And in the portion *Nitzavim, And if thou shall return unto the Lord thy God*, etc., *then the Lord thy God will bring back thy captivity and have compassion upon thee* (Deut. 30:2–3). And in the portion *Ha'azinu,* . . . *to observe to do all the words of this Tora, because it is not a vain thing for you, because it is your life, and through this thing ye shall prolong your days upon the land* (Deut. 32:46–47).

From these passages six principles emerge concerning our Redemption contrary to the opinion of the Christians. The first is that the neglect of the Tora will bring curses and exile upon them [the Jews], while its observance will make their standing in the land [of Israel] permanent, [which is] the opposite of the opinion of the Christians who say that our exile is for the sin of killing their Messiah. The second, that it was because of the neglect of the commandments that our king was exiled and our rule was discontinued, while they say that this was caused by the killing of the aforementioned. The third is that it is destined for us that even if we sin and go into exile, if we turn back to Him, blessed be He, He will gather us and bring us back to our land, etc., that is, this depends on our repentance, and if we do turn back to him, blessed be He, He will inevitably bring us out of the exile. The fourth is that our turning back to Him, blessed be He, consists of the observance of the commandments of the Tora, the opposite of their opinion that the Tora has been exchanged. The fifth is that the Redemption will consist of the bringing back of all of us to our land, and He will circumcise our hearts to love the Lord our God and to observe His commandments. And from this it can be seen that Jesus, who did not fulfill the commandments, was not the Messiah.

Also it is written, *Only be strong and [very] courageous, to observe to do according to all the Tora which Moses My servant commanded thee; turn not from it to the right or to the left* (Josh. 1:7). And so at the end of the book, *Be ye very courageous to keep and to do all that is written in the book of the Tora of Moses that ye turn not aside therefrom to the right or to the left* (ibid., 23:6). *When ye transgress the covenant of the Lord*, etc., *then ye shall perish quickly from off the good land which He hath given unto you* (ibid., v. 16). In this two principles are explained: one, that one must not turn aside from the Tora of Moses to the right or to the left, that is, to do evil or to do good; and the second, that those who transgress the covenant of the Lord will be exiled from the Land of Israel, etc., the opposite of the opinion of the Christians.

Also it is written in Kings, in the testament of David to Solomon, *Keep the charge of the Lord thy God, to walk in His ways*, etc., *as it is written in the Tora of Moses*, etc., *that the Lord may establish His word*, etc., *[that] there shall not fail thee [a man] on the throne of Israel* (1 Kings 2:3–4). And it is written, *As for this house which thou art building, if thou wilt walk in My statutes and execute Mine ordinances*, etc. (1 Kings 6:12), *then I will establish [the throne] of thy kingdom over Israel for ever*, etc. *But if ye shall turn away from following Me ... then will I cut off Israel out of the land* (1 Kings 9:5,6,7). And it is written at the end of Kings, *And the king of Assyria carried Israel away unto Assyria, and put them in Halah*, etc., *because they hearkened not to the voice of the Lord their God, but transgressed His covenant,[even all] that Moses the servant of the Lord commanded* (2 Kings 18:11-12). Therefore, two principles emerge from this: one is that the continuance of the rule of the House of David depends on the observance of the commandments of the Tora; the second, that the exile of Israel from their land came about because they transgressed the Tora.

Also it is written in Isaiah, *And He shall judge between the nations, and shall decide for many peoples* (Isa. 2:4), and Jesus hid himself even from Israel. And in the Gospel according to Matthew, chapter eight [sic!], he said, *I was sent only to the lost sheep of Israel* (Matt. 15:24). And likewise in chapter 43 [sic.], when he sent twelve disciples he said to them, *Go nowhere among the Gentiles, and enter no town of the Samaritans but go rather to the lost sheep of Israel* (Matt. 10:5–6).[1]

Also it is written, *He shall judge the poor with righteousness ... and he shall smite the land with the rod of his mouth* (Isa. 11:4). From this we derive ten principles. The first is that the Messiah will come and will smite and slay with the breath of his lips, whereas Jesus was smitten and did not smite. The second is that he will multiply peace until *the wolf shall dwell with the lamb* (ibid. v. 6). and in the

---

1. Here R. Shem Tov agrues that, contrary to Isaiah's prophecy about the Messiah, Jesus did not come to minister to the Gentiles but only to the Jews.

Second Temple, and even more so after Jesus, wars multiplied. The third one is that *They shall not hurt nor destroy in all My holy mountain* (ibid. v. 9), and the opposite happened: the city and the Temple were destroyed. The fourth is that *The earth shall be full of the knowledge of the Lord* (ibid.), and in the Second Temple all the sages were slain; and, moreover, according to the opinion of the Christians, Israel did not know and did not recognize Jesus that he was God. The fifth is what he said, *Unto him shall the nations seek* (ibid., v. 10), and this did not happen in the Second Temple, nor with Jesus, for Israel was in darkness, and the Gentiles even more so. The sixth is, *And his resting place shall be glorious* (ibid.), and the Christians say that Jesus received contempt and disgrace from the people. The seventh is that in the days of the Messiah, *The Lord will set His hand again a second time to recover the remnant of His people...from Assyria* (ibid., v. 11), but in the Second Temple Israel were not redeemed from Assyria and from the rest of the countries; only a few of them from Babylonia, and even more so after the coming of Jesus when Israel were exiled from their land. The eighth, *The envy of Ephraim shall depart* (ibid., v. 13), refers to the Ten Tribes, and in the Second Temple there was not one of them, and at that time the quarrels multiplied in Israel. The ninth, *And they shall fly down upon the shoulder of the Philistines to the west, together they shall despoil the children of the east* (ibid., v. 14), and this has not been fulfilled. The tenth, *And the Lord shall utterly destroy the tongue of the Egyptian sea*, etc., *And there shall be a path for the remnant of His people* (ibid., vv. 15–16), and this, too, has not been fulfilled.

Also it is written in Jeremiah, *Thus saith the Lord: There shall not be cut off unto David a man to sit upon the throne of the house of Israel; neither shall there be cut off unto the priests and the Levites a man before Me to offer burnt offerings, and to burn meal-offerings, and to do sacrifice continually... [and] as the host of heaven cannot be numbered, neither [the sand of the sea] measured, so will I multiply the seed of David My servant and the Levites [that minister] unto Me* (Jer. 33:17–18, 22). From this three principles emerge. The first is that there is no king but David, and if they say that he is Jesus, is it not that he never reigned in his life, but was killed? The second is that there is no burnt offering and no sacrifice, and no ministering priest, and the Christians say that it was uprooted from them and given to the masses of the people. The third is that He said that He will multiply the seed of David and the Levites, and in the Second Temple the family of the Hasmonaeans was lacking, as well as the seed of David.

Also it is written in Ezekiel, *Behold, I will take the stick of Joseph which is in the hand of Ephraim and the tribes of Israel his companions*, etc., *and I will make them one nation in the land, and one king shall be king to them all, and they shall be no more two nations . . . and My servant David shall be king over them* (Ezek. 37:19, 22, 24). And from this three principles emerge: One is that a time will come when all the tribes of Israel will be gathered in their land. The second is that all [of them] will become one nation in the land. The third is that he [the Messiah] will rule over them. And of this not one thing has come to pass thus far.

Also it is written there in Ezekiel, *This shall be the border whereby ye shall divide the land for inheritance according to the [twelve] tribes of Israel, Joseph receiving two portions*, etc. (Ezek. 47:13); *And ye shall divide this land unto you according to the tribes of Israel* (ibid., v. 21); *And these are the names of the tribes*, etc. (ibid., 48:1). Behold, he has let us know and described the portion of each tribe, as well as the property of the Levites, and this has not yet happened.

Also it is written in Joel, *And it shall come to pass afterward that I shall pour out My spirit upon all flesh*, etc. *And it shall come to pass that whosoever shall call on the name of the Lord shall be delivered* (Joel 3:1, 5). *I will gather all nations, and will bring them down to the Valley of Jehoshaphat, and I will enter into judgment with them there over My people Israel and My heritage whom they have scattered among the nations, and My land they have divided* (ibid., 4:2). And from this three principles emerge: One is that all flesh shall prophesy. The second, that He will vouchsafe signs in heaven and earth, and on the Mount Zion there will be a remnant. The third, that at the time of Redemption He will bring down all the nations to the Valley of Jehoshaphat there. And when has this happened?

Also it is written in Zechariah, *Behold a day of the Lord cometh*, etc., *and I will gather all nations against Jerusalem*, etc. *And the Lord shall be King over all the earth*, etc. *And it shall come to pass that every one that is left of all the nations*, etc., *shall go up from year to year to worship the King, the Lord of Hosts, and to celebrate the Feast of Tabernacles* (Zech. 14:1, 2, 9, 16). And from this five principles emerge: One is that all the nations will come to wage war against Jerusalem. The second, that those who are left will accept God, may He be exalted, as King. The third, that every year they will go up to worship Him, blessed be He. The fourth, that they will accept the commandments of the Tora and will celebrate the Feast of Tabernacles. The fifth, that if they will not go up the rain will not come upon them. And all this has not yet happened.

Also it is written in Obadiah, *And the captivity of this host*, etc., *and the captivity of Jerusalem that is in Sepharad shall inherit the cities of the South, and saviors shall ascend Mount Zion*, etc. (Obad. 20–21). And from this three principles emerge. One is that the captivity of the host which is as far as France and the exiles of Spain (Sepharad) will inherit the cities of the South. The second, that saviors will ascend from Mount Zion to judge Mount Esau. The third, that then the kingship will be the Lord's, and He will be King over all the earth. And all this has not yet come to pass.

Also it is written in Daniel, *At that time up shall stand Michael the great prince*, etc. *And at that time thy people shall be delivered*, etc. *And many of them that sleep in the dust of the earth shall awake* (Dan. 12:1-2).

Behold, the king of the south will arise, and the king of the
north shall attack him with violence, and
will come to the Land of the Hart, and
Michael will arise, and those that
sleep in the dust will awake.
And these things have never
happened but they will
come to pass at
the time of the
redemption.
BILA²

---

2. Acrostic of the Hebrew words *Barukh Adonai l'Olam, Amen*, that is, Blessed be the Lord forever, Amen.

Appendix VI

Grimmelshausen's Account

As the sixth and last appendix, I present a rather unusual source for Jewish Messianic beliefs. It is a description of those beliefs contained in a story by Hans Jakob Christoffel von Grimmelshausen (1622?–1676), the most important German novelist of the seventeenth century. Grimmelshausen was, above all, a satirist whose enduring fame rests on his *The Adventurous Simplicissimus* (1669). In a later novel, *The Enchanted Bird's Nest* (1672), he describes how his rogue of a hero, in pursuit of an amorous scheme, learns all he can about Jewish Messianic beliefs from the converted Jew Erasmus. The chapter in which he presents what he found out is, irrespective of its satirical intent, an excellent summary of the actual seventeenth-century German-Jewish Messianic beliefs after the Shabbataian debacle of 1666. Here we have the testimony of a Gentile author, whose intention was to heap ridicule on the Jews for what he considered their foolish Messianic expectations, and who, in doing so, gives us a picture, not of what the learned rabbis taught concerning the Messianic days, but of what the simple Jewish folk knew and believed about the expected Redeemer.

He [Elijah] was also supposed to bring the Messiah and his office, or future Messiah, and to assist him in his work.... Of the Mashiah and his office, Erasmus told me that the Jews believe that he will be a king of this world. With his great power and divine help he will miraculously bring them together again from all corners of the earth to which they were dispersed and will lead them back to the Promised Land. In this way, the Jews, hoping for a sort of temporal paradise on earth, confused the eternal life promised to the elect with the reign of the Mashiah or Messiah. They also firmly believe that God will awaken their dead; banish from among His people all trouble, hardship, and sickness; and rebuild with precious stones their holy temple in Jerusalem so that it will again look just as it did when the prophet Ezekiel had seen it. Thereafter the people of Israel will govern and rule over the entire world and possess all of its resources, treasures, and riches. God will rid them of inborn lust, of the desire and impulse to sin and do evil; indeed, He will dwell among them so that they will see Him face to face. God will lengthen their life span. They will reach Adam's or Methuselah's age, and he who went to heaven at the age of a hundred would be said to have died in early childhood. The Promised Land, cleansed by fire of the uncleanliness with which heathens, Christians, and Mohammedans had defiled it, will become larger and a thousand times more splendid and fruitful than it now is; once again it would be as it was when all twelve tribes with their twelve hundred thousand souls lived together there so well. Their Mashiah will govern forever, and at the beginning of his reign all Jews will be his guests in Jerusalem. At his table they will drink the most delicious wine, grown in paradise and carefully kept in Adam's cellar for just that purpose. The biggest beasts, birds, and fish that God had ever created will be slaughtered, among them the ox Behemoth (Job 4) that crops a thousand mountains every day, and what he crops during the day grows again at night. His mate had been made frigid and barren by the Lord lest this breed of immensely big beasts multiply and ruin the whole world, but the ox himself had been castrated and fattened and preserved by Him for the pious Jews of the future. And so, too, the great cruel bird Bar Yuchne[1] will be turned into roasts. So huge was she that a single egg which had once dropped from her nest felled three hundred cedar trees and, when it broke, flooded, drowned, and carried away sixty villages. Of no less service would be the whale Leviathan (about which Job also speaks). In order to keep it from multiplying, God had also castrated it; but the female He had done away with and salted for the table of those God-fearing Jews, who would return to the Holy Land with their Mashiah....

Let me end this chapter with what of all this foolishness seems to me the most foolish. The Jews believe that the archangel Michael will blow a big horn three times when their Messiah comes. At the first sound the Messiah, son of David, will appear with the prophet Elijah to reveal himself to the children of Israel. Everywhere in the world the Jews will hear the sound of the horn and know that God is visiting His people and the final salvation is near. The Christians and other nations, however, will know only terror, lament, and misery, while the Jews girding their loins will gaily get up and march in great joy with their Mashiah to Jerusalem.

Upon the second blowing, which will be a very long blast, all the graves in Jerusalem will open. God will revive all the dead; then, too, the Messiah son of David, and Elijah the prophet, will awaken from his death the pious and poor Messiah ben Joseph (who lived with the sick and the lepers of Rome and perished in an encounter of the Israelites). And the kings of all nations will lift the Jews who still dwell among them upon their own shoulders and upon their chariots to bring them to Jerusalem.

And when the archangel Michael sounds his horn for the third time, God will lead out the numberless Israelites who live beyond the rivers Gason, Lachlach, and Chobar and in the cities of Juda,[2]

---

1. Bar Yokhni ["Son of the Nest"], a gigantic bird, is referred to several times in the Talmud. In later writings it is stated that this bird will be used as food for the pious in Messianic times. Later authorities identify Bar Yokhni with Ziz, cf. Louis Ginzberg, *Legends of the Jews* 5:139.

2. The names of the rivers Gason, Lachlach, and Chobar, and the cities of Juda, mentioned by Grimmelshausen, are taken by his informants from 2 Kings 17:6, where we read that Shalmaneser took the captive Israelites to Assyria, "and placed them in Halah [= Lachlach] and in Habor on the river Gozan and in the cities of the Medes." The cities of the Medes have been corrupted into the cities of Juda. In the Middle Ages the mythical Sambatyon river was identified with the river Gozan— e.g. Nahmanides on Deut. 32:26. As for the Children of Moses and the ten tribes of Israel who were believed to have been dwelling beyond the Sambatyon, see above, chapter 19.

and they will go to Paradise with the other children of Moses. During this exodus of the ten tribes of the Israelites, God's glory and majesty will surround them like clouds, in columns, and yes, God Himself will walk ahead of them. In front, behind, and alongside will be nothing but fire and flame, and for the Christians and other nations on earth nothing will be left to sustain their lives.

(Grimmelshausen, pp. 243—48)

Epilogue

And for two thousand years the Messiah sustained the Children of Israel, and they kept the Messiah alive by their fervent faith and their unceasing hope that he would come any day. Throughout that long period, the Gentiles accused Israel of having killed the Messiah. They hounded and persecuted them, forced them to flee and to wander from country to country, tortured and slaughtered them.

Finally a new era dawned. In some countries light spread, and Israel was allowd to sit down at the table with the Gentiles. The food they offered them was sweet on their tongue, and as they gorged themselves they began to sing Gentile songs, and forgot Jerusalem. And they no longer yearned for the Messiah. Consequently, the light of the Messiah grew dimmer and dimmer and dimmer. Not long thereafter, the Gentiles assembled in a great conclave and decided that, after all, Israel was not guilty of killing the Messiah.

And the Holy One, blessed be He, observing sadly the doings of His world, said:

"My children, you surely did not kill My Messiah, even though you did lose faith in him. If his life depended only on you, he would be no more. But I shall reveal to you a secret: I have never ceased longing for My Shekhina, and I, too, am waiting for the Messiah to reunite Me with her. My longing alone is enough to sustain him. Your ancient sages taught that the Messiah will come only in a generation which is either all pious or all wicked. No such generation can ever arise. But he will come, not for your sake but for Mine.

                                                                    (R.P.)

Chronological List
of Sources

While the date of some of the sources listed below can be pinpointed with accuracy, of others there are only rough estimates. Occasionally the uncertainty is such that all one can say is that the work in question was written between two far-apart dates, say between the seventh and tenth centuries. The difficulty is compounded in the case of a work which was in the course of formation for many centuries. A Midrash may have been put in final shape several centuries after the material contained in it was first assembled. In such a case I assigned it to the century in which it was finally redacted. The Babylonian Talmud, which I thus assigned to the date of its redaction (sixth century), contains sayings, teachings, legends, etc. quoted in the names of sages who lived as early as the first century B.C.E. The same is true for the Jerusalem or Palestinian Talmud, and for almost all Midrashim.

Century	Title or Author
8th B.C.E.	Isaiah
7th–6th	Jeremiah
6th	Ezekiel
	Deutero-Isaiah
	Zechariah
5th	Malachi

2nd	Ben Sira (180 B.C.E.)
	Daniel (l64 B.C.E.)
	1 Enoch (l50 B.C.E.)
	Sibylline Books (l40 B.C.E.)
	1 Maccabees (100 B.C.E.)
1st	Psalms of Solomon
1st B.C.E. – 1st C.E.	2 Maccabees
1st C.E.	2 Baruch
	Philo of Aleandria (20 B.C.E.–50 C.E.)
	4 Ezra (ca. 70 C.E.)
	Josephus Flavius (38–100)
	Apocalypse of Abraham
	Revelations
lst or 2nd	Testaments of the Twelve Patriarchs
2nd	Mishna
	Tosefta
	Seder 'Olam Rabba (?)
3rd	Targum Onkelos
4th	Genesis Rabba
	Canticles Rabba
	Ruth Rabba
	Sifra
	Sifre Numbers
	Sifre Deuteronomy
	Mekhilta diR. Yishma'el
	Jerusalem or Palestinian Talmud (see Y.)
4th to 12th	Midrash Tehillim
	Midrash Hallel
5th	Leviticus Rabba
	Lamentations Rabba
	Mekhilta diR. Shim'on ben Yohai
	Pesiqta diR. Kahana
	Sefer Hekhalot
6th	Babylonian Talmud (see B.)
7th	Targum Yerushalmi
	Targum Jonathan
	Midrash Fragment (Marmorstein)
7th–8th	Eleazar Kallir
7th–9th	Sefer Zerubbabel
7th–10	Sefer Eliyahu
	Pirqe Mashiah
	Pereq R. Yoshiyahu (?)
	Pesiqta Hadta (?)

8th	Pirqe R. Eliezer
	Ecclesiastes Rabba
	Seder Eliyahu Rabba and Zuta
8th—9th	Midrash Alpha Beta diR. Akiba
	Midrash Alpha Betot
9th	Pesiqta Rabbati
	Halakhot G'dolot
	Midrash Mishle
9th—10th	Midrash Tanhuma
	Sa'adya Gaon (882—942)
10th	Ma'ase Daniel (ca. 940)
	Aggadat B'reshit
	Midrash Zuta on Shir haShirim
	Midrash Haser w'Yeter shebaT'NaKh
10th—11th	Hai Gaon (939—1038)
11th	Rashi (1040—1105)
	Aggadat Mashiah
	B'reshit Rabbati
	Midrash Konen
	Midrash vaYosha'
	Midrash Leqah Tov (Pesiqta Zutarta)
11th—12th	Exodus Rabba
12th	T'fillat R. Shim'on ben Yohai
	Sefer haYashar
	Maimonides (1135—1204)
	Midrash 'Aseret haSh'vatim
	Midrash Abba Gorion
	Nistarot R. Shim'on ben Yohai
	Numbers Rabba
	Otot haMashiah
	Rigord of St. Denis
12th—13th	Sefer Hasidim
	Ibn al-Athir (1160—1233)
13th	Zohar (The Book of Splendor; 1270—1300)
	Yalqut Shim'oni
	Midrash Tehillim
	Abraham Abulafia (1240—after 1291)
14th	Midrash haGadol B'reshit
	Yalqut haMakhiri
	Midrash Gadol uG'dola
14th—15th	Maharil (c. 1360—1427)
15th	Yohanan Alemanno (1435—c. 1504)
	Abrabanel, Isaac ben Judah (1437—1508)
	Ladino *Romances*

16th   Yitzhaq Luria (1535–1572)

16th–17th   Hayyim Vital (1542–1620)
                    Abraham Azulai (c. 1570–1643)

17th   Naphtali Hirsh ben Elhanan Bacharach
                    Jacob Sasportas (1610–1698)
                    Shabbatai Zevi (1626–1676)
                    Nathan of Gaza (1643/44–1680)
                    Yalqut R'uveni
                    Yalqut Hadash
                    Shivhe R. Hayyim Vital
                    Joseph della Reina (?)

17th–18th   Doenmeh Notebook
                    Midrash Talpiyot

18th   Israel Ba'al Shem Tov (c. 1700–1760)
                    Shivhe haBeShT

18th–19th   Levi Yitzhaq of Berdichev (1740–1809)
                    Nahman of Bratzlav (1772–1811)
                    Numeous Hasidic stories
                    Malbim (1809–1879)

20th   Modern Jewish writers

Abbreviations and
Annotated Bibliography

Abrabanel, Isaac ben Judah (1437–1508), *Y'shu'ot M'shiho* ("The Salvations of His Messiah"), Karlsruhe, 1828. Interpretation of Rabbinic dicta on the advent of the Messiah.

Abraham, Y'huda Leib, *Mid. RIBaSh Tov* ("Midrash of the Ba'al Shem Tov"), Kecskemét, 1927. Legends about the Ba'al Shem.

Abulafia, Abraham (1240–after 1291), *Sefer haOt* ("Book of the Sign"), ed. Adolph Jellinek in *Jubelschrift zum 60. Geburtstage des Prof. Dr. H. Graetz*, Breslau, 1887. Hebrew part, pp. 65–88. A "prophetic" writing by the Spanish Kabbalist.

Aggadat B'reshit ("Legend of Genesis"). Edited by Solomon Buber, Cracow, 1903; reprinted New York, 1959. Homiletic Mid. compiled about the 10th cent.

Aggadat Mashiah ("Legend of the Messiah"). Reprinted in BhM :141–43. A Mid. fragment contained in the *Mid. Leqah Tov* of R. Tuvya ben Eliezer (11th cent.).

Alemanno, Yohannan (1435–c. 1504) *Sefer Sha'ar hatlesheq.* (Book of the Gate of Desire), Livorno, 1790.

Amora, pl. Amoraim. Talmudic sages of the 3rd to 5th cent.

Apocalypse of Abraham. Edited by G. H. Box, London: Society for Promoting Christian Knowledge, 1918. Written originally probably in Hebrew toward the end of the 1st cent. C.E.

Asch, Shalom, *From Many Countries*, London: Macdonald, 1958. Short stories by the famous Yiddish author.

Ashkenazi, Eliezer, ed., *Sefer Ta'am Z'qenim* ("Book of Meaning of Old Men"), Frankfurt/M.: I. Kauffmann, 1854. A miscellany, containing a responsum of Hai Gaon (939–1038).

Ashkenazi, Yitzhaq, *Otz'rot fun Idishen Humor* ("Treasuries of Jewish

Humor"), New York: Tel Aviv Publishers, 1929. Jewish anecdotes in Yiddish.

Attias, Moshe. *Romancero S'faradi* ("Sephardi Romancero"), Jerusalem: Kiryat Sefer, 1956. A collection of Sephardi poems in Ladino and Hebrew.

Azulai, Abraham (c. 1570–1643), *Hesed l'Avraham* ("Grace to Abraham"), Amsterdam, 1685. Analysis of the principles of the Kabbala in the spirit of Yitzhaq Luria.

B.—*Babylonian Talmud*. Compiled in Babylonia, c. 500 C.E. After the Bible the most important authoritative source book of Jewish religion, and the main subject of study throughout Jewish history. In our source references, the abbreviation B. is followed by the name of the tractate and the folio number of the quotation.

B.C.E.—Before the Common Era.

2 *Baruch*, also known as Apocalypse of Baruch. Apocryphal work written originally in Hebrew in the early 1st cent. Included in Charles.

Bassin, M. *Antologi: Finf Hundert Yor Idishe Poezi*. New York: Dos Idishe Buch, 1917.

Benayahu, Meir, ed., *Sefer Toldot ha Ari* ("Book of the History of the Ari"), Jerusalem: Makhon Ben-Zvi, 1967. Contains the Hebrew text of reminiscences about R. Yitzhaq Luria, written by his disciples.

Ben Sira. The Wisdom of Shim'on ben Jeshu'a ben Sira. Included in Kahana. The earliest example of extra-Biblical Jewish wisdom literature, written in Hebrew, c. 180 B.C.E.

Berdach, Rachel, *The Emperor, the Sages, and Death*, New York–London: Thomas Yoseloff, 1962. Philosophical novel about conversations between Frederick II and a Jewish sage.

BhM. See Jellinek, Adolph.

Bialik, Hayyim Nahman, *Kol Kitve H. N. Bialik* ("Collected Writings of H.N.B."), Tel Aviv: Dvir, 1945. Works of the foremost modern Hebrew poet.

Bloch, Chajim, *Die Gemeinde der Chassidim* ("The Community of the Hasidim"), Berlin-Wien: Benjamin Harz, 1920. Hasidic stories, reworked in German.

Brainin, Reuben, *Hayye Herzl* ("Life of Herzl"), New York, 1919. Hebrew biography of the founder of modern political Zionism.

B'reshit Rabbati ("Greater Genesis"), ed. H. Albeck, Jerusalem: Mekize Nirdamim, 1940. An 11th-cent. abridgment of the *Mid. B'reshit Rabba*, written in the same century by R. Moshe haDarshan of Narbonne.

Buber Martin, *Gog and Magog*, Frankfurt/M. und Hamburg: Fischer Bücherei, 1957. Novel set in the world of the early Hasidim.

———, *Tales of the Hasidim II. The Later Masters*, New York: A Schocken Book publ. with Farrar, Straus & Young, 1948. Hasidic stories retold in Buber's style.

C.E.—Common Era.

Cant. Rab.–*Canticles Rabba* (in the original hebrew: *Shir haShirim Rabba*). Aggadic Mid. on the Song of Songs, the product of Palestinian Amoraim, redacted in Palestine not later than the middle of the 6th cent. Forms part of the standard editions of the *Mid. Rab.*

Charles, R. H., ed., *The Apocrypha and Pseudepigrapha*, 2 vols., Oxford, 1913. The most complete scholarly edition of the extracanonical Jewish writings in English translation, with critical apparatus.

Daniel. Late Biblical book, written partly in Hebrew and partly in Aramaic, and dating from about 164 B.C.E., featuring apocalyptic visions.

Doenmeh Notebook from the 17th or 18th cent., publ. by G. Scholem in *Sefunot* 9 (1965), p. 201. The Doenmeh sect believed in the Messiahship of Shabbatai Zevi even after his apostasy, and its members converted to Islam.

Eccl. Rab.–*Ecclesiastes Rabba* (in the original Hebrew: *Qohelet Rabba*). Exegetical Mid. on the book of Ecclesiastes, compiled in the 8th cent. Forms part of the standard editions of the *Mid. Rab.*

Ehrman, B., *Sefer P'er v'Khavod* ("Book of Praise and Glory"), Munkacs, 1912. Photostatic reprint, 1970. Collection of stories about Hasidic rabbis in a mixture of Hebrew and Yiddish.

Eisenstein, J. D. See *OM.*

Encyclopaedia Judaica, Jerusalem, 1972. 16 volumes.

1 Enoch. Apocryphal book, written in Hebrew or Aramaic in c. 150 B.C.E., and containing apocalypses and other material. Included in Charles.

Ex. Rab.–*Exodus Rabba* (in the original Hebrew: *Sh'mot Rabba*). Partly exegetical and partly homiletical Mid., put in final shape in the 11th or 12th cent., but containing much older material. Written in Aramaic and Hebrew. Forms part of the standard editions of the *Mid. Rab.*

Ezek.–*Ezekiel.* Biblical book written in Babylonia by the prophet and priest Ezekiel in 593–571 B.C.E., although it bears sign of some later editing.

4 Ezra (or *Esdras*). An apocalypse, that is, revelation of the future, written in Aramaic c. 70 C.E. Included in Charles.

Festinger, Leon, Henry W. Riecken, and Stanley Schachter, *When Prophecy Fails*, Minneapolis: University of Minnesota Press, 1956. Study of the reaction of people to "disconfirmation" of sectarian prophecies.

Frisch, Efraim, "Die Legende von Kuty," in Karl Otten, ed., *Schofar: Lieder und Legenden jüdischer Dichter*, Neuwied am Rhein: Hermann Luchterhand Verlag, 1962.

Gen. Rab.–*Genesis Rabba* (in the original Hebrew: *B'reshit Rabba*). Exegetical Aggadic Mid. on the Book of Genesis, product of Palestinian Amoraim (4th cent. C.E.), written partly in Hebrew and partly in Aramaic. Forms part of the standard editions of *Mid. Rab.*

Ginsburger, M., *Pseudo-Jonathan*, Berlin: S. Calvary, 1903. Aramaic version of the Pentateuch, better known as *Targ. Yer.*

Ginzberg, Louis, *Eine unbekannte jüdische Sekte* ("An Unknown Jewish Sect"), New York: Im Selbstverlage des Verfassers, 1922. Reprinted Hildesheim—New York: Georg Olms Verlag, 1972.

———, *Legends of the Jews*, 7 vols., Philadelphia: Jewish Publication Society of America, 1909—46.

Greenberg, Uri Zevi, *Sefer haQitrug w'haEmuna* ("Book of Denunciation and Faith"), Jerusalem—Tel Aviv: Hotza'at S'dan, 1937. A collection of poems.

Grimmelshausen, Hans Jakob Christoffel von, *Courage the Adventuress & the False Messiah*, transl. and intr. by Hans Speier, Princeton, N.J.: Princeton University Press, 1964.

HaAretz. Israel daily, Tel Aviv. Item about "Messiah Banquets" in the Apr. 8, 1977, issue.

Haberman, M., *Mahb'rot Immanuel*, Tel Aviv: Sifrut, 1946.

Hai Gaon (939—1038). See Ashkenazi, Eliezer, *Sefer Ta'am Z'qenim*.

Halakha, pl. Halakhot. The traditional Jewish law, going back through the medieval law codes to the Talmud, the Mishna, and ultimately the Bible.

Halakhot G'dolot ("Great Halakhot"), ed. by Azriel Hildesheimer, Berlin: Mekize Nirdamim, 1888. A Halakhic code, written in the 9th cent. by Simon Kayyara.

Herzl, Theodor. See Patai, Raphael, ed., *The Complete Diaries of Theodor Herzl*.

Higger, Michael, *Massekhtot Q'tanot* ("Small Treatises"), New York: Bloch, 1929. Collection of Midrashim and other ancient Jewish writings.

Ibn al-Athir, 'Izz al-Din Abu al-Hasan 'Ali (1160—1233), *al-Kamil*. An annalistic history of the world. As quoted by Hayyim Schwarzbaum, "The Messianic Movements of Alroy, Molcho, and Reubeni" (in Hebrew), *Mahanayim* 81 (1963).

Idelsohn, Abraham I., *Gesänge der orientalischen Juden*, Jerusalem-Berlin-Wien: Harz, 1923.

———, *N'ginot Y'hude Teman*, Jerusalem-Berlin-Wien: Harz, 1924. Collections of traditional folk melodies.

'Iny'ne Shabbatai Zevi ("Matters of Sh. Z."), ed. Aharon Freimann, Berlin: Mekize Nirdamim, 1912. Writings by the adherents of the false Messiah.

Isa.—Isaiah. Biblical book containing in most of its first 39 chapters the prophecies of Isaiah, who lived in the latter half of the 8th cent. B.C.E. in Jerusalem. Chapters 40—66 were written by one or more anonymous prophets who lived in the middle of the 6th cent. B.C.E. The unknown author(s) of these chapters is (are) often referred to as Deutero-Isaiah.

Jellinek, Adolph, *Bet haMidrash*, 6 vols. 2nd ed., Jerusalem: Bamberger & Wahrmann, 1938. A collection of minor Midrashim in the original Hebrew or Aramaic, with introductions.

Jer.—Jeremiah. Biblical book containing the prophecies of Jeremiah, whose activity fell into the last 40 years of the Kingdom of Judah (626–586 B.C.E.).

Josephus Flavius (c. 38–c. 100 C.E.), *Antiquities of the Jews.* Loeb Classical Library. Account by the Jewish historian, written in Greek, of the history of the Jews from earliest times to the Roman-Jewish war.

————, *Wars of the Jews.* Loeb Classical Library. Invaluable account of the Roman-Jewish war of 67–70 C.E., which ended with the fall of Jerusalem.

Kadaner, Jacob, *Sefer Sippurim Noraim* ("Book of Terrible Stories"), Munkacs: M. Herskovics, 1912. A collection of Hasidic stories.

Kafka, Franz, *Parables and Paradoxes*, New York: Schocken Books, 1961.

Kahana, Abraham, ed., *HaS'farim haHitzonim* ("The External Books"), 4 vols., Tel Aviv: M'qorot, 1937. Contains most of the extant Apocrypha and Pseudepigrapha in a Hebrew translation.

————, ed., *Sefer haHasidut* ("The Book of Hasidism"), Warsaw, 1922. Hasidic texts.

Kallir, Eleazar (7th or 8th cent.), *BaYamim haHem* ("In Those Days"). Lamentation for Tish'a b'Av, printed in the *Mahzor* (holiday prayer book) according to the Roman rite, Bologna, 1540.

Kleinman, M. S., *Sefer Or Y'sharim* ("Book of the Light of the Straight"), Piotrkov, 1924. Reprinted Jerusalem, 1957/58. Hasidic stories.

Lam. Rab.—Lamentations Rabba (in the original Hebrew: *Ekha Rabbati*). Aggadic Mid. on the Book of Lamentations, written in a mixture of Hebrew and Aramaic, redacted in Palestine about the end of the 5th cent. C.E. Forms part of the standard editions of the *Mid. Rab.*

Lev. Rab.—Leviticus Rabba (in the original Hebrew *VaYiqra Rabba*). Homiletical Mid. on the Book of Leviticus, written in Hebrew and Aramaic in Palestine. Composed in the 5th cent. C.E. Forms part of the standard editions of the *Mid. Rab.*

Levi Yitzhaq of Berdichev (1740–1809), *Imre Tzaddiqim* ("Sayings of the Tzaddiqim"), ed. Tz'vi Hasid, Zhitomir, 1899. Sayings and stories of the famous Hasidic rabbi.

Löwinger, Adolf, "Die Auferstehung in der jüdischen Tradition" ("Resurrection in Jewish Tradition"), in Max Grünwald, ed., *Jahrbuch für jüdische Volkskunde* ("Yearbook of Jewish Folklore") I, Berlin-Wien: Benjamin Harz, 1923, pp. 23–122. A detailed study of the subject.

Luria, Yitzhaq (1535–1572). The leading Safed Kabbalist, whose teachings are contained in the works of Hayyim Vital and others.

M.—Mishna. The basic law code of Judaism, compiled by R. Y'huda haNasi in Palestine about 200 C.E. Forms the basis of both the Babylonian Talmud (see B.) and the Palestinian Talmud (see Y.).

Ma'ase Daniel ("The Story of Daniel"). Hebrew translation included in Y'huda Ibn Sh'muel, *Midr'she G'ula.* Earlier translation in BhM

5:117–30. For a German translation see Zotenberg. A Persian-Jewish apocalypse, written in 940.

Ma'ase diR. Y'hoshu'a ben Levi ("Story of R.Y.b.L."). Reprinted in BhM 2:48–51. A Mid. fragment of Essene origin, redacted in later centuries.

Ma'asiyyot v'SihotTzaddiqim ("Stories and Talks of Tzaddiqim"). Published anonymously by the son of R. Avraham Nissan haLevi of Lemberg (Lvov). Warsaw: Levin-Epstein, 1924. Stories about Hasidic rabbis.

Macc.–Maccabees, Books 1 and 2. 1 Macc. is a historical work about the exploits of the Maccabean family from c. 175 to 134 B.C.E. Written in Hebrew in Palestine, 100 B.C.E. 2 Macc. is an abridgment, written between 125 B.C.E. and 70 C.E., of a lost book written by Jason of Cyrene in c. 150 B.C.E. dealing with the history of the Jews from 175 to 160 B.C.E.

Maharil (Ya'aqov ben Moshe Moellin, c. 1360–1427), *Hilkhot Shabbat* ("Rules of the Sabbath"). Halakhot by the foremost Talmudist of his generation.

Maimonides (Moses ben Maimon, 1135–1204), *Commentary on the Mishna*, ed. Joseph Kafih, Jerusalem: Mosad haRav Kook, 1964. The classical Mishna commentary of the greatest mind of medieval Jewry.

———, *Epistle to Yemen*, ed. Abraham S. Halkin, New York: American Academy for Jewish Research, 1952. Advises the Jews of Yemen to reject the pseudo-Messiah who arose in Yemen.

———, *Guide of the Perplexed.* Numerous editions and translations. The greatest religio-philosophical work produced by medieval Jewry. Original written in Arabic.

———, *Sh'mona P'raqim* ("Eight Chapters"). An introduction to the Mishna tractate *Avot* ("Sayings of the Fathers").

———, *Treatise on Resurrection*, ed. by J. Finkel, New York: American Academy for Jewish Research, 1939. A rationalist's view of the traditional beliefs about Resurrection.

———, *Yad haHazaqa* ("The Strong Hand"), also known as *Mishne Tora* ("Second Tora"). The great Halakhic code of Maimonides.

Malachi. Biblical book of a minor prophet who lived in the first half of the 5th century B.C.E.

Malbim (Meir Loeb ben Y'hiel Mikhael, 1809–1879), *Commentary on Daniel.* Part of the author's Bible commentary, designed to show the unity of the Written and Oral Law.

Marmorstein, Arthur. "Les Signes du Messie," *Revue des Études Juives* 52 (1906), pp. 176–86. A Midrash fragment composed c. 628–38.

Marx, Alexander. "The Correspondence between the Rabbis of Southern France and Maimonides about Astrology," *Hebrew Union College Annual*, v. 3 (1926), pp. 311–58.

Mekh.–Mekhilta ("Compendium"). Title of two Midrash collections. See following.

Mekhilta diR. Shim'on ben Yohai ("Compendium of R. Sh. b. Y."), ed. D. Hoffmann, Frankfurt/M., 1905. Halakhic, exegetical Mid. on the Book of Exodus, redacted in Palestine in the 5th century C.E.

Mekhilta diR. Yishma'el ("Compendium of R. Y."), ed. M. Friedmann, 1870. Halakhic, exegetical Mid. on Exodus, compiled and redacted in Palestine about the end of the 4th century C.E., but containing, in the main, Tannaitic material from the school of R. Yishma'el (2nd cent. C.E.).

Michelsohn, Abraham S. B. H., *Sefer Shemen haTov* ("The Book of Good Oil"), Piotrkov, 1905. Hasidic stories.

Mid.–Midrash, pl. *Midrashim*. Generic term denoting the extensive literature of legends, commentaries, homilies, ethical teachings, Biblical exegeses, sermons, proverbs, etc., produced by Jewish sages and rabbis in Hebrew and Aramaic from the 4th to the 14th centuries. See following entries.

Mid. Abba Gorion (or *Guryon*). Printed in BhM 1:1–18. A Mid. on the Book of Esther, written in the 12th cent.

Mid. Alpha Beta diR. Akiba ("Mid. of the Alphabet of R. A."). Printed in BhM 3:50–64. Probably from the 8th or 9th cent.

Mid. Alpha Betot ("Mid. of Alphabets"). Printed in Wertheimer, *Bate Midrashot* 2:419–59. Probably from the 8th or 9th cent.

Mid. 'Aseret haSh'vatim ("Mid. of the Ten Tribes"). Printed in OM. Probably from the 12th cent. Purporting to be a letter written by Prester John to the Pope in Rome.

Mid. Gadol uG'dola ("Mid. of Great [*m.*] and Great [*f.*]"). Printed in BhM 3:121–30. From the 14th cent. at the latest.

Mid. haGadol B'reshit, ed. Mordecai Margalioth, Jerusalem: Mosad haRav Kook, 2nd printing, 1975. Voluminous Mid. on Genesis, written in Yemen in the 14th cent. by R. David ben Amram of Aden. Contains material from older sources, some of which were lost since.

Mid. Hallel. Printed in BhM 5:87–110. From the Middle Ages.

Mid. haNe'elam ("The Hidden Mid."). Part of the Zohar.

Mid. Haser v'Yater shebaT'NaKh ("Mid. of the Missing and Superfluous in the Bible"), ed. Wertheimer, Jerusalem, 1930. Probably from the 10th cent.

Mid. Konen ("Mid. 'He established'"). Printed in BhM 2:23–29. Composed not earlier than the 11th cent. Deals with Creation, Paradise, Hell, etc.

Mid. Leqah Tov ("Mid. Good Teaching," also called *Pesiqta Zutarta*, or "Small Section"), by R. Tuvya ben Eliezer (11th cent.), ed. Solomon Buber, 2 vols., Vilna, 1880. Exegetical-Aggadic Mid. on the Five Books of Moses and the Five Scrolls.

Mid. Mishle ("Mid. on Proverbs"), ed. Solomon Buber, Vilna, 1893. Compiled in the 9th cent., probably in Babylonia.

Mid. Rab.–Midrash Rabba ("Great Mid."). Collective name of the "Rabba" Midrashim on the Five Books of Moses and the Five Scrolls, dating from the 4th to the 12th cent.

Mid. Talpiyot, by R. Eliyahu haKohen, Warsaw, 1875. First ed. Smyrna, 1736. A Kabbalistic collection of Midrashim.

Mid. Tanhuma, Warsaw: Levin-Epstein, n.d. Mid. on the Five Books of Moses, from the 9th–10th cent.

Mid. Tanh. Buber. A different version of the preceding, ed. Solomon Buber, 1885, reprinted New York, 1946, 2 vols.

Mid. Tehillim, ed. Solomon Buber, Vilna, 1891. Aggadic Mid. on the Psalms also called *Shoher Tov* ("Good Friend"). Contains material from the 4th to the 12th cent.

Mid. vaYosha' ("Mid. 'And He Saved'"), Printed in BhM 1:35–57. Written or compiled in the late 11th cent.

Mid. Zuta ("Small Mid.") on *Shir haShirim* (Song of Songs), ed. Solomon Buber, Berlin, 1894. From the 10th cent.

Midrash Fragment, ed. Marmorstein in *Revue des Études Juives* 52 (1906), p. 184. See Marmorstein.

Midrash Fragment, ed. Wertheimer in his *Bate Midrashot* 2:503–4.

Milhamot Melekh haMashiah ("The Wars of King Messiah"). Printed in BhM 6:117–20. A Mid. fragment based partly on material dating from the 7th cent.

Mintz, Jerome R., *Legends of the Hasidim*, Chicago: University of Chicago Press, 1968. Hasidic legends collected in New York.

Nahman of Bratzlav (1772–1811), *Sippure Ma'asiyyot* ("Stories of Tales"), Berdichev, 1815. I used the Warsaw: die Velt edition for the story in ch. 7, and the Jerusalem, 1973, edition for that in ch. 12. Hasidic stories by the great-grandson of the Ba'al Shem Tov, founder of Bratzlav Hasidism.

Naphtali Hirsh ben Elhanan Bacharach (1st half of 17th cent.), *'Emeq haMelekh* ("Valley of the King"), Amsterdam, 1653. Detailed presentation of the Kabbalistic doctrine of Yitzhaq Luria.

Nathan of Gaza (1643/44–1680), *D'rush haTanninim* ("Treatise on the Dragons"), Ms. Halberstamm 40, f. 99b. Excerpt published in Hebrew in G. Scholem, *Major Trends*, p. 418, n. 26. A mystical treatise by the foremost adherent and prophet of Shabbatai Zevi, the false Messiah.

Nistarot R. Shim'on ben Yohai ("Mysteries of R. Sh. b. Y."). Printed in BhM 3:78–82. A Mid. fragment containing allusions to the first Crusade, hence written in the 12th cent.

Num. Rab.–Numbers Rabba (in the Hebrew original *BaMidbar Rabba*). A combination of two different Midrashim on the Book of Numbers, both exegetical-homiletic, and both written in the 12th cent. Forms part of the standard editions of the *Mid. Rab.*

OM–Otzar Midrashim ("Treasury of Midrashim"), ed. J. D. Eisenstein, New York: J. D. Eisenstein, 1915. Collection of 200 minor Midrashim, with introductory notes.

Otot haMashiah ("Signs of the Messiah"). Printed in BhM 2:58–63. Apocalyptic Mid. fragment, dating probably from the 12th cent.

Patai, Joseph, "Herzl's School Years," in *Herzl Year Book* vol. 3, New York: Herzl press, 1960.

———, *Lelkek és Titkok* ("Souls and Secrets"), Budapest: Mult és Jövö, 1937. Second, augmented edition of the author's short stories about the world of the Hasidim.

Patai, Raphael, *Adam waAdama* ("Man and Earth"), Jerusalem: Hebrew University Press, 1942–43, 2 vols. Comparative study of ancient Jewish custom, belief, and legend centering on the relationship between man and earth.

———, "The 'Control of Rain' in Ancient Palestine," *Hebrew Union College Annual* 14, Cincinnati, 1939. Study of Biblical and Rabbinic rainmaking rituals and related beliefs.

———, *The Hebrew Goddess*, New York: Ktav, 1967. Study of the female divinity in Jewish religion. Second enlarged ed. New York: Avon Books, 1978.

———, *The Jewish Mind*, New York: Scribner's, 1977. Study of the psychology of the Jews, including the Jewish I.Q., talents, Nobel-Prize record, mental health, etc.

———, *Man and Temple in Ancient Jewish Myth and Ritual*, 2nd ed., New York: Ktav, 1967. Study of the role of the Temple and the Righteous in the Talmudic belief system.

———, *Myth and Modern Man*, Englewood Cliffs, N.J.: Prentice-Hall, 1972. Study of modern myths and their role in contemporary life.

———, *Sex and Family in the Bible and the Middle East*, New York: Doubleday, 1959. Comparison of Biblical and modern Middle Eastern mores.

———, "What Is Hebrew Mythology?" *Transactions of the New York Academy of Sciences*, Nov. 1964, Ser. II, vol. 27, no. 1. Introductory statement on the scope and characteristics of Hebrew mythology.

———, ed., *The Complete Diaries of Theodor Herzl*, 5 vols., New York: Herzl Press and Thomas Yoseloff, 1960. Annotated edition, in the English translation of Harry Zohn, of the diaries of the founder of modern political Zionism.

P'er v'Khavod, see Ehrman, B.

Pereq R. Yoshiyahu ("Chapter of R. Y."). Printed in BhM 6:112–16. Mid. fragment from the Middle Ages.

Pereq Shalom ("Chapter of Peace"). Printed in Michael Higger, *Massekhtot Q'tanot*. A Mid. fragment on the value of peace. See Higger.

Persian Jewish Legend, see Zotenberg.

Pes.–Pesiqta ("Chapter"). Name of several Midrashim. See following entries.

Pes. diR. Kah.–Pesiqta diR. Kahana, ed. by Bernard Mandelbaum, New York: Jewish Theological Seminary, 1962, 2 vols. Homiletical Mid. on the festivals of the year, written in Palestine, probably in the 5th cent.

Pes. Had.–Pesiqta Hadta ("New Chapter"), printed in BhM 6:36–70. A Mid. from the Middle Ages.

Pes. Rab.–Pesiqta Rabbati ("Greater Chapter"), ed. by M. Friedmann, Vienna, 1880, reprinted Tel Aviv, 1963. Mid. on the festivals of the year, composed beginning with the year 845. In addition to the above edition, I also used the Shklov, 1806, edition.

Philo of Alexandria (also known as Philo Judaeus, c. 20 B.C.E. – 50 C.E.), *De confusione linguarum* and *De praemiis et poenis,* Loeb Classical Library. Two treatises by the famous Hellenistic Jewish philosopher.

Pirqe Mashiah ("Chapters of the Messiah"). Printed in BhM 3:68–78. Mid. fragment of Persian provenance, dating from the 7th to 10th cent.

Pirqe R. Eliezer ("Chapters of R. E."). Many editions. I used the Warsaw, 1879, edition. Apocalyptic Mid. written in Palestine in the early 8th cent.

Psalms of Solomon. Pseudepigraphic book, written in Hebrew, c. 63 B.C.E. Contained in Charles.

R—Rabbi. Title of a sage, master, or teacher in Talmudic and later times.

Ra'aya Mehemna ("The Faithful Shepherd"). Part of the Zohar dealing with the interpretation of the commandments. Written in Aramaic in the 1290s or the early years of the 14th cent. by an anonymous Kabbalist, and included in the standard editions of the Zohar.

Rakats (or Rokotz), J. K. K., *Siah Sarfe Qodesh* ("The Talk of Holy Seraphim"), Lodz, 1929; reprinted Brooklyn, 1954. Hasidic stories.

Rashi—R. Sh'lomo ben Yitzhaq (1040–1105). The greatest commentator of the Bible and the Babylonian Talmud. Lived in Troyes, France. His commentaries, printed in many editions of the Bible and in all standard editions of the B., are indispensable in studying these primary sources of Jewish religion.

REJ—*Revue des Études Juives,* Paris.

Revelation. The only apocalypse in the New Testament, written originally in Hebrew, Aramaic, or Greek, by a Judeo-Christian, in the late 1st cent. C.E.

Rigord of St. Denis (French chronicler of the 12th cent.). Latin text printed by Fritz Baer, in *Monatschrift für Geschichte und Wissenschaft des Judentums* 70 (1926).

Rubashov (later Shazar), Zalman, "Ma'ase R. Yosef della Reina" ("Story of R. Y. d. R."), in *Eder haY'qar* dedicated to S. A. Horodetzky on his 75th birthday, Tel Aviv: Dvir, 1947, pp. 97–118. Yiddish version of R.

Leib ben Ozer Rosenkranz, based on the Hebrew text of R. Sh'lomo Ayllon (c. 1655—1728), of the story of a famous Jewish magician.

Rubin, Ruth, *Voices of a People*. New York/London: Thomas Yoseloff, 1963. Collection of Jewish folk songs.

Ruth Rab.—Ruth Rabba. Aggadic Mid. on the Book of Ruth, written in the 4th cent. by Palestinian Amoraim. Part of the standard editions of the *Mid. Rab.*

Sa'adya Gaon (882—942), *Emunot w'De'ot* ("Beliefs and Opinions"), ed. Y'ruham Fischel, Leipzig, 1859. One of the major works of medieval Jewish philosophy.

Sasportas, Jacob (1610—1698), *Tzitzat Novel Tz'vi* ("The Fading of the Flower of Zevi"), ed. I. Tishbi, Jerusalem: Mosad Bialik, 1954. Polemical work against the Messianic claims of Shabbatai Zevi.

Scholem, Gershom, *Major Trends in Jewish Mysticism*, New York: Schocken, 1941. The classical introduction to the subject.

Seder 'Avodat Yisrael ("The Order of the Service of Israel"), Roedelheim, 1868; reprinted New York: Schocken, 1937. Standard Jewish prayer book, arranged by Yitzhaq ben Arye Yosef Ber.

Seder Eliyahu Rabba and Zuta ("Great and Small Order of Elijah"), also known as *Tanna diVe Eliyahu*, ed. M. Friedmann, Vienna, 1904; reprinted Jerusalem, 1960. Didactic, ethical Mid., compiled prior to the 9th cent.

Seder 'Olam Rabba ("Great Order of the World"). Chronological Mid., mentioned in the Talmud and ascribed to the 2nd-cent. Tanna R. Yose ben Halafta. Published in several editions.

Sefer Eliyahu ("Book of Elijah"). Printed in BhM 3:65—68. Apocalyptic Mid. fragment of Persian provenance, dating from the 7th to 10th cent.

Sefer Hasidim ("Book of the Pious"), by R. Y'huda ben Sh'muel heHasid (c. 1150—1217), ed. J. Wistinetzki, Berlin: Zvi Hirsch Itzkowski, 1891. Moral teachings interspersed with legends.

Sefer haYashar ("Book of the Straight"), ed. Lazarus Goldschmidt, Berlin: Benjamin Harz, 1923. Anonymous heroic Mid., written in Spain in the 12th cent., telling about the exploits of early Biblical heroes.

Sefer Hekhalot ("Book of Heavenly Halls"), also known as *Sefer Hanokh* ("Book of Enoch"). Printed in BhM 5:170—90. A Mid. discussing the heavenly halls as shown by Enoch-Metatron to R. Yishma'el. Probably written before 500 C.E.

Sefer P'er w'Khavod. See Ehrman, B.

Sefer Zerubbabel ("Book of Z."). Printed in BhM 2:54—57. Apocalyptic Mid. fragment, written probably in the 9th cent., or, according to others, in 638. A different version is printed in Wertheimer, *Bate Midrashot* 2:497—505.

Shivhe haBeShT ("Praises of the Ba'al Shem Tov"), Tel Aviv: Talpiyot, 1961. Stories about the Ba'al Shem (c. 1700—1760), founder of

Hasidism, written by one of his disciples.

Shivhe R. Hayyim Vital ("Praises of R. H. V."), Jerusalem, 1966. Stories about the foremost disciple of Yitzhaq Luria.

Shoher Tov. See *Mid. Tehillim.*

Sibylline Books. Apocalyptic writings in oracular form, dating from 140 B.C.E., attacking the enemies of Israel and foretelling the Redemption. Included in Charles.

Sifra, ed. A. H. Weiss, Vienna, 1862. Halakhic Mid. on the Book of Leviticus, compiled in Palestine not earlier than the end of the 4th cent. C.E.

Sifre Deut. ("S. Deuteronomy"), ed. H. S. Horowitz and Louis Finkelstein, Berlin 1934–39. Halakhic Mid. to the Book of Deuteronomy, arranged and redacted probably not before the end of the 4th cent. C.E.

Sifre Num. ("S. Numbers"), ed. M. Friedman, Vienna, 1864. Another edition by H. S. Horowitz, Leipzig, 1917. Halakhic Mid. to the Book of Numbers, arranged and redacted in Palestine, probably not before the end of the 4th cent. C.E.

Silver, Abba Hillel, *A History of the Messianic Speculations in Israel,* New York: Macmillan, 1927. Study of the efforts to foretell the date of the coming of the Messiah, from the 1st to the 17th cent.

Socrates Scholasticus, *Historia Ecclesiastica. The Ecclesiastical History of S. S.* Revised with Notes by A. C. Zenos. Select Library of Nicene and Post-Nicene Fathers, 2nd Ser., vol. 2, New York, 1890; repr. Grand Rapids, Mich: Wm. B. Eerdmans, 1957.

Sofer, Ya'aqov, *Sippure Ya'aqov* ("The Stories of Jacob"), Husiatyn: F. Kawalek, 1904. Small collection of Hasidic stories.

S'udat Livyatan ("The Leviathan Banquet"). Printed in BhM 6:150–51. Mid. fragment related to the *Pirqe Mashiah.*

T.–Tosefta, ed. by M. S. Zuckermandel, Pasewalk, 1881, reprinted Jerusalem, 1937. Collection of Tannaitic traditions and teaching not included in the Mishna.

Talmud. See B. and Y.

Tanna, pl. Tannaim; Tannaites. Palestinian Jewish sages and teachers who lived in the 1st cent. B.C.E. and the 1st and 2nd cent. C.E., and whose teachings are contained in the Mishna and the Tosefta.

Targ.–Targum. Generic term denoting various Aramaic translations-paraphrases of the Bible or parts thereof. The oldest and most important of them is the *Targum Onkelos,* redacted in the 3rd cent. C.E.

Targ. Jonathan. Aramaic translation-paraphrase of the Prophets. Originated in Palestine in Tannaitic times, redacted in Babylonia in the 7th cent.

Targ. Yer.–Targum Yerushalmi ("Jerusalem Targum"). Aramaic translation-paraphrase of the Pentateuch, put into final shape in the 7th cent. See Ginsburger.

Testament of Judah. See Testaments of the Twelve Patriarchs.

Testament of Levi. See Testaments of the Twelve Patriarchs.

Testaments of the Twelve Patriarchs. Composite pseudepigraphic work containing much material from the 1st or 2nd cent. B.C.E., but compiled in the 1st or 2nd cent. C.E. Included in Charles.

T'fillat R. Shim'on ber Yohai ("Prayer of R. Sh. b. Y."). Printed in BhM 4:117–26. Apocalyptic Mid. containing allusions to the Crusades. Dates from the 12th cent. at the earliest.

Vital, Hayyim (1542–1620), *Sefer 'Etz Hayyim* ("Book of the Tree of Life"), Warsaw: Jacob Zeev Unterhandler, 1890, 3 vols. Contains elaborations on the teachings of Vital's master, Yitzhaq Luria.

——, *Sefer haHezyonot* ("Book of Visions"), ed. A. Z. Aescoly, Jerusalem: Mosad haRav Kook, 1954. Autobiographical notes, descriptions of dreams, etc., by the foremost disciple of Yitzhaq Luria.

Wassermann, Jakob, *Die Juden von Zirndorf,* Berlin-Wien: S. Fischer Verlag, 1918. Story of Jewish fate by the well-known German-Jewish novelist.

Wertheimer, Sh'lomo Aharon, *Bate Midrashot* ("Houses of Legnds"), 2 vols., 2nd ed. Avraham Yosef Wertheimer, Jerusalem: Mosad haRav Kook, 1952–53. Collection of minor Midrashim.

Wiesel, Elie, *One Generation After,* New York: Random House, 1970.

Y.–Yerushalmi. The Jerusalem or Palestinian Talmud. Written partly in Hebrew but mostly in Aramaic, and compiled in the late 4th cent. C.E. Considered less authoritative, and hence is much less studied, than the B. Quoted by tractate and folio of the Venice, 1523, edition.

Yalqut Hadash (New Collection), by Israel ben Binjamin of Belzice (17th cent.). Various editions. Kabbalistic collection of legends.

Yalqut haMakhiri ("The Makhiri Collection"), by Makhir ben Abba Mari (14th cent.), ed. by Y'huda Z'ev Kahana Schapira, Berlin, 1892; reprinted Jerusalem, 1964. Anthology of Aggadic Midrashim.

Yalqut R'uveni ("The Reubeni Collection"), by R'uven Katz (d. 1673), Warsaw: Levin-Epstein, 1889. Kabbalistic collection of legends and miscellaneous material based on the weekly portions of the Pentateuch. First published in Wilmersdorf, 1681.

Yalqut Shim'oni ("The Shim'oni Collection"), by R. Shim'on haDarshan of Frankfurt. The best known and most comprehensive Mid. collection, compiled in the 13th cent.

Yemenite Apocalypse. Printed in Y'huda Ibn Sh'muel, *Midr'she G'ula.*

Yemenite Midrash. Printed ibid.

Y'huda Ibn Sh'muel, *Midr'she G'ula* ("Midrashim of Redemption"), Jerusalem–Tel Aviv: Mosad Bialik-Massada, 1954. Collection of Midrashim dealing with the Messianic age and events.

Zech.–Zechariah. Biblical book, one of the twelve minor prophets. Contains in chapters 1–8 prophecies of Zechariah dated 520–518 B.C.E., to which are added, in chapters 9—14, apocalyptic prophecies of anonymous authorship.

Zevin, Sh'lomo Yosef, *Sippure Hasidim* ("Stories of Hasidim"), Tel Aviv: Avraham Tziyoni, 1957, 2 vols. Collection of Hasidic stories.

Zohar (The Book of "Splendor"), by Moses de Leon. The central work in Kabbalistic literature, written in Aramaic between 1270 and 1300 in Spain. The edition I used is that of Vilna: Rom, 1894, 3 vols.

Zotenberg, Herman, "Geschichte Daniels" ("The Story of Daniel"), in Adalbert Merx, ed., *Archiv für wissenschaftliche Erforschung* 1, Halle, 1870, pp. 385—427. A Persian Jewish legend.

Zukerman, William, *Refugee from Judea*, New York: Philosophical Library, 1961. Short stories.

MANUSCRIPTS

In addition to the printed sources listed above, also several hitherto unpublished Hebrew manuscripts were excerpted, translated, and quoted. They are fully identified on pp. 27, 162, 328, 330 and 332.

Index